A Lesser Life

·SYLVIA·ANN·HEWLETT·

A Lesser Life
The Myth of Women's Liberation

MICHAEL JOSEPH LONDON

First published in Great Britain by Michael Joseph Ltd
27 Wrights Lane, Kensington, London W8 5DZ
1987

British Library Cataloguing in Publication Data

Hewlett, Sylvia Ann
A lesser life: the myth of women's liberation
1. Women—Europe—Social conditions
2. Women—United States—Social conditions
I. Title
305.4'2'094   HQ1587
ISBN 0-7181-2795-1

Typeset in Linotron 202 11½/13pt Perpetua by Wilmaset, Birkenhead, Wirral
Printed in Great Britain by Billings & Sons Ltd, Worcester

For Richard

Contents

Acknowledgements

For me this is a special book in that it represents a unique coming together of the personal and the professional. It therefore gives me particular pleasure to acknowledge the extensive help I have received from family, friends and colleagues.

My greatest debt is to my husband, Richard Weinert. This book could not have been written without his constant support, which spanned the gamut from intellectual to domestic. He read all six drafts of the book and was my most rigorous and most constructive critic. Even more important, over the course of the last three years he has spent numerous evenings and weekends cooking meals and looking after the children so that I could work. If every career woman had such a partner, much of this book would be redundant.

A special word of thanks is due to our children – Shira, Lisa, David and Adam. They helped me out with daily doses of love and were generous enough to be proud of a mother who sometimes worked too hard and too long. Besides which, it was their births and their childhoods that prompted the questions that lie behind this book.

I am also indebted to many others. I have depended on my editor, Pat Golbitz, for her fierce commitment to the book, which sustained me through the agonies of redrafting. My agent, Molly Friedrich, contributed generous amounts of time, judgement and friendship. Few authors receive such wholehearted support and I am deeply grateful.

My greatest intellectual debt is to Betty Friedan, Lenore Weitzman, and Sheila Kamerman. Their ideas – and their scholarship – inform the arguments in this book and I am pleased to pay tribute to their work.

Over the last three years I have relied on the encouragement of my colleagues at the Economic Policy Council. I would like to express my appreciation to: Robert O. Anderson, Doug Fraser, Charles Barber, Ray Marshall, Jack Sheinkman, Henry Kaufman, John Sweeney, Alice Ilchman, Albert Shanker, Ed Luck, Dan Burton and Rose Carcaterra.

I would also like to thank Elizabeth Jakab, Joyce Kozloff, Charles Perrow and Benjamin Kalman for thoughtful comments on early drafts of the book, and Margie Simmons for sharing her time and expertise. Pam Laber, Judy Farrell, Marthe Abraham and Marie Sauveur provided invaluable assistance throughout the lifespan of this project; and Wendy Atkin, Kathryn Bregman, Roy Brown, Frances Beinecke, Tru Helms, Abby Hirsch, Helen Knight, Ruth Spellman, Thelma Weinert and Marcia Welles gave generous amounts of support and affection. I thank them all.

I also wish to acknowledge all those people I interviewed. Business leaders, journalists, government officials and hundreds of working parents in five different countries gave freely of their time and their energy. In a critical sense they made this book possible and I am grateful.

Finally, my heartfelt thanks go to my parents, Vernon and Jean Hewlett. Before it became fashionable, they taught me to strive for both a career and a family, and any success I have found is grounded in their unconditional love.

New York City
September 1985

Note: Names marked by an asterisk* in the text are pseudonymous.

Preface to British Edition

Are American women the most liberated in the world?

I once thought so. I grew up in Britain, and like most Europeans, viewed American women with awe and respect. They seemed to be so rich and powerful. As a young woman my models were Gloria Steinem and Jane Fonda; given my druthers I would have combined their attributes into a heady American brew.

My youthful view reflected the conventional wisdom. For two centuries America has been seen by its own citizenry and by foreigners as a land where women are born free, where they enjoy a degree of freedom and independence unparalleled in the rest of the world. In the early nineteenth century the French aristocrat and social critic Alexis de Tocqueville pointed to the superiority of American women. 'I have nowhere seen women occupying a loftier position,'[1] he wrote in 1830. In more recent times women in the United States have had the benefit of many more civil rights and much more education than their contemporaries elsewhere. And, as if to clinch the matter, there is the women's movement, which has been so much more vocal in America than in other countries. The prominence of feminism in the United States would seem to confirm the advanced status of American women.

When I left Britain to go to Harvard University as a graduate student at the end of the 1960s, I felt doubly lucky. Not only had I come to America – to foreigners always the land of opportunity – but I felt that I was destined to be part of that golden generation of women who were going to find a place in the sun. By the early 1970s the women's movement was maturing, doors were being flung open, and the barriers to professional achievements for women were falling. I felt confident that I could have it all: career success; marriage; children. A few years later, when I actually dealt with the problems of bearing and raising children in liberated America, I learned what most women learn: it's damn tough. In fact, it was (and is) much tougher than I had expected, given the popular image of the new American superwoman – strong, efficient, cheerful, working, raising her kids, having it all.

While living in America, I stayed in close touch with my sisters in Britain, two of whom were also working and having children around the same time I was. They didn't seem to have as hard a time as me. At first I thought this was most likely due to differences in type of job, career ambitions, lifestyles, and so on. But as time went on, I began to wonder.

So I decided to look into it. And the more I looked, the more shocked – and dismayed – I became. For, despite all those new female MBAs, MDs, astronauts and TV anchorpersons, modern American women suffer immense economic vulnerability. They have less economic security than their mothers did and are considerably worse off than women in other Western democracies.

Way back in the 1950s a traditional division of labour gave women a substantial degree of financial security. Maybe many were stuck in bad marriages, but the man did go out every day and earn enough to support his family. In exchange the woman ran the home and brought up the children. With the social and sexual revolutions of the 1960s, all this changed. Divorce became common – in fact it became three times more common – and women could no longer count on marriage to provide the economic necessities of life.

This, of course, is a worldwide trend evident in Britain as well as in America, but the rate of divorce in the United States is now two to twenty times higher than in other advanced nations, and the degree of financial insecurity and injury women suffer as a result of divorce is far higher in America than anywhere else in the world.

Accompanying the breakdown of traditional marriage in the late sixties and seventies was a dramatic rise in the proportion of women who worked. This was part cause, part consequence. The weakening of marriage forced women into the labour force, while the combination of working and earning money enabled more women to free themselves of unsatisfying marriages.

Again, this was part of a larger trend; in Britain and throughout the advanced world women have entered the work force at an extremely rapid rate in recent years. How have they fared in the work place? Not well, and American women have fared worse than most. The United States has one of the largest wage gaps in the advanced industrial world (women still earn a mere 64 per cent of the male wage) and is one of the few countries where the gap between male and female earnings hasn't narrowed over the course of the last fifty years.

The plain truth is that modern American women, liberated or not, have little economic security as wives and mothers, or as workers. They are squeezed between the traditional and modern forms of financial security to an extent which is unknown in other societies.

In Britain and the other Western democracies, women have a much better shot at economic viability. Marriage remains a considerably more dependable institution than in America, and, therefore, traditional forms of economic security mean more. On the work front, wage gaps in Europe have been closing, and women's wages relative to men are now 2 to 30 per cent higher than in the US.

But that's not all. These other advanced democracies have also instituted family support systems, such as paid maternity leaves, child allowances, subsidised day care, and free health services, all of which considerably ease the lives of working parents. In contrast, the majority of working mothers in the United States have no right to maternity leave, and Reagan's social spending cutbacks have reduced even further the low level of public support for child care. These problems of childbearing and child rearing are critical as 90 per cent of women have children at some point during their lives.

In other words, while women in Europe have better maintained the security of marriage and have steadily improved the material conditions of their lives – by increasing the scope of family support systems and by narrowing earnings differentials between men and women – women in America have become more and more vulnerable. Despite their legendary claims to power and privilege, American women actually face a bad and deteriorating economic reality.

The *Wall Street Journal* put its finger on the nub of the problem: 'Aglow with talent and self-confidence, young women who came of age in the early 1970s breezed through college, picked up their law degrees and MBAs and began sprinting up the corporate ladder.'[2] There was only one snag: these same women found their careers 'sabotaged by motherhood'.[3] Although most of these women joyfully chose to become mothers and would have a hard time seeing their babies as saboteurs, the *Journal* was quite right.

Those of us who reached maturity in America in the 1970s were expected to clone the male competitive model in the labour market while raising our children in our spare time. Compounding this double burden were gratuitous psychological pressures, for we were also expected to raise these children according to wildly inflated notions of motherhood. We were the lucky generation of superwomen who got to combine the nurturing standards of the 1950s with the strident feminism of the 1970s. But, as I discovered when I struggled to bear and raise children mid-career, the rigid standards of the 1950s 'cult of motherhood' are impossible to combine with the equally rigid standards of America's fiercely competitive work places. Mere mortals such as I end up trapped between the demands of the earth mothers and those of the hard-nosed careerists, and because these demands are incompatible and contradictory, we are ultimately unable to satisfy either. Neither hired help nor supportive husbands can insulate American mothers from these antagonistic pressures.

My own difficulties led me to pose the central questions of this book. How did the most independent and best-educated women in the world come to have the worst conditions of life? And why has the American women's movement failed to deliver on these critical economic fronts?

To help me better understand this great American paradox, I decided to look closely at four Western democracies: Britain, France, Italy, and Sweden; all nations that have produced better conditions of life for the majority of their female citizens. I chose these particular countries because they represent a range of political values; I wanted to examine traditional Catholic societies as well as secular welfare states. But despite their differences, all these countries are affluent Western democracies and constitute a legitimate peer group to compare with America. I also chose them because I knew them well. I grew up in Britain, I have lived and worked in both France and Italy, and I have done research in Sweden. This first-hand experience enabled me to interpret the mass of data I collected.

As well as understanding these problems I wanted to develop some practical policies capable of improving the situation. So I decided to turn to some major players in the American economy. Since 1981 I have been director of the Economic Policy Council (EPC), a powerful private-sector think-tank made up of business leaders, labour leaders, economists, educators, and policy analysts. I persuaded the EPC that family life in America was in the midst of revolutionary change and that this was throwing off problems that had major economic as well as social implications. In 1983 I set up a policy panel at the Council which included former President Gerald Ford and twenty-five senior corporate executives. Its mission was to investigate the problems facing working women in America and to recommend policies that would help resolve these problems.

This exercise I thought would produce realistic solutions, not pie in the sky. The panel members, while sympathetic to the problems in hand, were not professional do-gooders but hard-headed members of the Establishment who had a firm grip on economic and political reality. I wanted to find out what could be done in present-day America, not what might be done in Utopia.

A Lesser Life was published in the States in March 1986. It received massive attention from both the quality and the popular media and provoked a series of fierce debates.

One of the first reactions came from the women's movement. In the main feminists were feisty, riled up and hopping mad. Robin Morgan opened the offensive in a March issue of *Ms* magazine. In it she described my book as full of 'tediously familiar right-wing anti-feminism', and accused me of 'blaming the victim' because I point out that feminist organisations have neglected to support motherhood. Eleanor Smeal (president of the National Organization of Women) dismissed my analysis as being 'very uniformed' and full of 'cheap shots at the movement', while Betty Friedan joined the bandwagon in a March issue of *Time* magazine and dubbed *A Lesser Life* a 'deceptive, backlash book'.

I did have some feminist defenders. Erica Jong in *Vanity Fair* declared that my book was the kind of work that 'could start a revolution' and 'serve as blueprint for a new era of feminist activism'. And Elinor Guggenheimer (president of the Child Care Action Campaign), in a letter published by the *New York Times* in May, supported one of my basic contentions that none of the feminist organisations has ever given meaningful support to mothers or children. 'The women's movement has given short shrift to child care. To date I know of no conference held by a woman's advocacy group where a major address on child care has been given, nor of any feminist publication whose major focus has been on child care.'

In the heat and energy of this debate, no one contested my central findings that modern American women are in lousy economic shape. The data are dramatic:

Two out of three adults in poverty in America are women.
One quarter of all women earn less than the poverty level when working full time.
In 1985 American women earned 64 per cent of the male wage, up only one cent since 1939.
And, a real shocker:
Women in the US are worse off than their Western European sisters.

Despite hostility from the élite ranks of the women's movement, the reaction from the heartland was overwhelmingly positive. Ordinary women in the mainstream of American society connected strongly and passionately with the themes and voices of my book.

Over the course of three months in the spring of 1986 I was part of a snow-balling media tour. On the TV and radio talk shows, in book-signing sessions in shopping malls, in hundreds of letters written in response to my book, I heard directly from the women of this vast country. They know what the score is.

For a lucky few the 1970s did constitute the decade of liberation. Doors were flung open, and young privileged women beat a noisy path into the male worlds of medicine, law and corporate management. But the vast majority were left behind to cope with a deteriorating economic and social reality. The economic reality is that most women still earn very little on their own, and the social reality is that contemporary women are more likely to be on their own.

The women who called in on the talk shows, who sat in the TV audiences, and who read articles about my book in *Family Circle* and *People Magazine* understood these facts. If you listen to the voices of housewives, working mums, divorcées and widows, to a remarkable degree they tell the same tale. It is almost impossible to raise a family and earn a decent living in liberated America. Despite all the new freedoms, in their gut most women feel immensely vulnerable.

Mothers of young children connected with particular passion with the themes of *A Lesser Life*. Anne Eggebroten of Newport Beach, California, shared her reaction in a letter:

I am so grateful to you for pinpointing the causes of the crisis in which I find myself.

You have it exactly: I am trapped between the powerful cult of motherhood of the 1950s and the current feminism which encourages us to copy the male competitive model and become identical to men.

I cry as I read Chapter One of *A Lesser Life*. I cry for your anguish and my own. You see, I never thought I would become a full-time mother. In eighth grade I wanted to become a geologist. In high school I dreamt of being a writer. I spent the next nine years in pursuit of degrees in medieval English and in 1979 I began my first college teaching job. It only lasted a year as a full-time position. My first child was born and I couldn't find affordable childcare so I cut back to spend time with Ros. Once Ellen was born I took a whole semester off. It was risky, but there was no maternity leave policy where I worked and I knew there was no way I could return to teaching immediately after birth with a newborn baby and a toddler to look after. As it turned out, postpartum exhaustion plus germs from nursery school triggered a long bout of illness. I asked for another semester of unpaid leave and was fired. I am now an unemployed PhD frankly too tired to hit the job market again until my children are much older. Will there be a job slot for me when I am forty years old? I doubt it. In this profession it is almost impossible to get back on the train once you have got off.

Carrying a heavy, sick baby up and down the room to put her back to sleep, trying to avoid the clutter of unsorted laundry and left-over food, I understand the trapped feeling that so many homemakers have had – even as they enjoy those baby smiles. I cannot even type this letter but have to write it out in long hand because my sleepy infant wakes at the sound of my typewriter.

Although I grew up assuming that I would not waste my time on such a menial occupation as childcare, I now have new respect for women who devote their time to raising children. I see both the difficulty and the value of surrounding small people with stimulation, safety, patience and support. It is a pity that mothering has been so devalued in our society.

Some of the most poignant letters came from women suffering the economic fall-out of divorce. The case of Jacquelyn Porter of Owensboro, Kansas, is typical:

I am living *A Lesser Life* and thousands of other women can echo my plight. Until recently my family was living the great American dream: Dad, Mom, three kids, nice house, two cars, even a dog. Then, as of 13 January 1986, I became a statistic – a white, middle-aged, divorced female with a job earning $10,750 a year (which, as you know, is below the poverty line). I was one of those foolish women who put all her faith and trust in the man of her dream. He has already remarried.

The court awarded me $100 a month maintenance for five years and $50 a week child support. A paltry reward for nineteen years of being a loyal wife and homemaker! I was totally unprepared for these economic difficulties, they make the emotional trauma pale in comparison.

These sad stories from the heartland of America share a critical characteristic: one way or another, these women have been derailed by motherhood. Which is why they responded so strongly to my book.

In *A Lesser Life* I show that the most urgent problem facing modern American women is reconciling the demands of childbirth and child-rearing with those of earning a living. For modern working mothers conditions are onerous and getting worse. Consider the following facts:

Sixty per cent of working women in America have no right to job-protected maternity leave. And yet these days women do not work for pin money; they need to hang on to their jobs to buy groceries and pay the rent.

Half the babies under one year of age have mothers in the work place but, perversely, federal funds for day-care assistance have been cut by a quarter since 1980.

The plain fact is American women take a nosedive when they become mothers. Pregnant workers are routinely fired; others are defined as 'new hires' when they come back to work after childbirth and lose seniority rights; and large numbers of new mothers fail to find affordable child care and are forced to take third-rate jobs with short hours close to home. Overall, American women lose a fifth of their earning power in the two years following childbirth.

To date American feminism has given little attention to issues of motherhood and children, which is why so many feminists were defensive in their reaction to my book. For many early leaders of the women's movement 'family' was part of the problem, not part of the solution. In the late sixties and early seventies feminists were trying to escape the boundaries of traditional domestic roles. The focus of the struggle was to win formal equality of rights between the sexes – to get out there and clone the male competitive model.

Many of the battles fought in the 1970s were important. We American feminists did manage to open up the marketplace and women gained new access to jobs, education and credit. But, as we dressed for success in our business suits and little string ties, we tended to forget that 90 per cent of women choose to have children, and that women would remain seriously handicapped in the work place unless we established a new system of family supports. Other Western democracies have done much better on this front partly because the social reform brand of European feminism has concentrated on dealing with woman's double burden in the home and in the work place.

British women can take comfort from the fact that they can rely on an important range of family supports that are denied their American sisters. A British working woman who gets pregnant is entitled to a maternity allowance, 29 weeks' leave (at least six weeks of which is paid), a guarantee of her job back and a £7-a-week child allowance. In addition, she receives an elaborate bundle of free medical services (pre-natal care, hospital delivery, post-natal care in the home) through the National Health Service. None of these benefits exist for American working women.

However, there is no need for complacency. British women have managed to close the wage gap between men and women a little, and relative earnings for women are higher than in the US, but progress has been slower than in other Western European countries. The fact that in Britain the gap between male and female earnings is 26–34 per cent (depending on which estimate you use), whereas in Sweden this gap has shrunk to 19 per cent shows how much is left to be done. Part of the problem is that too little public money has gone into day care and nursery schooling. Like their American counterparts, British women with young children are often forced to take third-rate part-time jobs because they simply cannot afford to buy high-quality child care on the private market. Women continue to pay a big penalty when they become mothers.

The problems faced by working mothers are not going to go away. On both sides of the Atlantic two-thirds of all new jobs are now going to women, and the fastest growing segment of the labour force is women with pre-school children. Easing the lives of working parents, ensuring a better start in life for our children – these are among the central problems of our age. Solving these problems not only benefits women, but as many Western European nations have discovered, such policies also comprise wise planning for the future. For children are not just an expensive hobby that women can indulge in if they so desire, today's children are the citizens and the workers of tomorrow, and we all have a vested interest in making sure that they have a decent start in life.

1. A Personal View

Until I had children, I was profoundly confident of my ability to find fulfilment in both love and work. Having grown to maturity on the crest of the modern women's movement, I expected nothing less. In the early seventies women were rapidly breaking down the male monopoly on career achievement, and I, like millions of educated men before me, was encouraged to believe that I could build a successful career *and* lead a rich personal life. When the political activists of my generation told me that American women had never had it so good, I believed them; when they told me I could dictate my terms to life, I believed that, too.

It is hard to remember how bright and shining the future seemed in those years. For me it seemed particularly dazzling because of the dreary hopelessness of my early life. I was raised with five sisters in a narrow-minded, unemployment-ridden mining community in South Wales. My father was a struggling teacher who was (in the absence of sons) intensely ambitious for his six daughters. Although we were brought up in straitened circumstances – no refrigerator, telephone or car – we were encouraged to think big and, above all else, get ourselves an education. And most of us put together enough effort and determination to do precisely that. But it was a hard, lonely struggle, and my memories of childhood and adolescence are grounded in a harsh reality. At the age of seven my most valued skill was an ability to peel potatoes very fast; at fourteen I was a social outcast because my wardrobe (none of us sisters ever had new clothes – we wore other families' cast-offs) and my career aspirations meant I had little in common with my working-class contemporaries. But hard work and doggedness paid off. At seventeen I won a place at Cambridge University and went off to start a successful academic career at that élite institution.

In 1967 I won a graduate fellowship to Harvard University and sailed across the Atlantic to the country that, to me, as to so many other immigrants, had

1

always been the Promised Land. I was not disappointed. The Great Society was then in full swing; America was eradicating poverty and urban decay. The younger generation was repudiating the materialism of middle-class life and working up a great cleansing anger over the immorality of the Vietnam War. Blacks and women were beginning to claim their birthright as free and equal human beings. I still recall the exhilaration I felt being in the right place at the right time – America in the latter part of the twentieth century. I was destined to be part of that special generation of women who were going to reap the benefits of all this progressive social change. While I could not quite believe that the world was at my feet, it seemed clear that the barriers to professional achievement for women were falling. We were now allowed to join the mainstream and compete on equal terms with men for power, status and material rewards. At the very least, I thought, I was not condemned to repeat my mother's life and see my best years slip away in endless domestic drudgery.

In the early seventies I returned to England to complete my PhD at London University, but in 1974 I decided to make my home in America and accepted my first professional appointment as assistant professor of economics at Barnard College, Columbia University. Two years later I got married, and in 1977, at the age of thirty-one, I had my first baby. Lisa was a very wanted child, and I was profoundly happy to have a beautiful, healthy daughter. However, the first few months of her life turned out to be a difficult period, full of frustration and failure. First of all, I was trying to breast-feed. But, since my teaching job at Barnard, a prestigious women's college, offered no maternity leave (paid or unpaid), I had to be back at work within ten days. Despite an immense effort, I failed to combine my demanding job with breast-feeding. When my milk supply dried up and I reluctantly had to substitute bottle for bosom, I felt that I could not now bond adequately with Lisa, that I had flunked the first test of motherhood.

More serious challenges soon followed. As a conscientious new mother I read the child-rearing manuals and found, to my dismay, that much of the experts' advice was incompatible with a professional existence. Most books simply assumed that the mother was available to her child sixteen hours a day. Besides physical care, there were such complex duties as 'architect or designer of the child's world and daily experiences' and 'consultant, someone to provide constant advice and assistance to the child'.[1] Only by fulfilling these roles could a mother ensure an adequate start in life for her child. I failed to find any child-rearing book that expended more than two pages on the problems of the working mother; most experts were more or less hostile. Benjamin Spock told me that unless a mother absolutely must work, it makes no sense for her to 'pay other people to do a poorer job of bringing up [her] children'.[2] Meanwhile, Berry Brazelton, an eminent paediatrician in the United

States, argued that 'two mothers are not as good as one' and urged mothers to delay their return to work.[3] I felt that Brazelton should have a word with my employer. Others were a little more generous, grudgingly conceding that work is permissible if a mother arranges her work hours to overlap with the child's nap time.[4] But Lisa, as is the habit of many babies, napped briefly and erratically. Burton White, the author of this particular piece of advice, clearly had not tried collapsing his work schedule into an unpredictable three-hour day – his wife had stayed home to look after their four children.

I found my first brush with the child-rearing experts an undermining experience, but I remained determined to qualify as a good mother. Had I not succeeded in other, more difficult spheres? Every minute I was not actually in my office or in class, I earnestly took care of my child, trying to compress into early morning, lunchtime and evening hours the elaborate responsibilities of motherhood. At the same time I was striving to be especially conscientious on the job, staying late, taking work home, and generally assuming extra duties. My great fear was that, given my new maternal role, I would no longer be seen as a committed professional.

A typical working day when Lisa was three months old went like this: I was up at 5 a.m. to feed and change Lisa (she was a very small child and it took months before she would sleep through the night). From six till eight was a precious period when I tried to cram in all kinds of 'quality time', attempting to 'lay the foundations of intelligence' in my three-month-old child in the way suggested by Burton White in *The First Three Years of Life*.[5] As well as the more obvious things, like encouraging Lisa to kick, gurgle and coo, I was supposed to move her about the house in an infant seat, do complicated things with steel mirrors (just seven inches from her face),[6] devise simple toys from cooking utensils to encourage her to use her hands as tools,[7] and train her sight by teaching her to follow a dangling ring 'with successive fixations' of her eyes.[8] This latter test could easily be flunked by the mother, for, as Rudolph Schaffer put it, if the ring 'is moved too suddenly, or is left static too long, the visual attention of the infant will flag'.[9] Poor Lisa, her infancy must have been rather arduous; I certainly didn't allow her to just lie around being a baby.

My husband, Richard, came on duty about 7 a.m., made breakfast for everyone, and cleaned up. At eight our part-time baby-sitter arrived, and by nine I was teaching a class. I tried to cram all my work responsibilities into the morning and early-afternoon hours, often going home to bring Lisa into the college for lunchtime department meetings, and relegating my own lunch to a sandwich eaten on the run. From three thirty till six was 'quality time' again with Lisa. From six till eight I coped with dinner and laundry while Richard put Lisa to bed; then, from eight till midnight I ground away at my research. In addition to my normal job responsibilities I had taken on a major writing assignment which I crammed into the later evening hours so that it would not encroach on my time with Lisa. As a result, I was always desperately short of sleep.

I had further complicated matters by electing to employ a baby-sitter part time rather than full time. I did this partly to save money and partly because I did not want to be accused of handing my baby over to a stranger. As a result of this part-time baby-sitting arrangement, any lunch-hour work commitment plus those that happened to fall after three thirty had to be undertaken with Lisa *in tow*. It is hard to exaggerate how wrenching it is to try to carry out work responsibilities with a baby in attendance. Simple tasks like dictating a letter or meeting with students become impossible if there is a fussy (and often messy) baby in the room, and colleagues were simply not amused if Lisa started to wail or filled her nappy in the middle of a meeting. Although to a non-parent these chaotic scenes seem to verge on the farcical, living through them was truly a nightmare and I cannot now understand how I endured the constant physical and psychological stress of trying to combine motherhood and career in this way.

When Lisa was four and a half months old, I capitulated and hired a full-time baby-sitter. I did this not out of any consideration for myself or Richard (though by this stage both of us were wretchedly tired) but because I was encountering tremendous disapproval and hostility at work and I knew that I could not take Lisa to my office any longer. The final straw was a note I found on my desk that spring. It was from a colleague down the hallway, and it read: 'Dear Professor Hewlett, I would like to point out that we at Barnard are not running a crèche but a college.' I was surprised and hurt: Weren't we supposed to be providing role models for our women students? But I was also cowed. I never took Lisa to work again except for the annual Christmas party.

A word on why I was dependent on private baby-sitters. When Lisa was born, I made inquiries about what child care was available on campus. I discovered that the only service offered by Barnard College was for toddlers. This service cost just under $1,000 a year and took children aged eighteen to thirty months for two hours, two mornings a week. I did not think I could use it even when Lisa was old enough since regulations required that mothers attend with their kids for the first six weeks of class! I remember being a little surprised. The toddler-care service was clearly not designed for the women who worked at Barnard College; we needed day care, not another set of responsibilities. Maybe it was meant for the non-working wives of male faculty members.

When I look back on this situation several years later, I realise that only one other person in my department had ever actually had a baby and that I was

4

surrounded by people (many of them women) who, for one reason or another, had opted not to embark on conventional family lives. Any thoughts I may have had about this being an unusual state of affairs are dispelled by a look at the statistics. By the age of forty 90 per cent of all American women have had children, but among professional women the story is different. Surveys of lawyers, business executives and other professionals show that less than half the career women of my generation have had children.[10] In many cases work pressures seem to have ruled out the possibility. These same women often tend to resent working mothers, viewing their struggles to bear and raise children as an illegitimate effort to have their cake and eat it.

My sister Helen, who lived in England, in Manchester, and taught in a secondary school, also had a baby in 1977. I was surprised to learn that she was entitled to an eight-month maternity leave, six months of it on full salary. At the time I didn't know anything about policies in other countries, and, after thinking about Helen's situation for a while, I decided that it must be some sort of special deal. I saw Britain as being rather backward on women's issues and decidedly 'unliberated'. Why, English people still talked about manpower and chairmen when they referred to women and weren't even self-conscious about doing it! I could not imagine that progressive America had anything to learn from the world I had left behind. In spite of all my American advantages, however, it was clear that I had not been able to cope successfully with the dual roles I had so joyfully undertaken. Instead, I had lost the precious beginnings of my daughter's life in a fog of desperate exhaustion. This was, I felt, a personal failure on my part. I knew there had to be a way to be superwoman and succeed on all fronts. I just hadn't been able to find it yet.

Two years later, in 1979, I attempted to have a second child. From the very beginning this second pregnancy was difficult. I was more than usually nauseated, I swelled up at an alarming rate, and I experienced frightening bouts of cramping. My obstetrician calmly and authoritatively told me not to worry, everything was in order. I found it hard to believe him, and at the end of the third month I sought a second opinion, carefully selecting a senior woman obstetrician at a New York City teaching hospital, who, I felt, would take my apprehension seriously. The consultation did not turn out as I had hoped. The doctor examined me quite brusquely, and afterwards, when we were seated in her smart Fifth Avenue consulting room, she glanced at her watch and told me that she had only two minutes to spare. I tried to assemble my thoughts and blurted out some of my worst anxieties: that I was feeling much too uncomfortable for this stage in pregnancy; that I was frightened by the intermittent cramping; and that I was afraid I might miscarry. The doctor smiled condescendingly and said that she was sure everything was normal and that, since I seemed to be getting a little obsessed with this pregnancy, why didn't I take up swimming or maybe even a little gentle jogging to take my mind off my aches and pains? Surprised and offended, I made one last stab. Did she think I should cut back on my work load during the remainder of my pregnancy? 'Good heavens, no!' she said heartily. 'This isn't the nineteenth century!'

A few weeks later the sonogram I had in connection with amniocentesis (a test carried out on older pregnant women to detect any chromosomal abnormalities in a fetus) showed that I was carrying twins. While Richard and I were delighted with the news, I now felt somewhat justified in my forebodings. I did some reading and found out that twins were often born dangerously early. Back I went to my calm male obstetrician and asked again, should I stop working or at least cut back to part time? 'Not at all, my dear, college teaching isn't hard labour.' He pinched my cheek and sent me home. I was immensely depressed; I yearned for some authority to tell me to take time off and concentrate my energies on growing those babies. Despite reassurances from the doctors, in my gut I felt that this pregnancy was in trouble. I talked it over *ad nauseam* with Richard, who gently encouraged me to follow my instincts. If I was so worried, I should stop working.

But it wasn't that simple. Since I appeared to have no legitimate medical problem, I could not request a leave of absence; I would have to resign. It had taken ten years of hard, grinding work to arrive at my present job and it would be extremely difficult to find another comparable position since the academic job market was shrinking. Besides, I was only eighteen months away from being considered for tenure at Barnard College, which would bring with it an associate professorship and a lifetime's job security. I agonised but finally decided to stick at my career. The truth was that, without external validation of physical problems with the pregnancy, without a doctor's approval, I could not throw in my job. I simply did not have the courage to take the decision into my own hands and deliberately destroy my professional prospects. I did not take the woman doctor's advice and start jogging, but I did try to put my worries to the back of my mind and concentrate on coping with the tasks in hand, which included a two-year-old child, a full-time job and a painful and malfunctioning body.

Later that year, on November 17, at about 6.30 p.m., I was sitting in my office in a state of total exhaustion. Earlier that afternoon I had given a seminar to the assembled faculty, a rather tension-ridden event where I exposed my most recent research to the critical comments of my colleagues. This seminar was extremely important because it marked the beginning of my tenure review and would help decide whether I was eventually promoted or let go. I was slumped in my chair, trying to summon up enough energy to go home, when water began to trickle down my legs. My mind was a little befuddled and at first I didn't know what it was. Then, as the trickle turned into a stream, I realised in horror that my waters had broken, that it was much too early to go into labour (I was in the sixth month of my pregnancy), and that this might mean the death of my two babies. By now my boots were filled with water and a great puddle was spreading across my office floor. I stumbled out into the corridor and, discovering that no one was in the building except me, made my way, dripping, shivering and sobbing, across the cold dark campus to nearby Broadway. I hailed a cab and asked to be driven to hospital.

Hours later my now grim-faced male obstetrician told me that if my body did not go into contractions, and if the amniotic fluid replenished itself, I had a very small chance of saving the babies. The more probable outcome was that over the course of the next forty-eight hours I would go into labour spontaneously and the babies would be born. Given their age and size (about one and a half pounds each), they would have no chance of survival.

I spent two days in limbo, lying flat on a hard hospital bed, sick with fear and praying to some ill-defined deity for the lives of my children. Then the technicians did a sonogram, and, to my great joy, not only were the babies alive but they were floating around in what seemed like plenty of amniotic fluid. But on the morning of the third day I awoke to find something strange and hard protruding from my vagina. It was an umbilical cord, and it was lifeless. No blood pulsed through the lifeline to the baby; it was stiff and dry like a withered stalk. One of the children was dead. I frantically rang the bell for a nurse, and everything started happening at once. Doctors and stretchers arrived, and I was rushed to the delivery room. 'What are you doing?' I cried. 'The other baby is still alive and I want to keep it inside me!' One of the doctors on duty patiently explained that they had no option but to induce labour. With a dead baby in my uterus there was considerable danger of maternal infection. Both babies had to be delivered. One was dead; the other would die. I hit my head against the steel railing of the bed and screamed at them not to touch me. It was Richard who finally persuaded me that I had no choice. We could have more babies, he said, but there was only one of me.

Later that morning I started a 'normal' fourteen-hour labour. I screwed up my eyes and plugged my ears so that I would not see or hear my dead and dying children being born – but I felt them warm and wet against my thighs. Although my obstetrician claimed that a natural (i.e. undrugged) labour was quicker and safer, to my dying day I will never understand why he couldn't or wouldn't knock me out with anaesthesia for the birth. I should have been spared such gratuitous agony.

7

Afterwards, for quite a long time, life was truly hard to bear. First, there were the physical ironies. My breasts swelled up hard and hurtful, full of milk for my dead babies. Several weeks later my breasts were still leaking milk, providing a constant reminder of my loss. But I needed no reminder. I mourned my children with an intensity that frightened me. In addition to my grief I was coping with an overwhelming sense of responsibility. Night after night I lay awake going through various scenarios in my head. I found at least four or five ways in which I thought I might be directly to blame. If only I had given up work I would not have miscarried. If I had sought a third medical opinion I might have found a doctor who could have saved the pregnancy. Or if I had chosen an obstetrician attached to a teaching hospital perhaps one of the babies could have been saved by access to a 'state of the art' neo-natal unit. I was riddled with guilt; I had failed to protect my babies and therefore had no pity on myself. For a while I believed that I was living proof of the conservative wisdom that women could not have both careers and babies.

As I gradually recovered and my life became happier, the dreadful sense of blame ebbed away. In retrospect it seems that I will never know for sure why I miscarried, but I now believe it would probably have happened even if I had given up my job.

My anguish during that dark winter of 1979–80 prompted me to do some reading and thinking about pregnancy. I discovered that my case was not unique. Twenty per cent of all pregnancies end in miscarriage, and for older women, who have often waited many years to start a family, miscarriage is almost always profoundly upsetting. In an interview, obstetrician Alan Berkeley of New York Hospital told me that in his practice many older patients who experience a miscarriage go through such anguish that they often reorganise their lives (resign from their jobs, change the pace of their lives, move to the suburbs) in order to decrease the likelihood of losing another pregnancy.[11] If one adds to the toll of miscarriage the difficult burdens of infertility, it becomes obvious that childbearing in the latter part of the twentieth century is far from being an easy or automatic process, whether or not the mother is in the work force. However, I was beginning to realise that for many working women the problems of pregnancy are compounded by the indifferent and often harsh attitudes of institutions and employers. Modern superwomen are meant to have children on the side, 'in their own time', and the less said about the matter the better. In America, unlike, say, Italy, there is little appreciation of the fact that having children is a social imperative as well as a private choice, that children are a nation's collective future. In America, children tend to be defined as private consumption goods. If working women choose to have them, then it is up to them to cope as best they can on their own.

The reaction at work to my loss of the twins ran true to form. I was allowed two weeks off for the 'procedure' (as one colleague called it) and was then expected to resume a full work load. Very few people ever referred to my loss. They found it embarrassing and a little messy, hard to mix with professional small talk. However, two women colleagues from different departments whom I hardly knew did seek me out. Pamela* invited me to meet her for lunch off-campus and in a quiet voice (as she glanced around the restaurant to make sure no one else was listening) told me of the day ten years before when she had miscarried in the middle of a lecture. She had left the room trailing blood and fled to the toilet, eventually depositing a bloody bundle in the bin. She had never told anyone at work what had happened for fear that her professional image would be compromised. She still dreamed about the baby she had lost and never replaced. She clasped my hand and said in a choked voice that she understood how I felt.

A few days later Susan* came to find me in my office. She had given birth to a stillborn child five years before. That tragedy made her want to reach out to me. Susan's story was chilling. The stillbirth had been followed by two subsequent miscarriages and it had taken her four years to give birth to a healthy infant. She had been fired from three different jobs over this period because no institution had been willing to give her a leave of absence to deal with the various pregnancies. Her husband had been unemployed for part of this time, so she had had no option but to try to continue working. Like Pamela, and for the same reason, she had kept her childbearing problems a secret. Susan offered to take over some committee duties for me and before she left we held each other and cried. I was deeply touched by these brave and lonely women, each hiding her grief as if she had committed a crime. They were afraid of professional repercussions and ashamed of showing their maternal vulnerabilities in the work place. By this point I was bitterly aware of the fact that they would have received considerably more sympathy from their colleagues and support from the college if, instead of losing a child, they had broken a leg on a skiing holiday.

When I returned to work after losing the twins, the head of my department called me into his office and, after offering his condolences, got straight to the point. He strongly advised against my getting pregnant again until the tenure issue had been resolved (and that decision was still more than a year away). He implied that he would not be able to answer for the consequences should I be so headstrong and emotional as to get pregnant before then. But I was past caring whether I was endangering my prospects for tenure. I had finally decided to follow my instincts, and what my instincts told me was that I desperately needed to replace my babies. Two months later I became pregnant again.

This time I sought out a specialist in high-risk pregnancy. In my third month I was sewn up – that is, my cervix was secured with stitches to minimise the chance of another miscarriage. For the remainder of the pregnancy I was under strict medical orders. I would carry out most of the basic functions of my job but was not to take on anything stressful or physically taxing. It was an immense relief to be able to 'take things easy' now that I had the imprimatur of a higher medical authority. I spent much of those months semi-horizontal on a daybed in my office. Students and colleagues came to me, not vice versa. My son, David, was born prematurely, but alive and well, at the end of the seventh month. Richard and I were overjoyed; it was, even with the additional problems of coping with a premature baby, the happiest of endings. As usual I had to return to work quickly, this time two weeks after the birth, and the expectation was that I should perform as though I did not have a family care in the world.

By now I had become deeply perturbed by the difficulties of combining a career with childbearing in the liberated Promised Land of my adopted country. My concern was especially acute because I knew that I was a privileged person. Seventy per cent of women in the American work force go to work out of economic necessity; they are single, widowed, divorced, or are married to men who are either unemployed or low-paid. I was not poor, black or single, and I had an abundance of marketable skills. What happened to working mothers who were more vulnerable than me?

As for myself, why had I gone on working if I was so bent on having children? I was, after all, married to a man who was able to support all of us.

There were some obvious reasons. I loved my job. I was good at it, and working made me feel useful and effective. But there were other, much more powerful reasons. I knew from looking around me that professional women who took a few years off to have children rarely made it back 'on track' and often spent their mature years in second-rate jobs. Did I really want to be someone else's research assistant when I was forty-one? My own institutions, Barnard College and Columbia University, seemed to have an abundance of female lecturers and assistant professors but few in the more senior ranks.[12] Most faculty women seemed to fall by the wayside in their thirties as they struggled, unsuccessfully, to both raise a family and live up to the competitive pressures of their profession.

I was also afraid of divorce. Richard and I had a strong and loving marriage, but I knew the statistical odds (at least half of all American marriages fail), and I had too many friends who had been left not only jobless and poverty-stricken but literally 'holding the baby' in the aftermath of divorce. I had endured too much economic insecurity in my childhood to want to expose myself (and my children) to that kind of risk. Stories about the sad plight of what are termed 'displaced homemakers' distressed and frightened me. My future in terms of both job satisfaction and earning power seemed to depend on sticking with my career during my thirties; my job was also my only insurance against divorce.

In the wake of my childbearing experiences I decided to form a committee with other women staff members to press for the adoption of a maternity policy at Barnard College. We had modest demands – a three-month leave, a small reduction in the teaching load during the first year of a child's life, and the ability to stop the 'tenure clock' during the same period (the system in American universities whereby, after six or seven years, assistant professors have their positions reviewed and it is decided whether they will be offered permanent jobs as associate professors or whether they are fired). We failed.[13] Our proposal was never defeated *per se*; it was simply allowed to die. My committee kept on meeting, and we kept on getting our draft document back for revisions and additional information, and nothing ever happened. It was like petitioning a brick wall.

Our biggest surprise was to find that the feminists on the faculty disapproved of maternity policies. To comprehend our astonishment, it is necessary to understand that Barnard College was and is a national bastion of women's rights. The college is understandably proud of its Women's Center (with its rape crisis centre, its abortion counselling service and its steady stream of national and international visitors); its annual 'The Scholar and the Feminist' conference, which produces some of the finest feminist scholarship in the country; and its fierce determination to remain independent of Columbia University precisely because it thinks that Barnard stands for values and academic standards that are important to women and that these values and standards would be swallowed up if the college were to merge with the larger university. Barnard College is one of the few top rank American colleges to have an undergraduate major in women's studies, and there is a powerful group of feminist scholars who teach in this area and are active at the Women's Center. In our naïve way we thought that all this emphasis on women's rights and feminist values had to translate into concrete support for the working mothers on the teaching staff. It did not.

Many of my feminist colleagues did not have children and were less than enthusiastic about families. Indeed, one of them publicly accused me of trying to get a 'free ride' when I spoke out at a meeting for a college maternity policy. Didn't I understand that if women wanted equality with men, they could not ask for special privileges? She and her (childless) colleagues were passionate in their insistence that liberated women should strive to copy the career patterns of men – to become male clones.

In the event, the Barnard Women's Center gave very lukewarm support to the proposed maternity policy. The director of the centre (who was personally supportive) apologetically explained to me that maternity leave was a divisive issue among feminists. If this was the other side of the coin of liberation, I thought, heaven help the working mother. It was clear our sisters wouldn't.

By 1980 my difficulties in having children mid-career had made me a less idealistic and less ambitious woman. I had become aware of an enormous gap between the aspirations of modern American women and the practical reality of their lives. Despite the achievements of the women's movement, my generation was a long way from being able to combine work and family life in the way that is taken for granted by the majority of men. As a social scientist I began to want to understand better the contradictions that so adversely affect the lives of American working mothers. For a while this new interest of mine was no more than a hobby. I was preoccupied with the care of two small children and my work as an academic economist. However, I was able to do a certain amount of research and travelling and discovered (to my amazement) that most Western democracies have made more progress in helping women shoulder their dual burden than has liberated America. I became determined to discover why this was so. Several years later I became director of a powerful private-sector think-tank, the Economic Policy Council, set up to explore important economic problems, and obtained some funding to set up a policy panel on women and work in America. I finally found myself in a position to push these questions further. All of which led to this book.

By the early eighties my experience had already led me to one important conclusion: women of my age in America are at the mercy of two powerful and antagonistic traditions. The first is the ultradomesticity of the fifties, with its powerful cult of motherhood; the other is the strident feminism of the seventies with its attempt to clone the male competitive model. Both these traditions can be found in other industrialised societies, but they are pale reflections of the American prototype. Only in America are these ideologies pushed to extremes. An American woman trying to fulfil the demands of both traditions is obviously in something of a dilemma. It is not easy to be simultaneously the earth mother–goddess and the hard-bitten, hard-nosed corporate executive. And her attempt to manage both roles is further undermined by the fact that American society, having produced the strongest and most antithetical dual roles for women, has left them with the weakest support systems with which to mediate these roles. Successive governments have repeatedly failed to provide the maternity leaves and child-care facilities taken for granted by working parents in other advanced countries.

Just trying to meet the demands of the cult of motherhood can prove to be an almost impossible task. Take, for example, the ways in which modern

American mothers are expected to give birth without drugs and to
The earth mother–goddess 'American-style' has her roots in the fift.
countercultural rebellion and feminism both added to the burdens o

The highly domestic women of the 1950s were encouraged to gl
specialness of being female, particularly in the unique ability of wome
children and suckle their young. According to Betty Friedan, influential author
of *The Feminist Mystique*, 'they were told to choose with free intelligence to have
babies, to bear them with proud awareness that denied pain, to nurse them at
the breast, and to devote mind and body to their care'.[14] In the 1960s the
Flower Children of the counterculture added their own special brand of
earthiness. Rebelling against the lifestyles and the values of affluent Middle
America, they led the return to a more natural state. College-educated young
women of this period abandoned foundation garments and make-up, ate
macrobiotic foods, and stopped shaving their legs and their armpits. Natural
childbirth and breast-feeding were emphasised as part of this back-to-nature
trend.

In the seventies feminists latched on to natural childbirth as a way in which
women could assert control over their bodies. They rhapsodised about birth
being the ultimate 'whole body orgasm' and hammered away at the need for
women to reclaim this precious experience from the space-age technology of
male obstetricians. Most of us were persuaded to believe that real women give
birth naturally and without pain.

Why did the earth-mother syndrome become particularly influential in
America? Natural childbirth, for example, had been pioneered in Europe. The
great leaders in the field – Grantly Dick-Read, Fernand Lamaze, and Frederick
Leboyer – lived and practised in England and France.[15] But it was in the
United States that the movement found exceptionally fertile ground in which
to plant its ideology. The ultradomesticity of the 1950s and the radical chic of
the 1960s joined with the new feminist desire to glory in woman's ability to
control her own body to produce new standards and new pressures for
modern American women.

My own experience was typical. During my first pregnancy Richard and I
took Lamaze classes, faithfully immersing ourselves in the techniques and
philosophy of the natural childbirth movement. We absorbed the message that
modern obstetrical practices were at best unnecessary and at worst a
conspiracy on the part of the male medical establishment to deny women the
'great experience' of birth. Specifically I was told to avoid using pain-killing
drugs during labour. A healthy woman undergoing normal childbirth would
only detract from her own experience and the well-being of her baby by using
such crutches. After all, if my head were in the right place, I would be able to
cast out fear and use the simple techniques of natural childbirth to reduce the

pains of labour to 'mild discomfort'. Surely I was enough of a woman to face this!

Fired up by such a worthy cause, I interviewed obstetricians until I found one who was suitably gung ho about natural childbirth. When my due date came, I went into labour right on schedule. And that was about the only thing that happened according to plan.

I remember it clearly. At noon on 8 November (I was about four hours into labour and had just been admitted to the hospital) I began to experience serious pain. I was startled and a little apprehensive. This wasn't supposed to be happening. It would probably stop soon, I thought. Instead, it got worse. Richard wanted to help, but since I was hooked up to an impressive battery of machines, the only way he could get near me was to kneel on the floor and lean over a set of wires to put his arms around me. Thus encouraged, I tried very hard to 'think about daisies and pant like a dog' in the way I had been taught in my Lamaze class.[16] But things got steadily worse. When I entered the second 'accelerated' stage of labour (during which the uterus acts like a piston to propel the baby out), the pain became so intense that the puffing and panting went by the board and I lost all semblance of control. For seven excruciating hours pain invaded and devastated every intimate part of my body. Each contraction lasted an average of a minute and a half and hit at thirty-second intervals. I groaned and I writhed, and, as each contraction crested, my cries of pain turned into a long, continuous shriek. By early evening I had had it with nature and was thoroughly disgusted with all those male advocates of painless childbirth. I implored Richard to get some help. I no longer cared what kind of drug was administered as long as it was strong enough to produce relief from the appalling pain. At some level I was also very frightened. Normal labour was supposed to result in mild discomfort; obviously, in my case something had gone horribly wrong. Perhaps the baby was coming out the wrong way or had a grotesquely swollen head.

Richard summoned the obstetrician. He was not at all worried. He was, however, disapproving. Couldn't I pull myself together? After all, I was dilated seven centimetres and I had to hang in there for only another two or three hours. His sole concession to my pain was to allow the nurse to administer a little Demerol. It did not help; it merely sent me to sleep between contractions. I awoke, every minute or so, in the middle of the racking pain at the height of a contraction and with no time to brace myself. I could not bear any more and after a particularly cruel contraction I implored Richard to get me knocked out.

But our obstetrician was fast losing patience with both of us. After disgustedly surveying his screaming patient, he called Richard out into the corridor and stated baldly, 'Your wife is hysterical. It is my judgement that much of her behaviour is an attempt to impress you. If you leave the room, she will calm down and begin to co-operate in her delivery.' He then quoted a phrase or two from Nietzsche, intending to underline the moral weakness of women.

Richard practically spat at him and decided to take matters into his own hands. He found the hospital's consultant anaesthetist, browbeat the obstetrician into giving a (grudging) consent, and arranged for me to be given an epidural (a local anaesthetic which cuts out all sensation in the lower abdomen but leaves the rest of the body unaffected).

Within minutes I was a different person. The incredible, unbearable pain just drained away. I became calm and reasonable, even joyful. The epidural left me completely conscious and with a great deal of control over my body, so that when the time came, I was able to help push my baby out. Lisa was born pink, noisy and beautiful. Back in my room the three of us celebrated the splendid moment of birth with a bottle of champagne.

Of the thirteen women in my natural childbirth class, three had caesareans and seven of the remaining ten (myself included) had unexpectedly painful experiences. All seven of us succumbed to some type of medication and remembered their experiences of birth as dominated by agonising pain. Only three of the thirteen had been able to deliver their children according to the Lamaze blueprint, and subsequently many of us had to deal with bouts of depression. At some level we truly believed that we were the weaklings that had failed.

When I was calm enough to look back at Lisa's birth with some objectivity, I was amazed at how completely I had swallowed the natural childbirth trip with all its unrealistic expectations. I thought that I had learned the Lamaze techniques so well that I would not be one of your ordinary run-of-the-mill women whose pain would be 'greatly reduced' – I would be one of your superwomen whose pain would be 'totally eliminated'. In retrospect it all sounds a little nutty, but the pressures for American women of my generation to prove their womanhood by giving birth without drugs and without pain were and are quite intense.

For more than a decade 'experts' in the natural childbirth movement told us that 'with proper training of husband and wife over 90% of mothers neither need nor ask for drugs'[17] and that 'a mother who has had any medication is mentally confused, "drunk" from drugs and not to be trusted with the baby'.[18] So asserts Dr Robert A. Bradley, natural childbirth enthusiast and author of *Husband-coached Childbirth*, a highly influential book well-known in America. He even claims that the use of medication in labour produces 'shortened attention span and memory, inability to handle stress, impaired reading ability and hyperactivity' in children.[19] He proudly describes the son of one of his patients: 'Now 13 years old, Greg has won a spelling contest. His keen memory is undoubtedly related to his unmedicated birth and to being breastfed immediately by his mother.'[20] However, there is, as even Dr Bradley admits, *no scientific proof of any connection between medication during childbirth and subsequent child development.*[21] The object of most of his writing seems to be to shame women into undergoing natural childbirth.

The natural childbirth movement elsewhere has been much less stringent in its demands on women for ideological purity and has focused much less on a drug-free 'birth experience'. For example, at the Westminster Hospital in London, the standard natural childbirth course gives a realistic appraisal of the role of pain-killers in labour and spends as much time teaching prospective parents how to care for the child once it is born (feeding schedules, bathing techniques, medical care) as it does on pregnancy and childbirth. All of which would seem to leave both mother and father better prepared for actually having a child.

What most new-wave enthusiasts in America or, for that matter, Britain, forget is that modern medicine got into the business of childbirth in the first place because the bearing of children through the ages has been an appallingly hurtful and dangerous experience for women. In Genesis we are told that 'in sorrow thou shalt bring forth children',[22] and until the medical advances of the last century this dictum held true.

The proponents of natural childbirth have a great deal to say about the good old days. Traditional peasant societies are seen through a rosy, nostalgic haze as cultures where women, supported by a midwife and a community of other women, dropped their babies simply and easily on the earth. This was the golden age before the advent of the medical establishment conspiracy, a time when women had complete control over their bodies. An appealing image, but unfortunately historical reality was a good deal less attractive.

For example, in seventeenth- and eighteenth-century Europe not only was infant mortality appallingly high – children had only a 50 per cent chance of living until they were twelve months old – but women had a 10 per cent chance of dying in childbirth and a 20 per cent chance of being permanently injured by the incompetent interference of untrained midwives.[23] As historian Edward Shorter has put it, '. . . the actual midwives of traditional Europe intervened furiously in the natural process of birth. Constantly tugging and hauling at the mother's birth canal, at the infant's head and at the placenta, they were captives of a folkloric view that the best midwife is the one who interferes most.'[24] Common procedures included puncturing the sac of amniotic fluid with a (dirty) fingernail, a practice that greatly increased the likelihood of lethal maternal infection.

In contemporary primitive societies pregnant women are almost invariably malnourished and overworked as well as prey to fear and superstition. In some tribal societies the woman in labour is forced to swallow live crabs;[25] in others she is merely suspended from the ceiling by a bamboo rope.[26] But whether the superstitions of the culture are gentle or harsh, it is impossible to escape the terror induced by the fear of death – for oneself or for one's child. Infant and maternal mortality figures for present-day peasant societies are as bad as for premodern Europe. If having a child entails risking one's own life, or if the newborn child has only a 50 per cent chance of living, it is hard to approach the experience of birth with joyous anticipation. For anyone who has lived in poor, backward parts of the Third World and seen at close range the misery endemic in these societies, it is difficult to swallow the chic literature of the natural childbirth movement with its halcyon vision of the past and the 'noble savage'.

Yet the power and pervasiveness of an ideology can sometimes overcome even first-hand experience. I myself was a research economist in West Africa and Latin America for periods of time in my early twenties and worked with very poor people – the Ewe tribe of the Volta delta and the shantytown dwellers of Recife and Natal. Yet because this slice of my life preceded marriage and children, I somehow was not able to integrate this experience with the ideology of the natural childbirth movement in America. It was only in retrospect that I was able to put the two together.

Along with natural childbirth, the earth mothers of post-war America have emphasised the importance of breast-feeding. Once again the ideological pressures to prove one's womanhood through this natural act are impressive. When Lisa was born, I, along with millions of others, read Karen Pryor's classic preparation for American motherhood, *Nursing Your Baby*. It told me that 'a good nursing relationship is valuable, perhaps essential for the emotional growth of the infant, and possibly of the mother as well'[27] and that breast-fed infants are happier because they have more affectionate mothers 'who were naturally more apt to breastfeed'.[28] Since the emotional as well as the physical well-being of my child seemed to be at stake, I became extremely anxious to breast-feed Lisa. It never occurred to me (then, at any rate) to question any of the experts' assumptions.

But as was the case with childbirth, breast-feeding, albeit a natural act, also turned out to be more difficult and painful than I had anticipated. My first problems resulted from the fact that I left the hospital twelve hours after Lisa's birth. My gung ho obstetrician came to see me the morning after the birth, slapped me on the back, and told me I was as right as rain and, of course, I should go home immediately. One result of my precipitous departure from the hospital was that I failed to learn any of the relevant breast-feeding techniques from the nursing staff. Over the course of the first days of Lisa's life I had (in sequence) cracked nipples, massive engorgement of both breasts, and mastitis (a painful staph infection of the breasts). Such a collection of aches and pains might have forced a less committed mother to succumb to the dreaded bottle, but I had absorbed the teachings of the feminine mystique and just knew that breasts were best. I gritted my teeth and soldiered on. Things went from bad to worse when, out of necessity, I went back to work ten days after birth. Karen Pryor and the other experts warned me of the dangers of skipping too many breast-feedings until the baby was three months old and the milk supply firmly established. Sound advice, but extremely difficult to put into practice if you happen to be working. (In the latest edition of her book Pryor spends a mere one and a half pages on the problems of working women.)[29] If I was to survive the working day, I simply had to delegate one of the night-time feedings to my willing husband, and often, despite my constant rushing between home and office like a headless chicken, I missed a daytime feed as well. I tried all the conventional ruses (pumping my breasts in the ladies' toilet, drinking beer and eating potatoes), but my milk supply gradually and remorselessly dried up. I felt that I had failed again, failed my baby and failed myself. If only I had been better organised or less selfishly concerned with sleep, I could have or should have been able to do it all.

The difficulties involved in feeding my second child made my first experience pale by comparison. By this time I was both more exhausted and less ideological. However, since David was premature and allergic to formula, there were medical reasons that made breast-feeding advisable. The logistics were formidable. David was so small and immature that he both required frequent feeding and couldn't suck very well. The recommended solution to these problems was to pump my breasts and feed him the breast milk through a special teat at two-hour intervals. But pumping my milk and then feeding David took close on an hour. Unless I could speed up the pumping process, just feeding my baby threatened to consume half of all my time. The obvious solution was to get an electric pump. A few days before I returned to work (two weeks after the birth), Richard telephoned the New York branch of La Leche League and asked if we could rent an electric breast pump. (La Leche League is a group founded in 1956 which advocates and supports the cause of breast-feeding.) At first the woman who answered the phone at the league could not have been more helpful. She asked concerned questions about David's birth weight and digestion problems and was just getting into feeding schedules and how best to use an electric pump when Richard let slip that one reason I needed this equipment was that I was about to return to work. The conversation turned icy. In hostile tones she told Richard that the league disapproved of nursing mothers working and, as a matter of policy, would neither rent nor lend us any equipment.

18

Richard and I were stunned, appalled and, finally, outraged. How could this group of self-righteous women deny help to a frail infant (David at this point weighed under five pounds) on the ground that they disapproved of the mother's work commitments? But I swallowed my indignation. David *needed* this equipment. I called them back. I was not choosing to return to work so soon, I explained meekly; rather, it was that I was forced to return if I wanted to keep my job. The ladies found this argument irrelevant. Anyone who was interested in keeping her job was obviously not worthy of their attention.

In the end, after much searching around, we rented an electric breast pump from a medical equipment shop. The proprietor was interested only in a modest rental fee and asked no questions about maternal work commitments or family values.

When I look back at my breast-feeding experience, I can see that it involved many of the same pressures as natural childbirth. In both cases I was driven to attempt the impossible by experts imbued with a zealot faith in complete motherhood. This ideology clearly grew out of the fifties. The earth mothers of this ultra-domestic era had every reason to elaborate maternal responsibilities, in particular the roles of childbearing and breast-feeding. These are, after all, the only functions that are unique to women. But while complete motherhood may have been harmless in an era when most women with young children stayed at home, it can be downright pernicious today. In the modern world it collides with the demands of a rigorous and inflexible world of work, where there are few concessions to maternal roles, natural or not. Today millions of mothers in America do not stay at home; they work, mostly because they have to. In 1984, fully 48 per cent of children under one year old had mothers in the work force.[30] The majority (more than 60 per cent) of these women have no right to time off for pregnancy or childbirth.[31] Moreover, given the inadequacies of public child care in the US, women with small children are under constant domestic stress. It is hard enough for them to arrange and pay for decent child care without, in addition, being made to feel guilty about failures to perform on the natural childbirth and breast-feeding fronts.[32] One professional woman I know still worries about the fact that she gave birth to her son by caesarean section. Her chief consolation, several years later, is that 'at least I breast-fed Jason until he was sixteen months old. I made up to him for my failure to give birth naturally.'[33] However, she paid a high price for her commitment to breast-feeding. She had to give up a career she loved and replace it with a variety of temporary, low-paying jobs.

The degree to which the child-rearing professionals in America continue to be out of touch with reality is astounding. For example, a widely read manual on breast-feeding, *The Complete Book of Breastfeeding* by Marvin Eiger and Sally Olds, devotes fewer than two pages to the working mother.[34] The advice it does offer is both patronising and irrelevant. We are told that 'nursing couples' (this is a term which in breast-feeding manuals refers to mothers and infants; fathers are left out in the cold) are homely souls who require a lot of rest and need to pamper themselves. My favourite passage is one which states that, however ecstatic the nursing couple, 'the time will come when you want to go out and do things. Once the baby is three to four weeks old, there is no reason why you can't get out for an occasional visit with friends or a trip to a drive-in movie.'[35] When my babies were three or four weeks old, I was already (albeit reluctantly) back at work, and the thought of putting my baby in the car and driving off into the sunset in search of that perfect recreation for the 'nursing couple', the drive-in movie, struck me as simply absurd. Richard didn't think much of the idea either.

The complications attendant on and following David's birth prompted me to do some soul-searching about my goals and the manner in which I was trying to accomplish them. It was very clear to me that my children came first. I still wasn't reckless enough (or courageous enough!) to throw in the sponge with my career, but I did make a decision to cut down on the amount of work I did for my job, even though I realised this might endanger my academic future. I stopped volunteering for extra duties within the department, I resigned from some optional college committees, and I temporarily gave up any attempt to do research. In addition, if David and Lisa were sick, their needs took precedent over any work commitment. In short, I established my priorities in much the same way as any working mother does. I continued to fulfil the basic functions of my job and was conscientious in fulfilling my obligations to colleagues and students, but I systematically eliminated extra work effort in order to save some of my best energies for my children. I was ruthless in sticking to this compromise, and by and large I was at ease with my decision.

It is a good thing I felt comfortable with my decision because when David was six months old, I was turned down for tenure at Barnard College, Columbia University. Everyone was surprised, especially since I had in the end been unanimously recommended by my department and by the Appointments and Tenure Committee of Barnard College. It was the final committee, the Ad Hoc Committee of Columbia University, that turned me down. No one will ever know why since this committee meets in secret and gives no reasons for its decisions. I can't help suspecting that it had something to do with my struggles to bear and to rear children while holding my job. There were student demonstrations and faculty appeals, but the decision stuck and I was given notice.

Quite unexpectedly there was a happy ending, which is not usual in cases like these. Within weeks of the tenure decision I received several job offers, and I moved into a policy position – directing the Economic Policy Council. The new position actually turned out to be well suited to my abilities and was both more lucrative and more flexible than academia. Apart from this practical fall-out, I also coped with the massive psychological rejection of having failed to get tenure (seven years' hard work down the drain!) with a considerable amount of equanimity. It was, after all, so very, very much less painful than losing the twins.

My problems following Lisa's birth had prompted feelings of depression and failure. I viewed my inability to perform my diverse roles with ease as my fault, the result of my own inadequacy. Somehow I simply hadn't been able to measure up. After the loss of the twins and David's premature birth, with all the special agonies that followed, I started to become angry. It seemed clear that the stresses of this exceedingly difficult period had little to do with my shortcomings but rather were a result of the attitudes of the society I lived in. I came to the bitter conclusion that at least some of my anguish had been unnecessary. Why had I been told that childbirth did not hurt? Why had I felt so much pressure to breast-feed? Why wasn't I entitled to maternity leave? And why did the commonplace complications of pregnancy have so little legitimacy in the work place?

Becoming a working mother seemed to elicit the worst from all sides of society. It was as if I had entered some kind of forbidden no-man's-land where every hand was turned against me and women like me. My place of work, supposedly an enlightened institution, had established its rules and regulations as if childbearing and -rearing had no place in the life of a professional woman. My feminist colleagues were opposed to any kind of maternity policy because, in their view, such policies smacked of special privileges in an era when liberated women were supposed to be behaving exactly like men in the labour market. My earth-mother 'sisters' at La Leche League, on the other hand, were prepared to deny me (and my premature infant) the use of equipment they had available because I was not, in their eyes, taking motherhood sufficiently seriously and devoting all my time to nursing my baby. Obviously the demands of these two groups of women were mutually incompatible; taken together, they guaranteed failure for mere mortals like me.

In most other modern societies working mothers are not put under these special and exaggerated pressures. For example, French mothers often prefer to breast-feed their babies, but they do not feel that their womanhood is at stake if they fail to do so. Nor does anyone else. Even more important, working mothers in Europe take for granted a set of social support structures which enable them to choose to breast-feed if they so desire. Free and extensive post-natal care; a statutory right to generous maternity leaves (five months minimum in Italy, for example, at 80% pay)[36]; provisions for breast-feeding time during the working day (in Italy again two paid one-hour breaks per day till the first birthday)[37] – all these rights and services are built into the fabric of European society.

Not only does contemporary America provide few of these support systems in comparison with other industrialised countries, but it also does rather badly in comparison with its own recent history.

A case in point concerns my former employer. After my failure to get a maternity policy approved at Barnard College, I did some research into the history of the college and discovered that more than fifty years ago, in 1932, the trustees adopted a maternity policy which offered a woman faculty member expecting a child the right to 'a leave of absence for half a year on full salary or for a full year on half salary'.[38] Reporting on this new policy in the autumn of 1932, Virginia Gildersleeve, the Dean of Barnard College, said, 'One of the most perplexing problems thrust upon women by the economic and social changes of recent years has been the necessity of combining marriage, motherhood and careers. It is of the greatest importance that our teachers should be normal and interesting human beings with as full and rich lives as may be. Neither the men nor the women on our staff should be forced into celibacy, and cut off from the great source of experience, joy, sorrow and wisdom which marriage and parenthood offer.'[39] For these reasons, Dean Gildersleeve was 'much gratified by the enlightened and progressive action of the trustees in passing a maternity policy'.[40]

Fine-sounding, noble thoughts, and we recognise them immediately since we heard them expressed so many times in the 1970s. The policy initiative is less familiar. Barnard's maternity policy seems to have lapsed in the late 1940s, and my own efforts to establish a similar though considerably less generous policy in the late seventies failed. Indeed, the committee I formed has only just completed its work, for it took until the summer of 1985 to get a minimal maternity policy readopted by Barnard College.

My professional history is clearly not an isolated case. Most women academics have found it impossible to progress to the senior ranks of their profession, and, at least at Barnard, things seem to have got worse rather than better in recent years. When I went for my interview at Barnard College in 1973, all three of the tenured professors in the economics department were women. Now only one out of four tenured professors at the college is a woman – and that after a decade of militant feminism at Barnard.

Barnard College – because it is a college for women – is a particularly distressing example of what are national trends. In 1984 only 4.2% of full professors at Harvard were women, 3.2% at Princeton, 2.6% at Stanford and 3.9% at Yale.[41] This situation cannot be blamed on a scarcity of qualified women – the pipeline is full of women. Almost a third of PhDs at American universities are awarded to women, and more than a quarter of junior faculty members are women.[42] At least some of these women do not make it to the top of their profession because they have the audacity to become mothers and proceed to raise children in a work environment that makes few concessions to maternal roles. Since they were busy earning their PhDs in their twenties and need to bear children before their biological clocks run out, many of these women are forced to raise their families in their thirties. Many – perhaps a third – have to deal with complications of miscarriage, prematurity, and infertility without missing a beat on the work front, and even those who are blessed with easy pregnancies find raising children – in the absence of subsidised day care and other support structures – an immensely strenuous activity. The end result is that these women find their energies hopelessly stretched in their mid-thirties, precisely the time when academic careers (and many other careers) are either made or broken. In short, they fail for much the same reasons as I did.

One final comment on my profession: even if a woman is lucky enough to be promoted, she is unlikely to be paid as much as her male colleagues. The salary picture in the Barnard economics department is instructive. In the autumn of 1984 the department had two full professors, a woman and a man. They had similar publication records and similar reputations in their respective fields. In some ways the woman was senior to the man because she was a few years older and had held a tenured position longer than him. Yet she was paid $45,000 a year and he was paid $59,000 a year.[43] Barnard's commitment to equal rights for women seems to be largely a verbal accomplishment. It is not allowed to interfere with the economic facts of life. But in this respect the college merely mirrors the nation.

Between the Devil and the Deep Blue Sea

2. *The Economic Fall-out of Divorce*

Once upon a time women could rely on marriage to provide a financially secure way of life. Leaving aside emotional issues such as 'Did the married couple really live happily ever after?' it is clear that marriage used to be a practical division of labour. The husband directed his best energies to building a career, while the wife worked hard at creating a home, an occupation which she saw as a lifetime career. Until quite recently this was a reasonably safe arrangement. Some marriages may not have been 'made in heaven', but most of them were enduring and provided a better standard of living for women than paid employment.

But times have changed. The divorce rate has risen sharply all over the Western world and America's divorce rate is by far and away the highest – currently almost twice that of Sweden, Great Britain and West Germany, and between three and twenty times higher than that of Catholic nations like France and Italy.[1] In America in 1940 there was one divorce for every six marriages, while in 1980, there was one for every two marriages,[2] and demographers predict that two out of every three new marriages will end in divorce.[3] While marriage used to be a safe bet, for today's women it cannot be relied upon to provide a lifetime's job security.

Take Julie Davenport.* Until six years ago, Julie was a traditional housewife. For two decades she had been a dedicated wife, mother, and housekeeper. She was proud of her accomplished children and proud of the prosperous life she had built with her husband Bill. For fifteen years, ever since the children were born, they had lived in a five-bedroomed house in Chappaqua, an affluent New York suburb. It was a good life. They had a live-in maid and a part-time gardener and took two holidays a year. Julie lacked for nothing.

In the autumn of 1978, one day short of their twentieth anniversary, Bill Davenport announced to his wife that he had fallen in love with another woman and wanted a trial separation. Two days later Bill moved out, leaving Julie with two teenage children. As Julie put it, she felt as though she had been 'tossed on the scrap heap'.

By the spring of 1979 Bill had stopped paying the bills. He now wanted a legal separation and a divorce. Julie was reluctant, so his strategy became, in Julie's words, 'If I cut her off and starve her, she will settle for anything.' Six months later Julie, hounded by debt collectors and unable to keep up the mortgage payments on the house, went to court, and Bill was ordered to pay the costs of running the house plus support payments of $325 a month.

For the next two years the Davenports fought over the terms of the separation agreement. Although Julie hired an expensive lawyer, she failed to prove that Bill had any assets other than their house, but she did establish that he earned $120,000 a year in his management consultancy business. They settled in 1981. Julie got the house, which she immediately sold. After she had paid off the mortgage and some back debts, she cleared $90,000. She was also awarded $26,500 a year in child support and maintenance until their youngest child left for college – an event which was just two years down the road. Under New York's divorce laws Julie was not entitled to long-term alimony.

Today, at age forty-nine, Julie lives in a one-bedroom rented apartment on West Eighty-third Street in Manhattan. She is short of money, tired, lonely and bitter.

In 1983 support payments stopped. She had $10,000 a year to live on (the interest income on her profit from the house) in a country in which the median wage for a man in full-time employment in 1984 was $23,218.[4] So Julie returned to nursing, a profession she had prepared herself for some twenty-five years ago. She now holds a job at a large teaching hospital. She works rotating shifts (one-third nights, one-third evenings and one-third days) and earns $20,000 a year. She now fervently wishes that as a young woman she had trained for a career that is decently paid. As she says, 'I never imagined I would have to support myself nursing.'

Bill, meanwhile, has remarried and is living with his 28-year-old wife and new baby in a luxurious house in Saddle River, New Jersey. Julie estimates that his income is now in the $150,000 range, and with that, she says with angry emphasis, 'He is able to buy not only the latest-model wife but also our children.' For the last year Julie and Bill's two children have elected to spend most of their holidays with their dad. 'Who can blame them?' says Julie. 'Their father has a pool, a tennis court, and a stay-at-home wife who cooks gourmet meals . . . He also has a large house so they can have their own rooms when they stay with him. Why, at my place they have to sleep in sleeping bags on my living-room floor and are often alone evenings because of my shift work.'

Despite her troubles, Julie is an appealing woman – slim, attractive and obviously capable. I asked her about the men in her life. She looked startled, then amused. 'You obviously don't know what the market is like for single women my age. Believe it or not, there are about four of us to every one of them [eligible men], and those that exist are looking for sprightly young blondes. No man I know is interested in a used wife with stretch marks on her belly and slightly sagging breasts.'

Julie is convinced that the good part of her life is over, although she probably has another thirty years to live. She points out, 'My ex-husband is going to get richer and richer and will spend his middle age in comfort surrounded by a growing family. I, on the other hand, am going to get poorer and more lonely. I've lost my partner, my house, my friends, my status, and even my children. I have nightmares about being old, poor and arthritic, and it's all because I did what I was supposed to do and spent my best years being a loyal and loving homemaker. It's not my fault that the rules changed mid-game. I guess I feel cheated.'[5]

Julie Davenport's case is not unusual. Indeed, by the standards of the modern world her story is not even particularly pathetic. After all, she got the house and an impressively high (if short-term) maintenance award. In addition, Julie is a trained nurse and was able to find a job. But there are many 'displaced homemakers' in much worse shape than Julie.

'Displaced homemaker' is a term coined in America in the mid-1970s to describe some of the more poignant victims of the breakdown of traditional marriage – former full-time housewives who have lost their sources of income and self-esteem through divorce (or, in some cases, widowhood).[6]

A typical displaced homemaker is fifty-two years old and has invested two to three decades in her home and family. As one magazine article put it, 'She has barely finished eighth grade, has high blood pressure, varicose veins, gynaecological problems, little stamina and her self-confidence is in shreds.'[7] The US Labor Department estimates that there are anywhere from 4 to 15 million displaced homemakers in contemporary America.[8] The figures are vague because, unlike in Great Britain, they are not eligible for even basic social security and therefore the federal government has no need to make an accurate estimate of their number. Little, in fact, is being done for them. Because housework is an unpaid job, homemakers do not qualify for unemployment benefits; if their children are over eighteen they are not eligible for any form of family allowance; usually they are not old enough to collect an old age pension. But what of alimony, the traditional unemployment insurance of marriage?

Folk wisdom about divorce in the United States has it that alimony provides divorced women with meal tickets for life. Or, as one famous legal opinion put it, alimony converts 'a host of physically and mentally competent young women into an army of alimony drones who neither toil nor spin and become a drain on society and a menace to themselves'.[9]

However, over the last fifteen years two things have happened to the divorce laws in America which have served to undermine the economic position of divorcing women. Divorce comes under state rather than federal law in the United States and, although the grounds for divorce differ slightly from state to state, most have enacted some version of no-fault divorce, usually described as 'irretrievable breakdown of marriage', and most have adopted equitable or equal division of property laws. The main practical effect of these amendments has been to reduce drastically alimony as a source of long-term income maintenance for the divorcing wife.

Alimony in America has always been rather less common than folklore would have us believe. One study finds that as early as 1919 alimony was awarded to only 32 per cent of divorcing women.[10] It seems that for most of this century alimony has been a prerogative of the affluent classes. Only well-off ex-husbands were required to pay alimony. Despite this qualification, middle- and upper-class women who had been left by their husbands found that alimony did provide a measure of financial security in the wake of divorce. All this changed with the advent of no-fault divorce, where economic need and the wife's potential for future self-sufficiency replaced past behaviour and status as the grounds upon which alimony was to be awarded. This is much as in Britain, except that in Britain the welfare of any children involved is the most important factor. Consequently, since children tend to stay with their mother, the British system still favours women.

In the early days in America no-fault divorce was thought to improve women's lot. It was embraced by feminists in the first heady days of women's liberation as the enlightened path to singleness. No longer would marital break-up lead to a public and perhaps humiliating airing of grievances. But experience has shown that no-fault is a bad economic bargain for women because it tends to reduce alimony as well as acrimony. For example, in California, it has triggered a drop in the 'overall frequency of alimony awards'[11] and a noticeable 'decrease in the percentage of open-ended awards and an increase in "transitional awards".'[12] According to one eminent judge, lower settlements follow naturally, if not inevitably, from no-fault. 'Because fault-finding required negotiation,' he says, 'it benefited the non-faulting party which was generally the woman. The husband had to *give* in order to get the divorce. It somehow resulted in a fairness. He had to give more than he would have otherwise.'[13]

As American states have moved toward no-fault divorce, they have also moved toward equitable division of property laws. These cut even deeper into an ex-wife's long-run financial security.

New York State is a case in point. In 1980 it became the forty-first state to amend its divorce laws so as to provide for the 'equitable' distribution of property acquired during the marriage. It replaced the common-law principle that awarded property to the spouse who held title to it, no matter that the division might seem unequal or that the titleholding spouse might seem undeserving – this compares with the British system whereby common property is usually split fifty-fifty between husband and wife. Many women's groups originally supported equitable-distribution legislation on the ground that wives would be awarded a more equal share of the property, but at least some feminists are now ruefully admitting that 'the [new] law is primarily a device to deny women alimony'.[14] True, wives now have a slightly better shot at a fair division of property, but the new laws have eliminated alimony, replacing it with maintenance – a temporary award designed to help wives (or, in rare cases, husbands) get back on their feet.

And even on the property front wives are not doing all that well. A study analysing twenty-six of the first equitable distribution cases decided by the courts in New York State found that seventeen favoured the husband, seven were ambiguous, and two were pro wife.[15] *Segal* v. *Segal* is an example of a pro-husband case.

Sandra and Lenny Segal had been married for twenty-five years when in 1978 he left her for his new girlfriend (who was the same age as his eldest daughter). Lenny had made it big in Sandra's father's company, and by the time of the separation he was earning a six-figure income and held considerable assets in addition to their house, which was in both their names. Sandra, who had spent her adult life being a wife and mother, knew that the divorce settlement was critically important to her. She had no skills and no track record in the labour market; how could she land a job, let alone earn a living? So she borrowed money from her parents and hired an expensive lawyer. He advised waiting for passage of the new divorce laws, telling her, 'You will get a fair deal out of equitable distribution.' She took his advice, but it didn't help. In the spring of 1984, after a long and messy court fight and a revolving door of expensive lawyers, accountants, tax experts, and economists, Sandra's divorce was settled. She was awarded half the house which the judge instructed her to sell immediately, and $100 a week in maintenance. She was not awarded legal fees or any other costs, and her bills for the divorce proceedings totalled $65,000. Sandra was desperate. She took the only job she could find, working as a shop assistant in a fashion boutique owned by a friend. She now earns $15,500 a year and is expected to work Saturdays.

In the divorce hearings Sandra's expensive lawyers and accountants had produced evidence (proof, she thought) that Lenny had at least $600,000 in stocks and bonds. The judge dismissed the evidence on the ground that it was insufficient. Her lawyers also produced evidence that Sandra's parents had paid the original deposit on the house and argued that the house was rightly hers. The judge decided that 'in-law help' was irrelevant to the question of ownership. Her lawyer hired an economist to ascertain what her services as a housewife had been worth over those twenty-five years. The economist constructed elaborate flow charts and testified that Sandra had performed $230,000 of work for her husband over the years. The judge was thoroughly contemptuous of this exercise. He tossed the charts aside, saying they were not worth the paper they were written on.

Sandra, an elegant, poised woman, can hardly control her voice when she talks about her divorce judgement. 'You know, he [the judge] had the gall to tell me that in mid-life both my ex-husband and I were starting new lives and new careers. He [Lenny] was setting up a new real estate venture, while I was starting a new job in retail business. He forgot to mention that Lenny is working with thirty years of business experience and six hundred thousand dollars of capital he got out of my father's company. My "new career", on the other hand, will barely keep me above the poverty level. To imply that we have an equal shot at earning a living is a parody of the real situation.' Sandra paused and then added, 'They may have changed the laws, but they sure haven't changed the judges.'[16]

Three aspects of equitable distribution are particularly negative for women. First of all, the burden of proof is on the partner who doesn't hold title to the marital property. This is almost always the woman. If a wife can't prove the existence of an asset or can't prove she deserves a share in the asset, she doesn't get a share in the asset. Obtaining such proof means hiring accountants, appraisers, tax and pension specialists, and, of course, a very good lawyer. The cost of contesting a divorce has therefore escalated – $60,000 or $70,000 is not an unusual amount – and obviously many wives do not begin to have access to that kind of money. In short, the spouse with the 'deep pocket' – most often the man – gets to dictate what an equitable division of property looks like.

Secondly, and more fundamentally, the vast majority of divorcing couples own few assets, and even if the property is divided in an equitable manner, it does not mean as much to the woman as alimony. According to Manhattan matrimonial lawyer Benjamin Kalman, 'In such a situation the wife-mother may well get the house, but that is all she gets, and many may then have nothing for everyday living expenses.'[17]

Finally, a great deal of discretion is left in the hands of the judge. According to a 1983 report published by a task force of the New Jersey Supreme Court, judges make an assumption that divorced women often remarry and thus regain lost economic ground.[18] In fact, women remarry significantly less often than men do. Judges also assume that women can get good jobs and earn decent salaries. As we shall see in the next chapter, they don't. Judges also consistently 'overestimate the earning power of women who have been out of the job market for many years' and fail to appreciate the 'particular employment problems of the displaced homemaker'.[19] Not only are judges unaware of how much women earn in the labour market, but according to the New Jersey study, they also systematically underestimate the cost of feeding and clothing a family. This is because 'judges do not do the grocery shopping and are not really aware of the cost of items'.[20] It seems that the judge that ruled on the *Segal* v. *Segal* case had a mind set that was typical of his profession.

If one compares the American rulings with Britain for a moment, one sees that in Britain also much is left to the discretion of the judge. However, the court's expectations of the wife's earning power is rather more realistic: she will be expected to undergo retraining, and maintenance may well be linked to the period of a suitable course that will give her a chance to return to the job market. The court will, though, always take into consideration the fact that the wife has to look after very young children who cannot be left during the day or that she has been out of the job market for a number of years. British courts do not *assume* in the same way as their American counterparts appear to do that women will automatically be able to get themselves jobs and maintain a reasonable standard of living when the main breadwinner has gone.

For American women, the bottom line is that a decreasing minority of divorcées get any kind of income support after the breakdown of marriage. No-fault divorce seems to have increased the economic vulnerability of wives, and so has the move to equitable-distribution laws. Today fewer than 14 per cent of divorced American women are awarded alimony. Most of these women are awarded alimony on a temporary basis, and many never collect what they are entitled to. In a 1980 survey of maintenance orders only a third of the women collected the full amount of the court-ordered support, another third collected less than the full amount, while the final third 'never received a penny of the support ordered'.[21] In summary, *fewer than 10 per cent of American ex-wives actually collect any alimony payments.*

Despite these facts of life, the alimony myth dies hard. Even in sophisticated circles it is commonly believed that ex-wives are often freed from worldly cares while their former husbands struggle to support them. Even lawyers and judges who should know the most about divorce because their speciality is matrimonial law 'seem genuinely to believe that the majority of all divorced women are awarded alimony'.[22]

One result of these misconceptions is that women often have unrealistic notions about life after divorce. Divorce lawyer Benjamin Kalman told me that 'women still enter my office with completely distorted conceptions of what they are entitled to . . . Some wives are still capable of saying to an absconding husband, "I will take you for everything you have plus your testicles, which I want handed to me on a silver platter." ' Kalman paused for a moment and then said, 'Frankly I don't see husbands being taken for a ride. . . . The law, in its operational effect, overwhelmingly favours men.'

I asked Kalman why the myth was so persistent. 'People get these ideas from *Dallas* and from Hollywood, where a few starlets have gotten large settlements and their hotshot lawyers have publicised the cases in the popular press. Palimony is a good example. A lawyer on the West Coast made a big splash with the *Lee Marvin* case, and everyone's girlfriend started to imagine she could cash in. Not so. The great majority of palimony cases have no legal basis and are thrown out of court.'[23]

Scholars in the field seem to agree with Kalman. In one study sociologists Lenore Weitzman and Ruth Dixon came to the conclusion that 'the persistence of the alimony myth is largely due to the visibility of middle- and high-income divorce cases'.[24] The publicity surrounding these cases encourages everyone to believe that wives are left in the lap of luxury after divorce.

Last time I was in a suburban supermarket I picked up a copy of a popular tabloid called *Globe*. The headline read GLEN CAMPBELL: MY LOVES COST ME $7 MILLION.[25] It told the story of how Campbell had been forced to settle $7 million on two ex-wives. This story may be typical of Hollywood, and it is perhaps the image of American divorce settlements which has travelled the Atlantic but it has nothing to do with the reality of divorce for ordinary American women.

So far we have been talking about the plight of ex-wives. What happens when these ex-wives also happen to be the mothers of small children?

Rose Barroso* separated from her husband six years ago, when her son, John, was five years old. Although she had worked as a secretary before marriage, she had spent her married life at home looking after the household, her husband and her child. In 1979 at the time of the divorce Rose was awarded child support but no alimony, and after the separation she found a job as a waitress. The job was hard, unpleasant, and badly paid ($3.50 an hour with no fringe benefits); its only saving grace was that the hours were 6.00 p.m. to 1.00 a.m., which allowed Rose to look after her child and do her domestic chores during the day. Her sister, who lived in the adjacent building, came over for a few hours every evening to bridge the gap between the beginning of Rose's job and John's bedtime. Rose repaid her sister by looking after her sister's child at weekends. In 1982 Rose took a new job as a secretary at the local school. It is not as badly paid as her former job (she now earns $12,000 a year), and it does provide some health and retirement benefits (John has had bronchitis quite a lot recently, and health insurance has become essential – except for poor families on welfare, there is no free health service in the United States), and since Rose works an 8.00 a.m. to 3.30 p.m. day, she can be with her child when school finishes.

Rose's ex-husband is supposed to contribute $200 a month in child support according to the terms of the separation agreement, and most of the time he does pay on time. He also sees John regularly for a few hours each weekend, and every other week John sleeps over at his father's house on Saturday night.

Rose's greatest concern is money. She and John barely survive on what she makes plus the child support, and she hates it that her son has to do without many things he needs. However, she says, 'For another few years I am stuck. Until John is older, it is useless to look for a better job because that would mean longer hours and a longer commute; he is too young to become a latch-key kid and spend hours on his own until I come home from work.' Rose does not think that her separation agreement was particularly unfair. Her ex-husband is more reliable than most divorced men she knows. However, she did point out that his income is now slightly more than double hers, and he has only himself to look after.[26]

Rose is right to think that her ex-husband is more responsible than most divorced men. The financial profile of most single mothers in America is bleak. Most of them are worse off than she is. At least part of the problem is the irresponsibility of divorced fathers.

In 1983 children from households headed by single women constituted almost a quarter of the entire population of children of the United States, but they made up a half of all poor children.[27] Divorce can depress a single mother's income as much as 70 per cent, and since nine out of ten children of divorce live with their mothers, the children suffer accordingly. Shockingly few divorced men help support their children. According to a 1982 Census Bureau survey, 41 per cent of custodial mothers are not awarded any child support in the first place, and of the 5 million single mothers who are legally due child support, only a third receive the full amount. A further third collect a small proportion of the award, and the remainder collect nothing.[28] Custodial mothers who do receive child support average $150 a month, a sum which is clearly not enough to make a great deal of a difference in the modern world.[29] The bottom line – *60 per cent of divorced fathers contribute nothing at all to the financial support of their children.*

One particularly shameful finding of the research in this field is that most divorced fathers can afford to comply with the court orders and are able to live quite well after doing so. In other words, most divorced fathers cannot plead poverty; *the money is there*. The data show that if an ex-husband earns $40,000 a year, he is as unlikely to pay child support as one who earns $14,000 a year.[30]

A poignant example of the low priority the legal system and divorced men attach to their children is contained in a survey of child-support practices in Denver. This study found that two-thirds of the fathers were ordered by the courts to pay less for child support than they reported paying on monthly car payments. While most were current on their car payments, more than half were delinquent in their child-support payments.[31]

In recent years there have been a variety of attempts, at both the federal and the state level, to grapple with the problem of default in child-support payments (which has reached record levels; in 1984 unpaid child support totalled $4 billion). In August 1984 the American Congress passed the Child Support Enforcement Amendment, which requires states to set up a system for withholding money from the pay cheques of parents whose support payments are a month or more overdue.[32] While this act is helpful, it fails to provide the custodial parent with an income while the state goes after the defaulting parent.[33] Besides, even if all child-support awards were collected on time, a larger problem would not be solved. The plain facts are that the level of awards is low and falling[34] and that only 59 per cent of custodial mothers are awarded child support in the first place. The present American system of child support is simply not capable of going far to meet the real long-run costs of raising a child. Estimates of how much this costs range from $71,000 to $160,000.[35] In the wake of divorce most of these expenses are picked up by single mothers.

Abby's relationship with her ex-husband is, unfortunately, more typical than that of Rose. Abby Gaynor* is a schoolteacher with two children, Ben and Jessica, aged twelve and eight. When she and her husband divorced in 1979, Abby thought that finances would be tight but possible. Her teaching job paid $23,000 annually and, although she had no alimony, she had been awarded $650 a month in child support – $7,800 a year. Although her living expenses were high because she lived in New York City, she estimated that these two sources of income would just be enough to enable her and her children to get by. There was only one problem: her ex-husband did not pay child support most of the time. By the autumn of 1983 he was in arrears by $20,000. Abby says, 'It is difficult to know which is worse: Bob's financial irresponsibility or his failure to maintain contact with the children.' Since the divorce he has never taken the children for a complete day. As Abby puts it, 'He says he can't think of things to do with them.' During this entire four-year period the older child, Ben, stayed the night twice at his father's house, and the younger child, Jessica, stayed three times. The pattern is that every now and then Abby's ex-husband will call and ask to see the children for a few hours. Sometimes he doesn't call for months. Despite the financial and emotional difficulties his behaviour has caused them, Abby never tries to prevent the children from seeing their father. 'His relationship with them is very imperfect, but he is the only father they will ever have and they need to know him,' she says.

For the first two years after the divorce Abby's financial position was precarious. During this time she took a second job, working holidays, weekends, and sometimes evenings for a debt collector's. Her economic problems were finally resolved last year when she remarried. Two salary cheques enable the family to live comfortably once again. Abby feels extremely fortunate. In her experience divorced women with dependent children often fail to find second husbands.[36]

Abby's perceptions are accurate. Older divorcées, particularly those with dependent children, are casualties of a marriage squeeze.[37] The plain fact is there are many more available women in America than available men. According to a 1984 study, 'After age 24, the prospects for women [finding a mate] deteriorate rapidly, with the odds in favor of men growing from a 20% male advantage at 25–29 to an advantage over 13 times greater by age 60–64.'[38] At ages forty to forty-nine (Julie Davenport's age-group) 'there are fewer than three suitable men available for every 10 college-educated women'.[39] All these glum statistics boil down to a remarriage rate for divorced and widowed men which is twice that of women in the twenty-five to forty-four age bracket, while in the older age bracket, forty-five to sixty-four, the remarriage rate for men is four times the rate of women that age.[40] According to the Bureau of the Census, only 18 per cent of divorced women in America eventually remarry.[41]

There are several reasons for this imbalance. First, men's tastes for younger women leads most divorced men in their forties to remarry women significantly younger (ten plus years) who have never been married rather than divorcées in their forties. Secondly, the fact that women live, on average, nine years longer than men creates a shortage of men in the older age brackets and dramatically reduces the number of potential mates for middle-aged women. Thirdly, baby-boom-generation women, now in their thirties, are particularly disadvantaged because the group of men immediately their senior is much smaller – a result of the low birthrates of the depression and war. These women have an even smaller pool of older men to draw upon.

If divorced women derive little financial security from ex-husbands, and if divorcées in their thirties and forties are unlikely to remarry, it becomes obvious that women like Sandra Segal may have no choice but to seek economic salvation in the labour market. Indeed, the new divorce laws instruct them to do precisely this.

The new litany tends to be: Any woman who wants to can get a job and be self-supporting. Therefore, she doesn't need any long-term supplement to her income. In a recent legal decision a Florida appeal court denied a 48-year-old housewife's request for continued alimony (she had been divorced for two years) with this statement: 'In this era of women's liberation movements and enlightened thinking . . . the woman is as fully equipped as the man to earn a living and provide for her essential needs.'[42]

But as we shall see in the next chapter, the earning capability of divorced women is low. Not only is a divorcée faced with the lower wage rates typical of women's jobs (and the median wage of year-round full-time women workers in the USA is only $14,479), but often she is going back into the labour force after years (sometimes decades) spent being a full-time housewife. It is extremely hard to get a job if you are older and inexperienced. If you have any skills, they are likely to be obsolete in the modern work place. If you are lucky enough to get a job, it's likely to be low-level, badly paid, and have few prospects for advancement. Add to this the fact that many divorced women (60 per cent) are single parents. Inadequate and expensive child care provides further constraints on the kind of employment a divorcée can get or accept. All these factors severely depress her earning capability at a point in life when her ex-husband is usually rising rapidly in his career.

Contemporary American divorce laws supposedly have the goal of equal or equitable treatment. And 'most judges appear to view the law's goal of equality as a mandate for placing an *equal burden* of support on men and women whose position and capacity for support are, by virtue of their experience in marriage, typically *unequal*'.[43] Many ex-wives are simply not equipped to bear an equal burden. If they are older or if they have young children, they are severely handicapped in a job market which already discriminates heavily against women.

All the evidence demonstrates that in the economic arena divorced women – and their children – fare extremely badly, while divorced men do considerably better. A study by Stanford sociologist Lenore Weitzman shows that just one year after divorce the standard of living of the ex-husband has risen 42 per cent while that of the ex-wife – and often her children – has fallen 73 per cent.[44] According to Weitzman,

divorce is a financial catastrophe for most women: in just one year they experience a dramatic decline in income and a calamitous drop in their standard of living. It is difficult to imagine how they survive the severe economic deprivation: every single expenditure that one takes for granted – clothing, food, housing, heat – must be cut in one-half or one-third of what one is accustomed to . . . It is not surprising that divorced women report more stress and less satisfaction with their lives than any other group of Americans.[45]

The economic consequences of divorce for women seem to be much more severe in the United States than in other advanced countries. For, not only is divorce more common in America than in, say, France or West Germany, but its impact is not softened, as it is in most European countries, by social policies expressly designed to lighten the load on single parents. As one Norwegian woman explained:

> Everyone knows that divorced parents need more money and more social support because of the additional pressures involved in raising children as a single parent. . . . So, as soon as I got divorced *my income went up*: both the local and national government increased my mother's allowance, my tax rate dropped drastically as I was now taxed at the lower rate of a single head of household, and my former husband contributed a significant sum for child support. . . . It also helped to have the possibility of 24-hour day care and a husband who was willing to take some of the responsibility for parenting during the week.[46]

These support policies for divorced mothers are not limited to the welfare states of Scandinavia. In France a newly divorced woman is eligible for a special social security payment for a year after divorce or until the youngest child is three; reimbursement for children's health expenses; a family allowance; a variety of special tax deductions; and government retraining programmes which pay 90 per cent of the minimum wage.[47] Even in Britain, a single mother (or father, for that matter) can claim an extra One Parent Benefit on top of the Child Benefit for which all women with children under sixteen, regardless of income, are eligible.

Many European countries (e.g. Sweden and West Germany) have instituted a system whereby the government guarantees the custodial parent (usually the mother) a minimum child-support payment. If the non-custodial parent (usually the father) fails to come through with child support, the government steps in, pays the mother the minimum amount, and then tries to collect from the father by such mechanisms as attaching his salary.[48] The systems adopted in many European countries, then, have one major advantage over the American Child Support Enforcement Amendment in that they guarantee a base income for custodial parents and their children.

In view of the economic distress visited on the majority of divorced women, it is disheartening to see how unrealistically their problems are portrayed in

39

American popular culture (which is also, incidentally, the main source of the European view of American culture). In the novels, plays and films dealing with the 'older' (over thirty-five) woman who gets divorced, reality is generally kept firmly at bay. For instance, in the film *An Unmarried Woman* Jill Clayburgh, abandoned by her husband, continues to live with her child in a large and lavish apartment on Manhattan's Upper East Side. She appears to have no financial anxieties whatsoever. Every day she blithely takes an extremely long taxi ride down to her part-time job in a funky SoHo art gallery which couldn't possibly pay enough to cover even her cab fare. Her greatest dilemma is deciding whether to spend August in New York searching for her true identity or in Vermont with new boyfriend Alan Bates, risking her precarious new independence. Would that all newly divorced women faced such problems!

As we have seen, most divorced women are overwhelmed by the grim economic consequences of marital breakdown. Not only do women bear the direct costs of divorce – their own standard of living takes a nosedive – but they also bear almost all the costs and take almost all the responsibility of raising the children of divorce. A recent study at the University of Pennsylvania finds that in America 49 per cent of children in the custody of their mothers do not see their fathers at all.[49] It is easy to see how the pressures on mothers in the immediate aftermath of divorce can become so intense that they find it difficult to perform their parental roles, becoming inconsistent and punishing erratically. The children start playing up and the result is often a battle for survival. One divorced mother described the constant harassment as 'like being bitten to death by ducks'.[50] It is hardly surprising that these women have problems holding down a job, let alone building up a career.

3. The Wage Gap

Say the words 'American working women', and our minds immediately conjure up images of superwomen, those television anchorpersons, astronauts and executive vice-presidents so beloved by the American media. Barbara Walters and Sally Ride are modern heroines, and the press would have us believe that the US is full of glamorous career women, all earning six-figure incomes.

Fortune magazine, for instance, ran a spread on vivacious Linda Taylor. A graduate of Harvard's Business School, Linda is in her mid-thirties and on the fast track. She has just been promoted to chief investment officer of the United Mine Workers' $2.3 billion pension and health fund and now earns more than $100,000 a year. Linda is also the mother of three children. To keep her household running smoothly, Linda employs a staff of three – housekeeper, nanny, and weekend substitute (who takes over housekeeping and child care on Saturday and Sunday). The annual payroll of Linda's domestic staff totals $27,000.[1]

Forbes had a story on dynamic Lorraine Mecca. Five years ago this enterprising 34-year-old former English teacher invested $25,000 from her divorce settlement in her fledgling Micro D Inc. of Fountain Valley, California – a wholesale operation that sells computer software. In the first nine months of 1983 Micro D had sales of $50 million and a net of $859,000. The company went public in July 1984, raising $25 million. Lorraine is now a wealthy woman.[2]

Would that Linda and Lorraine were representative of working women in American, or for that matter, British society. Unfortunately reality is a lot less glamorous. Despite the enormous expansion of the female labour force in the United States in recent years – the number of women working has doubled since 1960 – there has been little improvement in women's economic position.

Only 7 per cent of employed women in America work in managerial positions, and only 10 per cent earn more than $23,000 a year. Three-quarters of American working women continue to be employed in traditional 'women's jobs' and spend their time waiting on tables, typing letters, cutting hair, emptying bedpans and cleaning offices. Most are badly paid. In 1984, one out of every four women earned less than $10,000 a year when working full time.[3] In many cases, some women's salaries fail to lift them above the poverty line, and this produces much hardship in a day and age when women's wages no longer constitute pin money. Today 45 per cent of the working women of America are single, divorced, separated or widowed and have no option but to take prime economic responsibility for themselves (and often their children). The low earning power of women helps explain why 35 per cent of single mothers fall below the poverty line.

A critical measure of how well women are doing in the labour market is the wage gap, which is the difference between male and female earnings. The wage gap in America is extremely wide and has not shifted in fifty years.

In 1939, when Franklin D. Roosevelt was president, *Gone with the Wind* was awarded the Academy Award as best picture, and Joe DiMaggio was star of the baseball field, American women earned sixty-three cents to every man's dollar.[4] Presidents have come and gone, *Gone with the Wind* is on cable TV, and DiMaggio is a legend. But women's earning power hasn't changed much. Today women earn sixty-four cents to a man's dollar.[5] America has women astronauts and women vice-presidential candidates – indeed, fully 45 per cent of the US work force is now female – yet the gap between male and female earnings is as wide as it was half a century ago.

In 1984 women who were employed full time the year round earned, on average, $14,479, while similarly employed men earned $23,218. A woman with four years of college still earns less than a male high school drop-out.[6]

Mary Engle works at the Ms and His Unisex salon in Pennsauken, New Jersey, mostly cutting hair. She is single and twenty-six years old and has been working at the salon on Center Street for eight years, ever since she finished her training at the Maison de Paris beautician school in Haddonfield, New Jersey.

With salary and tips she earns about $10,000 a year, the average wage for a female hairdresser of her age with a high school diploma. Average, that is, for a woman, not average for a man.[7]

According to 1980 census data female hairstylists between ages twenty-five and thirty-four earn $3,677 less than male hairstylists of similar age and educational background. Female hairdressers between ages thirty-five and forty-four earn $7,603 less than their male counterparts.

Engle's wage-earning experience is mirrored in virtually every occupation. Male lawyers between the ages of twenty-five and thirty-four earn, on average, $27,563 a year; the figure for female lawyers is $20,573. Bus drivers average $15,611 if they are men but $9,903 if they are women. As for shop assistants, males average $13,002 a year while females average $7,479 a year.[8] America seem to have eliminated sexist terminology without doing anything about economic inequality.

The wage gap pursues women even into old age. There are 16 million women over sixty-five years old in the population of America. In 1982 their median income was $5,365, compared to $9,188 for men.[9] It seems that if you are a woman, you have a 60 per cent shot at being poor in old age, and since women live on average to be seventy-nine, old age can last a long time. The main reason for the disparity between the incomes of elderly men and women is that since the jobs women hold are rarely good enough to qualify them for private pensions, only 11 per cent of women over sixty-five collect company pensions.[10]

Perhaps one of the most extraordinary and, for American women, most disturbing facts about the wage gap in the USA is that it is actually much wider – and more stubborn – than elsewhere in the industrial world. As the British economist Peter Sloane puts it, 'In most countries for which data are available the average gender wage differential narrowed significantly during the 1970s'; only in the United States did the sex wage differential 'remain fixed as if through some divine law'.[11]

In Sweden, where women are among the highest paid in Europe, they earned just over 81 per cent of male earnings in 1980, up from 71 per cent in 1970.[12] In Italy women's wages as a percentage of men's wages increased from 74 per cent in 1968 to 86 per cent in 1982; in West Germany women's wages rose from 69 per cent in 1968 to 73 per cent in 1982; in France they rose from 76 per cent in 1964 to 78 per cent in 1982; and in Denmark they rose from 74 per cent in 1968 to 86 per cent in 1982.[13] Even in Britain, where women are among the lowest paid in Europe, their wages as a percentage of men's increased from 54 per cent in 1970 to 66 per cent in 1982.[14] Across the board in Europe, however, the wage gap is narrowing and traditional Catholic societies as well as the Scandinavian welfare states have made more progress than America on this critical front.

The low earning power of American women workers as compared with their European peers is particularly surprising when one takes into consideration the educational picture. American women are the best-educated in the world. Of current four-year college students in the United States 52 per cent are female, and half of all master's degrees and a quarter of all professional degrees go to women. Indeed, the average American woman worker is now slightly better educated than her male colleague, having completed a median of 12.65 years of schooling, compared to 12.57 for men.[15] In Europe women continue to lag behind men in educational attainment. In Italy, women make up 41 per cent of students in higher education, in France the figure is 45 per cent, and in Britain only 39 per cent.[16] One would therefore expect the wage gap in these countries to be wider, not narrower. All of which adds to the mystery of why American women do so badly in the work place.

Perhaps the biggest surprise about American working women is that women at the very top of the pile, the superwomen of media fame, are not in fact closing the economic gender gap. Census data show that more women in America hold executive and professional positions than ever before – the percentage of managerial jobs held by women rose from 14.5 per cent in 1960 to 28.9 per cent in 1980[17] – yet over these two decades, when executive women made such impressive numerical gains, the wage gap between men and women executives actually widened. In 1960 women managers earned 58 per cent of the male wage; in 1980 they earned 55 per cent.[18] Women are simply not making it into upper management; they remain heavily concentrated in the lower half of the corporate pyramid. It is calculated that women make up about 50 per cent of entry management and 25 per cent of middle management.[19] But although business began recruiting and promoting women in substantial numbers in the early 1970s – far enough back to give them time for considerable career advancement – they account for only a tiny percentage of upper management in the United States. Estimates are in the 1 to 2 per cent range.[20] There seems to be a revolving door for women at the bottom of the managerial career ladder.

Finally, the difference between the starting salaries of men and women in America has actually widened in recent years. Gordon Green, a demographer at the Bureau of the Census, has found that the wages of white women entering the job market were 3 percentage points farther behind comparable white men in 1980 than they were in 1970. This is 'despite the growth of affirmative action and educational gains by women'.[21]

A favourite indoor sport among economists is debating the reasons behind the wage gap. Those on the liberal left of the discipline emphasise the fact that women are paid less because they are discriminated against; those on the conservative right stress that the home and family responsibilities of women depress their earnings potential.[22]

Discrimination against women in the labour market shows up in a variety of ways. The most overt kinds of discrimination occur when a woman is paid less than a man for doing the same job, or when a qualified woman is denied access to a job or promotion to a better job on account of her sex. These forms of discrimination have been illegal in America since the passage of the Equal Pay Act in 1963 and Title VII of the Civil Rights Act in 1964. In fact, in this respect, the United States has led the world. Britain, the first member of the EEC to introduce equal pay legislation, did not pass an Equal Pay Act until 1970 and its Sex Discrimination Act until 1975; France did not have an Equal Pay Act until 1972 and Italy its Anti-discrimination Act, covering equality of both pay and opportunity, until 1977.

The efficacy of equal pay legislation is debatable – the evidence suggests that legislation 'far from being responsible for improvements in female relative earnings has tended to follow them'.[23] However, although discrimination on pay and opportunity on the grounds of sex has far from disappeared, progress has been made both in the United States and in Europe. For example, in America between 1962 and 1982, the proportion of women among engineers rose from 1 to 6 per cent; among physicians from 6 to 15 per cent; and among bus drivers from 12 to 47 per cent.[24] The figures for Britain are not exactly comparable, but, to give some idea, the proportion of women at Assistant Secretary (just below Under Secretary) level in the Civil Service rose from 4.8 per cent in 1975 to 6.3 per cent in 1983; the proportion of women members of the Institute of Bankers rose from 4.2 per cent in 1975 to 20.6 per cent in 1983; women made up 16.6 per cent of hospital doctors and 12.9 per cent of General Practitioners in 1975 and in 1981 the figures were 20.6 per cent and 16.5 per cent respectively. Small steps *are* being made.[25]

A less obvious form of discrimination against women, almost impossible to legislate against, is the 'pink-collar' ghetto, when women are segregated into low-paying jobs. These jobs are not necessarily low-skilled, but for a host of social and political reasons they are almost always low-paid – in Europe and in America. Concentrating on America, however, in the first place, women's occupations have often been overcrowded because of legal and social restrictions on the jobs open to women. Secondly, women's jobs have generally not been organised by trade unions, and this has weakened the earning power of these jobs. Thirdly, employers have got away with paying women less because many of them were, and to some extent still are, secondary wage earners within the family. Finally, women workers have often interrupted their work to bear and raise children. All these factors have depressed wages in women's fields. So powerful are these factors that any field dominated by women in the United States is almost guaranteed to have low wages. Indeed, there are certain occupations that used to be dominated by men and used to be well paid until women took them over.

For example, a century ago most clerical workers in the United States were male. They earned about twice as much as blue-collar workers. Today 80 per cent of all clerical jobs are held by women, and the average wage is far below that of blue-collar work. In fact, in modern America a secretary with eighteen years' experience earns less than a parking-lot attendant. A similar story can be told about bank tellers. Before the Second World War bank tellers were male, and the jobs they held were prestigious and well paid. Today this occupation is dominated by women, and bank tellers have lost both status and earning power.

Despite the changes of recent years, the United States labour market is still largely segregated by sex. In 1982, 50 per cent of employed women worked in only 20 occupations – out of the 427 occupations detailed by the United States Department of Labor. More than half of all employed women worked in occupations which were 75 per cent female, and 22 per cent of employed women were in jobs that were more than 95 per cent female.[26] Women still account for 99 per cent of secretaries, 97 per cent of typists, and 96 per cent of all registered nurses.[27]

Contrary to popular opinion, the entry of women into professional and blue-collar jobs has *not* reduced the overall degree of segregation. This is because the movement of a few women into predominantly male jobs has been overwhelmed by a flood of new women workers into predominantly female jobs. In other words, for every woman entering a traditionally male field such as law or motor mechanics, there are several women entering traditional women's fields.

Over the last two years there has been an increasingly vigorous attempt in the United States to combat this more subtle form of discrimination – the segregation of women into low-paying occupations – by applying the principle of equal pay for jobs of comparable worth. The argument is that women have been 'segregated into job classifications on the basis of sex, and, as a result, are paid less than employees in historically predominantly male classifications which require an equivalent [amount] of skill, effort and responsibility'.[28] The strategy is to conduct job evaluations, measure the value of different jobs to the employer, and come up with a numerical rating for each. If a secretary is rated the same as a plumber, then both jobs should command the same pay. Currently a score of states and municipalities are under pressure from public employee unions to pay women in low-paying occupations more by applying the principle of comparable worth.

Perhaps the most important legal decision came at the end of 1983, when a federal judge ordered the state of Washington to pay its women workers $800 million in back pay and wage increases on the basis of a comparable worth evaluation. Judge Jack Tanner ruled that the state practised 'direct, overt and institutionalised' discrimination against its women employees.[29] The Washington State ruling triggered scores of cases, and by the end of 1984 litigation was pending across the nation.

Comparable worth has been called the civil rights issue of the 1980s in America, and it is already a political football – supported by liberals, opposed by conservatives. In the 1984 election campaign it was endorsed by the Mondale–Ferraro ticket and opposed by the Reagan administration. Liberals see comparable worth as the best way of producing economic justice for women workers who are shunted into the lowest paid jobs, and they vigorously defend the use of job evaluations to determine the value of a job. 'This is done every day by American business and industry,' says Eleanor Holmes Norton, a former head of the Equal Employment Opportunity Commission. As she sees it, 'Women are doing valuable work which just happens to be underpaid because it is done by women.'[30]

Conservative critics respond that unlike the job evaluations of individual companies, which are useful internal measures that take into account the forces of supply and demand, comparable-worth plans like the one used in Washington State are not pegged to the market.[31] But many people – including Ray Marshall, economist and Secretary of Labor in the Carter administration – aren't sure that market forces work with much precision in internal labour markets. 'If you compare the predominantly male profession of engineer with the predominantly female profession of nurse, you find there is a shortage of both but the market's response is different. The wages offered to engineers go up, while nurses who will work cheap are imported from abroad.'[32]

The cost of raising wages for what have traditionally been women's jobs can be high. The Washington State settlement, if upheld by the courts, would cost an estimated $642 million in back pay and $195 million a year in raises. Another issue raised by opponents is that if comparable worth were applied on any scale to private business, it would increase the wage bill and the cost of production, bringing higher prices at home and hindering the ability of American firms to compete in overseas markets.

All this implies that the principle of comparable worth is not going to be accepted quickly or easily in the US labour market.

If occupational segregation is important in explaining the wage gap,[33] the other critical explanatory factor is the heavy load of family responsibilities borne by most working women.

Women attain much less seniority and earn much less money than men whatever occupation they are employed in. As a woman you don't have to be a waitress or a secretary to be badly paid; you don't even have to be discriminated against. You can attend the best professional schools, you can be hired by the most prestigious firms, and you can be treated the same as a man but still find that over a lifetime it is easy to earn a fraction of the amount earned by male contemporaries. The fact is most women bear weighty home and family burdens and need more than equality with men if they are to attain equal earning power in the marketplace. They need job-protected maternity leave, child care, flexitime and specially tailored career ladders.

*

Susan Fischer* works a three-day week as a programme officer at a private foundation in Washington. She is 39 years old, earns $23,000 a year and lives quietly with her husband and two small children in suburban Maryland. It's a pleasant enough life but not one that will set the world on fire.

I first met Susan some ten years ago. At the time she was single and fiercely ambitious. I remember being impressed by her professional zeal and by the fact that her recent book on trade policy had just won a coveted prize awarded by the American Economic Association. Susan dreamed of being the first woman president of the Council of Economic Advisers, and many people thought that she had a good chance of realising her ambition.

In her early thirties Susan got married, and over the course of five years she bore two children. Gradually her career options narrowed. Looking back, Susan sees two critical decision points. 'Just after I became pregnant with Anthony [her first child], Carter won the election and I was asked to go to the National Security Council to work on East–West trade questions. Saying no was one of the hardest things I have ever done. Imagine the excitement of actually working in the White House, being involved in some of the most difficult trade problems of the decade. But the decision was cut-and-dried. Of course I couldn't do it. I knew I wanted to take a six months' leave when my first child was born, and if I had accepted that job, it would have meant making a total commitment – sixty hours a week and no time off.' Susan paused and said reflectively, 'You know, that first pregnancy not only ruled out working at the National Security Council, it also cost me the job I was in. The organisation I worked for allowed you to take a six-month unpaid leave for childbirth but did not guarantee your job back. In the event, they filled my position when I was on leave.' Susan's expression became almost bitter as she remembered this period of her life: 'I tell you it is not much fun hitting the job market with a new baby at home, but Robert [her husband] was still in graduate school and earning peanuts. I had to find a new job.

'Four years later I was faced with another tough set of choices. I had changed course and was now working at a research foundation; the hours were regular, and I found it fitted in with family life much better than policy work.' Susan smiled. 'But you know me, I am ambitious and, I suppose, capable, and soon I was made a vice-president. In early 1980 the president of the foundation announced his intention to retire in eighteen months' time, and it suddenly hit me that if I went all out for it I could probably land his job. But Robert and I had just made the decision to have a second child so, instead of working for a promotion, I became pregnant and took a ten-week maternity leave.

'I was careful to take a short leave so as to not jeopardise my job. But this time I ran into another problem. We could not find decent child care. I tried hiring a full-time baby-sitter. I even brought over from Europe an old-fashioned nanny, but no one lasted more than a month. I guess we live too far out in the suburbs to attract live-in help. I then tried day care but found that the only centre that would accept a three- or four-month-old infant was forty miles away. Even if I had been willing to do all that driving, it would not have solved the problem of what to do with Anthony at the end of his short school day. In the end we put together a complicated child-care package by combining local part-time sitters with a live-in student. But despite all kinds of organisational effort, the package kept on breaking down. Vanessa would not take her bottle from the new Thursday sitter, or our in-house student decided to take an impromptu vacation. The tension and the guilt were overwhelming. Every time a sitter called me at work I found my hands shaking as I picked up the phone in anticipation of yet another crisis. My concentration became poor, and I just knew that I was not performing well on the job. When Vanessa was eight months old, I cut back to three-fifths time. At least I could now guarantee some quality time for my children.

'The repercussions of going part-time were serious, as I knew they would be; why else had I tried so hard to remain full-time? I could no longer be an officer of the foundation as they do not allow vice-presidents to work part-time. So here I am, almost forty years old and a lowly programme officer once again. I suppose I have become downwardly mobile.' Susan pulled a face and said with some humour, 'The guy they did promote to the presidency now earns eighty thousand dollars a year. When you stack that up against my paltry twenty-three thousand a year, I guess Vanessa comes out to be a pretty expensive baby.' Susan's face relaxed into a wide grin. 'But naturally her adoring mother thinks she is worth every penny of it.'

Susan wanted to add one more thought. 'The other day I caught myself thinking about how I will take up the threads of "my brilliant career" in my mid-forties, when Anthony and Vanessa are launched and don't need me so much. But that is just a pipe dream. No one wants a grey-haired lady on the staff of the National Security Council. Those slots are strictly for up-and-coming thirty-year-olds. I am trying to reconcile myself to reality, which is that I have fallen behind my generation and can never re-create the opportunities I once had. My career is permanently stalled.'[34]

A surprising aspect of Susan's story is that she took a total of only eight and a half months' leave for the birth of her children and that for twelve out of the last fifteen years she has worked full time. Yet childbearing has severely compromised her career prospects and her earning power. It doesn't take much to derail a career. A couple of leaves, a stint of part-time work will do it. Susan's story accurately reflects the mechanisms through which women – even well-qualified, ambitious women – fall behind in the American job market.

*

Some convincing research in the field (much of which has been done by conservative 'human capital' theorists) links earning power to the lifetime work histories of men and women.[35] According to this view, the wage gap can best be explained by the fact that working women bear a double burden – in the home and in the labour force. Domestic responsibilities, particularly those associated with child-rearing, interrupt and limit women's careers, permanently depressing female earning power. In the words of economist Solomon Polachek, the lower earnings of women are due to 'the division of labour within the family. . . . It is the wife who is shackled with the family responsibility, and it is the wife who forgoes wages and job opportunities to take on these responsibilities'.[36]

The typical American woman drops out of the labour force for nine years.[37] There are signs that this period is shortening as more and more mothers of small children stay in the labour market, but recent census data show that women are three times as likely as men to have their careers interrupted, and only 36 per cent of .currently employed women have worked continuously since leaving school.[38]

Human capital theorists argue that the wage gap can be largely explained by these interruptions that mark women's work lives. For example, when Polachek compares the difference between the re-entry wage – the wage a woman earns when she comes back into the labour force after a period of not working – with the wage she would have received had she stayed in the labour force, he finds that he can explain 50 per cent of the wage gap. Indeed, when he adds in the assumption that women will train less precisely because they expect to spend less time in the labour force, he claims to account for close to 100 per cent of the wage gap.[39] Polachek is not alone in stressing the depressing effect of interruptions on women's earnings. Other studies find that occupational tenure accounts for 25 to 44 per cent of the wage gap.[40] It seems that a two- to four-year break in employment lowers average earnings by 13 per cent while a five-year break in employment lowers average earnings by 19 per cent.[41] Economist Eli Ginsberg goes so far as to say that 'a continuous work history is almost a prerequisite for high or even good achievement'.[42]

Various kinds of circumstantial evidence lend support to theories that link the wage gap to women's family responsibilities. First, wage levels for women vary dramatically according to family status. Never-married women have complete wage parity with never-married men, while the wage gap between married men and women is extremely large. On average, *married women in America earn less than half the earnings of married men.* The number and spacing of children also affect the wage differential. Women with large families, with children spanning a broad age band, have the lowest wages of all.

Secondly, a greater proportion of single and childless women – with continuous work histories – are in professional, technical, and administrative 'male' jobs. Indeed, more than 50 per cent of the women in top management positions are childless. In contrast, married women with children crowd into low-paying 'women's' fields. These women tend to have large gaps in their work histories.

In the third place, black men do a great deal better in the labour market than women, whether they are white or black. In 1981 white women earned 60 per cent of the male wage while black men (who have two years less schooling than white men and women) earned 69 per cent of the wage for all men.[43] Since black men continue to be discriminated against in the labour market, the only way to explain these figures is to assume that the family responsibilities borne by women exert such a strong downward pressure on earnings that they outweigh even the disadvantages of being black. Gender seems to be a more powerful handicap than race in the labour market.

Finally, there is evidence drawn from the pattern of earnings over the life cycle. Age-earning profiles for men and women demonstrate the severely depressing effect of child rearing on female earnings. When women enter the work force in their late teens and early twenties, they earn somewhat less than men, but for a few years they do experience a fairly rapid rate of wage increase. However, in the twenty-five to thirty-four age bracket (the main childbearing years) their earnings fall way behind that of men. In other words, when one compares women's age earnings profiles with that of men, it becomes obvious that women miss out on the rapid upward mobility men typically experience in their late twenties and thirties. At this critical stage of most career paths, women have children (or at least 90 per cent of them do), and given inadequate (or no) maternity leave and the paucity and expense of child-care facilities, the majority of working women in America are forced to make drastic compromises in their work lives. Some leave the labour force for a number of years; others take third-rate jobs with short hours and little responsibility close to home. Economist Lester Thurow puts the problem succinctly: 'The years between 25 and 35 are the prime years for establishing a successful career. These are the years when hard work has the maximum pay-off. They are also the prime years for launching a family. Women who leave the job market completely during those years may find that they never catch up.'[44]

Thus, because of children-related handicaps, most American women – even highly educated ones – fail to take off into careers in their thirties. And when they are able to resume the all-out commitment necessary for career advance (usually around the age of forty), the structure of the labour market makes it extremely difficult, if not impossible, for them to get back on track.

Susan Fischer's case is not unusual. Her experience is typical of women trying to combine a career with raising a family. Forty-five per cent of American women returning to part-time jobs after having children 'find themselves moving down the occupational ladder into jobs which are worse paid or duller than those they had before their children were born'.[45] The consensus seems to be that interruptions, even if few and of short duration, exert a substantial downward pull on women's earning power.

The legal profession, which has more women than other élite occupations, is an interesting example of how family responsibilities continue to limit women's careers and their earning power. American women have clearly come a long way. More than a century ago, in 1873, the United States Supreme Court ruled that a young woman named Myra Bradwell was not constitutionally entitled to practise law. In his opinion Justice Joseph P. Bradley wrote: 'The natural and proper timidity and delicacy which belongs to the female sex evidently unfits it for many of the occupations of civil life. The paramount destiny and mission of women are to fulfil the noble and benign office of wife and mother. This is the law of the Creator.'[46] Columbia University did not admit its first woman law student until 1928, and as late as the mid-1960s only 5 per cent of the intake was female.

By 1984 almost 50 per cent of law school students were women, as were 30 per cent of associates at private law firms. But only 5 per cent of partnerships in these firms were held by women.[47] Women lawyers in America are still not making it to the centres of power, money, and prestige.

A study of the 71 women of the Harvard Law School's class of '74 by Jill Abramson and Barbara Franklin sheds some light on why this is so.[48] As they describe it, 'entering the job market when they did, at the height of the women's movement and armed with Harvard Law degrees, these women probably stood a better chance of finding success than any other group of women in the country. They certainly hoped to do as well as the 478 men in their class.'

Nine years later the results were startling: 23 per cent of the women from the class were partners at law firms, compared with 51 per cent of the men although roughly equal percentages started out in private practice. For most, partnership decisions have already been made (they were faced in the 1981–3 period). Abramson and Franklin find that for many of these women lawyers there is a definite trade-off between family responsibilities and career advancement.

Carolyn Lewis Zeigler, an associate in the litigation department of a New York law firm, is a case in point. 'When I hit thirty,' says Ms Zeigler, 'I said to myself, gee, it's time.' That was three years ago, and soon afterward Zeigler became pregnant with her first child, a daughter. Now she is pregnant again.

She has worked part time, usually three days a week, since the birth of her first child, and she anticipates keeping a part-time schedule until her second child turns three. She sees no way of carrying the full load of a fifty-hour working week while her children are little. Zeigler's decision to be a part-time lawyer has had a profound effect on her career. She has not become a partner; indeed, she will not even be considered for partnership until she returns to work on a full-time basis. She is now earning a fraction of what her male contemporaries earn. Her career is on hold.

Katherine Reed is another example. Ms Reed joined the New York firm Proskauer, Rose, Goetz & Mendelsohn in the mid-1970s. She did not stay long, for she found that the pace of work ruled out any kind of private life, let alone the possibility of husband and children. 'Proskauer did not discriminate,' says Reed. 'Everyone was forced to work an eighty-hour week.' She eventually switched to the legal department of a large corporation. This represented a step down in career terms because the potential financial rewards are lower. The biggest attraction of the new job was an 8 a.m. to 6 p.m. working day.

Of the forty-six women Abramson and Franklin interviewed from the class of '74, nineteen have children. These women found that in all spheres of legal work – private firms, government, legal aid, and corporate in-house – 'balancing maternity leaves and part time work with career advancement has proved difficult, and the demands of family life are one of the most common reasons cited by women who have left high powered jobs.' In addition, many of the women lawyers who do not have children strive to arrange their work lives so as to leave open the possibility of finding mates and having a family.

The conclusion of this study was that 'few of the women in Harvard's law school class of '74 turned out to be superwomen. They found that they could not stay on the fast track and develop satisfying personal lives.'[49]

The conventional wisdom used to be that the thousands of women entering the legal profession just have not had the time to make their way up through the ranks to partnership. Senior partners at law firms are fond of pointing out that they are hiring a veritable flood of women fresh out of law school; as soon as these women put in the necessary seven to nine years as associates, they say, there will no doubt be a flood of women partners.

It does not seem to be happening that way. True, a great many women are being hired as associates, but a far greater percentage of them seem to be leaving the fast track after four or five years than do their male counterparts.[50] Some are 'let go' or 'passed over' by the firm. Others, like Carolyn Zeigler and Katherine Reed, go part time or turn to less demanding jobs – in teaching, in government work, or on corporate legal staffs – to create more time for themselves or their families.

The career trajectories of the class of '74 make for a better understanding of the census figures cited earlier in this chapter: male lawyers aged twenty-five to thirty-five earn $27,563 a year, while their female counterparts earn $20,573. Even the best-trained and most ambitious professional women find that they have to make considerable career sacrifices – in terms of both status and salary – in order to have a family.

As we have seen, economists have advanced powerful arguments to support the theory that career interruptions wrought by housework and child care explain at least half the wage gap between men and women. Polachek takes this theory further and argues that much of the low earning power of women is caused not by employers discriminating but by 'the more implicit and subtle forms of societal discrimination taking place within the family.'[51] In plain language, working women are still stuck with most domestic chores, and this severely limits how well they can do in the labour market.

Looking after a home and a family is still an enormously time-consuming activity – sixty hours per week for a family of four, according to one survey.[52] This may have involved more physically strenuous work in the past but never more complex. Looking after the home in a modern industrial society includes the management of extensive relationships with shops, banks, schools, hospitals and government offices as well as housework and child care. It involves seeing that thousands of personal needs are met. The five-year-old needs a booster shot or a costume for the school play, name tapes need to be ordered for the seven-year-old, an appointment must be set up with the nursery school teacher to explain Johnny's stammering problem, and 300 family snapshots are waiting to be put into albums. Sometimes relationships with shops, schools or government offices are fraught with problems. The new car is a dud, teacher can't discipline the children, a credit card is lost or stolen – all add stress to everyday life at home.

Over the last fifteen years there has been a great deal of talk about men taking on more household responsibility. Magazines have discovered a 'fathering boom', and films like *Kramer vs. Kramer* have tried to convince us that modern men develop intimate nurturing relationships with their children. And it is true, some men have taken on considerably more housework and child care. I have interviewed men who take care of their children by day and work factory shifts at night, and my own husband takes 50 per cent of the responsibility for our children. But in the aggregate this increased participation by men does not add up to very much. Recent studies show that American men still do less than a quarter of all household tasks, and that married men's average time in family work has increased by only 6 per cent in twenty years despite the massive shift of women into paid employment.[53] One survey finds that the working week of American women is twenty-one hours longer than that of men.[54] Economist Heidi Hartmann claims that men actually demand eight hours more service per week than they contribute,[55] and Joseph Pleck hits the nail on the head when he describes 'men's characteristically low level of family work' as one of the key problems of contemporary life.[56]

An insurmountable obstacle to increased male responsibility for housework is the absence of men in many households. Any small progress that has been made in recent years toward raising the consciousness of concerned husbands and fathers has been cancelled out by the inroads of divorce. Approximately 50 per cent of children born into American households in the early 1980s will go through a divorce, and 90 per cent of those children will end up living with their mothers. As we saw in the last chapter, custodial mothers in America pick up nearly all the physical and financial responsibilities of rearing the children of divorce – their European peers do rather better, at least on the financial front.

Nora Ephron in her book *Heartburn* displays a jaundiced, if amusing, view of how much women have actually achieved on the household division of labour front. As she describes it, in the 1970s it was fashionable to sit down with your husband and draw up a list of household duties in order to divide them equally: 'This happened in thousands of households, with identical results: thousands of husbands agreed to clear the table. They cleared the table and then looked around as if they deserved a medal. They cleared the table and then hoped that they would never again be asked to do another thing. They cleared the table and hoped the whole thing would go away. And it did.'[57]

Ephron may have been bitter because her own husband left her when she was pregnant with her second child. Unfortunately her experience is not unique.

The division of household labour between men and women seems stubbornly resistant to change, and part of the problem is that women earn so much less than men. Married women in the United States when working full time earn less than half the wages earned by married men, and when you weigh in part-time workers, employed wives contribute only 26 per cent of the family budget. In view of this asymmetry it is hardly surprising that men have picked up so little domestic responsibility. It still makes economic sense for a family to put the husband's job first. When a parent has to leave the work force in order to take care of a child, it usually costs the family less for the mother to stay at home than for the father. But this is a vicious circle. As we have seen, by 'interrupting' her career, the mother permanently lowers her earnings potential.

A 'raised consciousness' on the part of a man is not enough. Many husbands have the best of intentions when embarking on family life. Over the long haul goodwill is often defeated by the economic facts of life. As French feminist

Simone de Beauvoir put it some thirty years ago, 'Many young households give the impression of being on a basis of perfect equality. But as long as the man retains economic responsibility for the couple, this is only an illusion.'[58] You cannot expect to change behaviour without first changing the economic logic on which this behaviour is based. In their book *American Couples*, Philip Blumstein and Pepper Schwartz demonstrate that 'money establishes the balance of power in relationships', and according to them, this shows up most crudely in who does what in the household.[59]

For women the wage gap sets up an infuriating Catch-22 situation. They do the housework because they earn less, and they earn less because they do the housework. The only way to break this vicious circle is to develop social policies that support women in their domestic roles so that they can do better in the labour market. Doing better in the labour market has to include limiting those interruptions that so severely depress women's earnings. High-quality, subsidised child care would enable many women to take fewer years out of the labour force when they have children and thus pay a smaller penalty in terms of a lower wage when they re-enter (remember, a two- to four-year break in employment lowers average lifetime earnings by 13 per cent for American women while a five-year break in employment lowers average earnings by 19 per cent). Indeed, generous maternity leaves with rigorous job-back guarantees would enable many women to bear children without paying any penalty at all in terms of earning power or seniority. In short, social policies that support women in their efforts to bear and rear children would go a long way toward narrowing the wage gap. And once the gap between male and female earnings narrows significantly, the household division of labour may well shift. An equal sharing of housework and child rearing between men and women will await the day when a woman's job is as important to the household economy as a man's.

In America over the last twenty years a great deal of energy has been channelled into devising ways of improving the economic position of women. In the 1960s and 1970s efforts were directed towards getting rid of overt discrimination. Title VII of the Civil Rights Act and Executive Order 11246 were used to sue firms that had unfair hiring practices or paid unequal wages for equal work. And much was accomplished as barriers fell and professional and blue-collar jobs were opened up to women. In the 1980s the main thrust seems to be towards utilising the concept of comparable worth to tackle occupational discrimination – the segregation of women in low-paid jobs. But all this activity on the anti-discrimination front has had little effect on women's earning power in America.[60]

Any attempt to eliminate discrimination in the job market is bound to be seriously limited because women's double burden at work and at home has not been dealt with. Unless women get some relief from their domestic responsibilities, they will continue to fare badly in the work force. In America, at least, such relief seems a long way away.

America's family support system is shamefully weak, and shrinking – subsidies for child care have been cut by 21 per cent since 1980. In the United States having a baby is viewed as strictly a private matter. Fewer than 40 per cent of working women have any maternity coverage, and in most cases such coverage is very limited.[61] And this is despite the fact that 48 per cent of babies under one year old have mothers in the work force.

The only federal provision for maternity leave is contained in the 1978 Pregnancy Disability Amendment to Title VII of the Civil Rights Act which decrees that an employer can no longer fire a worker *solely* because she is pregnant. But since 'the law is based on non-discrimination [it] names no special benefits associated with childbirth'.[62] A pregnant woman is merely eligible for the same fringe benefits as workers with other disabilities. This seems to boil down to the right to use temporary disability insurance for pregnancy.

Unfortunately this provision is less useful than it might be because American federal law does not require employers to provide disability insurance. In fact, only five states (California, Hawaii, New Jersey, New York and Rhode Island) require disability coverage. Thus the 1978 act, which was touted as 'solving' the maternity leave problem for American women, is a dead letter in forty-five states of the Union. Even those women lucky enough to live in the right states might still not be covered by disability insurance. For example, in New York State, government workers, farm workers, and workers in firms with fewer than fifteen employees are all excluded from the disability insurance requirement. And what does this disability coverage amount to? A few (usually six to ten) weeks of partial wage replacement at the time of a normal pregnancy and delivery, but no job protection.

If some 40 per cent of working women in America have some disability coverage for pregnancy and childbirth, what provision do they have for care of the infant during the first months of life? It is shocking but true that the laws are 'silent about any period of time a mother or indeed a father may wish to be at home to care for an infant child'.[63]

The shortcomings of the Pregnancy Disability Amendment as a national maternity policy seem obvious, yet it is all there is. Unlike other countries, pregnant women in the United States are not guaranteed leave from employment for a specific length of time at childbirth and therefore have no right of job protection if they do take some leave. Employers still routinely fire women if they take even a short leave of absence to have a baby. According to Arkie Byrd, attorney for the Women's Legal Defense Fund in Washington, D.C., 'It happens every day . . . and outside of sexual harassment, the largest number of employment discrimination cases handled by the Fund involve pregnancy.'[64]

In addition, the United States does not guarantee health coverage to women for their own medical expenses or that of their newborn children at the time of birth. Since one-third of single women and one-quarter of married women have no health insurance, childbirth can be a very expensive proposition (costs range between $1,000 and $3,000). And even if women have some coverage for the medical expenses of childbirth, it is rarely comprehensive. None of the 100-odd working mothers I interviewed were completely covered for the expenses of childbirth.

The best maternity policies in the United State are to be found in large corporations as part of their employee benefits package. In a 1981 survey of 250 large corporations, 88 per cent reported offering some type of maternity leave.[65] The median length of maternity leave in these corporations is twelve weeks (six weeks' paid leave, six weeks' unpaid leave), and in most cases these leaves carry job protection guarantees. The most generous employers tend to be banks, financial institutions and insurance companies, and the least generous employers are in the retailing sector. A few companies have exceptionally good policies (by American standards): the Aetna Life and Casualty Company, for example, offers pregnant women employers as much as six months' leave at 60 to 100 per cent of salary.[66]

As good as some of the best corporate policies are, one should not lose sight of the fact that fewer than a quarter of American working women are employed by large corporations. For the vast majority there is no substitute for a statutory maternity policy that guarantees certain essential rights and benefits to working women when they give birth. In the modern world women often cannot simply chuck their jobs in when they have children; they desperately need to continue working to support themselves and their growing families. (Besides, their future earning power is affected by how much time they take off and whether this time is defined as job-protected leave or time out of the job market.) It constitutes 'cruel and unusual punishment' to present women workers with the choice of either losing their jobs or leaving their newborn children in the hands of (often inadequate) childminders. This is precisely the choice that faces more than half of America's working women. No other advanced industrial country forces this choice on its female citizens.

Carmen Santos* is a medical secretary, and for the last four years she has worked for a large teaching hospital in New York City. When I interviewed her, she had a twenty-one-month-old child and was six months pregnant with her second child. At the birth of her first child Carmen's disability insurance replaced two-thirds of her salary for a period of six weeks. She originally planned to go back to work when her child was three months old and had been told that her job was secure. Despite these assurances, Carmen was fired one week before she was due to go back to work. Her union made sure that she was first in line for any new job that came up, and five months later she found a job at the same salary in another department of the medical school. However, Carmen lost all the benefits she had built up in the job switch. In her new job she is defined as a 'new hire' and is not entitled to paid holiday for six months and cannot take part in the pension plan for another two years. In her old job Carmen had built up a considerable number of benefits: she had the right to three weeks' paid holiday (good by American standards) and had been participating in the pension plan for a year. 'It's a pity about the paid holiday,' Carmen said wistfully. 'It would have helped to tide us over the next six months.'

When her next child is born, Carmen plans to take another three months off. She would prefer to take less time, but the local woman who will do the bulk of the baby-sitting will not take babies younger than three months. Carmen is keeping her fingers crossed and hoping that this time she will get her job back immediately. Family finances are precarious. Together she and her husband earn $27,000 a year. Her husband's income alone is not enough to cover the basic expenses of food, shelter and transport. Carmen *has* to work.

In one respect Carmen feels that she is fortunate. Her medical plan is very comprehensive (it was negotiated by her union), and expenses for the birth of her first child amounted to only $300 out of her own pocket. She knows many couples who faced bills of thousands of dollars when they had a child. I told Carmen that America was the only advanced country that didn't completely underwrite the medical costs of childbirth. She didn't believe me.[67]

Gail Tobias* is a writer. For the last six years she has been one of the principal writers for a TV soap opera. In late 1983, at the age of thirty-five, Gail became pregnant with her first child. Gail's employer had no provisions for maternity leave in place, and so after extensive negotiation it was arranged that Gail should work right up to when she went into labour and then take two and a half weeks off for the delivery. One and a half weeks of this comprised Gail's paid holiday time; the other week was defined as leave at half pay. In the event, Gail had a difficult labour and eventually delivered her child by caesarean section. She therefore found it particularly difficult to be back on the job so soon after the birth. In Gail's words, 'I don't know how I lived through those first weeks back at work. I was exhausted and in pain from the surgery. I could hardly drag myself around. The worst thing was the lack of sleep. Annie woke to be fed at least three times a night, and by midday I was ready to kill for sleep. But somehow I had to work – and to smile and pretend to my boss that I didn't have a family care in the world.' Gail is convinced that she would have lost her job had she taken additional time off. 'I'm in a very competitive field, and they would have filled my slot easily and quickly.' Since she and her husband have recently bought a house, they could not manage without her salary. Gail's poor maternity coverage extended to medical costs. She estimates that $1,800 of the childbirth expenses were not covered by medical insurance.[68]

The experiences of many European women I interviewed throw Carmen's and Gail's struggles into sharp relief. Take Susan Arnbom who works as a secretary in Stockholm and has three small children. When each of her children was born, Susan was entitled to nine months' paid leave at 90 per cent of her salary plus a six-month job-protected, but unpaid, leave. Since her two youngest children were born within a year of each other, she chose to merge her maternity leaves into a consecutive two-and-a-half-year period. Her husband was also eligible to share parental leave with her, and he took a four-month leave at the time of the birth of their first child. However, child-related leave in Sweden does not stop there. A mother is also allowed to take off sixty days per year per child to stay at home and look after a sick child (albeit at a reduced rate of pay – less than 90%). In one year Susan took off about thirty days to take care of her children. And, as she says, 'If your child is sick you can also call the social authorities and they can send a woman to the house to look after the child. You have to pay for this but it is not much, it is less than the money you would probably lose by staying at home.'[69]

The French social services do not provide this particular amenity; however, maternity provisions are, by American standards, very generous. Annette Laborey is a programme officer at a cultural foundation in Paris. She is married with two young children. At the birth of each child she was entitled to and took a three-month leave at full pay. She was also entitled to a two-year unpaid leave. She took part of this leave when her first child was born, but when she had her second child, she decided to go back to work at the end of the three-month paid leave. 'With two children we needed my salary more, besides there was an excellent [public] crèche just around the corner from home, so day care presented no problem.' And this enables her to get on with her career. 'I never want to "work" at being a mother or to have to "look after" my children,' says Annette. 'I like just to live with them – bring them to work with me, play with them, have them around, but I would never want to devote my life to "looking after" them.'[70] And nor does she have to.

The United States is the only industrialised country that has no statutory maternity leave. One hundred and seventeen countries (including every industrial nation and many developing countries) guarantee a woman the following rights: leave from employment for childbirth, job protection while she is on leave, and the provision of a cash benefit, to replace all or most of her earnings.[71]

As we can see from Susan Arnbom's case, Sweden is particularly generous in its maternity policies. Since 1975 this Scandinavian country has provided a parental leave of nine months at the birth of a child which can be taken by either parent. It replaces 90 per cent of earnings up to a specified maximum, protects holiday entitlement and pension rights, maintains fringe benefits, and, most important, guarantees that a parent can go back to the same or a similar job.[72]

Italy has a package of benefits typical of the European Economic Community. A pregnant woman is entitled to five months' paid leave at 80 per cent of her wage, followed by a further six months at 30 per cent of her wage. Her job is held for both time periods. A woman is also allowed to stay away from work when her child is ill until the child is three years old. In addition, a woman worker is entitled to two years' credit toward holiday and pension rights each time she gives birth to a child.[73]

Britain, which is parsimonious by European standards, has the Employment Protection Act (enacted in 1975 and improved upon by the Employment Protection [Consolidation] Act of 1978 and the Employment Act of 1980) which provides: paid time off from work for pre-natal care; six weeks' paid maternity leave, during which time 90 per cent of earnings are replaced; and the right to leave work six weeks before a child is born and to return to work at any time before a child is twenty-nine weeks old and to be re-employed on terms 'not less favourable than those applicable if she had not been absent'.[74] There is in addition a one-off payment, called a maternity grant, of £25 for each child born for which every woman is eligible and an eighteen-week maternity allowance (dependent on National Insurance contributions and deductible from the six weeks' paid maternity leave). However, moves are afoot to amalgamate these two into one payment, to be called the statutory maternity pay, part of which would be earnings-related. A government proposal also currently under discussion is that there should be more flexibility as to when the maternity allowance is payable (currently eleven weeks before the baby is born and five weeks afterwards).[75] Many employers in Britain, particularly those in the public sector, provide additional maternity benefits to their employees.

It is interesting to note that the British maternity provisions (which are on the low end of the European scale) have been instituted during a period of public spending cutbacks and increasingly conservative policies. Even Margaret

Thatcher has had to recognise that in a world where more and more women are in the work force, pregnant women and newborn babies need protection, and the state is the only entity able to guarantee such protection. In this area private-sector initiatives are not enough. British women see their maternity benefits as critically important. Ruth Spellman, who works at the National Economic Development Office in London, put it this way: 'I cannot imagine how I would have dealt with those first months of my son's life without the provisions of my maternity leave. The Employment Protection Act is as important to women as gaining the vote. It makes it possible for you to keep your job without short-changing your kid.'[76]

I called a friend in London in the autumn of 1983 to talk about a conference we both were attending. She was not in her office, so I called her at home – rather apologetically since I thought she might be home from work because she was ill. 'Oh, don't worry,' Judy said breezily. 'I feel fine. I am at home because I just started my maternity leave. I actually won't be in the office until June, and I'm glad you called here because I wanted to talk to you about the paper I am writing for the manpower conference.' My initial reaction was interesting. I couldn't figure out what she was talking about. Why, her baby wasn't due for another six weeks, and June was seven months away! Despite the fact that I had done a great deal of research on maternity policies, and I knew that Britain, in common with the rest of Europe, had long statutory maternity leaves, I still couldn't absorb the fact that someone I knew – a committed, driven professional – was taking an eight-month leave to have a baby and was not the slightest bit guilty or defensive about it. Rather, she took it completely for granted. As Judy said later in the conversation, 'It's my right. It is every woman's right.' She paused and said reflectively, 'It's not even a big deal for employers. How many children am I going to have anyway? One or perhaps two. Fourteen months' leave is very little considering that I will spend forty-odd years in the labour force.' My conversation with Judy made me realise how little help my American compatriots expect to receive from public policy or from employers and how low their expectations are.[77]

Over the course of the last fifteen years most advanced industrial countries have undergone major economic and social changes which have resulted in a dramatic rise in the number of women working. In 1984, 63 per cent of American women, 59 per cent of British women, 77 per cent of Swedish women, and 55 per cent of French women were in the work force.[78] In all these countries a variety of 'push' factors have propelled women into paid employment. Rising divorce rates, inflation, stagnant real incomes, growing unemployment rates in male blue-collar occupations, and the heightened career aspirations of modern women – all are factors which have pushed women into employment. On the 'pull' side of the equation is the changing occupational base of advanced countries as economic activity increasingly tilts toward services. Business services (which range from word processing to cleaning offices), health care services (in hospitals, nursing homes, and social welfare offices), and food catering services have all expanded enormously in recent years in both Western Europe and North America. Two-thirds of the new jobs in these areas of the economy have gone to women. This has not happened by accident. As Marvin Harris has pointed out, women provide 'a literate and docile' pool of willing workers and are therefore desirable candidates for the information- and people-processing jobs thrown up by modern service industries.[79]

Women are joining the European work force at much the same rate and for much the same reasons as in America. But there is one major difference. In Europe working women are supported by an elaborate (and in most cases expanding) family support system which is a major factor behind their improved earning power. It is no coincidence that the country with the most developed benefits and services for working women – Sweden – is also the country with the smallest wage gap, while the country with the least developed benefits and services – the United States – is also the country with the largest wage gaps.

Working women in America bear the full brunt of the double burden because the United States does less than any other advanced industrial nation to provide support systems for families. And it is not just the advanced welfare states of Scandinavia that provide maternity leave, family allowances, and child care. Traditional Catholic nations such as France and Italy and conservative governments such as Britain's are all doing much more than the United States to provide benefits and services for working mothers. Most American women who work are hard pressed in their attempts to raise a family while continuing to hold down a job. Compounding these difficulties is the high rate of divorce, which has substantially lessened male participation in child rearing. These are the causes of the large wage gap in America and the reasons why, unlike in Europe, this gap does not appear to be narrowing.

Government policies have floundered while economists have debated the reasons behind the wage gap. The liberal left of the discipline emphasises discrimination, particularly the more subtle forms which segregate women in a 'pink-collar' ghetto. Economists on the right wing of the discipline stress the ways in which family responsibilities limit the earning potential of women.

The debate is often acrimonious because the left and the right have very different views of what should be done. Liberals press for rigorous enforcement of anti-discrimination legislation while conservatives tend to say that since women 'choose' to have families and 'choose' to limit their careers, low female wages are a result of individual choice and should not be interfered with by government (a line of argument which is bolstered by right-wing faith in free markets). However, this argument is a little silly. Of course, women 'choose' to have families but they do not also 'choose' to do all the child care or 'prefer' low-paying jobs. If working women in America had job-protected maternity leave, subsidised day care, and flexitime, they would then be better able to seek out high-paying jobs.

Anyway, these two explanations of the wage gap are not antagonistic; they complement each other. Women's careers are heavily conditioned and constrained by marriage and child rearing. Precisely because of this conditioning and these constraints, many women opt for low-paying jobs in the 'pink-collar' ghetto. Being a primary school teacher does fit in comfortably with maternal responsibilities, and a secretarial position is easy to find if you are expected to follow your husband to a new city.

On the policy front, both family support measures and anti-discrimination efforts are needed if women are to improve their earning power significantly. However, although anti-discrimination measures, particularly in the area of low wages for traditional jobs in the 'pink-collar' ghetto, are crucial in the battle for equal opportunity, women will never attain equal results as long as they are handling 80 per cent of all household responsibilities. American women still have a very long way to go; European women, aided by their countries' family support systems, are better off.

4. Children: The Other Victims

American women aren't the only ones squeezed between the devil and the deep blue sea; their children are right there with them. The breakdown of traditional marriage and the failure of women to achieve significant earning power in the job market are factors which severely affect the well-being of children in America today.

As a result of high rates of divorce, one-quarter of all American children are being raised – and largely supported – by their mothers. Indeed, it is estimated that 40 to 50 per cent of children born in the late 1970s will spend part of their youth in female-headed households. This is a large part of the reason why increasing numbers of children in the richest country in the world are growing up in poverty. Although women (particularly mothers) have entered the work force in unprecedented numbers, both as a cause and as a consequence of marital breakdown, few of them can ever expect to earn an adequate 'family' wage. The average income of single mothers is $9,000 a year. In fact, the majority (57 per cent) of female-headed households are defined as poor.[1]

Children who grow up in poverty are at risk in all kinds of ways: their health is more fragile, their life expectancy is shorter, their educational prospects are dimmer, and they are more often the victims of abuse and neglect than children growing up in adequate material circumstances. Child abuse in the United States has increased right in line with the children-in-poverty figures, and is perhaps the most painful illustration of the consequences of neglect. In New York City a 1983 task force reported an increase of 140 per cent in the incidence of child abuse between 1974 and 1982.[2] In all, forty-five states have seen an increase in reported cases, and in most of these states this increase has been accompanied by a cutback in child abuse prevention programmes.

The net result: today in child-centred America about 1 million children are abused and neglected, more than 44,000 are sexually abused, and 5,000 children die each year as a result of severe physical maltreatment.[3] Children are not doing well in contemporary America, and current social policies seem to be making the situation worse, not better. In 1983, 22 per cent of all American children fell below the poverty line, as opposed to 14 per cent just ten years ago.[4] Statistics such as these caused Representative Barney Frank (Democrat, Massachusetts) to remark that Ronald Reagan seems to believe that 'life begins at conception and ends at birth'.[5]

Early on the Sunday morning of 26 September 1982, as his brothers looked on and an upstairs neighbour heard his cries, Shawn Nicely was beaten to death. He was three years old. His killers were his own mother and father.

At the inquest the pathologist attributed Shawn's death to a combination of injuries, including internal haemorrhage, a laceration of the liver and lacerations and contusions of other internal organs. The pathologist also found a recent break in Shawn's right arm, one newly fractured rib, three previously fractured ribs, haemorrhaging on the tongue, bruised gums, a slight swelling of the brain from repeated blows to the head, and old scars on the buttocks, thigh, and upper back. All these injuries proved to be more than a small boy could take. At his death Shawn Nicely stood thirty-six inches tall and weighed thirty-one pounds.

Shawn's parents have since been convicted and jailed, his mother, Renée Nicely, for murder, and his father, Allen Bass, for manslaughter. Behind the courtroom verdicts is the story of Shawn Nicely and his twenty-one-year-old parents, who began having their children at the age of fifteen and who never married.

As is so often the case, Renée Nicely's childhood was also marked by poverty, parental strife and physical abuse. She dropped out of high school to have her first child, and by the time she was twenty she had three children under five. With no skills, no husband and no access to child care she was trapped on welfare and existed on a meagre AFDC income (Aid for Families with Dependent Children – a state benefit available to only the very poorest). Depressed, hopeless and angry, Renée took out her frustrations on her most vulnerable child, perpetuating and deepening the grim cycle of poverty and abuse.[6]

If 1 million children in the United States of America are the victims of abuse and neglect, a great many more suffer the consequences of poor-quality child care. Hundreds of thousands of pre-schoolers and 2 to 5 million schoolchildren spend large chunks of their parents' working days either unsupervised or in highly inadequate care.[7] As a result, the physical and psychological well-being of these children is often imperilled. A point which was brought home in the summer of 1984, when sex abuse scandals at child-care centres across the country shocked the nation.

Today more than 50 per cent of the mothers of pre-school children in America work, in contrast with 12 per cent in 1950, and 48 per cent of mothers with children under one year of age now hold jobs, up from 24 per cent in 1970.[8] Since most of these women work out of economic necessity, they cannot afford to use high-quality private child care, which, when it is available, can cost anything from $80 to $200 per child per week. Research shows that many mothers resort to a patchwork of informal arrangements, which typically involve relatives and friends as well as paid help. Many of these arrangements are inadequate for the child, and almost all of them produce a great deal of stress and anxiety for the parents.

Jeremy Morenzi is thirteen months old and despite his extreme youth already leads a very complicated life. He has two older brothers, and in order to meet basic family expenses, both his parents work. His mother, Debbie, teaches in a nursery school in New York City, and it is she, who has a more flexible job than his father, who orchestrates Jeremy's day.

At 8 a.m. every weekday Debbie takes Jeremy to Mrs Hopkins, an elderly neighbour, whom she pays $30 a week for 'watching' Jeremy in the mornings. Mrs Hopkins is sixty-eight years old and is a cautious, kindly woman who takes her duties seriously. Because she is too old and clumsy to run around after a toddler, she keeps Jeremy in an old crib with some toys rather than let him loose in the flat. As Mrs Hopkins explains it, 'this way he cannot come to any harm'. At noon Debbie picks Jeremy up, gives him lunch and takes him to school with her. She teaches a small group of four-year-olds in the afternoon and finds it possible to keep an eye on Jeremy at the same time. However, once again Jeremy is confined, this time in a playpen, so that he does not disrupt the activities of the older children. At 2.45 p.m. Debbie drops Jeremy off at either her friend Linda's house or her friend Nancy's house and catches a bus to her second job – teaching an after-school course at a private school. Three days a week Jeremy spends these late-afternoon hours with Linda, and two days a week with Nancy, playing with the children of his mother's friends. At 5.45 p.m. Debbie picks him up on her way home. Debbie repays Linda and Nancy for this afternoon baby-sitting by looking after their children at weekends.

Jeremy is too young to reflect on the pros and cons of his daily schedule, but his mother is unhappy, particularly about the mornings. 'I know Mrs Hopkins doesn't have the energy to look after a toddler properly,' she says, 'but what can you find for thirty dollars a week? At least I know that he is safe.' Debbie believes that her choices are a direct result of family finances. Ideally she would have liked to take some time out of the job market and look after Jeremy herself, but without her salary (small as it is) she and her husband could not cover rent, basic amenities and food. For the same financial reasons Debbie feels that she is locked into second-rate child care. A thoughtful and well-educated woman, Debbie cannot understand why nothing has been done to provide affordable child care to ordinary working families like her own. Everyone she knows is tortured by this issue. 'The women's movement seems to have won a lot of rights for gays, and this is well and good, but the women I talk to are in worse shape than they were ten years ago.'[9]

Jeremy is luckier, however, than many children: he has two parents. For, as we saw at the beginning of the chapter, the number of children in America who will spend at least part of their childhood in single-parent homes is growing at an alarming rate, and the majority of children from broken homes live with their mother.[10] The sorry but remediable truth about divorce is that much of the anxiety that follows it is centred on money. As one authority has put it, the most detrimental aspect of the absence of fathers from one-parent families headed by women is 'not the lack of a male presence but the lack of a male income'.[11] Two-thirds of divorced American fathers cease to support their children, forcing mothers to assume the entire financial burden for both themselves and their children. This economic pressure, in turn, means that these mothers have less time for looking after their children.

Children cannot successfully handle too many changes. In a widely respected study English psychiatrist Michael Rutter demonstrates that while children are able to absorb a single stress with no appreciable risk, as they are subject to additional stresses, such as moving, changing schools, mothers going out to work, new (and often imperfect) child-care arrangements, the adverse effects of divorce begin to multiply.[12]

It was eighteen months since her parents' separation, and twelve-year-old Laura was not coping well. In her new school she was skipping classes and refusing to do her homework. She was also increasingly hostile toward her father; just last Saturday she had stormed out of his house at lunchtime and refused to go back despite the fact that she was supposed to spend the entire day with him. Laura's mother was worried but also a little puzzled; after all, Laura had coped with the immediate aftermath of the separation very well. A few weeks later Laura finally unburdened herself to a sympathetic teacher. As she saw things, it was not her parents' divorce that was upsetting her but rather the new flat and the new school. In order to save money, her mother had sold the family home, and she and Laura had moved into a small flat on the other side of town. Laura felt depressed and humiliated by her new situation. 'I despise the tacky furniture and the tiny rooms, but most of all, I hate sharing a bedroom with my mother,' she declared passionately. Laura also desperately missed her friends and her teachers in her old school: 'I feel stranded. Since I am the only new kid in the seventh grade, no one will ever want to know me.' Laura blamed her father for her newly reduced circumstances and was very angry with him: 'He has lots of money. Why he just spent Christmas in Vermont skiing. Mom and I, on the other hand, have to pinch and scrape and live in this mean little apartment.'[13]

If American mothers had more adequate incomes after divorce, many of these negative changes could be avoided. Part of the problem is the non-payment of child support by divorced fathers. Only a third of all fathers liable for child support comply with the terms of the awards, and a third pay nothing at all.[14] But even more important is the low earning power of working women. In 1984 one quarter of working women, when working full time, earned less than $10,000 a year.[15] For such women getting a job is not a route out of poverty. As the Catholic bishops described the situation in late 1984, 'Hundreds of thousands of women both hold full-time jobs and are still poor.'[16]

The provision of high-quality and affordable child care from the public pocket emerges as central to any solution to the problems facing children whether these problems involve parental abuse, divorce or working mothers. Experts agree that if poor parents in America today had ready access to free day care, there would be a dramatic reduction in child abuse with its terrible toll. Child deaths associated with abuse fall off dramatically after the age of six, indicating that troubled parents can cope with their children better once the children are out of the home for part of the day. The New York City task force cited earlier in this chapter found that 60 per cent of fatalities arising from child abuse occur among children less than two years of age.[17] In a similar, though less chilling, vein, the negative repercussions of divorce for children would be mitigated by access to high-quality subsidised child care. The question of how to care for her children often constitutes *the* major unresolved problem for a newly single mother, and inadequate alternative care often prevents her from earning enough money to put the household back on its feet.

Karen, a black divorced mother I interviewed, recalled with horror the years when her two children were too young to go to school. 'When George left me, the kids were eighteen months and three years old. I tried so hard to hold a job down, not only for the money but because I liked my work as a legal secretary, and it was a way of rebuilding my self-respect after the separation.' Despite her determination, Karen was fired from three jobs – for arriving late, for absenteeism, and for bringing her youngest to work with her on two occasions. The basic problem was that her baby-sitting arrangements kept breaking down. 'I lived in Brooklyn at that time, and I couldn't find day care. I wasn't eligible for subsidised care since I was working, and I could not afford the private day-care centres.' Karen resorted to a multiple arrangement package comprising her sister-in-law (who covered the mornings) and a neighbour and local teenager (who split the afternoons). Karen paid a small wage to the neighbour and the teenager but repaid her sister-in-law in kind by looking after her two-year-old nephew at the weekends. But Karen's child-care package was subject to recurrent crises. Her sister-in-law moved away and left her with no one to take care of the baby in the mornings (this was the point at which she tried taking her baby to work), the neighbour was always getting sick, and Karen had to fire the teenager for negligence: the three-year-old fell out of the first-floor window while she was baby-sitting. Karen will never forget the phone call she got at work from the hospital emergency room saying that her child had had an accident; fortunately, it turned out not to be very serious. After the accident Karen gave up her struggle and went on welfare until her youngest was old enough for public kindergarten. 'It was the only way to be sure that my kids were safe.'[18]

As we have seen with Jeremy's mother Debbie, the problems of day care are not limited to single mothers. *All* working mothers, even if they have husbands and decent salaries, need better access to quality child care if the next generation is not to be short-changed. The United States has a large deficit in child-care facilities at *every* economic level. As Annice Probst, executive director of the Preschool Association in New York, has put it, 'The system simply fails many people. There is insufficient care for low-income families, there are middle-income families who have trouble paying the full cost of care, and there is a shortage of quality centres at any price.'[19]

It is extremely difficult to obtain an accurate picture of child care in America because there is no systematic collection of data at the national level. However, the child-care deficit is most severe for infants and toddlers. This is because mothers of very young children have entered the American work force at a particularly rapid rate in recent years. Of mothers with children under one year of age, 48 per cent now hold jobs, and since a minority of these women are entitled to maternity leave, many of them need to find substitute care for their children from a very early age.

For young children (six weeks to three years) there are four types of care in general use. In the first place, there are family day-care homes which account for more than 40 per cent of the child care used by employed mothers.[20] Family day care generally comprises informal arrangements whereby a neighbourhood woman cares for several children in her own home. Only a small proportion of this kind of care is licensed – estimates are in the 10 per cent range – and a very small number of family day-care plans are subsidised by the government.[21] The cost of family day care ranges from $40 to $70 per week per child, and the standard of care is very uneven. However, this is the only kind of care most parents can afford.

Secondly, there are day-care centres, which provide approximately 10 per cent of the child-care services used by working mothers. Half these centres cater specifically for poor, usually single-parent, families and are subsidised out of public funds. These have been severely affected by the Reagan budget cuts: the money set aside for them has been cut by 21 per cent since 1980.[22] The other half are private day-care centres which serve an upper-middle-class market and can cost anywhere from $80 to $200 per week per child.

Profit-making child-care chains, with branches all over the country, have grown significantly in America in the last couple of years. For example, Kinder-Care Learning Centers, Inc., which is the largest, now has 850 centres in forty states.[23] These establishments cater to an affluent clientele (middle-class, professional) and are aggressive, commercial enterprises. They have been criticised for being more concerned with making money than with the quality of the care they provide. It does seem that in the interests of keeping costs down these child-care chains pay their staff such low wages (their teachers are paid, on average, $7,000 per year) that there is a very high staff turnover, which cannot be beneficial for the children in their care. According to a report of the National Council of Jewish Women, half of all privately owned centres for pre-school children provide inadequate care, and as a group they are less good than the non-profitmaking centres.[24]

Thirdly, some professional and upper-middle-class women (perhaps 5 per cent of all working women) choose to employ full-time baby-sitters in their own homes. This arrangement costs between $120 and $250 per week. Although this kind of money is high for child care, it certainly isn't high as a wage, which is why private baby-sitters are often new immigrants with few skills and little education.

Finally, there are the packages of multiple informal arrangements, where parents piece together a mixture of their own time, relatives' time, neighbours' time, and paid help to provide enough child care to get through the working day. Many working parents resort to this desperate juggling act when they cannot find high-quality day care or, more usually, when they simply cannot afford it. Approximately a third of all children under three with working parents are cared for in such a package. Remember the nursery-school teacher Debbie and her thirteen-month-old son, Jeremy, whom we met at the beginning of this chapter? Her package of child-care arrangements comprised Mrs Hopkins (paid help), herself and Linda and Nancy (neighbours). The disadvantages of this kind of solution are that the child is subject to many different people, the quality of care is erratic, and juggling all these arrangements is always very stressful for the parents concerned, especially since they can easily break down. Karen, the single mother we described earlier, was clearly not able to make her package work and was forced to give up her job and go on welfare until her children were old enough to attend school. The advantage of packaged arrangements is, of course, that the cost is low (in Debbie's case $30 per week for Mrs Hopkins; in Karen's case $40 per week split between the teenager and the neighbour), and it is therefore the only feasible solution for many working parents. In her survey research in one particular area, Westchester County, Sheila Kamerman found that a package comprising relatives, neighbours and paid help was the most common child-care solution. 'More than half of the pre-school children experience 2 or more types of care each week and half of these are exposed to 3 or 4 types of care during a routine week.'[25] All this adds up to a great deal of strain for parents and children.

A variation on the multiple arrangement package occurs when parents manage without any paid help by working different shifts and relying on relatives to fill in the gaps.

Eileen is a registered nurse currently working twenty-four to thirty-six hours a week on private duty. When I interviewed Eileen, her daughter was twenty-two months old. Prior to the birth of her child Eileen was working in a large teaching hospital. She was entitled to a three-month leave of absence but, in the event, failed to go back to her job because she was unable to find affordable child care despite an intensive search. Eileen needed to work; her income was essential to maintain an adequate family standard of living. She therefore began private-duty nursing, working nights and weekends. By coordinating her hours with her husband's shifts and her mother's and mother-in-law's days off from work, she always had a family member available to look after the baby. From Eileen's perspective, this family package is far from ideal: the baby rarely sees her parents together, the parents rarely see each other, and sometimes Eileen doesn't see her baby for a three-day stretch as the child is left at one or the other of the grandmothers' houses for a long weekend while the parents cope with their shift work. The other problem is that these arrangements will probably limit their family to one child. As Eileen puts it, 'None of us could deal with this crazy schedule if there were more than one child.'[26]

Good quality child care for three- to five-year-old children is slightly easier to find, but only if you have a high enough income to pay for both nursery schooling and considerable additional baby-sitting. Nursery school enrolment in America has doubled over the last decade, and 35 per cent of three- and four-year-olds now attend nursery school.[27] Unhappily for low-income working parents, more than 90 per cent of nursery schools are private, and tuition costs range from $1,500 to $3,000 per year. Another severe disadvantage is that most of these schools operate for only three hours a day, a schedule which does not begin to cover normal working hours. For women with jobs, nursery school has to be part of a more complicated and more expensive package.

Another problem is that nursery schools remain geared to enriching the development of the children of at-home mothers, and many stubbornly refuse to adapt their schedules so as to also provide convenient child care for modern working parents. The tradition of regarding the nursery school as a positive experience and day care as an unpleasant necessity dies hard. And so, the American system of child care is divided into the following: (insufficient) public day care for low-income families, private part-time nursery schools for the affluent, and 'potluck for those families who fall into neither category'.[28] In America, because publicly funded day care is only open to the poorest, it still tends to be thought of as a cheap custodial operation for the weakest members of society, not to be confused (or combined) with education.

When my son David started nursery school in the autumn of 1983, his schedule was as follows:

Week 1	School hours	9 a.m. to 10 a.m.
Week 2	School hours	10 a.m. to 11.30 a.m.
Week 3	School hours	9 a.m. to 11 a.m.
Week 4	School hours	9 a.m. to 12 noon

In short, it took this particular nursery school almost a month to work up to a full three hours a day. This schedule has been in place for twenty years and is based on the premise that since nursery school is the first time the child and the mother are separated, it is necessary to ease them into the school routine very gradually. This assumption is out of date. Two-thirds of the mothers of children in David's class worked, and all the easing-in process did was create enormous problems for us working parents as we struggled to put together a patchwork of extra baby-sitting in the morning hours. David, who at the age of three was an old hand at being in a group of children, couldn't understand why he was being sent home so early.

I did ask the school for one concession: could we drop our child off a little early, between 8.30 and 8.45 a.m.? This would enable either me or my husband to bring David to school before going to work. The school administrator I talked to dismissed this suggestion out of hand, telling me condescendingly that 'this nursery school organises its programme for the benefit of the children, not of the parents'. It is obviously to the child's advantage to be taken to school by a parent rather than by a casual baby-sitter hired for the purpose of getting a child to school precisely at 9.00 a.m. It is also extremely nice for the parent to be able to take a child to his or her first school. What this reaction really shows is how deeply the schools disapprove of working mothers – despite their numerical dominance! So much so that they make it gratuitously difficult to match school schedules with the working day.

Over the last two years I have kept a log of when the schools of my children have requested my presence – for conferences, for special assemblies, for birthday celebrations – and the favourite time slots are 10.45 a.m. and 2.30 p.m. It is hard to think of less convenient times for a working mother (or father) to take a couple of hours out of the office.

Because of the expense of nursery schools and the short duration of the nursery-school day, many working mothers in America (almost half) keep their children in family care until they are old enough to go to state school (either kindergarten or first grade).[29] There has been a significant (and welcome) growth in numbers of state-sponsored kindergartens over the last few years, but since most kindergartens are half day, they pose many of the same scheduling problems for working parents as nursery schools. This leads us into the whole question of the mesh between the American schooling system and the world of work.

In 1983 the National Commission for Excellence in Education released its report on the American educational system entitled *Nation at Risk*. Part of the explanation given in this report of why the United States is witnessing 'a rising tide of mediocrity' in education is the fact that American children spend so little time in school; the American school year is about 25 per cent shorter than that typical of other advanced countries. In Britain and other industrial countries it is not unusual for secondary school students to spend eight hours in school 220 days per year. 'In the US by contrast the typical school day lasts 6 hours and the school year 180 days.'[30] In the 1950s and 1960s the nation probably didn't suffer too much from the abbreviated school year. After all, mothers were available to supervise homework, to chauffeur children to enriching after-school activities, and to look after children during the long school holidays.

In America today working parents who think that they have solved their child-care problems because Bobby and Jane are finally old enough for full-time school are faced with a decade of trying to deal with those hours before and after school (7.30 a.m. to 8.30 a.m., 3.30 p.m. to 6 p.m.), those nine to twelve weeks of summer holidays, and other sundry breaks. No one knows for sure how working parents cope with their children over this long haul, but only a tiny fraction of schools offer after-school or before-school facilities. It is estimated that between 2 and 5 million schoolchildren aged six to thirteen are latchkey kids – that is, they return home every day to empty houses because both parents are working.[31] Sometimes they spend their time with friends or siblings, but the fact is they are without adult supervision for several hours each working day. In a recent survey of working parents 23 per cent admitted that they regularly left their children alone.[32]

Many children find the experience of being latchkey kids unpleasant – full of fear, loneliness and conflict. According to one study, approximately 25 per cent of latchkey children have experienced serious problems coping with looking after themselves for hours at a time. 'Fear levels were high enough to cause hiding, sleeplessness and nightmares. Isolation was intense enough to cause depression or strong feelings of rejection. The responsibility placed on them was overwhelming enough to cause bitterness, resentment and anger.'[33]

Tracy grew up in Danbury, Connecticut, with her parents and sister. She lived in a nice house in a neighbourhood considered safe. At the age of five, when she started school, her mother returned to work. Tracy was expected to care for herself from the time she arrived home from school at 3.15 p.m. until her mother arrived at 5.30 p.m. Tracy's sister, who was seven years older than her, went to a private school across town and arrived home after their mother.

On the face of it, Tracy's experience was uneventful. During the thirteen years she had to care for herself there was never any reason for her to call the police or even a neighbour for that matter. She was well behaved and followed her mother's rules. But although Tracy was physically safe, she had a difficult time dealing with the experience. 'I felt short-changed. Mom cared enough to stay home when my sister was little, but she didn't care enough to stay home with me.'

Tracy was also very frightened of being by herself. 'The house seemed so large and was full of shadows in the late afternoon. There were lots of small, unexplained noises, and I would turn on the TV to block them out.' Because she was so afraid, Tracy spent a great deal of time playing in cupboards, where she felt safe. Even though her parents were home in the evening, Tracy was often too frightened to go to sleep at night and suffered from insomnia and nightmares.[34]

The American educational system makes life extremely difficult for working parents. No attempt is made to mesh school hours with work hours, and many school administrators either ignore or are actively hostile to the constraints that jobs impose on mothers. It would be a relatively simple process to make a few changes in the educational calendar. For example, lengthening the school year and the school day would considerably ameliorate the burdens of working parents. It would also enhance the lives of their children. More hours of schooling would both upgrade educational performance and ensure that children were left unattended for fewer hours of the week.

In the late 1960s and early 1970s there was a major legislative push to provide day care and nursery schooling for America's children. It was supported by, among others, the American Federation of Teachers, led by Albert Shanker, who thought that both day care and nursery schooling should be undertaken by the state school system. As Shanker saw it, the declining birthrate left the country filled with underutilised school buildings and qualified teachers without jobs. It therefore made a lot of sense to put these resources to work in providing desperately needed child care.[35] Unfortunately the Comprehensive Child Development Act of 1971 was vetoed by President Nixon, and the family services bill of 1975 failed to get through Congress. Shanker's ideas were never realised.

Thus the world of work and the educational system remain particularly incompatible in America. Children spend 25 per cent fewer hours in school than their European counterparts, while employed adults have much shorter holidays than European workers. Workers in France and Sweden have five weeks' paid holiday a year, plus public holidays, while in West Germany workers average more than four weeks off a year. Indeed, among the member countries of the EEC the standard minimum annual leave is four weeks.[36] In America, on the other hand, workers average two weeks' annual leave a year plus public holidays, and about 20 per cent of workers (many of them women) have no right to paid leave at all.

How did this situation come about? Limited amounts of time off in the United States seems to be a function of the country's rigorous work ethic and free-market system, which has little tolerance of social benefits or state interference in private-sector activities. Originally the school year in the United States was developed on an agricultural calendar when America was largely a nation of farmers. As the country became more urban, families (or, more precisely, mothers) were expected to span the gap between the work and the school day, filling in with supervised play, piano lessons, Boy Scouts, etc. This arrangement, which places a considerable educational burden on mothers, works only when women are able and willing to stay out of the work force in large numbers. It is obviously not working today. The gap between the school and the work day – a gap which is much wider in America than in Europe – merely serves to increase the miseries of millions of latchkey kids.

Europe also has an agrarian past (indeed, a quarter of the French and the Italian populations still work on the land), but in modern times education has been defined by both governments and citizens as a serious business to be undertaken by professionals in the schools, not by amateurs at home. This approach has been reinforced by the fact that European countries have not been as affluent as the United States and therefore have not been able to afford to keep so many young people at school until their mid-twenties. Thus there is a more rigorous approach to education at the primary and secondary levels which requires long hours of schooling.

But America is no longer top dog in the economic universe. Several European countries have higher per capita incomes than the United States, and America can no longer afford to take such a haphazard approach to education. This is especially true since a critical component of the American system supplied by at-home mothers is less readily available now than in the past.

What are other advanced industrial nations doing to meet the needs of working parents and their children? In most of these countries, even the most progressive, there is a lag between the demand for and the supply of public child-care facilities. This is because women have entered the work force at an extremely rapid rate in recent years, just as they have in America. It has been hard for governments to keep pace with the changing social and economic realities. However, the services that are in existence are considerably more elaborate than those available in America. And many European governments have committed to trying to catch up with demand as quickly as possible – which is a good deal more than can be said for the United States.

We met Susan Arnbom in Chapter Three. Susan works as a secretary in Stockholm. She is also the mother of three children, aged seven, three and two. During the working day Susan's eldest child, Eric, is at primary school, which gets out at 4 p.m.; he then attends after-school activities at the same school. The younger two are enrolled at a government-sponsored day-care centre. The fee for this facility is income-adjusted, and Susan pays the same for her two children as she would for one. The day-care centre is located in the block of flats where Susan and her family live and is open from 7 a.m. to 6 p.m. The centre takes a total of twelve children, who are supervised by four adults. The facilities are bright, airy and well equipped.[37]

Approximately one-third of all children under seven years old in Sweden are in some form of state-sponsored child care.[38] The options range from municipal childminders (who look after three to four children in their homes and are paid for and licensed by local government) to various types of day-care centres. A further third of Swedish children under seven are cared for privately, most commonly by unlicensed childminders who take children into their own homes. Priority in allocating state day-care places is given to single mothers and low-income families.[39]

Child care in state day-care centres is of very high quality. The centres are generally open ten to twelve hours a day five days a week. Costs are paid by the state (50 per cent), local government (40 per cent), and parental fees (10 per cent). Fees are charged on an income-related basis, so that a parent earning $500 a month or less, for instance, may leave a child nine hours a day five days a week for as little as $16 a month, while parents earning $1,325 or more a month would pay $122. This fee includes three hot meals a day plus snacks.[40]

In France out-of-home child care is taken for granted partly because of the long history communal care has in the country; the first child-care centres were started in the early nineteenth century. In modern times the *écoles maternelles* (free public nursery schools) have been accepted as the norm. Since the 1950s they have taken nearly all three- to six-year-olds. Since these nursery schools have short hours, *Haltes-garderies* (part-time day-care centres) have been set up to make up the difference in hours between the nursery school day and the average work day. Parents can pay for meals and extra care at these centres, which are often attached to the *écoles maternelles*.

Publicly run crèches cater for children aged six months to three years. While the actual cost of crèche care per child is about 500 francs a week, parents pay on an income-adjusted basis, and parental fees can range anywhere from 35 francs to 50 francs a week. The remainder is paid for from a variety of local and national funds. The crèches are generally open from 7 a.m. to 7 p.m. five days a week. The quality of care is excellent, and there are very long waiting lists for places. Some of the excess demand is filled by government-licensed *nourrices*, who charge approximately the same as the crèche, or else by private *nourrices*, who can be very much more expensive. In addition, grandmothers still play an important child-care role in France.

In 1980 the French Ministry of Education estimated that 35 per cent of two-year-olds, 90 per cent of three-year-olds, and 100 per cent of four-, five-, and six-year-olds were enrolled in crèches and state nursery schools.[41]

In Italy the state provision of day care and nursery schools is a recent development. However, by 1980 nearly 70 per cent of three- to six-year-olds were attending nursery schools.[42] Most of these are run by private non-profitmaking and church organisations, although there are increasing numbers of state nursery schools. State-run nursery schools are free; private ones charge income-related fees, which are kept low through large government subsidies.

Crèches for under threes are also predominantly privately run. Free state-run crèches are increasingly available and now serve 10 to 25 per cent of this age-group. Relatives also continue to play an important child-care role in Italy.[43]

In Britain the picture is not as good. Only 0.1% of the country's estimated 3.5 million under fives have access to crèches (which take children aged three months to five years) provided by the local Social Services departments, so inevitably these places are reserved for children from single-parent families and children at risk.[44] About 38 per cent of three- to five-year-olds attend state nursery schools, although the provisions for these vary enormously from local authority to local authority – with inner London, Newham, Manchester and Birmingham providing for the highest percentage of children (50 per cent).[45]

The most popular form of care for the pre-schoolers in Britain is, however, the registered childminder, of which there are approximately fifty thousand. In the London borough of Camden, there are 268 registered childminders who are permitted to take in as many as three children, including their own, for a fee they negotiate with the parents. Registering themselves with the local authority entitles childminders to the use of equipment like strollers and high chairs, free milk for the children and access to facilities such as toy libraries. In recent years the DHSS has been encouraging the use of childminders for the under threes – taking the view that the home environment is a more personal (as well as cheaper) place in which children can be cared for than local-authority-run crèches.[46]

Although far from perfect and much less widespread than in most other European countries, the British system of child care does have one major advantage over the American system: crèches and childminders all have to be registered with the local authority and they are carefully monitored – in Britain there have been none of the scandals of sexual abuse in day-care centres in New York and California that shocked Americans recently.[47] On the whole, the parents who do use the network of childminders in Britain are reasonably happy with it. As Liz Bailey of London, an economist in her thirties, says: 'One thing that you have to accept when your child is cared for by another person is that sometimes the child may even express a preference for that person. You will feel jealous at times. And sometimes my daughter complains that she has to get up early to go to the childminder and that she doesn't have enough time to play with her toys. But on the whole I think she has benefited from it, and I think that now she has the feeling that there are a lot of caring adults.'[48]

Most advanced industrial countries, however (welfare states such as Sweden and Denmark, traditional Catholic countries such as France and Italy) have made considerable progress toward providing state or state-funded child care. This has been done to ease the lot of working parents, primarily mothers, but it has also been done to ensure their nation's future prosperity. For example, by the end of the 1970s France was spending more than 4 per cent of its gross national product on subsidies to pre-school children, not because French society is particularly keen on women's rights (France, in fact, is quite traditional in its attitudes toward women) but because French policy-makers consider these expenditures a good investment in the nation's future.[49] The French logic is impeccable: if government neglects the needs of two- and three-year-olds, it is likely to create expensive problems later; after all, it is possible to pour all kinds of public money down the drain at the primary- and secondary-school levels if pre-schoolers are allowed to suffer. Many governments recognise that the quality of their human resources is directly linked to facilitating a decent start in life for children. Only America is actually *decreasing* state support for children. Since 1980 an additional 3 million children have fallen into poverty, 700,000 poor children have been struck from the Medicaid rolls (entitling them to free health care), and 200,000 have lost their day-care subsidies.[50]

There is a substantial body of research (ironically, much of it undertaken in the United States) demonstrating that 'more than half of intelligence measured at age 17 develops before age 5'.[51] The pre-school years are the ones in which general learning abilities develop more rapidly than at any other period. According to psychologist Benjamin Bloom, 'Failure to develop appropriate achievement and learning in these years is likely to lead to continued failure throughout the remainder of the individual's school career.'[52] Reinforcing this viewpoint is the work of Martin Deutsch, which shows that higher intelligence scores are found among children who have pre-school experience than in those whose initial contact with school was in first grade.[53] Finally, the research of Katrina de Hirsch demonstrates that many 'intelligent but educationally disabled children . . . would not have required help had their difficulties been recognised at early ages. . . . Early identification would have obviated the need for later remedial measures.'[54]

Some of the most persuasive evidence of the positive effects of early-childhood education comes from the Perry Preschool Project of Ypsilanti, Michigan. This project began in the 1960s and closely tracked the lives of 123 impoverished black children, half of whom were given one to two years of high-quality pre-school education. Researchers have found that the children with the pre-school experience, now in their late teens, stay in school longer, have better earnings prospects, are less involved in crime, and get pregnant less often than their peers who began school later. Their lives appear to have been changed for the better, and so has their community, in terms of lower crime rates, lower expenditures for special education, welfare, and criminal justice proceedings, and higher tax revenues from the participants' earnings. The administrators of the Ypsilanti project took the unusual step of trying to calculate their net rate of return and estimated that the benefits of the project amounted to seven times the cost.[55]

The Ypsilanti project is, however, but a drop in the ocean. The deterioration in the American educational system is such that the National Commission for Excellence in Education was prompted to comment that 'if an unfriendly foreign power had attempted to impose on America the mediocre educational performance that exists today, we might well have viewed it as an act of war'.[56] Today 13 per cent of American seventeen-year-olds are functionally illiterate, and the average achievement of high school students on most standardised tests is lower than it was twenty-five years ago.[57] All this has extremely negative implications for the quality of the country's future work force. However, it is difficult to blame all these problems on a deterioration in the formal educational system – America spends more public money per capita on education than Britain, West Germany, France or Italy.[58] America has had a total blind spot as regards nursery care and pre-school education and finds it difficult to see that investing in child care and child health may be as important as investing in secondary and tertiary education.

When we think of childhood, our mental images rarely include physical abuse, latchkey children, or single parenthood. Western culture has been called child-centred, and our poets and novelists have seen childhood as a paradise, a time of innocent family fun. John Betjeman describes it as 'the peace before the dreadful daylight starts of unkept promises and broken hearts'.[59] Many of our classic children's books begin, as *The Railway Children* begins, with a description of an ideal family situation:

They were just ordinary suburban children, and they lived with their Father and Mother in an ordinary red-brick-fronted house, with coloured glass in the front door, a tiled passage that was called a hall, a bathroom with hot and cold water, electric bells, french windows, and a good deal of white paint, and 'every modern convenience'.

Mother was almost always there, ready to play with the children, and read to them and help them to do their home-lessons. Besides this she used to write stories for them while they were at school . . . and she always made up funny pieces of poetry for their birthdays and for other great occasions, such as the christening of the new kitten, or the refurnishing of the doll's house, or the time when they were getting over the mumps.

These three lucky children always had everything they needed: pretty clothes, good fires, a lovely nursery with heaps of toys, and a Mother Goose wall-paper. . . . They also had a Father who was just perfect – never cross, never unjust, and always ready for a game.[60]

For many of us this kind of family is no more than a contemporary dream. Today this 'classical family of Western nostalgia'[61] – the nuclear family of breadwinning father, dependent wife and two or more children – constitutes a mere 6 per cent of the population of the United States of America,[62] and 10.9 per cent of the population of Great Britain.[63] We are more likely to see it pictured on a box of cornflakes than in our own lives. Yet in America, and to a lesser extent in Britain, social policies still work on the assumption that children grow up in such families and have no unmet needs.

The Women's Movement

5. *Image and Reality*

Americans are condescendingly sure that women in their country are much better off than women anywhere else in the world.

In a *New York Times* piece in December 1983 American writer Kati Marton smugly reports:

It's good to be home. After nearly six years abroad, I am struck first of all by what a good time it is to be a woman in America. Speak not to me of a gender gap. I have lived for the past four years in London. I now feel a surge of new life akin perhaps to what a ghetto child might experience contemplating an endless expanse of green space . . .

The country I have just left is light years away from all of this. Life for a woman in Britain can be an energy-sapping experience.[1]

Energy-sapping or not, if you are interested in increasing your earning power or trying to have a child while working, British women are in better shape than their American sisters.

New York Times correspondent R. W. Apple, back in the States after many years overseas, is astonished by American women 'whose role has changed out of all recognition in a single decade'. He confesses to being gripped by the sight of 'female forest rangers, female bulldozer operators and female partners in hundreds of law firms all across the country'.[2] Apple obviously has not read the studies which document how and why women are not becoming partners in hundreds of law firms across the country.

These New World women, who, everyone is agreed, are the most liberated in the world, actually face major economic handicaps. As we now know, they have to cope with the consequences of the highest divorce rate and the largest earnings gap (between male and female earnings) in the advanced world. The female experience in backward, 'energy-sapping' Britain and the rest of Europe is a much better deal, at least if one focuses on the material conditions of life. American women are big on image and short on substance.

Our perception of the powerful American woman has undoubtedly been shaped by the modern women's movement, which has been larger, noisier, and more visible in the United States than in any other country in the Western world. America's liberated women still become dewy-eyed at the memory of those heady days in 1969 when feminists stormed the Atlantic City beauty pageant. Dumping padded bras, curlers, girdles, false eyelashes, copies of *Playboy* and *Family Circle* and shorthand notepads into a 'freedom trash can', they placed a Miss America crown on the head of a live sheep and sang:

> Ain't she sweet,
> Making profit off her meat.[3]

Later that year members of the Women's International Terrorist Conspiracy from Hell (WITCH for short) disrupted a fashion show for brides by singing (to the tune of the 'Wedding March'):

> Here come the slaves,
> Off to their graves.[4]

In August 1970, 10,000 feminists marched along Fifth Avenue and Kate Millett declared, 'Today is the beginning of a new movement. Today is the end of millenniums of oppression'. The same summer 1,000 women marched in Boston, and 2,000 in San Francisco. In Miami women smashed crockery at a 'liberation garden party' while in Philadelphia's Rittenhouse Square feminists prepared themselves for the struggle by taking free open-air karate lessons. Back in New York City's Duffy Square, Mary Orovan made the sign of the cross at a ceremony honouring Susan B. Anthony, intoning, 'In the name of the Mother, the Daughter, and the Holy Granddaughter, Ah-Women. Ah-Women,' while the crowd waved placards reading REPENT, MALE CHAUVINISTS, YOUR WORLD IS COMING TO AN END.

All very stirring stuff, and in some important ways the women's liberation movement has managed to reconstruct the language and the consciousness of the American nation. There has been an impressive increase in personal and sexual freedom for women, the career aspirations of élite women have been permanently raised, and there has been a dramatic rise in the number of women lawyers, doctors and managers in eighties America. But if women are allowed to be ambitious in this new liberated age, and if they have become free not to have children, the fact remains that they have not made a dent in the wage gap, and many are increasingly unable to reconcile motherhood with their professional aspirations. In short, very little of this feminist agitation has boiled down to policies that help American women deal with the concrete realities of their daily lives; for the majority, these realities centre on reconciling motherhood with a job.

The European experience has been different. In some ways European women seem to have made much less progress than their American counterparts. As Kati Marton, author of the 'energy-sapping' Britain article, correctly points out, there are fewer women executives in the City of London than on Wall Street, and British men still find it difficult to get their tongues around the term 'Ms'. But despite the fact that European society has not reconstructed its consciousness, many Western European countries have instituted generous maternity leaves, pushed ahead with public child care, and made considerable progress in closing the gap between male and female earning power. It is also true that there are more women in high public office in Europe than in the United States: Geraldine Ferraro, failed Democrat vice-presidential candidate, is the closest any American woman has come to the political status of Mrs Margaret Thatcher.

Why has the experience of European women been so very different from that of women in the United States? Part of the explanation lies in the goals and objectives of feminism on either side of the Atlantic.

The central emphases of the American movement have been on equal rights and on sexual freedom. Most American feminists have stressed the importance of acquiring an equal set of legal rights and of achieving control over one's body. The assumption has been that once women possess the same rights as men and can choose not to have children, they achieve true equality of opportunity and are able to compete for jobs, income and power on the same terms as men.

For a century and a half much of the energy of American feminism has been channelled into the struggle to win formal equality of rights between the sexes. In the nineteenth and early twentieth centuries the main goal was to win the right to vote; in the modern period the central struggle has been over the Equal Rights Amendment (ERA). Most recently abortion and birth control rights have been added to the core agenda. Eleanor Smeal (president of the National Organization for Women, one of America's most vociferous feminist organisations, from 1978 to 1983 and re-elected in 1985) underlines these priorities in her 1984 book, *Why and How Women Will Elect the Next President*, in which she lists the ERA and abortion as the two most important issues for contemporary American feminists.[5]

In Europe various groups of social feminists have conceived the problem of the female sex quite differently. For them, it is not woman's lack of legal rights that constitute her main handicap, or even her lack of 'reproductive freedom'. Rather, it is her dual burden – in the home and in the work force – that leads to second-class status. The goal of the social feminists has therefore become one of lightening this burden by instituting family support systems – many of which were described in Chapters Three and Four – that make this dual role less oppressive for women. Their conviction is that because women are wives and mothers as well as workers and citizens, they need special compensatory policies if they are to accomplish as much as men in the world beyond the home. Equal rights are seen as only a small part of the story. As Anna-Greta Leijon, the current Swedish Minister of Labour, points out, 'If children cannot receive good care while their parents are away working, the right to work becomes illusory for most women.'[6]

One thing is immediately apparent: these contrasting visions of the female problem place a very different weight on the issue of motherhood. American feminists have generally stressed the ways in which men and women should be equal and have therefore tried to put aside differences. This has led them to sidetrack issues of motherhood. When it comes to the special functions of women in the bearing of children, there has been a tendency to focus on reproductive freedom and the right to choose *not* to have a child, since that is what would permit women to approximate men. The critical problems of having children or of being a mother are ignored or played down.

Social feminists, on the other hand, have placed motherhood centre stage. The essence of the female problem, in their view, is to reconcile the demands of childbirth and child rearing with those of the work place and the wider community. They believe that men and society at large should provide systematic support to women in recognition of their dual role as mothers and workers. The logic of this view is simple and compelling. Ninety per cent of women have children, and in the absence of support structures it is precisely during the childbearing years that women fail to make the grade in the career struggle. In Chapter Three, when we examined wage differentials in the American economy, we found that the earnings gap between the sexes widened considerably when men and women reached their late twenties and thirties. Women simply fell behind in the job market when they bore and raised their children, and they rarely caught up.

Of course, not all American feminists have been equal rights enthusiasts and not all European feminists have concentrated on material realities. Social feminists have played a small role in the United States, and equal rights advocates have been present in Europe. But it is true that the overwhelming preoccupation of the American women's movement has been on equal rights and reproductive freedom, while the central focus of most European feminists has been on the material conditions of life, specifically on the support structures necessary to reconcile women's maternal and work responsibilities.

This difference between feminists, between the equal rights enthusiasts and those that stress material realities, is more than a theoretical distinction, for these two groups of feminists have very different political priorities. A recent furore in California over maternity leave highlights the clash between these two visions of feminism.

In the summer of 1984, just after Geraldine Ferraro had been selected as the vice-presidential nominee at the Democratic National Convention in San Francisco, the *New York Times* ran an article entitled 'Maternity Leave: Is It Leave Indeed?' It told the story of Lillian Garland's fight both to have a baby and to keep her job:

Miss Garland, a receptionist at the California Federal Savings and Loan Association here [in Los Angeles], gave birth to Kekere Yuri Latik Gamer on February 12, 1982. The delivery was by Caesarean section, and Miss Garland's doctor certified that she would be medically able to go back to work on April 21st. But when Miss Garland presented herself at the bank, ready to resume work, she was told her job had been filled – and there were no openings for her.

'I just felt faint, I was cold all over,' said Miss Garland. 'It never occurred to me that I might lose my job because I'd had a child. I was in total shock. I don't think a woman should have to choose between having a baby and having an income.'

Things got worse for Miss Garland after she lost her job: lacking income, she was evicted from her apartment, and had to sleep on a woman friend's couch. Without resources to care for the baby, she lost custody to the child's father.

Finally, Miss Garland called California's Department of Fair Employment and Housing for help. The lawyers there told her that what Cal Fed had done was illegal. Under the department's interpretation of a 1979 California law, every woman is entitled to up to four months' unpaid leave, without losing her job, for medical disability caused by pregnancy or childbirth. But Cal Fed – joined by the California Chamber of Commerce and the Merchants and Manufacturers Association, an employers' group with 2,900 members employing about 3 million workers – decided to use the Garland case to challenge the law.

Requiring employers to give disability leave to pregnant women, they argued, is a form of sex discrimination singling out women for preferential treatment. If disabled men do not have the right to reinstatement, they said, neither should women who have just had babies.

Federal District Judge Manuel L. Real, in a March 21 ruling, accepted that argument and declared the California law null and void. The case is now on appeal to the United States Court of Appeals for the Ninth Circuit, and more than 200 pending cases like Miss Garland's – that is, cases of women whose pregnancy cost them their jobs – are frozen in the Fair Employment Department. Many legal observers believe the question is ultimately headed for the United States Supreme Court.

Throughout the nation, the Garland case has set off a bitter debate ... The issue is whether the law must always treat men and women the same, or whether the law, and the business community, should accommodate the unique childbearing capacities of women workers ... The idea offends many employers. 'I don't believe that picking out a small select group of people and giving them preferential treatment is a good thing,' said Richard E. Bradley, vice president of the Merchants and Manufacturers Association.

Dianne Feinstein, the Mayor of San Francisco, supports this reasoning. 'What we women have been saying all along is we want to be treated equally,' she said, shortly after Judge Real struck down the California law. 'Now we have to put our money where our mouth is. What we were asking was to create a special group of workers that, in essence, is pregnant women and new mothers. I just don't happen to agree with that. *I don't think the work market has to accommodate itself to women having children* [my italics].[7]

Most women's rights groups in America, including NOW (the National Organisation for Women), are siding with Cal Fed and against Miss Garland – a situation that many European feminists would find incomprehensible.

Does Mayor Feinstein realise that the US is the only advanced democracy that doesn't provide paid maternity (or parental) leave as a matter of national policy? In the world today 117 nations, including Britain, France, Italy, West Germany and Canada, provide some sort of statutory maternity leave, in the simple belief that allowing mothers to recuperate from childbirth, allowing infants to spend the first few weeks of their lives with their mothers or fathers, and producing circumstances in which working women feel able to become mothers, is actually good for society – and for the economy.

Does Mr Bradley realise that we are not talking about a small, select group of people? Women constitute 53 per cent of the population and 45 per cent of the American work force. As we have noted before, 90 per cent of these women will have children, and most of them have no option but to try to hang on to their jobs during their childbearing years.

Does Lillian Garland realise that many of her feminist contemporaries think that she should not have had the right to take maternity leave and get her job back? That they think that she has less right to a leave for childbirth than if she were incapacitated in a skiing accident? After all, anyone can have a skiing accident, but only women can have babies, so if you apply the principle of equal treatment, skiing accidents qualify and childbirth doesn't. It is my guess that if she knew where NOW stands on this issue, she would pass up feminism and throw equal rights out of the window.

Does NOW realise that women are not men? Only women can have babies; it is both the privilege and the responsibility of the female sex. To ignore this biological difference, as many American feminists choose to do, is to commit a double folly. In the first place, it ensures that most women will become second-class citizens in the work place. For *without public support policies few women can cope with motherhood without hopelessly compromising their career goals.* Secondly, society has to suffer. For a child cannot be compared with a new car or a holiday, some private consumer good that a woman can choose to spend resources on if the fancy strikes her. The decision to have a child is both a private and a public decision, for children are a nation's collective future. For failing to create decent conditions for the bearing of children, and for depriving those children of parental contact in the first few weeks of life, the richest nation in the world will have to pay a huge price in the future. As we saw in Chapter Four, neglected children grow into problem-ridden, unproductive adults.

Eleanor Roosevelt, wife of Franklin D., once said, 'Women are different from men, their physical functions are different, and the future of the race depends upon their ability to produce healthy children.'[8] Because of this belief in the importance of motherhood, Mrs Roosevelt was indifferent to women's suffrage and was a lifelong opponent of the Equal Rights Amendment (ERA). She thought that if men and women had to be treated equally, it would undermine the protective laws she and other social reformers had sought for women in the work place – factory safety standards, minimum wage laws, a forty-eight-hour working week, elimination of night work, and exclusion from dangerous work.

Mrs Roosevelt was so irritated by the equal rights emphasis of mainstream American feminists that she refused to be labelled a feminist herself. The fact that she avoided the term doesn't, of course, mean that she didn't act like a feminist a good deal of the time. She thought women were every bit as capable as men. However, Mrs Roosevelt got to grips with the fundamental issue that feminism should not be equated with equal rights and that sometimes women have to be treated unequally if they are to have a fair deal as mothers and workers. This broader concept of feminism has had a larger following in Europe than in the United States, and because of this, feminism has been a more constructive force in Europe than in America.

6. Equal Rights Versus Social Benefits

In order to understand how equal rights have come to take such a central position in the thinking of the American women's movement today, it is important to take a historical perspective. For, the equal rights issue has been fundamental to the movement ever since it began some 150 years ago. It has been the thread which binds the early agitation for women's rights in the 1830s and 1840s, the suffrage movement of the late nineteenth and early twentieth centuries, and the women's movement of the 1960s and 1970s. Yet American women in the 1980s still await constitutional acknowledgement of their equal rights.

The initial period of feminist activity in America coincided with the beginning of industrialisation. In the 1830s and 1840s the textile mills, food-processing factories, shoe factories and other nascent industries of the north-east of the country attracted large numbers of women workers. Historian William Chafe underlines the importance of industrialisation as a trigger for feminist agitation: 'Although the industrial revolution did not directly cause feminism, it provided the context for the first collective assault on traditional ideas about women's place.'[1] In the new industrial order working women were even more exploited than they had been in the agricultural production process. While the pioneering women of the mid-West were often accorded rough equality with men, in the new factory system women often worked as hard as men for half the male wage rate.

At the same time more affluent women were beginning to resent their second-class status. The anti-slavery movement provided the catalyst. Many middle-class women were active in the abolitionist movement, which defined slavery as a religious abomination and a national disgrace. But what was the condition of these slaves? They could own no property and indeed themselves were treated as property. They had no legal rights to their own children, no right to vote, no right to payment for the work they performed for their masters, no redress against abuse or violence, and no access to education, skilled work or independent social status of any kind. It could scarcely have escaped the attention of the married women working for abolition that despite their relative comfort and security, precisely the same restrictions applied to them. The turning point came with the exclusion of women from effective participation in the World Anti-Slavery Convention in London in 1840.

The American women's rights movement was formally launched in 1848, at a convention in Seneca Falls, New York, organised by Elizabeth Cady Stanton and Lucretia Mott. The resolutions adopted by the Seneca Falls Convention were based on the principle that 'woman is man's equal, was intended to be so by the Creator, and the highest good of the race demands that she should be recognised as such'.[2] This convention and the subsequent public debate called for a broad range of new rights and freedoms for women. Stanton, Susan B. Anthony, Lucy Stone and other activists demanded equal rights for women in marriage, education, industrial employment and politics. Radical in sentiment and small in numbers, these early feminists had only limited influence on government policy.

A later wave of nineteenth-century feminism attracted widespread support but for a much more limited goal: the vote. Ever since the Seneca Falls Convention, suffrage had been a central demand of feminist activists. In the last two decades of the nineteenth century the right of women to vote was turned into a respectable and legitimate political issue. Instead of presenting the vote as an assault upon the family and traditional ideas of 'woman's place', feminists increasingly portrayed it as a means of bringing women's natural moral and spiritual concerns to bear upon government. The rationale for enfranchising women shifted from Stanton's natural rights argument that men and women were equal and therefore citizens with identical claims to a demand for suffrage which rested on female righteousness. Women deserved the vote not because they were equal to men but because they were virtuous, maternal, devout, sober and respectable. In the words of Jane Addams, it was a way for women to become the housekeepers of the nation.[3]

Stanton herself was impatient with the single-mindedness and conservatism of the late-nineteenth-century feminist movement. Refusing 'to sing suffrage evermore', she continued to advocate trade unions for women workers, divorce reform and birth control.[4] She even went so far as to publish *The Woman's Bible*, which attacked traditional church teachings on the status of women. But Stanton paid for her heresy. Suffragists feared that Stanton's radical feminism would damn their chances for success, and, to avoid the Stanton stigma, they isolated and ignored her, and instead conferred the role of figurehead on Susan B. Anthony, despite the fact that Anthony did not join the feminist movement until three years after Stanton had originally proposed women's suffrage.

The battle to win the vote was enormously costly. Feminists abandoned all other policy goals, cultivated conservatism, and devoted fifty-two years to a ceaseless campaign. By the time the vote was granted in 1920, the long channelling of feminists' energies into the limited goal of suffrage had exhausted the women's movement. By then many feminists had forgotten what the vote was for. Those who had assumed that the right to vote held the key to improving women's economic and social position were disappointed by the events that followed their victory in 1920. There was no noticeable progress towards equal status. Those women who used their vote (and only a third of them did) tended to vote the same way as their fathers or husbands. The enfranchisement of women was a political non-event.

Part of the problem lay within the movement. In the early twenties there was a serious split between equal rights enthusiasts who wanted to push for an equal rights amendment and social reformers who wanted to preserve and expand protective legislation for working women. This schism prevented the feminists from putting together a coherent plan of action. Contributing to this impasse was the economic and political climate of the day. During the twenties there was a communist scare, and feminists were suspected of being Bolshevik sympathisers, while the thirties in America were dominated by the Great Depression. During these grim years questions of economic survival overshadowed women's rights. The net result was that feminist issues faded from public view. It was forty-five years before women became militant again.

The American feminist revival of the 1960s and 1970s displayed once more a steadily mounting concern with the equal rights of women. In its early stages the new women's movement had two parts, distinguished by their structure and style. The first was a highly decentralised network of consciousness-raising groups which flourished in the early seventies. Typically these groups lacked any formal structure, they tended to dissolve and re-form frequently, and they focused their energies on personal relationships and sexuality.

The second part of the movement encompassed national women's organisations and included the National Organization for Women (NOW), the National Women's Political Caucus (NWPC) and the Women's Equity Action League (WEAL). These were set up as formal organisations with elected officers, constitutions and boards of directors.

When the movement began in the late 1960s, consciousness raising was intended to politicise the personal aspects of people's lives. But the participants were too privileged, their concerns were too private, and the groups were too ephemeral for them to develop a unified public voice. Besides, the focus was on individual redemption, not on promoting social change. In the event, consciousness raising prompted emotional and behavioural changes without mobilising energy for political action.

The consciousness-raising group I belonged to in the 1970s was typical. It met sporadically between the autumn of 1975 and the spring of 1977. Sometimes it met as often as twice a month, and once a whole summer went by without a meeting. The membership was also somewhat fluid, but the group remained roughly the same size (about seven of us) with a slightly different mix of people for its eighteen-month life-span.

As was the case with many of these groups, mine was essentially a circle of friends. We had three things in common: we lived in Manhattan; we were all professionals struggling to overcome various barriers to career success; and we were all infected with the spirit of women's liberation and saw ourselves as feminists. We were otherwise a diverse group. Our professions ran the gamut from struggling artist to editor to teacher; some of us were married, others were single, and about a third of the women in the group were mothers. Our ages ranged from twenty-eight to fifty-three, and in keeping with such chronological diversity, some of us were just beginning our careers while others among us were established. The guiding purpose of the group was to examine our various attempts to reconcile the personal and the professional sides of our lives and to help one another do a better job at integrating these two elements.

We had some procedural rules, which we thrashed out when we set up the group. The meetings rotated around the members' homes, and each session had a different 'lead person'. This position also rotated around the group. The job of this lead person was to present an issue or a problem and then to monitor the discussion to make sure that everyone had a chance to talk and that no one became overly critical or judgemental of anyone else in the group. Consciousness raising was, after all, an exercise in supportive interaction.

Our sessions ranged over a great variety of topics from how to integrate stepchildren into one's life to attitudes toward ambition. The focus was overwhelmingly personal; we looked to our relationships, to our childhoods, to our interior worlds to explain our problems in life. I remember one session with great clarity.

It was mid-January 1977, and it was Lila's* turn to host the meeting. We all met at her house at 8.30 p.m. for dessert and coffee. Some of us had not been to Lila's home before and were startled at how luxurious it was. She and her immensely successful husband lived in a glorious town house just off Park Avenue. It had wonderful fireplaces and panelling and seemed to be full of antiques. The thing that impressed me most was that Lila and her family seemed to occupy the entire five floors (at the time I was living in a hole in the wall in an unfashionable part of Upper West Side). The group met in the downstairs library. The room was furnished with bottle-green leather couches, Turkish rugs and shelves full of books, and looked out on to a peaceful, floodlit winter garden. I still remember the scene; it was quite magical.

Lila herself seemed totally incongruous. A pretty but unkempt woman, she simply was not credible as the mistress of this splendid mansion. She was wearing an old, shapeless skirt and a creased silk blouse which was much too tight and clearly pre-dated her most recent pregnancy. I was mesmerised by this blouse; throughout the evening the buttons over her bust kept on popping open, and Lila kept on fastening them up – to no avail.

Our topic for the evening was money: how much we made; how much we would like to make; how we shared money with our partners; whether we felt anxious, dependent or vulnerable in this sphere and, if we did, what we should do about it.

Joanna,* who was the lead person for the evening, opened the session with, 'I feel more nervous about this topic than about any other we have covered. I guess people these days are just much more secretive about money than they are about anything else.' She cleared her throat and went on rather hesitantly. 'I want to begin by making a confession. Last Saturday I was at Bloomingdale's getting some basic stuff for the apartment – you know, sheets and towels, that kind of thing. When I had finished, I peeked into one of those new designer boutiques on the second floor and some mad impulse came over me. I found myself buying this incredibly expensive sequinned evening blouse that we couldn't even begin to afford. But that's not the worst of it. I then took it home and hid it in the wardrobe in the spare bedroom so that Bob wouldn't see it.' Joanna paused and then let out a long sigh. 'How's that for immature, irresponsible behaviour?'

We all murmured sympathetically, recognising too readily and a little painfully the scene she described. Molly* pushed Joanna to analyse her behaviour a little: 'But did you hide the blouse from Bob because you really couldn't afford it – after all, you earn a good salary – or because you had neglected to ask his permission before buying it?'

This hit a chord in Joanna, and she responded eagerly. 'That's exactly what I have been asking myself. You know, I think that maybe I can afford the blouse. I just got a raise at Harper and Row [the publishing house Joanna worked for as an editor], and there is enough money left over after my share of household expenses to allow for the occasional extravagance. But you see, Bob still earns twice as much as I do despite the fact he holds a similar position [Bob was an editor at another publishing house], and I feel that I ought to ask his permission before making any major purchase. Every now and then I rebel and end up acting like a child hiding forbidden goodies under the bed.'

Lila had been listening intently and decided to join in the discussion. 'I really connect with that business of earning less than your partner. Rick* has been so successful recently that he now earns five times more than I do. I work so hard for my thirteen thousand dollars a year [Lila taught music in a private school], yet it hardly pays for the baby-sitter, let alone anything else. Rick hates my splurging out on clothes, and I've no self-control in shops, so last winter I just decided never to go into department stores again so that I wouldn't be tempted.' Lila paused and smiled triumphantly. 'It works! I order all household things by phone, and this way I avoid spending anything on me.'

I looked at Lila in amazement. My eye travelled from her creased and ill-fitting blouse (some more buttons had popped open) to the opulent furnishings. Just one of those rugs would have bought Lila a mink coat. 'But, Lila,' I said, 'are you saying that you and Rick can't afford to buy you any clothes?'

Lila nodded sadly. 'Well, you see the house and the kids pretty much take up everything we earn, and then Rick has to dress well because his position in the corporation demands it. I feel that it is up to me to economise.'

The rest of us looked at one another wide-eyed and decided not to push Lila any further just then; we moved on to the next person.

Looking back at this consciousness-raising session, I now think of all the things we did not bring up. For example, why did Joanna's husband Bob earn twice as much as she despite the fact that he had a very similar job? Why was Lila's teaching position so badly paid despite her impressive qualifications? Why didn't we focus on these issues and talk about a strategy for helping Joanna and Lila improve their earning capacities? So much of the guilt and the dependency we were talking about seemed to be triggered by the asymmetry in economic power between these women and their husbands. But we were entirely wrapped up in our own interior worlds and in our relationships. We never thought to go to the outside worlds of institutions and politics to explain our problems.

Consciousness raising was the single activity most universally associated with the American women's liberation movement in the late 1960s and early 1970s. In fact, for many women, their weekly 'rap' sessions constituted their *only* feminist activity. But while consciousness raising was meant to politicise the personal aspects of people's lives, it never quite made that transition. The new awareness seemed to lead most commonly to emotional and behavioural changes. As psychologist Phyllis Chesler reported, 'Some women started living together; some began living alone for the first time . . . Some women left their husbands; others began to live with a man . . . Women stopped giggling and competing with each other for male attention . . . Some women stopped going

97

to beauty parlours and began to value their time; they needed fewer adornments to "make up" for being female.'[5] There is, however, little evidence to show that the consciousness-raising experience mobilised many women to push for changes in government policy.

The problem was that consciousness raising tended to shift the burden for change away from society and towards the individual woman. It encouraged women to look to themselves, or to that small group of women with whom they shared consciousness, as the source of their 'liberation'. In short, consciousness raising was an approach that took the emphasis away from broad-based social action in favour of personal redemption.

In her best-selling book *The Cinderella Complex* Colette Dowling describes a dramatic collapse of ambition. Her protagonist leaves New York City, where she has just spent four years as a self-sufficient single parent, and goes to live with her three children and her new male friend in a small rural community in the Hudson Valley.

Gradually her ambition ebbs away. She launders, bakes, rakes, mulches, and plays helpmate to her man. She becomes increasingly less motivated and less effective as a writer. By the end of a year she and her children are completely financially dependent on her male friend.

Dowling sees this collapse of independence as a psychological phenomenon. She describes her protagonist as yearning to return to an infantile state of dependency so as 'to avoid the strain involved in undertaking an authentic existence'.[6] No mention is made of the practical difficulties of being a free-lance writer in a small rural community. Without an office or a library, far removed from the contacts and the network that make up the stuff of a professional writer's existence, it is easy to see that any person (male or female) might become unproductive. Dowling also fails to stress the real burdens of looking after a rambling old house and three children, burdens which don't seem to have been shared by the male friend.

Dowling focuses exclusively on the inner consciousness of her protagonist. The great stumbling block that prevents career success is 'the deep wish to be taken care of by others',[7] which Dowling sees as the chief force holding women down today. Like Cinderella, women 'are still waiting for something external to transform their lives'.[8] According to Dowling, women have only one real shot at liberation, and 'that is to emancipate themselves from within'.[9]

Dowling's emphasis on consciousness raising and personal redemption is characteristic of the American women's movement. She encourages women to get their heads in the right place and look to themselves as the source of their salvation. The material conditions of life or broad-based social change play no part in this vision of women's liberation.

*

So, while consciousness raising had little political impact, contemporary American feminists have sought policy action through national organisations and their local chapters. There can be no doubt that the priority of these organisations has been to win equal rights for women.

NOW was formed in October 1966 by Betty Friedan and a few other women activists. It revived and carried forward the nineteenth-century tradition of equal rights feminism, and its stated purpose was 'to take action to bring women into full participation in the mainstream of American society *now*, exercising all the privileges and responsibilities thereof in truly equal partnership'.[10] NOW had an élite constituency and a liberal agenda. It was populated by middle- and upper-middle-class women, and these women wanted equal educational and job opportunities, equal pay, and the abolition of all legislation which discriminated against women. Its initial strategy was to push the infant Equal Employment Opportunity Commission (EEOC), and to act on sex discrimination complaints being filed under Title VII, the 'equal protection' clause of the 1964 Civil Rights Act. Another national feminist organisation, WEAL (Women's Equity Action League), was established in 1970 to advance the cause of women's participation in political parties and in government.

These groups claim success in pursuing equal rights for women in the marketplace and in education, specifically in securing employment and educational opportunities and in gaining access to credit. In the 1960s the effect of these feminist organisations on these areas of government policy was limited; however, their influence grew in the seventies: for example, pressure from women's organisations played an important role in the passage of the 1974 Equal Credit Act. The most conspicuous failure of feminist organisations in America has been their inability to achieve ratification of the Equal Rights Amendment.

If the dominant goal of the American feminist movement has been equal rights, it has attempted to achieve this goal with a two-pronged strategy. First, feminist leaders have tried to protect the purity of the movement by avoiding alignments with interest groups, such as political parties and trade unions, outside the movement. Secondly, they have set themselves the task of uniting sisterhood in independent mass-based organisations, believing that the common bond of gender is enough to hold together a coherent movement.

This strategy has a historical root. Throughout the suffrage campaign feminists followed a policy of organising outside the major political parties. For example, the National American Woman Suffrage Association (NAWSA), a non-partisan organisation founded in 1890 for the purpose of winning the vote, refused any permanent party alignment, remaining 'obdurately non-partisan'.[11] While NAWSA supported Woodrow Wilson in 1913 because he appeared sympathetic to their cause, the organisation showed its disappointment with the Democratic Congress by organising campaigns in 1914 and 1916 to defeat Democratic congressional candidates.

Having won the vote, feminists debated the question of whether women should move toward integration into the established parties or maintain their identity as an independent political force. Some prominent feminists within the League of Women Voters (the organisational heir to NAWSA) urged women to become active participants in the Republican and Democratic parties; while a separatist faction advised women against joining parties, arguing that party politics was by nature a corrupt and unsavoury enterprise that would force women to abandon their reformist ideals and thereby destroy their unique contribution to politics. As one commentator said in 1922, 'A woman who joins one of these parties simply becomes an imitation man, which is to say, a donkey. Thereafter, she is nothing but an obscure cog in an ancient and creaking machine, the sole intelligible purpose of which is to maintain a horde of scoundrels in public office.'[12]

Ultimately the league advised women to become non-partisan and all-partisan; this seemed to boil down to a rejection of the established parties as appropriate vehicles for expressing women's demands. The most active political arm of the feminists became the Women's Joint Congressional Committee, which co-ordinated feminist lobbying activity for a variety of women's organisations but remained outside the party system.

The effectiveness of this separatist strategy depended on whether women would retaliate at the polls against a politician who was unresponsive to their demands. This threat was used to some advantage in the early 1920s, but feminists' influence on politicians dropped precipitously once it was discovered that electoral retaliation from women was an idle threat.

At the same time women could exercise little internal influence within the party structure because their separatist strategy had prevented feminists from making inroads into the party organisations. The result: impotence. In 1925 a Democratic committee woman was able to write in *Harper's Magazine*: 'I know of no woman who has a following of other women. I know of no politician who is afraid of the women's vote on any question under the sun.'[13]

With the revival of feminism in the 1960s the separatist tradition reappeared. Many of the modern proponents of women's liberation expressed 'an overt female separatist viewpoint, which calls for women to isolate themselves from men in order to come to terms with what it means to be female'.[14] Just as the black power movement used the slogan 'Black is Beautiful', the women's liberation movement coined the phrase 'Sisterhood is Powerful'. Both slogans were meant to convey a sense of group identity. The term 'sisterhood' has been used to promote 'female solidarity, respect for women as women, support for all women by women'.[15]

Thus American feminists today have chosen not to form any continuous alignment with political parties, trade unions, or other power blocs, but instead have formed a series of non-partisan interest groups, the most important of which is the National Organization for Women (NOW), who adopted in 1978 a resolution 'to remain independent and free from political party pressure, yet [be] able to endorse individual candidates who support NOW's positions'.[16] This policy of endorsing individual candidates has not worked very smoothly or effectively. For example, dissatisfied with President Carter's level of commitment to the ERA, NOW held off and did not endorse him until the last moment in the 1980 election. As a result, this large and influential women's organisation failed to mobilise against Reagan, who posed a clear threat to women's rights.

The decision to avoid partisan alliances is directly related to NOW's stated purpose, which is to serve the interests of *all* women regardless of their class, their race, their religious background, their party affiliation, or their sexual preference. Thus radical lesbians, whose participation in NOW is often viewed as a political liability, are welcomed on the ground that women's rights are indivisible. The premise is that all women, no matter how diverse they are in other respects, share the common problems of their sex. Working on this assumption, the NOW leadership has avoided permanent alignments with political parties or any other interest group whose membership and goals are less inclusive than their own.

If feminists were merely seeking to keep public debate on women's issues alive, then the umbrella strategy might be a good one. National conventions of NOW and the other feminist organisations provide excellent platforms from which to dramatise women's grievances. But if the goal is to effect policy change, then the strategy of maximising the coalition works only for those issues that unite women on the basis of gender alone. The equal rights issue in America has come closest to fulfilling this condition. However, as may be seen from the American ERA battle, going after equal rights is not a foolproof strategy. Women, after all, do not share a common economic status, religious background, or cultural heritage and therefore do not constitute a coherent class. Their ability to mount a unified campaign for a common goal is consequently limited. For projects the benefits of which are less inclusive than equal rights, the umbrella coalition simply cannot be a very effective pressure group.

An organisation like NOW, based on the principle of universal sisterhood among women, faces serious difficulties in promoting policies that benefit only certain groups, such as pregnant women, women who need day care for their children, or retired women. Umbrella organisations are forced to promote many issues at the same time to satisfy their diverse membership, and consequently, resources must be divided among many campaigns. Eventually, struggling to hold the coalition together becomes the leadership's primary task.

At a national conference on 'Women and the American Economy' in 1975, Betty Friedan called into question the feminists' strategy of going it alone. She argued that the American women's liberation movement she had helped found was only the beginning: 'the questions we face now cannot be solved by women alone'. Women now need to develop economic alliances with 'old people, young people, heart-attack-prone executives, trade unionists, Blacks and other minorities'.[17] Friedan was essentially arguing that the utility of the separatist strategy was exhausted, and that it was essential for the women's movement in America to develop more functional specialisation and align itself with other organisations and institutions.

Such a trend is beginning. For example, the late seventies saw the emergence of a coalition between feminist organisations and other interest groups (Planned Parenthood, the American Civil Liberties Union) to counteract groups pressuring Congress to limit Medicaid funds for abortions. More recently the Child Care Action Campaign, set up in 1983, has sought to align the feminist organisations with groups such as churchwomen, trade unionists and child development specialists in an effort to come to grips with the urgent problem of child care in America. However, it is too early to tell whether these coalitions will be effective in promoting their policy goals.

Despite these early signs that the American women's movement may at last be beginning to move towards co-operation in social policy areas, the historical momentum strongly emphasises equal rights via a separatist strategy which unites the sisterhood. This has been seen as the key to women's liberation in America. In Sweden, however, the principle of equal rights soon lost ground to other more concrete issues when the social feminists became a powerful force in the early years of this century.

Swedish social feminists believe that a preoccupation with equal rights is wrong-headed. Their own focus has been on developing support systems for women that allow them to be more effective as wives, mothers and workers. The view of these social feminists is that women deserve unequal treatment in the labour market. As Anna-Greta Leijon, the Swedish Minister of Labour, puts it, 'We think it compatible with equality that women should now be overcompensated in various ways.'[18] She is specifically referring to the elaborate benefits and services that the Swedish government has put in place to ease women's dual role at work and at home.

Another point of contrast between America and Sweden is that Swedish social feminists express little faith in the possibility of changing social conditions by altering individual consciousness, which was, as we have seen, a particular emphasis of the American movement during the early 1970s. One Swedish woman journalist told me, 'What good does it do an individual to raise her consciousness if she then cannot find a well-paid job because of the structure of opportunities in the labour market, or because of the lack of child-care services? Getting your head in the right place is not enough if material conditions interfere with your ability to reconcile work and family life.'[19] In the opinion of many Swedish feminists, the line of causality runs from the conditions of life to individual consciousness, not the other way around. That is to say, if material reality permits women to become effective wives and mothers *and* productive workers in the world beyond the home, then and only then can they develop their consciousness and fulfil their human potential.

Swedish social feminists believe that consciousness raising is not just ineffective, but is actually counterproductive. Because it shifts responsibility away from society and toward the individual, it tends to de-emphasise political action in favour of highly personal experiences. These self-help solutions to problems – even when they don't work – relieve the pressure on government to seek collective solutions to women's problems. Remember Joanna and Lila? Their consciousness-raising experience encouraged them to seek solutions to problems in their personal relationships rather than in a more public arena.

Swedish women point to a second negative effect of consciousness raising: it breeds divisiveness. An attempt by women's organisations to reconstruct their members' consciousnesses can be guaranteed to generate hostility from women who do not want to be reconstructed. In large measure American feminists have alienated traditional women because they have asked them to alter their values and their identities. Engineering a clash between a 'liberated' and a 'traditional' vision of the world can obstruct practical policy initiatives.

A final difference between feminism in the United States and in Sweden is the American movement's separatist strategy. In Sweden, by way of contrast, feminists have chosen to work through a women's section established in virtually every party, union, and professional, social and religious organisation in the country. The typical pattern has been for groups of feminists operating within these larger interest groups to press for better conditions for women workers, women lawyers, retired women, or women students rather than to unite and campaign for women as a class. This strategy has been enormously effective. For example, the women's section within the Social Democratic Party has persuaded this powerful political force to recognise the special needs of women. This commitment by the dominant political party to equality of economic result has led to the extensive parental leaves and the elaborate child-care facilities that we associate with modern Sweden.

Visitors to Sweden often remark that despite the high visibility of women's issues in the media and in public debate, it is hard to detect a women's liberation movement as such. This is because Swedish feminism is deliberately low-key. The strident tone of the American separatist movement has been avoided. Instead, Swedish social feminism has become embedded in virtually all of the country's social, political and economic organisations.

These distinguishing characteristics of Swedish feminism have their roots in the late nineteenth century, when two branches of women's political activity emerged. Equal rights activists became concerned with advancing women's legal rights, especially property rights, while a group of social reformers tried to improve the living conditions of working women.

The suffrage question was less important to nineteenth-century Swedish activists than it was to American feminists in this period. There seem to be two reasons for this. First was the early preoccupation of Swedish feminists with improving women's material circumstances. To many nineteenth-century Swedish feminists, winning the vote seemed a great deal less important than winning equal property rights and the ability to earn a subsistence wage in factories.

An equally important reason was that in Sweden the issue of the vote for women was subordinated to the issue of universal suffrage. Hence women's interests were bound up with those of larger organisations seeking general universal suffrage, such as the Social Democratic Party, formed in 1889 to represent the industrial working class, and the Liberal Party, established in 1902 to represent the lower middle classes and urban intellectuals. The battle for the vote was thus a battle that cut across the sexes and was led by the nation's two largest political parties. In the event, universal male suffrage was legislated in 1909 and women received the right to vote ten years later.[20]

Thus the struggle to enfranchise women in Sweden was carried out within the major parties, rather than being fought, as it was in the United States, outside the party system.[21] In Sweden, when universal adult suffrage became a leading political issue, the women's suffrage movement as such faded away. In this way feminism entered the arena of mass politics, and this early integration of women's activists and women's issues into the major parties helped overcome a separatist bias in the original women's movement.

As the twentieth century progressed, social feminists gained ascendancy over equal rights activists in the Swedish women's movement. Significantly they worked not only through political parties but also through the trade unions. For example, in 1960 the National Federation of Employers (SAF) agreed with the National Federation of Labour (LO) that women should receive equal pay for equal work, and that all low-paid work should be upgraded.[22] Since then this policy of solidarity, as it is called, has dominated the wage-setting process and has been largely responsible for the dramatic narrowing of the gap between male and female earnings in Sweden. The Liberal Party has argued that such collective bargaining agreements between management and workers do not have the legal force of a national law guaranteeing women's equal rights, but the Social Democrats see legal remedies as only appropriate for élite career women. They do not think that legal measures are effective for ordinary working women, whose interests are best served when they pool their strength in the collective bargaining process. The social feminists continue to place their faith in solidarity wage policies and in improving the already impressive array of Swedish family support policies described in Chapters Three and Four. In the spring of 1984 Anna-Greta Leijon told me that despite the extended economic recession in Sweden and severe budget constraints, 'This government intends to press ahead with the rapid expansion of child-care facilities. No issue is more important to our women workers.'[23]

'Of course I want equal opportunities but I don't like the petulance in this business of "women's issues",' said Conservative MP Anna McCurley in an interview in the *Guardian*, '. . . I find my shrieking sisters a bit of a pain in the neck. I do loathe the idea of being a second-class citizen and I'll do everything to ensure that it is overturned, that legislation is not maintaining the old traditional roles. That's what I'm here to do. But not to bare my bosom about abortion and sexual harassment. I find that very tedious and I don't mind saying that publicly.'[24] Here McCurley is displaying a scornful attitude towards American-style women's liberation, but her views on women's position in society seem quite close to that of many European social feminists.

Despite a long radical-intellectual tradition in women's thought stretching back to Mary Wollstonecraft's *Vindication of the Rights of Women* (1792) and before, and the strident militancy of the Suffragette Movement in the late nineteenth century, in Britain some of the most useful work towards improving the material condition of women's lives has been done by individuals and groups of women who would flinch at the term 'feminist'. These women chose to work within the current political and social framework and, like the Swedish social feminists, they concentrate on providing the support structures that women need to fulfil their dual role in the home and in the work place.

There are many women's organisations in Britain with a long and proud history of improving conditions of life for women, among them the Women's Institute (a Canadian idea, imported in 1915) and the Townswomen's Guilds.

However, one of the earliest and most influential of these groups was the Women's Cooperative Guild, founded in 1883 and still active today with some 25,000 members.[25] The original purpose of the guild was educational and social. Women were encouraged to form discussion circles and co-operative groups, but by the beginning of this century the guild had developed into a vigorous political organisation.

In 1911 the guild was instrumental in obtaining the first British maternity policy which gave working women a thirty-shilling maternity benefit and four weeks of paid leave after the birth of each child. The guild also fought for reform of the divorce laws and was the first women's organisation to pass a resolution in favour of legalised abortions (in 1934). Although the guild presidents were educated and middle class, the members themselves were working class. (The powerful working-class mother in D. H. Lawrence's book *Sons and Lovers* was a keen participant in guild activities, seeing it as one of the few avenues of upward mobility.) As one historian has put it, 'The Guild was reformist, but its achievements were of more practical value to working class women than the unrealised and more radical objectives of other [feminist] groups'.[26]

Another important organisation in this early period was the Women's Labour League, founded in 1906 and closely aligned to the newly formed Labour Party. Among other things members were meant to support Labour Party candidates in local and parliamentary elections, and 'watch the interests of working women in their own neighbourhood, and strive where possible to improve their social and industrial conditions'.[27] Some of the many issues on which the League campaigned during the early decades of the twentieth century were: the compulsory provision of school meals, medical inspection and treatment for schoolchildren, the establishment of baby clinics and the provision of free milk to expectant and nursing mothers.

The First World War and the discovery that a large percentage of army recruits had to be rejected on medical grounds triggered a concern with the physical development of children – who would become the next generation of conscripts? The Women's Cooperative Guild turned its energies towards this patriotic concern, publishing, in 1915, a book called *Maternity* which consisted of reports from Guild members describing their experience of pregnancy, childbirth and child-rearing with a preface by Herbert Samuel, President of the Local Government Board. As Samuel put it: 'Under existing conditions we waste, before birth and in infancy, a large part of our possible population . . . It is the duty of the community . . . to watch over the health of the infant . . . The infant cannot indeed be saved by the state. It can only be saved by the mother. But the mother can be helped and can be taught by the State.'

Reviewed by *The Times*, *Maternity* caused an uproar, followed by a flurry of official activity. Clinics were set up, midwives were trained, doctors were appointed to attend expectant mothers and children under five, and hospital beds were set aside for complicated deliveries and sick infants – measures largely based on the suggestions of the Guild. Half of the costs were to be met by central government, half by the local authorities, and Guild members were instrumental in ensuring that local authorities carried out their new tasks. Thirty years later all of these maternity and child-health schemes were incorporated into the National Health Service.

Both the Women's Cooperative Guild and the Women's Labour League, therefore, greatly influenced official thinking in the areas of health and child care. A 1908 government report pointing to the importance of a mother's care to the survival of her child shows how seriously the issue was taken and emphasises the responsibilities of government to both mothers and babies: 'The children of the State are the business of the State; if it neglects that business there is nothing that will atone.'[28]

In recent decades these women's pressure groups have remained strong and have continued to focus on the material conditions of life. However, in the late sixties these established groups were joined by the more radical feminists of the women's liberation movement. In Britain some of the radical feminists are linked to socialism through the international socialist movement and the Workers Revolutionary Party. Others in the radical camp derive their focus – on equal rights, on consciousness raising, on problems of sexuality – from new-wave American feminism.

New-wave feminism in Britain, unlike in America, has no national organised structure. Rather, there are a large number of local self-help centres, workshops, battered wives' shelters, rape crisis centres, consciousness-raising groups, alternative ante-natal classes and feminist publications. Some are run by professionals, many by volunteers. However, although many of the women running these have separatist tendencies, they are at least tackling the problems of women today at 'grassroots' level – rape crisis centres and battered wives' shelters undoubtedly serve a very useful purpose at the sharp end of British society.

Not only did modern British radical feminists inherit the separatist sentiments of the American movement, but it was also against their socialist principles to work with any organisations that smacked of the Establishment, so that, until recently, they have shunned contact with parliamentary political parties, trade unions, etc. However, in the last few years some of the radical feminists have begun to realise that they cannot achieve their objectives without help – albeit from organisations with whom they do not see fully eye-to-eye – and self-conscious, radical feminists have begun to appear in the Labour Party, in the trade unions and in local government. Perhaps, though, their greatest contribution to an improvement in women's daily lives has been in educating and politicising women and in raising personal issues such as wife-beating to political status. 'We feel that the women's movement has, at the very least, raised the consciousness, and encouraged the self-organisation of thousands of women,' says Sheila Rowbotham, the feminist historian. 'In so doing it has also begun to challenge relations of power. We had remained independent of any of the left groups because we didn't want them to tell us what to do.' And so, for the most part, these radical feminists remain non-aligned.

The British women's movement, unlike the American movement, has a very strong working-class as well as a middle-class intellectual tradition, stretching back to the matchgirls' strike in the 1890s. When feminism underwent its resurgence in Britain in the 1960s, again working-class women were at the forefront of the battle for change. As one historian put it, 'The voice of the new movement was first heard not from the intellectual radical community but from the working class.'[29]

In the early spring of 1968 a group of fishermen's wives in Hull, under the leadership of Liz Bilocca, set up a committee to improve safety conditions on the trawlers. Middle-class women joined the confrontation, and a women's liberation group was formed. In June of the same year women sewing machinists at the Ford Motor plant at Dagenham staged a three-week strike for equal pay, and in London bus conductresses demanding the right to become bus drivers went on strike. This outburst of industrial militancy among working women shook up the complacent trade union movement.[30] A union committee called the National Joint Action Committee for Women's Equal Rights was established to press for more energetic action. Shortly afterward an equal pay bill was piloted through the House of Commons. It was supported by the Trades Union Congress and the Labour Party and became law in 1970.

While American-style radical feminists have conditioned the debate in Britain – by writing books, by keeping women's issues in the limelight – more concrete changes have been brought about by the established women's groups working within the political structure. 'Organisations like the National Council of Labour Women, the Child Poverty Action Group, the National Council for Civil Liberties and the TUC Women's Congress between them [have taken up] most of the legal and egalitarian issues which in America required separate and more specifically feminist pressure groups.'[31] As was the case in Sweden, the most effective women support groups in Britain are embedded within the established centres of political power – specifically the parties and the unions – not in separatist feminist organisations. Women working for these organisations have a very clear idea of how they see the future. Judith Walpole, desk officer at Conservative Central Office, recoiled from the word 'feminist' when I spoke to her, but stated that as a career woman with a family she actually supported much of what the less radical feminists stood for. She illustrated her position with this anecdote: 'The previous week a male colleague rushed across the room to tell me that two of the three candidates for the chairmanship of X committee were women. He remarked that I didn't look very pleased, at which I replied, "I'll only be pleased when it is so taken for granted that you don't feel it's necessary to rush across the room and tell me." '[32]

One especially effective group among these women's organisations which runs across the entire social and political spectrum is the Women's Rights Unit of the National Council for Civil Liberties (NCCL), which was set up in 1973. It consists of a small group of women, some paid and full time, others part time and voluntary, who have access to the lawyers and research facilities of the council. The Women's Rights Unit has a large number of affiliates in the trade unions and in the Labour Party and has many local branches. Over recent years it has been concerned with equal pay for work of equal value and sex discrimination in the marketplace, particularly with regard to part-time and home workers (the majority of whom are women). Britain now provides more training courses aimed at encouraging women to enter male-dominated occupations than any other country.[33]

The National Labour Women's Advisory Committee, a division within the Labour Party, is another active women's group in Britain. The Labour Party has worked hard to attract women voters and likes to be seen as the women's party. In 1974, together with the TUC, it drafted the influential 'Charter for Women', which was eventually incorporated into the 1975 Sex Discrimination Act.[34] More recently, in the winter of 1983, feminist Labour MP Jo Richardson introduced the Sex Equality Bill to Parliament as a Private Members Bill, in which she proposed paternity leave as a right for all new fathers and sought to mandate proportionate equal pay for part-time workers and home workers.[35] Despite widespread support in all parties, the bill was narrowly defeated. However, the Labour Party expect to reintroduce it in a future Parliament.

Even Margaret Thatcher and the Conservative Party have been qualified supporters of women's rights. For example, Thatcher backed the Equal Pay Bill of 1970, and in 1980 her government expanded maternity leave benefits (*see* discussion in Chapter Three). Since her government came to power they have pushed voluntary child-care organisations and community self-help groups, and in particular have funded an association to provide training equipment, funding and support for childminders. A current major concern of the Conservative Party is getting more women into public service. As Thatcher puts it, 'We in the Conservative Party hope that many more women will realise their potential by volunteering for public life, including Parliament . . . This will go some way towards ensuring that the important contribution women can make to the health of our democracy is recognised.' However, this is all against a background of massive public-sector cutbacks which have reduced the support structures available to women and children. Whereas the Reagan government in America does not even acknowledge the difficult needs of women in today's society, Thatcher is at least prepared to accept that something should be done. In the current financial and social climate in Britain, however, the government appears extremely unwilling to put public funds behind public policies.

The Italian approach to women's issues is similar to that of Britain. There is a long tradition of women's support groups working within the trade unions, the political parties and the Church. For example, as early as 1902 women workers were guaranteed a leave of absence after childbirth and time off from the job to nurse their babies.[36] Legal rights have come much more slowly. Italian women only won the right to vote in 1945, and it was 1970 before divorce became legal.

Since the Second World War two of the most important women's support groups in Italy have been the Union of Italian Women (UDI), a semi-autonomous satellite of the Communist Party, and the Italian Women's Centre (CIF), which is linked to the Christian Democratic Party. These two political pressure groups have pursued a variety of reforms to improve the material basis of women's lives. The 1971 Law on the Rights of Working Mothers is a case in point. Under this law it became illegal to fire a woman during pregnancy or during the first year of her child's life; maternity leave was extended to five months with 80 per cent of the wage replaced; mothers were given the right to stay away from work when a child is ill up until the child is three years old; and mothers were given two years' credit toward a variety of seniority rights each time they gave birth.[37]

The UDI and CIF were also largely responsible for the passage of the 1971 legislation which created 3,000 public nursery schools and an extensive network of public day-care centres. But perhaps most important was their sponsorship of the 1975 Family Charter, also supported by the Church, which gave extensive economic rights to wives. This law provides for common ownership of all family property by husband and wife, and it recognises unpaid farmwork and housework as an economic contribution to family income for inheritance purposes and in the event of separation or divorce.[38] Perhaps one of the most progressive pieces of legislation concerning women ever passed in Italy came from within the Establishment – an Establishment that understands that constructive legislation is needed.

As in Britain, these pressure groups which have been so successful in furthering the cause of women are not self-consciously feminist. These groups fight for concrete rights or services for women; they are motivated by material needs and tend to be politically conservative. In Italy they are both conspicuous and active. Abby Laber, who lives and works in Ferrara, tells of the support services this northern Italian city (population 150,000) offers to working women: 'For starters there is the local branch of the UDI. This provides an extensive library; a feminist newspaper which is geared to women's concerns; a drug abuse programme, and a three-person legal aid office which offers help in all kinds of areas – divorce, wife abuse, adoption, abortion, you name it.' Abby paused for a moment, then added, 'The odd thing is, Ansalda Sirolli, who runs the branch, does not like to be called a feminist. She told me that she has a normal life and a family and that this precludes a militant attitude toward men or an experimental lifestyle. I guess in Italy most feminists are thought to be pretty radical.'

According to Abby, other valuable services for women are provided by the *consultori* (health clinics that provide free gynaecological, obstetrical and paediatric care to women and their children). But most important of all are the subsidised day-care centres and nursery schools. 'These have expanded very rapidly since the early 1970s,' says Abby, 'and they're great; they make all the difference to working women. A quarter of all the babies in Ferrara and half of all three- to five-year-olds are now in these schemes. They are very popular.'[39]

In Italy the term *femminista* is reserved for the post-1968 women's liberation movement, inspired by the political radicalism of the late sixties and new-wave American feminism. The MLD (Women's Liberation Movement) and the Lotta Femminista (Feminist Struggle) were vocal and active in the 1970s but are less so now. The MLD has been particularly concerned with issues of sexual and personal freedom – divorce, abortion, and non-sexist education. These radical feminists have sometimes worked against, or shown no interest in, legislation that promised to improve the material conditions of women's lives. As Daniela Colombo said in an interview, 'The feminist movement has been more interested in abortion and sexuality than in work and family issues.'[40]

Feminists failed to support the Family Charter because they didn't like the language of the legislation and because it was not central to their own, highly personal, agenda. Yet, according to one Italian professor I interviewed, 'The Family Charter has produced more security for more women than any other piece of legislation in recent Italian history.'[41] No wonder the women in the political parties and in the Church find it hard to identify with the radical feminists.

Let us leave the last word to Laura Conti, a 35-year-old physiotherapist, a divorcée with a ten-year-old son: 'I used to belong to a women's group – everyone did. But after a while I began to think that the needs and problems of all women are not the same. The group was feminist, the main issue was wages for housework (this was in 1975/6) and consciousness-raising. I felt more and more isolated as I participated. Mostly because they were so antagonistic to power structures and to men. I liked parts of it but I got alienated from much of it . . . The feminist movement made sense ten years ago but not so much now.'[42]

It seems clear that feminism in three very different European countries has produced an emphasis on material reality which has been largely missing in America. The social feminists in Sweden and the women's support groups in Britain and Italy have devoted their best energies to improving the material conditions of women's lives. Working within the established centres of power – political party, union and Church – these pressure groups have been effective in promoting the benefits and services women need if they are to reconcile their maternal and work responsibilities.

Western Europe has also experienced some American-style feminism. Equal rights enthusiasts have retained considerable influence in Sweden's Liberal Party, and a preoccupation with consciousness raising and sexual liberation runs through radical feminism in both Britain and Italy. But despite this, the core of European feminism is centred on a practical concern with the concrete conditions of women's lives. This social feminist tradition is almost totally absent in modern America. Nothing dramatises this more than the issue of maternity leave, which has always been a top priority for social feminists in Europe. Italy developed its first maternity policy in 1902, Britain in 1911, and Sweden in 1939. As we learned in Chapter Three, as of 1983, more than one hundred countries had mandatory maternity policies, which, on average, gave working women the right to five months' paid leave.

The United States presents a stark contrast. It is the only advanced industrial country that still does not have a national maternity policy. The maternity coverage that does exist is so patchy that 60 per cent of American working women have no rights to any kind of leave when they bear a child. And as we saw in Chapter Five, in a recent California case, feminists actually lined up against a woman who lost her job when she took a disability leave for childbirth. This is a striking example of how completely American feminism has failed to connect with the material side of life and with motherhood.

In late February 1984 Women in Crisis, Inc. held its fifth national conference, called 'Women and Power', in New York City. The guest speakers were Congresswomen Geraldine Ferraro and Claudine Schneider.

In their opening remarks both Ferraro and Schneider talked about the economic and political power of women, how much they had and where the gaps were. They then talked about what they were doing in Congress to help women. Ferraro was an active supporter of the Economic Equity Act, which was first floated in 1981. It's an important document, which, unfortunately, is not getting very far in Congress.

In her talk Ferraro concentrated on issues of pension equity, while Schneider focused on equal access to education for women. Eventually the discussion was opened to the floor. After almost thirty minutes of questions on pension equity, equal pay, comparable worth, and the enforcement of equal opportunity and anti-discrimination laws, I decided that there was a serious gap in the discussion. *No one* had mentioned what is perhaps the fundamental problem of working women's lives: the difficulties inherent in integrating work and family life. The closest the discussion had come to even touching on the subject was a brief discussion of dependant-care tax credits.

So I asked a question: 'How can American women achieve economic equality without family support structures such as maternity leave, child allowances, and public day care? Only forty per cent of working women in this country are entitled to any maternity leave; is there any action being taken in Congress to expand this right? Hundreds of thousands of American pre-schoolers spend their days in overcrowded third-rate day care; are there any plans to extend the scope of quality public child care?'

Neither Schneider nor Ferraro seemed anxious to respond. After a long pause Schneider volunteered that 'there are tax credits for dependant care, and we are working to raise the maximum credit level'. I thought to myself, big deal. If there is no child care available in your neighbourhood, tax credits are meaningless, or if you don't earn enough to pay substantial taxes, tax credits are again meaningless. But feeling that I had heard their answer to child care, I decided to push the Congresswomen on maternity benefits. So I ran down the long list of Western democracies that provided statutory maternity leave and emphasised how generous and how extensive this leave was. I then asked how the richest nation in the world could be the only country without these benefits for its working women. I waited for an answer, but an awkward silence hung over the dais. Finally Ferraro said rather plaintively, 'All I can say is that nothing is being done at the federal level about maternity leave.' She then signalled she was ready for the next question and briskly moved on. The next question from the floor was on abortion – both Congresswomen responded eagerly. They were very well informed about the debate and listed recent court rulings and legislative action with practised ease.

After the conference I caught Ferraro as she was trying to hurry out. I managed to give her some information about the panel on family policy at the Economic Policy Council. She nodded her thanks and was moving toward the door when she looked back, caught my eye, and said, 'Maternity leave? I learned something.'

7. Women's Liberation and Motherhood

Motherhood is not going out of style. The vast majority of Western women are mothers by the end of their childbearing years. In 1980 only 10 per cent of American women aged forty to forty-four were childless. Women are having fewer children, and they are having them later, but more women in the United States are having at least one child than ever before.[1]

The only exception to this trend are top professional women (who are such a tiny proportion of all women that they scarcely affect the average picture). Many of these women are single or divorced, and a large proportion remain childless. Surveys of women executives and high-level professionals in America show that more than half reach the age of forty without having children.[2] In fact, census figures show that 20 per cent of all highly educated American women (women with graduate training) remain childless.[3] But although top professional women often do not have children, for many it is not a preferred choice, and some are prepared to go to extraordinary lengths to have a child.

Jenny Windler* is forty-five years old. Until a year ago she was the executive vice-president of a clothing manufacturing firm in New York City. She was number three in the firm and, with bonuses, earned $75,000 a year. In 1983 she gave up her job in order to adopt a child.

Jenny explains her decision in the following way: 'I have wanted a child for as long as I can remember. I was married for several years in my thirties, but it was an unhappy, restless relationship, and Jon did not want children, so those prime childbearing years passed me by. I guess I just buried myself in work.

'We were divorced in 1978. By that time I was thirty-eight and desperate to have a baby. So I hatched this plan to have a child on my own. I decided to work hard for two more years and accumulate a nest egg so that I could take some time off to be with my child. I then intended to hit the adoption agencies. By then I would be over forty and too old to cope with pregnancy.'

Jenny sighed and said with feeling, 'It's a good thing I didn't know then how difficult it was going to be.' By 1980, when Jenny was ready to adopt her child, she was forty-one years old, much too old to be a prime candidate for adoption. Besides, she was single. On both accounts she was frowned upon by the adoption agencies; in fact, most would not even consider her as a prospective parent. Jenny bent over backwards: she was willing to take an Oriental child or a South American child, she was willing to take an older child, and she was willing to spend a lot of money. But two years of exhausting effort went by, and still Jenny failed to find a child. In desperation she got on a plane and went to northern India, where she had been told it might be possible to adopt a child from one of the refugee camps. The adoption struggle took four months and featured court battles and mountains of red tape, but Jenny just refused to budge until she could leave with her new three-year-old daughter.

I asked Jenny how she had dealt with her job during this difficult period. 'I coped with the Indian trip by taking a leave of absence from my work,' said Jenny, 'but when I got back, I realised that Toby needed all of me if she was going to cope with the massive adjustments required of her. So I resigned from my job, and right now we are living on my savings.' Jenny smiled, and added, 'It's a good thing I did give up my job. I couldn't possibly have fitted it in. I haven't even gone to the toilet by myself in a year. Adopting a three-year-old presents all kinds of special problems.' But Jenny didn't seem to mind any of these problems. She looked very content.[4]

Afton Blake is a single woman in her mid-thirties. She is a psychologist and lives in a quiet neighbourhood in a house crammed with books and art. In 1981 she decided to have a child by artificial insemination. 'It was time to have a child,' she says. 'I was secure emotionally and not in a steady relationship with a man.' She thought first of asking a friend to co-parent with her, but she feared that such a set-up could turn into an awkward triangle. That left insemination.

She shopped around the sperm banks of California and eventually ended up at the Repository for Germinal Choice. After studying the catalogue of donors – with a view to picking out traits, values, and characteristics that appealed to her – she chose Number 28. The catalogue described Number 28 as having 'good intellectual and musical ability, a charismatic personality, and very good looks'. As Afton sees it, 'He is the kind of man I might have married.'

When she started artificial insemination, Afton was lucky and conceived straight away, but two months later she miscarried. Several more months of insemination followed before she conceived again. A year ago Afton Blake gave birth to a healthy boy she named Doron.[5]

Doron joins the 500,000 other children conceived in the United States since 1960 by artificial insemination. It is estimated that 1.5 million more Americans will be created this way by the year 2000.[6] Two-thirds of the women undergoing artificial insemination are single.[7] They want children but have failed to find Mr Right.

The feminists of the modern American women's movement made one gigantic mistake: they assumed that modern women wanted nothing to do with children. As a result, they have consistently failed to incorporate the bearing and rearing of children into their vision of a liberated life. This 'mistake' has had serious repercussions.

In the nineteenth century feminists held motherhood in great esteem. As Elizabeth Cady Stanton said in an address to the National Woman Suffrage Association in 1885, 'Surely maternity is an added power and development of some of the most tender sentiments of the human heart and not a limitation.'[8] But these early activists did not feel the need to focus on motherhood as a feminist issue. They tended to take their maternal duties for granted, an attitude facilitated by the fact that they were privileged women in an era when in affluent households most domestic responsibilities were delegated to servants. They therefore devoted little energy to thinking through what support structures women might need if they were to become both mothers and workers.

In the modern period the situation has been much more extreme as many new-wave feminists have been openly hostile to both mothers and children. They have identified the family and the biological function of motherhood as the central institutions of male power serving to enslave women in the interests of men.[9] Radical feminists have even envisaged a Utopia where childbirth through science could be removed from the domain of women's bodies.[10] Rather than help women cope with their double burden – in the home and in the work place – modern American feminists have encouraged women to avoid both marriage and children.

All five women who organised the Seneca Falls Convention in 1848 – Elizabeth Cady Stanton, Lucretia Mott, Martha Coffin Wright, Mary Ann McClintock and Jane Master Hunt – were married, and all had children. Stanton later wrote of this group that they were 'neither sour old maids, childless women nor divorced wives, as the newspapers declared them to be'.[11] Even unmarried, childless Susan B. Anthony warmed to the idea of babies. In a September 1857 letter to Stanton she wrote that reproduction was 'the highest and holiest function of the physical organism . . . to be a *mother*, to be a *father*, is the best and highest wish of any human being'.[12] Anthony often found herself holding babies and stirring puddings to allow her friend and collaborator Elizabeth Cady Stanton time off from her large family to write speeches and tracts for the feminist cause.

With the possible exception of Stanton (who found that the bearing and rearing of seven children did get in the way of political activity), these early feminists did not regard motherhood as a burden. Given the contemporary approach to mothering – that children should be seen once a day for nursery tea – they did not feel weighed down by their maternal roles. Childbirth itself might have been dangerous, but once the children were born, there were lots of servants to look after them. As we shall see in Chapter Ten, until the 1940s it didn't occur to anyone that children needed the constant presence of their own mothers for several years from birth onwards. As Emily Davies put it in the 1870s, 'An educated woman of active, methodological habits, blessed with good servants, as good mistresses generally are, finds an hour a day amply sufficient for her domestic duties. Nothing is gained by spreading it over a longer time.'[13]

There was, however, one small group of feminists in this early period who did see housework and child care as a basic cause of women's inequality. These social feminists were most active at the turn of the century, when, under the leadership of Charlotte Perkins Gilman, they defined a 'grand domestic revolution' in women's domestic lives. They demanded wages for women's household work and proposed a transformation in the design of American homes. They developed housewives' co-operatives, kitchenless houses, day-care centres, public kitchens, and community dining clubs. Gilman's suggestions included purpose-built blocks of flats for professional women and their families:

If there should be built and opened in any of our large cities today a commodious and well-served apartment house for professional women with families, it would be filled at once. The apartments would be without kitchens; but there would be a kitchen belonging to the house from which meals could be served to the families in their rooms or in a common dining-room, as preferred. It would be a home where the cleaning was done by efficient workers, not hired separately by the families, but engaged by the manager of the establishment; and a roof-garden, day nursery and kindergarten, under well-trained professional nurses and teachers, would ensure proper care of the children.[14]

Gilman argued for the communal raising of babies, believing that a child 'would benefit and grow up less shy if he spent certain hours a day among other babies, thereby learning that he is one of many'. As for the mother, she 'will love her child as well, perhaps better, when she is not in hourly contact with it, when she goes from its life to her own life, and back from her own life to its life, with ever new delight and power'.[15]

Gilman's novel perspective was influenced by her personal history. She had gone through a divorce and brought up a daughter in difficult circumstances.

Because her life had been less comfortable than many other nineteenth-century feminists, she had a firm grip on the difficulties inherent in combining domestic responsibilities with a professional existence. Writing at the peak of the suffrage controversy at the turn of the century, Gilman staunchly maintained that the right to vote was of relatively little importance in improving women's economic position. A more important goal was to develop support services that would ease women's household and child-rearing duties. In her eyes the existence of such services was essential if women were to participate fully in the mainstream of society. In Gilman's eloquent words:

We have so arranged life that a man may have a home, a family, love, companionship, domesticity and fatherhood, yet remain an active citizen of age and country. We have so arranged life, on the other hand, that a woman must 'choose'; must either live alone, unloved, uncompanied, uncared for, homeless, childless, with her work in the world for sole consolation; or give up all world service for the joys of love, motherhood, and domestic service.[16]

But one should not exaggerate the impact of this splinter group. These early social feminists were small in number and hardly made a dent on the consciousness of the day. In the half century preceding 1920 about 5,000 women and men participated in these experiments designed to revolutionise domestic work. Contrast this with NAWSA, which for twenty years had 2 million members. Turn-of-the-century feminist activity was clearly centred on the fight for the vote.

However, despite their low profile, the social feminists did provide an alternative vision of women's liberation which had more in common with European social feminism than did the mainstream American movement with its emphasis on equal rights.

Most of these ideas were lost in the 1920s and 1930s as feminists, particularly the social feminists, came under direct political attack. The years following the First World War in America were marked by unemployment, strikes and social unrest. The political climate of the day was brittle and tense, and it was thought that women might use their newly acquired right to vote to trigger unwelcome social change. The War Department spearheaded the attack in 1919 and 1920 by devising an infamous spider web chart, which represented feminist activities and their organisations as part of a 'red web' aimed at destroying America through pacifism and socialism. All the moderate women's groups, including the Young Women's Christian Association and the League of Women Voters, were smeared in this campaign. But the social feminists were especially threatening and came in for the heaviest attacks. They were accused of advocating 'free lovism', 'unnatural motherhood', and 'futuristic baby raising'.[17]

As early as the 1920s policy makers were considering the strategy of offering male workers the chance to buy small suburban homes on long-term mortgages as a way of achieving greater social and economic harmony. This would both tame male discontent and ensure that women were not tempted to try out dangerous feminist ideas. As one publication of the era put it, 'A wide diffusion of home ownership has long been recognised as fostering stable and conservative habits . . . The man owns his home but in a sense his home owns him, checking his rash impulses.'[18] If male workers were to be defined as home-owners, women were to be the home managers and consumers of the new age. This new philosophy was in place by 1931, when President Herbert Hoover convened the National Conference on Home Building and Home Ownership, which was aimed at men 'of sound character and industrious habits'.[19]

Despite the ambitious plans of the new social conservatives, the Great Depression and another world war intervened, and they had to wait until the late 1940s before circumstances were receptive to their ideas. As I shall describe in Chapter Nine, after the Second World War the suburban flight began in earnest and American women became even more grounded in their individual, labour-intensive homes. When women began to rebel in the late sixties, they took for granted the three-bedroom house with a kitchenful of appliances. They knew nothing about the earlier generation of social feminists and their rigorous questioning of the single-family home as an appropriate framework for a liberated woman.

New-wave American feminists have failed to come to terms with motherhood more thoroughly than their nineteenth-century sisters. The women's liberation movement has not just decided to ignore children; many contemporary feminists have reviled both mothers and babies.

Some feminists rage at babies; others trivialise or denigrate them. Very few have attempted to integrate them into the fabric of a full and equal life. When Betty Friedan wrote *The Feminine Mystique* in 1963, she described the deep well of frustration faced by housewives as 'the problem that has no name'. One might say that motherhood is the problem that modern feminists cannot face.

My own experience at Barnard College illustrates this point very well. The college, in refusing to develop a maternity policy, exhibited a profound indifference to the whole issue of reconciling professional and maternal responsibilities – this despite Barnard's reputation as a bastion of women's rights. My colleagues, many of whom were active feminists, were hostile toward such a policy and accused me of trying to 'take a free ride'. At the time I felt bewildered and betrayed. It was somehow a lot more difficult to take this kind of treatment from Barnard College than from some stronghold of male privilege. After all, if my liberated female colleagues did not think I deserved any time off to deal with miscarriage or premature birth, maybe they were right and I was just being self-indulgent. I have since discovered that their reaction to my predicament was part of a larger trend. The modern women's movement has not just been anti-men; it has also been profoundly anti-children and anti-motherhood.

The book titles of the movement in its early, more radical phase are illustrative: Jill Johnston's *Lesbian Nation*, which declares that heterosexuality is the female form of treason; Germaine Greer's *The Female Eunuch*, which finds an explanation for impotence in being female; Kate Millett's *Sexual Politics*, in which the personal becomes the political and sex is redefined as a power struggle; Kathrin Perutz's *Marriage is Hell*, which argues that marriage is precisely that; and Ellen Peck's *The Baby Trap*, which reveals how and why babies are incompatible with liberation. The slogans of the day were extraordinary: marriage was hell, sex was political, coitus was killing, married women were prostitutes, babies were traps, intercourse was rape, love was slavery, families were prisons, and men were enemies.

The 1972 manifesto of SCUM (Society for Cutting Up Men) captures the extreme spirit of the day:

> . . . there remains to civic-minded, responsible, thrill-seeking females only to overthrow the government, eliminate the money system, institute complete automation, and destroy the male sex . . . It is now technically possible to reproduce without the aid of males (or, for that matter, females) and to produce only females. We must begin immediately to do so. The male is a biological accident: the Y (male) gene is an incomplete X (female) gene, that is, has an incomplete set of chromosomes. In other words, the male is an incomplete female, a walking abortion, aborted at the gene state.[20]

Many groups of radical feminists put out similar statements.

It is well known that the first targets of radical feminist rhetoric were men. According to the manifesto of one group, the Redstockings, '*All men* receive economic, sexual and psychological benefits from male supremacy. *All men* have oppressed women.'[21] Men were Enemy Number One, but family, marriage, and children also came under direct attack because they were the mechanisms through which women's second-class status was perpetuated through time. 'Freedom for women cannot be won without the abolition of marriage.'[22] However, since women as wives and mothers play a central role in all aspects of family life, they too became prime targets of the movement. To be a nurturing and empathetic mother and to be a loving and supportive wife – the overriding goals of women who grew to maturity in the 1950s – were seen as signs of weakness and inadequacy. These attributes and these roles were to be stamped out in the brave new world of liberated women. The problem of being a woman could not be taken care of by getting rid of oppression or even by destroying the oppressors; it was wrapped up in *being a feminine woman*.

In the late sixties and early seventies significant numbers of young feminists rejected the whole package – marriage, motherhood and children – as a bad life choice for any woman. To be liberated came to mean wiping out all special female characteristics, leaving behind an androgenous shell of abstract personhood. Stripped of their men and their children, these unfettered women could then join the mainstream and clone the male competitive model in the marketplace.

At least some of the new-wave feminists were fleeing from the ultradomestic world of the 1950s. Betty Friedan was typical. When she wrote *The Feminine Mystique*, she was struggling to free herself from fifteen years as a suburban housewife, years which featured three children and a failed marriage. Her own salvation was wrapped up in dismissing homemaking as comprising 'tasks for feeble-minded girls and eight year olds',[23] and it was to be twenty years before she could look motherhood in the eye again. In her 1982 book *The Second Stage*, written when she was enjoying the pleasures of grandmother-hood, she acknowledges the central role of children and family in women's lives. Then she was able to say that 'the failure of the women's movement was its blind spot about the family. It was our own extreme reaction against the wife–mother role.'[24]

Gloria Steinem is an example of another genre – the modern feminist leader who has chosen not to have children. This decision is undoubtedly coloured by her personal history. In her powerful and touching essay 'Ruth's Song', Steinem describes her mother, Ruth, as 'a spirited and adventurous young woman who struggled out of a working-class family and into college, who found work she loved'. But all this was before 'she gave up her career to help my father'.[25] Ruth's first bout of mental illness 'followed years of trying to take care of a baby [and] be the wife of a kind but financially irresponsible man'.[26] Ruth's daughter Gloria has obviously done her best to avoid such traps as marriage and babies, and this is reflected in her feminist perspective. In her 1983 book *Outrageous Acts and Everyday Rebellions* Steinem collects together twenty-seven essays. They represent the best of her writing and are impressively diverse, ranging from a piece on 'The International Crime of Genital Mutilation' to a poignant essay entitled 'In Praise of Women's Bodies'. Aside from the description of her mother's life, not one page is devoted to motherhood, family, or children.

Most of the women who were on the cutting edge of the women's movement in the late sixties and seventies were trying to obliterate those bright and smiling housewife-mothers of the 1950s with their 'unique femininity' and their devotion to the bearing and raising of children. They were not impressed by woman's 'God-given sensationally unique ability to wear skirts'.[27] In many instances the doll-like creatures of the fifties did not wear well. During the counter-cultural rebellion of the 1960s millions of them were tossed on the scrap heap by their husbands and became pathetic 'displaced homemakers'; others dealt with the 'empty nest syndrome' by the liberal use of Valium and alcohol.

If the lives of the fifties generation of women had been less artificial (or more viable), modern women might not have had to rebel so radically. In any event, contemporary feminists 'threw the baby out with the bathwater'. Twenty-five years of the feminine mystique and a birthrate rivalling that of India meant that anything which smacked of motherhood became anathema to the modern women's movement.

We are often told that those 'libbers' alienated ordinary women because of their extravagant rhetoric and behaviour. They burned their bras, called respectable men chauvinistic pigs, and ordinary people lost interest. I don't find this explanation very convincing. Every revolution requires its polemics since oppressors are usually deaf to reasoned whispers. Much more negative than the language of the movement has been the fact that, especially in America, it has alternately ignored, reviled and lashed out at the most widely shared experience of women (after sex), motherhood. In so doing the movement alienated its main constituency. The great majority of women have children at some point during their lives, and few of these women ever cease to love their sons and daughters. For the majority of mothers their children constitute the most passionate attachment of their lives. It is absurd to expect to build a coherent feminist movement, let alone a separatist feminist movement, when you exclude and denigrate the deepest emotion in women's lives. It is difficult to build a women's movement on an anti-men platform, but it could probably be done. The modern world is, after all, populated with divorcées, widows, gays and singles, many of whom bear grudges against the male sex. But it is impossible to build a mass women's movement on an anti-child, anti-mother platform.

Despite this logic, modern feminists have not been restrained in their treatment of women with children. The views of Juliet Mitchell are typical. In *Woman's Estate* she describes women with families as inclined to 'small-mindedness, petty jealousy, irrational emotionality and random violence, dependency, competitive selfishness and possessiveness, passivity, a lack of vision and conservatism'.[28] It is almost necessary to remind oneself that this is a portrait drawn not by a misogynist but by a feminist. Mitchell goes further: if women in families are despicable, the family itself is, 'by its very nature . . . there to prevent the future'.[29]

*

Shulamith Firestone developed what was perhaps the definitive feminist view on the subject with her theory of history based on sex itself. According to Firestone, the elimination of sexual classes requires the revolt of women and the seizure of control of *reproduction*, just as the elimination of economic classes requires the revolt of the proletariat and the seizure of the means of *production*. There must be, she says, elimination not only of privilege but also of class distinction and sexual distinction. She goes on to advocate artificial reproduction, or at least its option. This would eliminate reproduction by one sex for the benefit of the both. In her scheme of things the dependence of the child on the mother would be replaced by dependence on a small group of adults.

Thus Firestone produces a social framework in which 'the tyranny of the biological family would be broken'.[30] But her framework implies that women can be freed only by the elimination of motherhood. With the proposal of such a utopian and unrealistic solution the problem is effectively shelved. It becomes a way of not coming to terms with motherhood. Although few feminists are as extreme in their views as Firestone, this tendency to brush motherhood to one side runs through the modern movement.

It is easier to find feminist positions on abortion, rape, the female orgasm, the rights of lesbians and genital mutilation in the Third World than to find out what feminists in America think about motherhood. In a popular anthology of writing from the women's liberation movement, *Sisterhood is Powerful*, only one out of seventy-four essays has anything to do with motherhood.[31] One can read an essay on 'The Politics of Orgasm' or digest a poem called 'Song of the Fucked Duck', but it is difficult to find anything on childbearing or child raising, which are central issues of most women's lives.

It is important to note, however, that hostility towards children has not been limited to the radical wing of the feminist movement in America. Whereas in Europe it has only really been a small number of separatists who have come out strongly against motherhood and the family, in America even the mainstream of the movement has been at best indifferent and at worst antipathetic.

For the last fifteen years the national feminist organisations in America (such as NOW and WEAL) have given top priority to the ERA and abortion. Issues such as access to credit, equal educational opportunities, and getting women elected to political office have constituted a second tier of goals. Child care has been at the bottom of the scale of priorities, and as we saw in Chapters Five and Six, maternity leave hasn't even made it on to the feminist agenda.

The various platforms of the movement generally include child care, but treatment of this issue is always perfunctory. For example, at the 1977 International Women's Year conference in Houston, child care was hardly touched upon. The burning issues of the conference were the ERA, abortion, and sexual preference.[32] In the thirty-page 'National Plan of Action' that resulted from this conference, child care occupied half a page.[33] At other meetings child care has been mixed up with issues of reproductive freedom and control over one's body. For example, the Congress to Unite Women called for the 'elimination of all laws and practices that compel women to bear children against their will'. This congress also strongly advocated 'research in extrauterine gestation'.[34] Mainstream feminists have generally treated motherhood as something most women want to avoid.

In an interview, child-care expert Dana Friedman talked to me about the six years she spent in Washington, D.C., lobbying, trying to get various pieces of child-care legislation through Congress. As Dana puts it, 'The feminist groups never took the lead on child-care issues. It's not that in the end they didn't sign off on child-care initiatives, but they never put any real effort into this area.' Dana paused and then said reflectively, 'It's as though they wanted to look good – they didn't want to be accused of not supporting government funding for child care. But they viewed child care as an issue that was too connected to motherhood – too related to the role they were trying to downplay. At the Houston conference, child care was number fourteen on a list of goals that had fifteen items on it. I think that's a pretty accurate reflection of the importance of child care to feminists – it is priority number fourteen.'[35]

Friedan in *The Second Stage* describes how many feminists thought that the 1970 White House Conference on Families was not worth attending. She also talks about the cold silence that greeted her appeal in the autumn of 1979 for the women's movement to come to grips with the practical problems of the family.[36]

The issue of women's control over their bodies has enabled some feminists to address and yet to avoid the issue of motherhood. Natural childbirth is a good example of this sleight of hand. In the 1970s it became a rallying point for feminists wanting to seem helpful on the childbirth front but all the while retaining an almost exclusive concern with the female experience. Childbirth became an occasion to glory in one's body and experience self-fulfilment, rather than a time of bringing a child into the world and becoming a mother.

The declared goal of one of the first 'birth centres' set up in California in 1971 was to form 'a sisterhood concerned with birth and its process . . . We are finding out about the natural capabilities of women . . . and have taken our birthright, freedom, and decided for ourselves what our rituals of birth will be.'[37] The enthusiasts in the natural childbirth movement are convinced that 'doctors are always enemies of women' and 'this is especially true of most obstetricians who elect to play the role of the Father and God to their patients, forcing women into the role of helpless, stupid, ridiculous little girls'.[38]

Thus childbirth (like rape and abortion) is reduced to yet another struggle for control over a woman's body or (like sex) is treated as though its only function were to give women a valuable experience. Some of the insights of the natural childbirth movement are valid. Hospital births probably did become too clinical in the middle decades of this century, and women were not consulted enough in the process of labour and birth, but the movement has produced burdens of its own. As I myself found out when I had children, all this emphasis on performing to prove one's womanhood, all this talk about the great 'birth experience' can set a woman up for failure, and it almost always obscures rather than facilitates coming to terms with the central issues of parenthood.

Helen* was thirty-one years old when she became pregnant with her first child in 1977, and she and her husband became tremendously involved in giving birth naturally. As Helen put it, 'We were so idealistic. Like many of our friends, we believed in women's liberation and felt committed to this movement that was going to allow us to gain control over our bodies and truly experience this great moment in life. The idea seemed so good, so warm, so attractive to give birth naturally, together as a couple.'

Helen and Jim went to Lamaze classes, learned that childbirth would not hurt, did their breathing exercises, and chose an obstetrician who could offer a Leboyer delivery. This was the last word in naturalness. It meant that delivery would take place in a quiet, darkened room; that a birthing chair would be used; that the umbilical cord would not be severed immediately; that the newborn baby would be placed on the belly of the mother and allowed to nurse; and that one of the immediate post-delivery experiences of the baby would be to float in a warm tub of water. Helen and Jim were very proud to have found one of the few obstetricians and one of the few hospitals in America that could offer a Leboyer delivery.

Despite all the joyous preparation and despite all the careful plans, the actual delivery of Helen and Jim's daughter was a traumatic experience.

Helen had an incredibly painful and extremely long labour – thirty hours. Acting on her instructions, the obstetrician administered no drugs and tried desperately to avoid a caesarean section. After twenty-nine hours of labour the baby went into acute distress, and the delivery scene took on the frantic quality of a real medical emergency. The fetal heart became erratic and actually stopped for a while. The obstetrician used forceps, surgical incisions, anything, to get the baby out. And when Laura was born she looked blue, battered and lifeless. The parents were not even told whether their child was a boy or a girl. The baby was snatched away by the medical team and immediately taken to another floor, where the infant intensive care unit was housed. Helen says she will always remember the appalling emotions that swept over her in the immediate post-delivery period: 'I felt that I had been butchered, I felt an overwhelming sense of bitterness and betrayal in being cheated out of the greatest experience of my life, and I felt a sense of utter failure.' Oddly enough, in this immediate post-partum period, Helen says quite frankly that she barely thought about Laura. So thoroughly had she absorbed the messages of the natural childbirth movement that the shattering of her own experience of birth was uppermost in her mind.

Worry about Laura came later when it was discovered that the baby had a heart problem and, at six months old, had to undergo corrective surgery. The medical experts told Helen and Jim that the heart problem was congenital, that it had nothing to do with the difficult birth. But Helen does not altogether accept this. 'Laura had to work so terribly hard to get born, and it was quite clear that this did produce tremendous strain on her heart.' She goes on to say regretfully, 'If only I had not been so ideological, so committed to avoiding a caesarean, we all might have avoided the dreadful anxiety of those early months of Laura's life.'

Helen's retrospective judgement of natural childbirth is tense and to the point: 'I now think that it can get in the way of good medical practice. If I were to have another child, I would be more realistic in my expectations and I would not martyr myself for the sake of any cause, however fashionable.'[39]

Helen and Jim were left with a sense of bitterness, their 'birth experience' had been 'spoiled' by pain, trauma and a sense of failure. But in a larger sense they were fortunate: their baby is now a loving child who is developing well – and giving birth to a healthy baby has to be the ultimate point of pregnancy and childbirth.

Even in the modern world, anguish and tragedy can surround the birth process. When I lost my twins in the sixth month of pregnancy, and when I faced the physical and emotional problems of prematurity, I thought that I had been singled out for pain. I felt that I should remind God that this was the latter part of the twentieth century and women were supposed to jog through pregnancy and give birth to their children with joy and ease. I thought that it was only in nineteenth-century novels that women suffered when giving birth to a child. But the miracles of conception and birth can still be fraught for women.

It is true that modern women don't die when giving birth to a child, and babies generally survive the ordeal of being born. (Interestingly, the infant mortality rate is considerably higher in the United States than in Europe.) But real problems of infertility, miscarriage and of birth itself continue to haunt women.

One ironic fact of modern life is that infertility rates are sharply on the rise. The last twenty years have seen a dramatic increase in sexually transmitted disease and an increase in the use of IUDs as a birth-control method. Both factors have served to boost the incidence of pelvic inflammatory disease in women, which in its turn has pushed up the infertility rate.[40] A not-so-welcome byproduct of the sexual revolution!

According to Dr Alan Berkeley, an obstetrician who specialises in high-risk cases at New York Hospital, 'fifteen per cent of [American] couples face some serious problem of infertility, and the risks increase significantly with age. The infertility rate for women starts climbing at age thirty, and a forty-year-old woman has a forty per cent chance of being infertile.' Modern medicine can bring the final infertility rate down to 5 per cent, but this is after months of unpleasant tests, procedures and surgery. In Berkeley's experience most couples don't give up until they have been having treatment for two to three years.

Miscarriage is also a continuing problem. Today 15 to 20 per cent of pregnancies end in miscarriage, an event which many women find difficult to take in their stride. As Dr Berkeley put it, 'Miscarriage can be profoundly disturbing, especially for a career woman in her thirties who has waited years for the right time to start a family. After losing a pregnancy, many of these women want a child so badly that they are willing to reorganise their lives. Some of them are even willing to throw in their job and go to bed for nine months if this will enable them to carry a child to term.'[41] His words brought back to me the desperation I felt when I lost the twins. For me, too, the need to replace those babies temporarily obliterated other aspects of life.

Finally, birth itself is not without its complications. Thirty per cent of deliveries in America are by caesarean section, and although some might be 'discretionary', the majority are performed for the safety of either the mother or the baby. For those women who have 'normal' vaginal deliveries, many will lose control in labour and experience intense pain. In short, they will fail to live up to the natural childbirth ideal. In Chapter One I pointed out that only three out of the thirteen women in my Lamaze class experienced childbirth as the easy, joyous event they had been taught it should be.

Thus, for the millions of women who are struggling with the anguish of infertility or miscarriage, or for those who merely 'fail' to give birth naturally, the emphasis of the women's movement on the 'great experience' of birth can seem like a cruel joke. What modern working women need when they finally get around to being able to have children is concrete support in the problems they face, not another lesson in consciousness raising.

*

128

Hostility toward mothers and children permeates the American women's movement. The full-time care of a baby is likened to 'spending all day, every day, in the exclusive company of an incontinent mental defective',[42] while pregnancy is described as 'the temporary deformation of the body of the individual for the sake of the species'.[43] Even Betty Friedan, a moderate in the movement, accused her generation of feminine fifties women of having a 'sick, sad love affair with their own children'.[44]

All this prompted a swift and fierce reaction not only from men (who were clearly labelled as Enemy Number One) but from women. Women might wish to be free, but not of their families. If accepting sisterhood meant abandoning husbands, children, home and love, then they would do without sisters. The American women's movement made a fatal error in ignoring the importance of the family and the home in the lives of the majority of women. To denigrate looking after the home and family as a worthwhile occupation is to belittle the lot of millions of women. By trying to attach to it a market value, feminists cheapened rather than enhanced the value many women believed it had. Marriage may produce new forms of bondage, but it also produces new forms of freedom, while the vaunted independence of the liberated and divorced often turns out to mean loneliness and penury. Children are demanding, but often bring joy and fulfilment and extend rather than narrow the boundaries of a woman's life. And employment, although it can bestow status in the marketplace, is for most women drudgery that limits rather than extends their opportunities. The women's movement forgets this at its peril.

8. *The ERA: A Test Case*

To European feminists the American women's movement's obsession with the Equal Rights Amendment is extremely difficult to understand, especially when many more pressing issues like maternity benefits and child-care support seem to have been given such a low priority. From the outside, indeed, the fact that, despite constant lobbying and hundreds of demonstrations, the supporters of the ERA have been unable to get it ratified appears even more extraordinary. How could some of the most highly educated and brightest women living and working in the country that has come to symbolise the free world possibly fail with such a simple demand?

During the 1970s and early 1980s I gave my support to the ERA, I contributed money, I signed petitions, I did a little canvassing. I too could not understand how or why it stirred up such intense controversy, and I couldn't begin to explain why it was repeatedly defeated, especially since the opinion polls told me that it had the support of the majority of the American people. Little did I think that by the time I had finished the research for this book I would have considerable sympathy for the anti-ERA campaign. Indeed, I could no longer be counted on to vote for the amendment. One unhappy supporter of the ERA hit the nail on the head when she said plaintively, 'The ERA seemed to be more popular the less people knew about it . . . the longer the fight dragged on the more doubts and fears surfaced about the nature of the amendment.'[1] That is exactly what happened to me. The more I understood about this piece of legislation, the less I supported it.

So, what is the Equal Rights Amendment? The exact wording has varied over the years, but the 1971 version read simply as follows: '1. Equality of rights under the law shall not be denied or abridged by the United States or by any State on account of sex. 2. The Congress shall have the power to enforce, by appropriate legislation, the provision of this article. 3. This amendment shall take effect two years after the date of ratification.' The advocates of the ERA want it instituted into the American Constitution; its opponents do not. An equal rights amendment has been introduced in every Congress since 1923 and has been given serious consideration on at least four occasions: 1946, 1950, 1953 and 1971.

At the time of the 1971 amendment the central issue in American domestic politics was civil rights. Indeed, some civil rights legislation had recently passed through Congress. So no one was surprised when, in October 1971, the US House of Representatives passed the ERA by 354 votes to 23, or when in March 1972 the Senate approved it by 84 votes to 8. Indeed ERA opponents were hard to come by.

In order for the ERA to become incorporated into the American Constitution, it has to be passed to the individual states for ratification within a time limit of seven years. They fell over themselves to approve it. Hawaii passed it with no opposition within hours of the Senate's approval, followed quickly by Nebraska. Delaware was in such a hurry to pass it that they voted for ERA an hour and forty minutes before the US Senate, which later led to a court challenge as to the validity of their ratification. Within three months twenty states had ratified the ERA, and within a year thirty states had signed on. At this point only eight more states were needed to produce the two-thirds majority which, under American law, would make the ERA part of the Constitution, and its supporters had until 1979 to pick up these additional endorsements.

In March 1973 – with six years to spare before ERA's time limit expired – leaders of the feminist organisations predicted that within two months they would have the eight additional states. They failed to anticipate one factor: Phyllis Schlafly and her orchestration of a grassroots STOP ERA movement.

Schlafly was a right-wing political activist who had become nationally known for her successful promotion of Barry Goldwater as the Republican party nominee in 1964. In early 1972 she decided to fight the ERA. As a traditionalist, she found the amendment immensely threatening to family life and to the established division of labour between men and women. And as a conservative, she found it dangerous. A firm believer in minimal government, Schlafly considered the second section of the ERA, which gives enforcement power to the US Congress, as bad as the first, which decrees a strict equality of rights under the law. According to Schlafly – and to many legal experts in the field – the first section would require states to make extensive changes in the laws in such areas as marriage, divorce, child custody and adoption, while the second section would give Washington the power to rewrite state laws if they did not measure up.

131

When the ERA was introduced into Congress in 1970, its sponsors omitted one modification, which had been part of the pending amendment for twenty years. This rider, introduced by Senator Carl Hayden, stated: 'The provisions of this article shall not be construed to impair any rights, benefits or exemptions conferred by law upon persons of the female sex',[2] in acknowledgement of the fact that women, in order to be equal, needed more and different rights than men possessed. In 1970, when the ERA was on the floor of the Senate, Senator Sam J. Ervin reintroduced these qualifications by proposing nine amendments that specifically retained preferential laws for wives, mothers, and widows and exempted women from the draft and from combat duty. But Senator Ervin's qualifications were unacceptable to the House of Representatives, and the version that eventually passed Congress in 1971 contained no exceptions.

Schlafly was particularly concerned by the fact that the version of the ERA sent to the states for ratification required absolute equality. She even went so far as to say that she would have supported the ERA had Congress left in the Hayden modification or the Ervin amendments. The omission of these riders meant that once the ERA was passed, the states would have to treat men and women in precisely the same way, so that, for instance, laws requiring a husband to support a wife would become unconstitutional. In her book *The Power of the Positive Woman* Schlafly wrote passionately about the network of laws that gives a wife 'her legal right be a full time wife and mother in her own home, taking care of her own babies'.[3] She cited an Ohio law which states that 'the husband must support himself, his wife, and his minor children out of his property or by his labor', and stressed that all these laws would be wiped out by the ERA.

Thus, Schlafly promoted the view that the ERA would weaken the family and make women more vulnerable. Most at risk were middle-aged housewives who had no independent source of income. These women had married in the fifties, when it was taken for granted that the wife would raise the children and look after the home while the husband would earn the family income. It was from this group of women that Schlafly drew most of her support.

An important implication of the ERA to Schlafly was that if it were ratified, the federal law that exempted women from the draft and excluded them from military combat would become unconstitutional. Most experts agreed with her on this issue. According to the House Judiciary Committee, under the ERA 'not only would women, including mothers, be subject to the draft, but the military would be compelled to place them in combat units alongside of men'.[4] To Schlafly this both flew in the face of the natural differences between the sexes and weakened national defence. She used as ammunition in her argument Pentagon studies which demonstrate that women have, on average, 60 per cent of the physical strength of men.

Schlafly stressed other effects of the ERA. She claimed that women's colleges receiving federal aid (and most of them do) would not be able to continue admitting women only because by so doing they discriminated 'on account of sex'. She also pointed out that protective labour laws for blue-collar women – such as those exempting women from compulsory overtime, allowing women extra rest periods and better rest rooms – would also become unconstitutional. This hit a raw nerve among working-class women, as many pro-ERA campaigners were to find out. My experience was typical:

In 1979 the American Economic Association (AEA) staged its annual meeting in Atlanta, Georgia. Many of us liberal economists were unhappy with the venue. Georgia was a state that still had not ratified the ERA and we were mortified that the AEA was giving its convention business to such a backward state.

To 'make up' for such poor judgement on the part of our professional organisation, many of us allocated part of our time in Atlanta to canvassing for the ERA. I went with two colleagues to take on the shift workers at a small textile plant on the outskirts of the city. Early one Friday morning a cab dropped us off in front of the factory. It was a raw December day with freezing drizzle spitting out of an overcast sky. We huddled together, our fashionable winter coats and high-heeled boots seeming both inadequate and incongruous in this bleak landscape.

At last a siren wailed and a few minutes later workers from the night shift came straggling through the factory gates in twos and threes. I stepped briskly forward holding out my leaflets and reciting my set piece: 'Please read about the ERA; it will improve conditions of life for all American women.'

The first group of women eyed me suspiciously, then pushed past – roughly. I retreated surprised and intimidated. I was shocked by the appearance of these women: the bulky starch-fed bodies, the careworn faces and bloodshot, exhausted eyes reminded me of the adults who peopled my childhood in South Wales. The minds of these women were clearly on things other than the ERA.

'Can you take little Chrissy today? Ma is laid up; it's her back again, and I've gotta take her in to the clinic,' said one to another as she struggled into her plastic raincoat. Her friend sighed. 'I guess I can, but drop her off with some milk and food; my old man's drinking again and we don't have much stuff . . .' Her voice trailed off. These women might have finished work at the factory, but they were about to start another job – dealing with the demands of needy families.

Eventually I engaged the attention of a black woman. Younger than most of the other workers, she accepted some pro-ERA literature and then looked at me antagonistically.

'You know, I've heard of you "libbers" and your ERA. I've seen that Schlafly person on TV and she says that equal rights for women is a bad deal because we would lose a whole lot. Like us girls get an extra break in the shift, and management can't force us to work overtime the way they force the men.'

As she warmed to her theme, her voice rose. 'You should try working in this lousy factory week in and week out and I bet you would want all the benefits you could get.'

I attempted a comeback. 'You know the ERA wouldn't necessarily take job protections away from women; the ones that mean anything would be extended to men. If women need special benefits, so do men.'

This factory worker was now really angry. 'If you think life's fair, you're crazy,' she snapped. 'I've got two kids under five and a husband who doesn't lift a finger. What's fair about that? Why shouldn't I get some breaks on the job?' She flung my pamphlets into the gutter and stalked off to the bus stop to wait in the freezing rain for her bus home.

I felt cowed and uncomfortable. It was the last time I canvassed for the ERA.

Schlafly also won support by describing what the ERA *would not do*. She pointed out that it applies only to government action and has no bearing on the decisions of private employers. Paul A. Freund of the Harvard Law School concurs: 'Unless equality is denied by a public agency or because of a law the Equal Rights Amendment by its terms has no applications. If we want to see more women in law firms, in the medical profession, in the Cabinet – and I, for one, do – we must turn elsewhere than to the proposed amendment.'[5]

Schlafly concluded that 'the ERA will add no new employment rights whatsoever, ERA will not add any new rights to those spelled out in the Equal Employment Opportunity (EEO) Act of 1972 which prohibits all sex discrimination in hiring, pay and promotion'.[6] Most experts in the field agree with her that the legislation already on the books gives American women as much employment protection as the ERA. And so, Phyllis Schlafly, making sure along the way that she had support from some legal heavyweights, dubbed the ERA the 'Men's Liberation Amendment', arguing that it would take significant old rights from women and give them to men without giving women any substantial new rights.

In the autumn of 1972 Phyllis Schlafly founded STOP ERA, installing herself as national chairman. Over the course of the next decade she was to turn the tide single-handedly against the ratification of the ERA. How she did this is an amazing story.

Part of it was that Schlafly proved to be an inspired campaigner and strategist with a flair for public relations. When Schlafly called a rally, women came – in the thousands. Her 'troops' – decorous ladies in pink, frilly dresses carrying fresh baked bread and other goodies – seemed to come out of the woodwork whenever the ERA was being debated or voted on. Often these rallies were spiced up by media events. When Ruth Clusen, president of the League of Women Voters, made a speech in Springfield, Illinois, announcing that the league would give $150,000 to support the Illinois ratification fight, the Reverend John Peck began prancing around the stage in a gorilla suit before presenting to Schlafly a sign which read 'Don't Monkey Around with the Constitution'. This was followed by Schlafly's announcing that *Playboy* had just contributed $5,000 to the pro-ERA cause. She then led her troops in a rendering of her composition 'Here Comes *Playboy* Cottontail'.[7]

But organisation and flair were not going to win the fight on their own. Phyllis Schlafly was facing stiff opposition. The entire Establishment from Jimmy Carter to Ted Kennedy to Betty Ford to Jane Fonda seemed to be prepared to use their influence and clout lobbying for the ERA.

During his presidency Carter put the enormous prestige of his office behind the ERA. As Bella Abzug points out, Carter wanted to be known as the president who had achieved equal rights for women.[8] In December 1976, just after his election, he personally telephoned wavering Illinois legislators to try to tip the balance in that state – to no avail. Carter used presidential clout in North Carolina, persuading Congressman Lamar Gudger to cast a key vote for the ERA in exchange for $1.6 million in federal funds for the Asheville Airport. Gudger got his airport, but Schlafly organised her troops in a 'prayer chain', and the ERA went down to another defeat in this state.[9]

In October 1979 Carter held an ERA Summit at the White House for hundreds of ERA leaders and officials from unratified states. The following month, November 1979, thirty-six women's magazines ranging from *Ms.* to *Vogue* ran articles discussing how the ERA would benefit women. The combined circulation of these magazines was 60 million.

This new level of Establishment support for the ERA was put to the test in Illinois in 1980. Eleanor Smeal, president of NOW, called the Illinois campaign 'the most extensive in the ERA's history'.[10] She organised a huge pro-ERA rally, roped in a whole host of film and TV stars and galvanised the politicians. Jimmy Carter invited members of the Illinois legislation to the White House and promised 'to do anything that would be helpful', and Mayor Jane Byrne and Governor James Thompson campaigned vigorously for ratification (Thompson is said to have offered jobs, roads, and bridges in exchange for votes).[11] It was a messy campaign. The ERA backers were accused of exerting unwarranted pressure, and at least one of these charges was substantiated.[12] However, despite all this pressure, that winter Illinois failed to ratify the ERA for the ninth time.

In retrospect it seems clear that as soon as Schlafly started to fight against the ERA, public support for this legislation began to ebb away. In 1974 only three states ratified. In 1975 only one state ratified and sixteen rejected it. In 1977 one more state passed the ERA, but nine states defeated it, and so on until 1979, when the ERA made American constitutional history by becoming the first amendment ever to reach its seven-year limit still unratified. Congress then took the unprecedented step of extending the time for ratification from the original seven to ten years, but this extension also expired without ratification. Particularly undermining for those who supported the ERA was that five of the ratified states had second thoughts and voted to rescind their initial pro-ERA votes. An inevitable debate ensued as to the legality of their action.

Some ERA supporters explained the success of the STOP ERA campaign by pointing to a right-wing conspiracy of anti-abortionists and born-again Christians. STOP ERA was even accused of having important links to the Ku Klux Klan and the National States Rights or Nazi Party.[13] Other ERA supporters were content to blame men, and feminists were inclined to see Phyllis Schlafly as a mere tool of conservative men: 'if it weren't Phyllis it would be some other Barbie Doll of the right'.[14]

Undoubtedly the religious and the political right swung behind Schlafly's position on the ERA. From an early point in the battle she had put together a powerful but unlikely coalition of Catholics, fundamentalists, and Orthodox Jews, all of whom feared federal interference in how they conducted their churches. But mainstream political support did not come until late in the game: until 1980 even the Republican Party supported the ERA. Nor has anyone been able to establish that Schlafly received major financial contributions from any of the obvious right-wing sources. Most ERA supporters concede that 'opponents of the ERA spend far less money than proponents'.[15]

The STOP ERA movement was successful not because it was better financed or more powerfully backed than the pro-ERA forces – the opposite seems to have been true – but because ordinary Americans believed that there was real substance behind the Schlafly campaign. Millions of wives and mothers wanted desperately to preserve what was left of the legal props that supported family life. They heard Schlafly loudly and clearly when she told them, 'Women's liberation has gone too far. Instead of giving freedom it has relieved men of their responsibilities as head of the family.'[16] They were terrified of any further erosion of their rights and privileges as wives and mothers and they had a hunch that the old-fashioned laws were more favourable to women than the no-fault-divorce and equitable-distribution laws which had seriously undermined a wife's right to alimony in so many states (*see* discussion in Chapter Two). Many women did not want to be treated equally;

they yearned for the guarantees and protections of the past. Schlafly's appeal was to those 'thousands of frightened women who fear ERA will destroy the American family, legalise rape, send mothers into combat ... and force contented housewives into jobs they don't want'.[17]

When you add in the legitimate fears of blue-collar women that they would lose their hard-won protective benefits, you have a powerful constituency ranged against the ERA. There was no need to explain away the STOP ERA campaign as yet another exercise in male oppression. Rational women – housewives and workers – had some sensible reasons that prompted them to oppose ratification of the ERA. Schlafly did tap specifically right-wing energies: states' rights and women in combat weakening national defence were both issues which appealed to conservatives. Schlafly also tapped some free-floating right-wing paranoia with her talk about 'perverts' (i.e. homosexuals) gaining the right to adopt children. But she would not have succeeded had she not spoken for many ordinary Americans – apolitical workers who feared the loss of protection, and those millions of mothers (and fathers) who found their deepest satisfaction in family life and were afraid that it would be undermined even further by the ERA.

In many ways Schlafly's position on these matters was inadequate. She saw the threat posed by the ERA and wanted to derail this piece of legislation, but she failed to complement this with constructive proposals herself. After all, women at home were already immensely vulnerable. The 1960s had wrought sweeping changes in American sexual morality and family life. By the late 1970s family life was crumbling, the divorce rate had risen to one in two of all marriages, and alimony and child support provided a woefully inadequate safety net. In short, the network of laws giving a wife a legal right to be a full-time wife and mother that Schlafly vowed to save were, to say the least, inadequate. As Lisa Wohl correctly points out in her 1974 *Ms.* article, 'Too often women wake up to find that this right gives them as much effective protection as the emperor's new clothes.'[18]

As for women workers, they too were inadequately protected. In the mid-1980s, 40 per cent have no health coverage and 60 per cent have no right to maternity leave.

Ratification might have accelerated the disintegration of traditional family security and wiped out what remained of protective legislation for women workers, but clearly the ERA could not be held responsible for the precarious nature of women's lives. Rejection of the ERA could not reverse larger social trends and magically re-create 'the classical family of Western nostalgia' which had reigned supreme in the 1950s.[19]

In short, if Schlafly wanted to make American women secure in their roles as wives and mothers, she needed to do more than stop the ERA (or ban abortion, for that matter). Modern American women, traditional or otherwise, need a new set of rights and benefits: tougher divorce laws, child allowances, maternity leave, independent health coverage, and adequate retirement benefits. They also need better jobs and higher pay, and it is in this area that Schlafly's nostalgic vision has been particularly damaging to American women. For she has failed to grasp the fact that the majority of wives and mothers in the United States now work – most of them because they have to. Schlafly has not helped these women in their struggle to earn a decent wage in the job market. In fact, by coming out against the equal pay or comparable worth concept, she has pitted her considerable forces against them. But, however incomplete and flawed Schlafly's position, she undoubtedly has the support of Middle America.

The liberal Establishment of America never appreciated the substantive base of the STOP ERA movement. It became chic to dismiss Schlafly's troops as dim-witted Barbie dolls who were being manipulated by sinister forces on the lunatic right. They were rarely credited with any point of view, let alone a sensible point of view. Yet Schlafly won in state after state over the course of a decade. Had the ERA backers better understood the concerns of Schlafly's grassroots supporters, they might have addressed the fears of Middle America and offered a constructive agenda of their own, thus avoiding the colossal waste of time, energy and resources that the battle to ratify the ERA turned into.

Perhaps if the issues had been better understood, the image of the pro-ERA campaign would have been better crafted. Schlafly, never a woman to mince her words, called feminists 'a bunch of anti-family radicals, lesbians and elitists',[20] and the women's movement seemed to go out of its way to prove her right.

The 1977 International Women's Year (IWY) Conference in Houston is a case in point. Although it was meant to cover the entire range of women's issues from pension rights to child care, this mammoth get-together was dominated by three 'hot button' resolutions – those covering the ERA, abortion and lesbian rights. To many, these issues became inextricably linked. Dorris Holmes, Georgia's delegate and state strategist for the ERA, warned, 'It will be harder to pass the amendment in conservative states if it is associated with the lesbian cause.'[21] Nonetheless, the homosexual rights resolution was approved at Houston by a large majority. The ensuing scene received a great deal of media attention. Lesbians in the galleries roared their approval: 'Thank you, sisters!' They sported buttons that read 'A Woman Without a Man is Like a Fish Without a Bicycle',[22] and released hundreds of pink and yellow balloons with the message WE ARE EVERYWHERE scrawled over them, which did not endear the conference to the Moral Majority.

A *Washington Star* editorial pointed out that the IWY priority list 'links many of the emotionally charged issues quite the way an increasing alarmed opposition fears. Yes, publicly financed abortion on demand, equality of everything for homosexuals, 24-hour day care, guaranteed incomes and unilateral disarmament'.[23] Nicholas Von Hoffman, newspaper columnist and ERA supporter, commented, 'The belief persists that the women's movement will celebrate the passage of the [ERA] amendment by banqueting on roast fetuses.'[24]

It is sobering to realise that the ERA was defeated not by a bunch of male chauvinist pigs, but by women who were alienated from a feminist movement the values of which seemed élitist and disconnected from the lives of ordinary people. Worst of all, many women suspected feminists of being contemptuous of their values and aspirations – which centred on family life.

The modern battle over the ERA has a historical parallel. In the 1920s there was a bitter feud between advocates of an equal rights amendment and supporters of protective legislation for women workers. In retrospect, this early fight looks like a dreary rehearsal for the modern struggle. Like the contemporary feud, it centred on opposing visions of what women need to improve their lot in life.

At the beginning of the century many social reformers, including important groups of social feminists at the Labor Department and in the Women's Trade Union League (WTUL), were convinced that woman's maternal and wifely roles, together with her natural weakness, required that the state step in to protect her in the work force. Alice Paul of the National Woman's Party fiercely disagreed. The position of the Women's Party was that 'if . . . a law is passed applying to women and not applying to men, it will discriminate against women and handicap them in competing with men in earning their livelihood'.[25] Arguments based on physical differences were dismissed categorically: 'This is a philosophy that would penalise all women because some women are physically weak.'[26] The stage was set for a debilitating struggle.

The body of protective legislation that was in place in the early 1920s was a mixed bag. Some of these protective laws imposed limitations on the kinds of work women could do. Occupations were forbidden to women on a variety of grounds: selling liquor, for example, might expose women to lewd men and threaten their innocence; grinding or polishing metal might clog women's lungs with dust; work in underground mines might coarsen women's gentle natures. Operating lifts, reading meters, carrying letters and driving taxis were all among the occupations denied to women during this period.

Other types of protective legislation attempted to regulate the conditions under which women could work. Most states passed maximum hour laws limiting the number of hours a woman could work in a day. At first it was ten hours, but by the 1920s it was down to eight. In addition, there were provisions for more hygienic working conditions, some attempts to mandate a minimum wage, and legal restrictions against compulsory overtime and night-time work for women.

The net effect of protective legislation on the well-being of women workers is difficult to assess despite numerous official commissions and a heated contemporary debate. On the whole, it seems that married women with family responsibilities supported the regulations which produced shorter hours and more pleasant working conditions. But other working women, particularly single women in badly paying jobs, would have traded in the shorter hours for a higher wage.

One interesting aspect of protective legislation in America was that it restricted and limited paid work for women, but it did little to support working women. In 1916, when the president of the American Association of Labor Legislation presented a plan to pay hospital expenses and cash benefits to women who withdrew from the work force before and after childbirth, it was shot down.[27] Critics protested that such generosity would give potential mothers an incentive to work, and the proposal was withdrawn.

Contrast this with Europe, where in the early years of this century protective legislation came to encompass maternity leave, the medical costs of childbirth, and certain additional types of health coverage for women and their children. By 1920 Britain, Italy, and Germany all had support policies in these areas.

In Britain the Maternity and Child Welfare Act of 1918 made it obligatory for local authorities to provide child welfare and ante-natal clinics – much later, under the 1936 Midwives Act, they were also obliged to provide trained midwives. In Italy, although women did not win the vote until 1945, they were already supported by extensive protective legislation passed as early as 1902. Under the terms of this legislation their work hours were limited to no more than twelve hours a day, they could not work night shifts, they were not allowed to work in unhealthy locations, and they were guaranteed a leave of absence after childbirth and time off to nurse the baby. All of which was leading the way to the sort of benefits Italian women enjoy today.

In post-First World War America, however, what little protective legislation there was split the feminist ranks. Because this legislation produced special treatment for women, it conflicted in a fundamental way with the continuing struggle toward women's equality. It was felt that women could not both be wards of the state entitled to special protection, and achieve equality with men. Starting in the early 1920s, Alice Paul's National Woman's Party led the fight to urge a constitutional amendment guaranteeing equality. The ERA was formally submitted to Congress in December 1923. It was based on the original arguments for women's rights made in 1848 at Seneca Falls: that women were equal to men and therefore were entitled to all human rights. As Paul put it, 'If you demand equality, you must accept equality.'[28]

Many social feminists in America were made extremely nervous by the ERA, believing that it jeopardised the gains from decades of struggle to improve conditions for working women. At first the Woman's Party was conciliatory and offered to accept changes in the ERA so as not to injure the '8 hour day and other social legislation'. But compromise was difficult when the best legal minds in the country were of the opinion that it was impossible to draft a blanket federal constitutional amendment that would not jeopardise the social legislation.

In the event, the Women's Bureau of the Labor Department, the National Consumers' League and the Women's Trade Union League pulled out all the stops in a fight to defeat the ERA. *Justice*, the newspaper of the International Ladies Garment Workers Union (ILGWU), was typical in its reaction to the amendment: 'To destroy industrial laws for women merely because the same laws do not exist for men is . . . the same kind of thing we would have been doing had we sought to deprive men of suffrage because women did not have it.' Phyllis Schlafly could not have put the case better.

However, as time passed, the position of the Woman's Party hardened, until the party withdrew its tacit support for protective legislation and became intent on passing an ERA at any cost – and in so doing lost much grassroot support. Mary Anderson, the director of the Women's Bureau, became increasingly incensed. She had begun her working life as a shoe worker and was deeply committed to protective legislation for women. She accused the 'theoretical feminists' of the Woman's Party of 'talking about things and conditions entirely outside their own experience or knowledge'. (She would have understood why those women in the textile factory in Georgia were hostile to the ERA.) She went on to urge that 'rights must be interpreted for women workers as something concrete, and we must start with the world where it is today . . .' Anderson concluded with the statement, 'I consider myself a good feminist, but I believe I am a practical one.'[29]

This schism in the feminist ranks wreaked havoc with the effectiveness of the movement. The ERA was introduced in Congress every year after 1923 but got nowhere, and all factions – equal rights advocates and social welfare enthusiasts – were discredited and weakened by the conflict.

In Europe, feminists avoided this bloodletting in the early decades of the century. In Britain in the 1920s and 1930s feminists concerned with extending equal rights worked through such organisations as the Fawcett Society, while those interested in welfare measures joined the Women's Cooperative Guild, the Women's Labour League, and other movements for social reform. But there was no sharp conflict between them. One reason was that the welfare current was clearly dominant, and as time passed, the egalitarian goals of the movement were muted in favour of piecemeal social reform. Another reason was that 'the new Labour Party acted as an umbrella organisation [pulling] together the different groups in the cause of effective action. Politicians were . . . willing to go along with reforms and substantial welfare gains were made'.[30] Some of these efforts culminated in the Children's Act of 1948, which helped provide an elaborate safety net for mothers and children.

In contrast, American feminism languished in this period. As historian Alice Kessler-Harris has described it, even during the Second World War the divisions between feminists persisted: 'Business and professional women continued to support the ERA and paid little attention to such mundane issues as day care. For them, the important thing, as always, was not resolving the home and family issues that might equalise work force opportunities for all women, but improving their own relative economic positions.'[31] When feminism was reborn in the 1960s, the equal rights advocates were dominant and were able to set the agenda for the contemporary movement.

Had the modern backers of the Equal Rights Amendment been more conversant with the history of American feminism, they would have had more respect for their opposition. For in the 1920s opposition to the amendment came from within the reform movement, from the trade unions, and from social feminists such as Mary Anderson. It was impossible to dismiss this liberal opposition as so much right-wing hysteria. Had they understood that feminists could have a legitimate problem with the Equal Rights Amendment, the pro-ERA campaign might have been differently crafted.

What is the legacy of nearly 150 years of American feminism? With impressive consistency the best energy of the movement has focused on attaining equal rights for women, rights which were to be won by a separatist strategy uniting sisterhood in mass organisations. In the recent phase of feminism the equal rights issue has been joined by issues of sexual freedom, but even the modern movement sees the ERA as the bedrock on which all other rights are to be inscribed.

Even in its own terms American feminism has had limited success. By screening out other demands, feminists did enfranchise women in 1920. But it was a limited victory, as they then failed to use the vote for any useful purpose. The separatist organisations of feminism failed to give them any lever on power, and the failure to agree on a substantive agenda after winning the vote meant that the movement fell apart after 1920.

In the modern period the failures of the movement have been more dramatic. The battle to ratify the ERA – the modern centrepiece of American feminist demands – was lost in a particularly humiliating way: it was defeated by women. The ERA battle casts the mistakes of the women's movement into stark relief. It points to failures in understanding. The chic, liberal women of NOW have mostly failed to understand that millions of American women like being wives and mothers and want to strengthen, not weaken, the traditional family structure. For them motherhood is not a trap, divorce is not liberating, and many of them find the personal and sexual freedom of modern life immensely threatening. In a profound way feminists in America have failed to connect with the needs and aspirations of ordinary American women.

But the ERA battle also points to failures in strategy. The separatist feminist organisations chose not to align themselves permanently with political parties, trade unions or professional organisations and therefore failed to connect with the real centres of political power. Feminists did not heed Eleanor Roosevelt's advice, which was 'Get into the game and stay in it. Throwing mud from the outside won't help. Building up from the inside will.'[32] In addition, the umbrella character of the movement meant that the demands of the radicals could not be ruled out of court, and the broad coalition feminists needed to ratify the ERA was needlessly scrambled with extraneous issues of sexual freedom.

If modern American feminists have failed to achieve the goal they themselves define as central to their mission, they have obviously missed out on that other agenda – the support system of concrete benefits and services so important to European social feminism.

This neglect of material realities goes to the heart of the difference between American and European feminism. The American movement has defined the problem of womenkind as that of acquiring a full set of legal, political and economic rights, and achieving control over one's body. The assumption is that once women possess the same rights as men and can choose not to have children, they achieve true equality of opportunity and are able to attain power, status, and money on the same terms as men.

In Europe social feminists have conceived the problem of the female sex differently. For them, it is not woman's lack of legal rights that constitutes her main handicap or even her lack of 'reproductive freedom'. Rather, it is her dual burden – in the home and in the work force – that leads to second-class citizenship. The goal of the social feminists has therefore become one of lightening this load by instituting family support systems. The conviction is that because women are wives and mothers as well as workers and citizens, they need special compensatory policies if they are to accomplish as much as men in the world beyond the home. Equal rights are seen as only part of the struggle.

These contrasting visions of the female problem place a very different weight on the issue of motherhood. By stressing equality, American feminists have put aside differences from men, including that of bearing children. This not only has little public appeal, it actually gets in the way of creating the support systems so desperately needed by housewives and low-income working women. American feminists still have much to learn from their European sisters.

The Aberrant Fifties

9. *Ultradomesticity: The Return to Hearth and Home*

In May 1983 I interviewed Faith Whittlesey at the White House. At that time she was assistant to the President for public liaison and dealt with policies toward women and children. I told her of my concern for working mothers in America and explained in vivid detail how very hard it was for them to deal with childbirth and child care in the absence of family support policies. Whittlesey listened carefully and tried to respond. She told me that Ronald Reagan was tremendously concerned about the care and nurturing of children and that he did in fact have a policy in this area. The policy was to lick inflation and encourage the economy to grow so that men could once more earn a family wage. A little puzzled, I asked her how she thought this would help. 'Oh,' said Whittlesey, smiling, 'the rest is easy. Once men earn a family wage, all those women can go home and look after their own children in the way they did when I was growing up.'[1] Everything, it seems, would be solved if we returned to the good old days of the fifties, when mothers stayed at home and dads were stalwart breadwinners.

The odd thing is that Reagan himself grew up in the twenties and had a working mother; she worked in a dress shop for $14 a week in order to help out with the precarious family finances.[2] You might imagine he would relate to the difficulties faced by contemporary working mothers. Instead, he clings to a vision of motherhood fifties-style which did not exist in the 1920s and does not exist today.

The fact is that the 1950s were profoundly aberrant. The trademarks of the period – an extended baby boom, a glorification of domesticity, a turning against careers for women, an impressive elaboration of the maternal role – all run counter to modern values and contradict previously existing trends.

Americans look back at this period and say to themselves, 'How quaint!' 'How bizarre!' almost as though they were describing the customs of some exotic tribe. What they often overlook is the fact that fifties America also looks

147

quaint and bizarre from the perspective of pre-war America. In films of the thirties and forties Joan Crawford and Katharine Hepburn played gutsy, intelligent women, women who had nothing in common with the dumb sex kittens of the 1950s. The dialogue in *Some Like it Hot* (starring Marilyn Monroe) is enough to make a modern American woman – or a thirties woman – grind her teeth. Monroe spends an indeterminable amount of time insisting to Tony Curtis that she has no brains at all in her pretty little head.

It seems that the fifties were not the olden days. They were different from the years before as well as the years after. And it is crucial to a full understanding of the ideologies which condition many of America's current attitudes towards mothers and children, both public and private, that we understand this special period in American history.

During the summer and autumn of 1949 the American popular press was preoccupied with a scandal surrounding Ingrid Bergman. The beautiful Swedish film star had abandoned her husband and daughter in Hollywood and gone off to Italy, where she was having a torrid affair with film director Roberto Rossellini. Rumour had it that she was pregnant by Rossellini and that her husband was refusing to agree to a divorce. In due course Ingrid Bergman gave birth to a son, Robertino, in Rome on 2 February 1950. Since Bergman was not yet divorced, let alone remarried, Robertino's birth certificate said that he was the son of Rossellini and of some unknown mother.

This illegitimate birth unleashed a storm of public protest in the United States. As film critic John Russell Taylor describes it, 'All the self-appointed protectors of public morality in the States were up in arms.'[3] The frenzy reached its climax when Senator Edwin C. Johnson of Colorado launched an astonishing attack on Bergman from the floor of the Senate. His tone was unmistakably one of personal betrayal. 'She was a sweet and understanding person,' he wailed, 'with an attractive personality which captivated everyone on and off the screen.'[4] Again and again the same tone recurred: How could she do this to us? – as though all the men of America were married to her and all the women of America somehow tarnished by her 'moral turpitude'.[5]

Although Ingrid Bergman married Roberto Rossellini as soon as she was legally able and went on to have twins by him – in wedlock – the American Establishment continued its persecution. The Swedish film star was repeatedly refused a visa by the State Department and was not allowed to re-enter the United States until 1957. Her political rehabilitation did not occur until 1972, when Senator Charles Percy put the congressional record straight by making a speech that paid glowing tribute to Bergman. This testimonial effectively blotted out Senator Johnson's denunciation of twenty years before.

When we look back on this furore, it is hard to understand what all the fuss was about. Hollywood was not exactly a bastion of wifely virtue. Film stars such as Mae West and Rita Hayworth had been flouting conventional morality for years. The problem for Bergman was that by the late forties she had come to epitomise the domestic virtues that were aggressively back in style. She played the placid, sweet girl and submissive woman in *Adam Had Four Sons*, the clear-eyed, idealistic heroine in *Casablanca*, and the warm-hearted, impulsive nun in *The Bells of St Mary's*. Post-war American audiences (and politicians!) adored her as the lovely, wholesome girl next door. They would not stand for it when she turned out to be an emancipated woman.

Ingrid Bergman had the misfortune to give birth to an illegitimate child at an extraordinary time in America's social history, a time when a new conservatism crept into the national consciousness, along with a strong desire to return to the hearth. However, the American post-war craving for 'Mom and apple pie' did more than wreck Ingrid Bergman's Hollywood career. It ran full tilt into the career aspirations of less celebrated women. For during this period millions of American women were prodded and pushed until they left the larger world of work and public affairs and became the doll-like creatures so well described by Betty Friedan in *The Feminine Mystique*. They became 'feminine women with truly feminine attitudes, admired by men for their miraculous, God-given, sensationally unique ability to wear skirts'.[6] They congratulated themselves that 'they looked and acted far more feminine than the "emancipated" girls of the 1920s or even the 30s'.[7]

Despite the considerable advances made by women in the first half of the century, in the late 1940s careers went out of fashion in America and women were expected to devote their prime years and their best energies to home and family. As the country wallowed in an 'orgy' of domesticity, the birthrate doubled, and the tasks associated with mothering grew to unprecedented levels.

To be a good mother in America in the 1920s and 1930s was a role that had finite limits. It involved providing wholesome food, hygienic surroundings and lots of discipline. To be a good mother in the fifties was a role that knew no bounds, as mothers became personally responsible for the psychological and cognitive development of their children. On the psychological front mothers were burdened with the fearful knowledge that only they stood between their child growing up to be normal or growing up to be a neurotic, screwed-up adult. On the cognitive front the post-war American mother was handed both a challenge and a threat. She was told, 'You have the capacity to rear a genius, a masterpiece,' but it was also clear that if this child failed to live up to his or her potential, it was very definitely the mother's fault.

Ingrid Bergman's behaviour therefore clearly fell far short of these exacting standards. However, this resurrection of domestic virtues ran counter to all historical trends in America. Indeed, for at least a century American women had been proud of their reputation for freedom and independence in the world beyond the home and were well in advance of their European sisters.

In the 1880s the English aristocrat Lord Bryce was mightily impressed by the worldly position of American women. As he put it, 'In America it is easier for women to find a career, to obtain work of an intellectual or of a commercial kind than in any part of Europe'.[8] And his opinion did seem to reflect real differences in the way the old and the new worlds treated their women. The Swedish feminist Fredrika Bremer in her novel *Hertha*, published in 1856, described America as the 'promised land of women'.[9] She argued, with considerable force, how Swedish women in the mid nineteenth century were much more confined to their homes and much less emancipated than their American sisters. Sigmund Freud, on fleeing Vienna in 1938, took off to England, rather than the United States, where, in his eyes, 'the women were less subservient to men'.[10] He felt ill prepared to abandon his European values in this regard.

Throughout the nineteenth century American women were not as protected as their European counterparts. In frontier settings their economic role was too important and they were numerically too scarce to yield much power to husbands, and among the immigrant groups that settled along the eastern seaboard, women were often more employable than their menfolk. During the first third of this century their relative position improved at a rapid rate. American women obtained the vote at an early date (1920, as opposed to 1928 in Britain, 1945 in France, 1946 in Italy and 1971 in Switzerland); economic growth and a rapidly expanding industrial technology promised to reduce their domestic chores to a minimum; education for women increased at a much faster rate than in Europe; and divorce and contraception became generally available.

The long history of the frontier helps explain this development of greater freedom for American women. In the virgin lands of the westward-moving frontier, life was extremely arduous as families attempted to carve out a living from the wilderness. Because they were equal participants in the family's struggle for survival, women earned the respect of their husbands, their children and their communities. As historian Joanna Stratton has described it, 'The pioneer family existed as a self-sufficient unit that took pride in its ability to provide for itself and persevere in the face of hardship. Men and women worked together as partners, combining their strength and talents to provide food and clothing for themselves and their children. As a result, women found themselves on a far more equal footing.'[11]

The importance of the pioneer woman was enhanced by the fact that she was in short supply. During the whole of the colonial period men outnumbered women, and until late in the nineteenth century women remained few and far between in the American West. In 1865 there were three men for every one woman in California, while in Colorado the ratio was as high as twenty to one.[12] The economic importance of women and their scarcity value led to the early emancipation of women in the western states. An Oregon law of 1850 granted land to both single and married women, and several western territories granted suffrage to women at an early date (Wyoming in 1869 and Utah in 1870). In many western townships women were elected to political office: Kansas City had had sixteen women mayors by 1900.[13]

Another important dimension of the American experience was the early extension of education to women. The doors of higher education opened earlier and faster to women in the United States than in Europe. The breakthrough for American women came during the 1860s, when women's colleges like Vassar and Smith were founded and universities like Michigan and Cornell became co-educational. In Britain my alma mater, Girton College, Cambridge, which opened in 1869 with an enrolment of six students, was the only British institution of higher education available to women until London University accepted women in 1879. On the Continent progress was even slower: the first German university to open its doors to women was Heidelberg, in 1900, by which time one-third of college students in the United States were women.

America maintained an impressive lead in higher education for women until the Second World War; indeed, by the mid-1930s in the US women made up 40 per cent of students in institutions of higher learning. In Germany just before Hitler took power, no more than 10 per cent of university students were female, in Sweden during this time period the figure was 17 per cent, and in Britain the figure was 22 per cent.[14]

In short, by the 1930s American women had developed a considerable head start over their European counterparts on the slow road to political and economic emancipation. This freedom and independence were to be pushed even further during the Second World War.

In the 1942–5 period, at the peak of the war, 14 million American men were in the armed services. There was a desperate need for women workers – to replace men in the production of essential civilian goods, and to 'man' the vastly expanded arms factories. In response to these pressures, almost 5 million additional women workers were drawn into employment during the war years, and the number of wives holding jobs doubled.[15] These women took up traditional female employment in such sectors as food and clothing, but they also took up newly vacant male jobs in chemicals, rubber, petroleum, steel, aircraft and munitions, where they proved to be indispensable to the war effort. In these male fields women were paid 50 to 100 per cent more than in the female sectors of the economy.

'Rosie the Riveter' became a symbol of patriotic endeavour, and a popular song was written about her:

> Rosie's got a boyfriend, Charlie;
> Charlie, he's a marine
> Rosie is protecting Charlie
> Working overtime on the riveting machine.[16]

At the height of the war effort Norman Rockwell painted a picture of Rosie the Riveter for the cover of the *Saturday Evening Post* (29 May 1943). He depicts her as Junoesque – confident, muscular, yet feminine. With her machine tools and painted fingernails she is clearly the kind of woman you could rely on in any kind of emergency.

US government policy encouraged women in their new work roles. The War Manpower Commission employed the J. Walter Thompson advertising agency to run its recruiting campaign for women workers. However, the call to the factories was not clothed in feminine rhetoric. Posters announcing production jobs promised women 'man-sized' jobs with 'man-sized' wages. War propaganda pictured women operating heavy machinery, while the *Ladies' Home Journal* placed the image of a female combat pilot on its cover. There was even some grudging recognition that since three-quarters of the new workers were married women, problems relating to child care were capable of affecting wartime production. In 1942 the American federal government contributed $400,000 to assist local communities in funding child-care centres, and by 1945, 100,000 children were enrolled in federally supported facilities.[17]

In 1945 American women were more powerful than they ever had been before, yet in the years following the Second World War a strange thing happened. America, that bastion of strong, independent women, became caught up in an orgy of domesticity, and millions of women embraced an existence that was totally centred on home and family. For the first time in the history of the country educated women were expected and encouraged to devote their prime years and expend their best energies on housework and motherhood.

These post-war years were marked by a series of retrogressive trends, making the 1950s a strangely aberrant period. To begin with, women got married and had children earlier than ever, cutting short their education and worklife. The average age for women to marry dropped to twenty in 1950, down from twenty-three in the 1920s and 1930s.[18] No other industrial country had such an early average age for marriage in the 1950s. The birthrate rose steadily so that by the end of the 1950s the rate of population growth in the United States was twice that of Europe and close on the heels of Africa and India. In this gigantic baby boom, which lasted until 1960, 'the birth rate for third children doubled . . . and that for fourth children tripled'.[19] In this era of burgeoning families even the divorce rate fell a little.

During this same period women lost ground in educational and career terms. In the early fifties women constituted 35 per cent of US college graduates, down from 40 per cent in the 1930s.[20] However, the clearest sign of retrogression was the decline in the proportion of high-achieving women. Of the people listed in the 1902 edition of *Who's Who in America*, 8 per cent were women; in the 1958 edition women constituted a mere 4 per cent of the total. As sociologist John Parrish wrote – rather dismally – in 1961, 'At this rate of decline there will be no distinguished American women relative to men, in another generation or so.'[21]

Contrast this with Europe, where women were gaining ground in the 1950s. During these years 16 per cent of British and French doctors were women, as were 13 per cent of Swedish doctors; the figure for the United States was 6 per cent. France is a particularly interesting case. Commenting on the French situation in 1954, sociologists Alva Myrdal and Viola Klein said that 'it is remarkable to what a small extent professional women are influenced by the size of their families in the pursuit of their careers'.[22] At this time 21 per cent of all professionals in France were women, and three-quarters of French women with university degrees were in the work force.

In the United States the picture was dramatically different. In the 1950s women with college degrees in the childbearing age group had a lower rate of employment than any other group of women, for the plain fact was women with college degrees were often married to prosperous men. And in America in the fifties, if the family could afford it, the wife stayed at home.

In summary, the proportion of American women who went on to have professional careers (as lawyers, doctors, or college professors) was smaller in the fifties than in the pre-war period, and American women were increasingly less career-oriented than their European sisters. The ambition of women, even at top colleges, was to graduate with a diamond engagement ring rather than with high academic honours. American women increasingly held 'jobs' before childbearing and after their children entered high school, but they rarely took up 'careers'. Women of the fifties in the US vested their best energies in their homes and in their children.

The paradox is that as they entered the post-war era, American women were the best educated and the most equal in the world. Why did they give up their independent ambitions and go home?

The post-war orgy of domesticity owed much to policies put in place by a government attempting to cope with the aftermath of the Great Depression and the Second World War. These policies provided a variety of incentives that greatly encouraged traditional roles for women.

In 1945 not only were Americans recovering from the dangers and dislocations of a major war, but they still had deep and painful memories of the Great Depression, which lasted much longer in America than in Europe. Looking at affluent liberal America today it is easy to forget the suffering and deprivation of the 1930–39 period, which were phenomenal. As William Manchester describes it, 'Millions stayed alive by living like animals. In the Pennsylvania countryside they were eating wild weed-roots and dandelions . . . City mothers hung around docks, waiting for the spoiled produce to be discarded and then fighting homeless dogs for possession of it . . . Whole families were seen plunging into refuse dumps, gnawing at bones and watermelon rinds.'[23]

In particular, the Depression wreaked great psychological havoc on American men, who found themselves out of work for many consecutive years, unable to perform their role as breadwinner and generally powerless to control their destinies. Joseph Pleck in his book *The Myth of Masculinity* argues that the Great Depression was the historical event in America that caused 'the single greatest crisis in the traditional and institutional basis of the male role, that of family economic provider'.[24]

Ten years of deep depression were followed by a bloody and destructive world war. Although America did not suffer the ravages that Europe did, four hundred thousand US servicemen lost their lives, and tens of thousands more were seriously injured. While Europe was preoccupied with massive programmes of rebuilding an infrastructure that had been all but destroyed by six years of war, in America the population could afford to look inwards at last and, come 1945, there was enormous pent-up demand across the country for a normal life – for a family, a house and a decent job. This became the stuff of the post-war American Dream.

But the men guiding US policy in 1945 were not sure that they could conjure up the jobs that were so desperately needed if the expectations of the returning soldiers were to be realised. There was a great fear that with the return of peace, the economic gains of the war years would vanish and the country would plunge once more into deep depression and massive unemployment. One strategy was clear to the economic planners: Encourage women to leave wartime employment and return to their homes. Jobs were going to become scarce, and they would be needed by the returning soldiers. As one commentator put it, 'The nation has a powerful responsibility to the returning soldier. The veteran has been promised his old job. He will get it.'[25]

In the event, the post-war scene in America was one of great prosperity. By the late forties the economy was growing at an impressive rate, and between 1945 and 1955 the American GNP more than doubled. During the early fifties, the years of the Korean War, the expansion as compared with the rest of the Western world was particularly breathtaking. But American policy makers had not expected this post-war boom. According to historian Richard Hofstadter, 'We [America] were surprised by the fact that instead of having a tremendous depression after the war which those of us who were mature in the 1930s thought surely was coming, we entered upon one of the greatest boom periods in history.'[26] Contemporary policy action was based on a gloomy view of the post-war period, and top priority was given to sending women workers home – quickly. By the end of 1946 4 million fewer American women were working than had worked at the peak of wartime production. The decline in women's employment was particularly pronounced in well-paid heavy industry, where returning veterans were particularly anxious to take back their jobs. Few women retained skilled craft jobs after the war. A document released by the Women's Bureau concluded sadly that 'only a few women have been allowed to continue in the newer fields of employment, and thus to continue to use the skills learned during the war'.[27]

Both persuasion and coercion were used to lure women away from their jobs. Traditionalists had a field day resurrecting a feminine vision of womankind that was directly at odds with the capable powerful image projected by Rosie the Riveter just a few years earlier. In 1946 Margaret Pickel, dean of Barnard College, declared solemnly in an article for the *New York Times Magazine* that women workers were decidedly inferior to men. Not only did they have less physical strength than men but 'by middle age, when men are at their best, a devoted woman worker is apt to degenerate into fussiness or worse'.[28] Meanwhile, a stream of vituperation was being directed at those mothers who still wanted to work. Mothers, argued Agnes Meyer in the *Atlantic Monthly*, were needed at home to restore a sense of security to an insecure world. She called on middle-class women to resist pressure to enter the work force and to renounce any job except that of housewife and mother. 'What ails these women,' she asked, 'who consciously or unconsciously reject their children? . . . The poor child whose mother has to work has some inner security because he knows that his mother is sacrificing herself for his well-being. But the neglected child from a well-to-do home, who realises instinctively that his mother prefers her job to him, often hates her with a passionate intensity.'[29] In rather more measured tones Ashley Montagu proclaimed in the *Saturday Review*, 'Being a good wife, a good mother, in short a good homemaker is the most important of all the occupations in the world . . . I put it down as an axiom that no woman with husband and small children can hold a full-time job and be a good homemaker at one and the same time.'[30]

Some women were happy to be told that they should go home at the end of the war. One female union leader announced her retirement plans with girlish enthusiasm: 'When the war is over I'll get a manicure, put on the frilliest dress I can find, pour a whole bottle of perfume over my head and then I will be glad to give up my union chair . . . to some boy who comes marching home deserving it.'[31] But when persuasion failed to work, coercion was used. Many women didn't graciously resign from their jobs at the end of the war; they were fired. In the two-month period immediately following V-J Day, women were laid off at double the male rate, and lay-offs were particularly drastic in the heavy industrial sector, where women did not leave at the end of the war because they very much wanted to hang on to their well-paid jobs.[32]

A less-than-subtle form of official coercion was the closing down of government-sponsored child-care centres which had made it possible for mothers with young children to work. Women protested against the disman-tling of these centres but to no avail. Federal support for child-care facilities ceased in March 1946, and by the beginning of 1948 all state support had ended. Public child care was terminated as part of a national movement to return children to their mothers and working mothers to their homes. 'The women, so lately the darlings of the nation's factories, were summarily sent home to stay.'[33]

The United States government policy did not rest only on sticks to drive women out of the work force. It also employed carrots to lure women back to hearth and home. Among the juiciest carrots were the GI Bill and the Highway Act.

At first glance the GI Bill and the Highway Act said nothing about women. The GI Bill, which was officially called the Serviceman's Readjustment Act of 1944, provided 14 million returning veterans with free college tuition, subsist-ence allowances (which were increased by 50 per cent if one had dependents), and extremely low-cost mortgages; while the Highway Act of 1944 pumped $1.3 billion of public money into a road network around and between cities. But the effect of these pieces of legislation was to subsidise, to the tune of several thousands of dollars a year per household, a particular kind of family – one that comprised a breadwinning husband, a homemaking wife, and one or more children. How precisely did this happen?

In the first place, through the GI Bill men received free education and training. They acquired a head start in the job market and were able to become good providers. It made little sense for couples to invest in the skills of a wife since she couldn't compete with all this free training. Secondly, since dependents were at least partially supported through the provisions of the GI Bill, this legislation encouraged early marriage and procreation. Why not avail yourself of free income? Finally, the roads provided by the Highway Act and the cheap financing provided by the low-cost mortgages of the GI Bill extended the possibility of living in a house in the suburbs to millions of young American couples. In just five years (1950–54) the suburban rings around the cities increased their population by 35 per cent.[34] This trek to the suburbs, which was to become the largest internal migration in American history, removed wives to distant locations far from most job opportunities. All these factors helped domesticate American women.

If the returning soldiers, frustrated by years of depression and war, yearned for home and hearth, wife and children, the GI Bill and Highway Act permitted gratification of these fantasies. A house in the suburbs, a doll-like wife with all the housewifely skills, a brood of high-achieving children, were magically conjured up and became the ingredients of the post-war dream. The 'classical family of Western nostalgia' was born.[35] But the dream was nourished by something more substantial than hope and fantasy. It was grounded in some special post-war policies: it was fuelled by massive government subsidies, and it was sustained by unprecedented economic growth. For if the American economy had not grown so fast in the 1945–60 period, those well-educated GIs would not have earned enough to support the large families of the period, no matter how generous the government subsidies. The sticks and carrots of these government policies could only work well in a context of growth and prosperity.

The ideal of family life that pervaded the American consciousness during this period is perhaps best exemplified by the work of the artist Norman Rockwell, who for many years had been depicting scenes from American life on the covers of the *Saturday Evening Post*.[36] In the late forties and in the fifties Rockwell was to achieve his greatest fame. His sentimental glorification of joyous domesticity and his unabashed delight in the suburban lifestyles of Middle America exactly matched the contemporary mood.

Government policies designed to get women out of the work force and into the home were buttressed by some powerful new ideologies. One grew out of the grim politics of the thirties and forties and saw state-supported child care as part of totalitarianism. Another was Freudian theory, which saw women as inferior and childish, with no prospect of happiness unless they relinquished independent work and adjusted to being wives and mothers.

Once the Second World War was over, firm discipline, rigid schedules and group care for children became thoroughly unfashionable in America.[37] These practices now smacked uncomfortably of the Third Reich and Stalin's Russia.

The mood of the day was to allow the children of the free world more freedom (under proper maternal supervision, of course) than children had ever had before. The cold war, which started up in the late 1940s, was, after all, a war about ways of life as much as markets and territory, and in these post-war years much political capital was made out of contrasting stereotypes of domestic life.

Child-rearing models on both the Fascist right and the Communist left were seen as threatening. Ever since the 1917 Bolshevik victory in the Soviet Union, American leaders had been suspicious of Communist baby-raising techniques. In the early 1920s Senator Reed of Kansas described a 'noxious plan [that] had reached its highest degree in Russia, there every child was looked upon as a ward of the state, motherhood and birth control were established by law and children were taken from their mothers' arms and turned over to public officers'.[38]

After the Second World War this type of hysterical reaction from the right was put to more systematic use and bent to the purposes of the cold war. Anti-Communist sentiment was used as yet another reason for why women should go home and rear their children themselves, and it constituted an additional nail in the coffin of government-sponsored day care. In 1947 the *New York World-Telegram* charged that state-supported child care was conceived by leftists operating out of Communist 'social work cells'. The campaign for day-care centres, the *Telegram* said, had 'all the trappings of a Red drive, including leaflets, letters, telegrams, petitions, protest demonstrations, mass meetings and hat passing'.[39] Much to the *Telegram*'s approval, New York's Governor Dewey refused to yield to pressure from women's groups. Instead, he called working women Communists, accused them of contaminating our free society, and, in early 1948, discontinued state support for child care.

Freudian theory, which swept through American middle-class life during this period, provided additional energy for the return to hearth and home. Many of Freud's disciples, who were in the main German and Austrian Jews, fled Europe in the 1930s and early 1940s and settled in the United States. Helene Deutsch, Paul Federn, Edward Hitschmann and Hanns Sachs were among the refugees from Hitler's Europe who became part of the rapidly growing psychoanalytical community in the States.[40] In the post-war period both serious scholarship and pop psychology in America became replete with Freudian ideology.

Modern Women: The Lost Sex, a 1947 best-seller by Ferdinand Lundberg and Marynia Farnham, is a case in point. This book declared: 'Careers produce the masculinisation of women and with it enormously dangerous consequences to the home, to the children who depend on it, and to the ability of the woman as well as the man to obtain sexual gratification.'[41] Lundberg and Farnham were of the opinion that 'Women would do well to recapture those functions in which they have demonstrated superior capacity. Those are, in general, the nurturing functions around the home.' To women who chose to enter 'fields belonging to the male area of exploit or authority – law, mathematics, physics, business, industry and technology – government should make it clear that such pursuits are not generally desirable for women'. If women, despite their natural bent, insisted on entering such fields, Lundberg and Farnham held that they deserved to be discriminated against. The psychic maladjustment that had led them to leave their homes made them intrinsically poor risks at the office. They were described as emotionally unstable, quarrelsome, and apt to ferment feuds on the job. In particular, they lacked 'the gift for teamwork that makes for coordinated research'.[42] As professionals they were indecisive; as union members they were disloyal. Worst of all, their interest in work distracted attention from what should have been a primary concern with the home and with their children.

A curious aspect of this inveighing against careers for women was that the inveigher was nearly always a career woman. Thus, when in 1944 Helene Deutsch published her two-volume *The Psychology of Woman: A Psychoanalytic Interpretation*, she attributed a woman's discontent with her feminine role to a 'masculinity complex'. According to Deutsch, women who 'had achieved eminence by activity of their own in various fields had done so at the expense of their feminine fulfilment'. The remedy: to relinquish any goals of her own and 'to identify and fulfil herself through the activities and goals of husband and son'. If she had to work, she was advised to do such things as 'the basic research for her male superior's discoveries. The daughter who devotes her life to her father is also making a satisfactory feminine sublimation'.[43]

Of course, Deutsch was not about to publish any of *her* scholarship under any name but her own, and she took care to hire a nurse for her own child so that he did not interfere with the development of her career. 'Immediately after her son's birth, Dr Deutsch hired a nurse, Paula, and installed her and infant Martin in a vacant room next to her office.'[44] Finding breast-feeding rather an exhausting business – despite its importance in Freudian theory – Helene Deutsch acquired two goats to provide little Martin with milk. These goats proceeded to graze and fight in the courtyard of the clinic where Deutsch worked, providing an endless source of amusement for visitors.

The contradiction between what Deutsch advocated as proper feminine behaviour and what she herself chose to do did not seem to strike anyone as peculiar. Post-war America was focused whole-heartedly on the necessity and desirability of women's fulfilling their 'natural' domestic role, and Deutsch's book was just that much more ammunition in a worthy cause.

*

Today it is hard to appreciate how thoroughly domestic American women became in the 1950s.

In 1957 Betty Friedan as part of her research for *The Feminine Mystique* surveyed her class at Smith College – the class of '42 – to find out what her classmates were doing with their adult lives. She found that these well-educated women were thoroughly immersed in being wives and mothers. Of the 189 women who returned Friedan's questionnaire, 179 were married, 6 were single, 1 was widowed and 3 were divorced. Only 11 did not have children. Indeed, on average these women had 2.9 children, and 52 had 4 children or more. The great majority of these Smith graduates were full-time housewives. Even those whose children were in school had few ambitions outside the home; they had absorbed the conventional wisdom of fifties America and did not think it was possible to have both a family and a career. As one 37-year-old housewife wrote in her questionnaire, 'The highly educated career-trained woman who is in mental competition with men must fight frustration in marriage and emotional chaos'.[45]

Only twelve out of these 189 women held full-time jobs, and only one had embarked on a serious professional career. A further handful worked part time 'directing the choir', 'teaching piano', or 'typing for husband'.

Magazines of the era were full of bright and smiling housewife-mothers, who cherished their 'unique femininity' and the 'receptivity and passivity implicit in their sexual nature'.[46] A 1956 article in *Look* magazine celebrated the new domesticity:

The American woman is winning the battle of the sexes. Like a teenager, she is growing up and confounding her critics . . . She works, rather casually, less towards a 'big career' than as a way of filling a hope chest or buying a home freezer. She gracefully concedes the top jobs to men. This wondrous creature also marries younger than ever, bears more babies and looks and acts far more feminine than the 'emancipated' girl of the 1920s or even 30s. Steel worker's wife and Junior Leaguer alike do their own housework . . . Today, if she makes an old-fashioned choice and lovingly tends a garden and a bumper crop of children, she rates louder hosannas than ever before.[47]

In the fifties the American media heaped scorn on feminists, the emancipated 'career girls' of yesteryear. The anti-feminist backlash extended to conceptions of women's education. High schools and colleges began to teach courses on such topics as mate selection, adjustment to marriage and education for family living. At one college 'The Theory and Preparation of a Well-marinated Shish Kebab' replaced 'Kantian Philosophy' in the curriculum.[48]

This approach to education was self-fulfilling. As education for women became increasingly watered down, the adult destiny of the female sex became even more predictable. Women became housewives and mothers, at least partially because they were ill-equipped to do anything else. No wonder there were fewer women lawyers, engineers, and college professors in America in the fifties than in the thirties!

It is almost shocking to modern sensibilities to realise that when Adlai Stevenson made a commencement address at Smith College in 1955, he graciously conceded that 'women, especially educated women, have an unique opportunity to influence us, man and boy'.[49] The founders of Smith College would have been infuriated by this remark, and so would today's students. In the mid-1950s it was taken as meant – a supreme compliment.

Freudian theorists did not stop at exterior phenomena; they redefined the very nature of women's sexuality as part of this retreat to the home.

The sex act itself came to constitute a model for female happiness. During intercourse woman's role was passive, receptive and accepting, based on the notion that sexual pleasure could come only from vaginal orgasm and from the phallus. The one prerequisite for sexual fulfilment was that the woman 'accept with deep inwardness and readiness ... the final goal of intercourse – impregnation'.[50] The desire to be a mother constituted the core of sexual pleasure, and the climax of the sex act really occurred when the mother nursed the child who had been conceived. For the fifties American mother breast-feeding became a complement to the act of creation. It gave her a heightened sense of fulfilment and allowed her 'to participate in a relationship as close to perfection as any that a woman can hope to achieve'.[51] (So began the glorification of breast-feeding that caused me such pain and grief in the late seventies.)

Thus the conventional view of the psychology of women in post-war America came to be an extension of Freudian theory. The woman who wanted complete fulfilment had only to extend the attributes displayed during intercourse to the rest of her life. Passivity, dependence and the desire to raise children constituted the formula for female contentment. Feminism was seen as a serious illness caused by – guess what – penis envy! 'The shadow of the phallus lay darkly' over those masculinised females who still wanted careers.[52]

Even the movie industry reflected the changing cultural mores. As film critic Molly Haskell has pointed out, the 1930s featured 'whole genres of working-women films' which supplied 'details about working women and jobs, salaries, what goes on in offices'.[53] During these years 'women careerists enjoyed great popularity with such actresses as Katharine Hepburn, Rosalind Russell, Bette Davis, and Joan Crawford playing commercial artists, writers, reporters, lawyers and businesswomen'.[54] In *Mildred Pierce* Joan Crawford played a bored middle-class housewife who 'opted out of her socially well-defined milieu to become a free agent and successful businesswoman'.[55] In those years Bette Davis fought a court battle with Warner Brothers for meatier roles, reinforcing her film heroine message that 'one's identity, regardless of gender, comes from work not from one's spouse [or] children'.[56]

The film stars of the fifties were very different. Marilyn Monroe, with her moist, candy-coloured mouth, voluptuous pop-up breasts, and cooing helplessness, catered shamelessly to 'a false, regressive, childish idea of sexuality ... and was never permitted to mature into a warm, vibrant woman'.[57] In *All About Eve* she was a sex object and nincompoop. In *Bus Stop* she played an ingenuous earth mother, and in *Gentlemen Prefer Blondes* she played a floozy who is most comfortable with older men. Debbie Reynolds as 'professional virgin' and Doris Day as 'happy housewife' round out the fifties conception of womankind.

The favourite plot in Doris Day movies went something like this. A glamorous, sexy woman gives her man a thoroughly hard time threatening his masculinity. In the last reel she discovers true love and undergoes a Pygmalionesque transformation into a submissive housewife. For the millions who sat through *April in Paris* (1952), *Calamity Jane* (1953), *The Pajama Game* (1957), and *Teacher's Pet* (1958) the message was loud and clear: a woman might be as free and as clever as a man, but her real destiny and happiness lies in being a wife and a mother. Popular TV series reinforced this image of joyous domesticity. *I Love Lucy* (1951–7), which was the first television programme to be seen in 10 million American homes, and *Ozzie and Harriet* (1952–66), which became US television's longest-running sitcom, depicted a world where women were silly, lovable housewives. Debbie Reynolds summed it all up in *The Tender Trap* (1955): 'Don't you think a man is the most important thing in the world? A woman isn't a woman until she has been married and had children.'[58]

Thus American social history in the post-war years is very curious. In the late forties and fifties the most educated and most independent women in the world became ultradomestic creatures who centred their lives on family and home. This revolutionary shift was due to the interaction of government policy with some powerful intellectual currents.

In the mid-1940s American policy makers urgently desired women to leave their wartime jobs and go home. The returning soldiers deserved to get their jobs back. Besides, economists were convinced that stagnation and unemployment were just around the corner, and women should not be allowed to compete with men for a finite (or even declining) pool of jobs. Complementing this push to get women out of the work force were the GI Bill and the Highway Act. These pieces of legislation provided free education for men (which enhanced their breadwinning capabilities), offered allowances for dependent wives and children, and subsidised homes in suburban locations far removed from most job opportunities. In short, government policy provided the carrots and sticks that encouraged women to stay at home full time.

In such an economic context the Freudian view of womankind – as passive wife and wholehearted homemaker – became immensely popular because it helped justify what was going on. The gutsy, emancipated women of the 1930s and war years had to be redefined if they were to become the keepers of the post-war American Dream.

This transforming of independent women into domestic dolls was not easy, and it would not have succeeded without one more ingredient: the emergence of a veritable cult of motherhood which was tremendously effective in convincing everyone that child rearing was woman's authentic calling. It is important to bear in mind that housekeeping and wifely duties had finite limits in the 1950s. Given the labour-saving equipment in suburban homes and the long hours worked by breadwinning husbands, housework was not capable of filling the lives of educated, energetic post-war women. So child rearing was recast and reformulated until motherhood became loaded with heavy responsibilities. As we shall see in the next chapter, it became a role capable of infinite expansion.

As droves of post-war American women became full-time housewives, they read the child-rearing manuals written by Benjamin Spock, Selma Fraiberg and Berry Brazelton. Who among them 'did not worry that their child's bedwetting, thumbsucking, over-eating, refusal to eat, withdrawal, lack of friends, inability to be alone, aggressiveness, timidity, slow reading, too much reading, lack of discipline, rigidity, inhibition, exhibitionism, sexual preco-ciousness, or sexual lack of interest was a sign of incipient neurosis'.[59] Motherhood, under the spotlight of the modern experts, became a full-time career, even a cult. As the *Saturday Evening Post* put it in 1962, to make a woman completely content, it takes a man, 'but the chief purpose of her life is motherhood'.[60]

10. The Rise of a Cult of Motherhood

It was late on Friday afternoon in February, and my weekly play group was meeting at Sarah's apartment in Manhattan. For the last two years seven women, who were both friends and neighbours, had brought their toddlers to play together for a few hours at the end of the week.

The play group was particularly important for those of us who had jobs. It was a substitute for the park bench (which none of us had time for) and provided a comforting support network. In emergencies we didn't hesitate to call on one another – to pick a sick child up from school or to take in a child or two when a baby-sitter failed to turn up. For all of us it had grown into an invaluable forum where we could share the indignities of toilet training or the anxieties induced by Charlie's most recent attack of croup or strep throat. By 1984 all such topics were taboo in smart Manhattan society. To talk about one's three-year-old at a party or in the office was a social *faux pas* of the first order; it might lead someone to suspect you of being 'just a housewife' – the contemporary non-person.

This particular Friday the women settled themselves around Sarah's dining-room table, which was laid with teacups and a big pot of Earl Grey tea. The children drifted off to Philip's room (Philip was Sarah's three-and-a-half-year-old) and were largely forgotten as the women launched hungrily into conversation.

Beth* had had something on her mind for two days. 'Hey,' she said eagerly, 'did anyone read that article in the *New York Times* on Wednesday where all those experts discussed how to teach your toddler to read?[1] Has anyone tried any of the new techniques they were talking about?'

Linda* had read the article and jumped in immediately with 'Don't talk to me about that article. It made me so angry I practically tore it up.'

Beth was surprised at the intensity of Linda's reaction and prodded her with a mild 'What do you mean?'

164

'Well, you see, I dislike that whole approach – the notion that mothers should try to get their kids on some cognitive fast track. It offends me. Imagine putting a three-year-old under that kind of pressure!' She paused and then added, 'Besides, who has time to fool around with multimedia techniques designed to teach simple skills that all children eventually pick up in school?'

Linda subsided. Her outburst was obviously related to the fact that she was the most career-oriented woman in the play group and spent a limited portion of the week with her children. A senior editor in the textbook division of a large publishing house, Linda still worked full time despite two toddlers. She had a stake in not taking these particular experts seriously.

Beth attempted a comeback. 'But Linda, some of these techniques don't take up much time, and they really work!' Warming to her subject, she went on to say, 'When Eric was two, I bought him a set of flash cards and those Fisher-Price magnetic letters. At that stage he was too young, and although I worked with him every afternoon, he didn't seem interested in learning. But last month I had a breakthrough. He finally asked for "those word games", and now we spend an hour or so every day learning the letters and sounds of the alphabet. You see it is just a question of persevering.'

Linda still looked unconvinced, so Beth had one last stab at converting her friend. 'Don't you think it will be wonderful if our kids can read before they hit kindergarten? You know, if I can give Eric that kind of advantage, I will really feel good about taking these years out of my career.'

I opened my mouth, intending to give Linda some support, but decided to close it again. I realised that this conversation was getting a little heavy. If Beth (one of the two non-working women in the group) was having trouble with her decision to stay at home and found teaching Eric to read an effective way of bolstering that decision, who was I to interfere? Besides, Beth's speech had served to trigger my own ever-sensitive store of maternal guilt. My children had never even owned a flash card, and it was also true that neither Lisa nor David could read. Their teachers assured me that both children were doing just fine, that when the time came they would learn easily, but in my heart of hearts I suspected that it was one of those areas where I was failing my children. They probably spent too much time with baby-sitters and not enough time with me.

Marcia* took over for me and stepped in with some evidence that supported Linda's policy of non-intervention. 'You know, Beth, I once heard a talk given by a child psychologist on precisely this subject. He said that it was wrong to encourage your child to read too early because the child might then focus exclusively on deciphering letters and words and lose the ability to concentrate on pictures, colours and shapes. I pushed Emily to read when she was four years old and she did it beautifully, but as soon as she could read, her artwork became much more restrained and rigid. It was as though all that struggling with words stifled her imagination, and she didn't have energy left over for anything else.' Marcia giggled. 'But I must admit that it's very convenient for me to revise my theories with Thomas [her second child]. Now I am working, there is no way I could find the time to teach him to read.'

She stopped for a while and then said more reflectively, 'I wish those child-rearing experts would let mothers off the hook. On the surface I can be very rational about decisions I make as a working mother, but in my gut I feel tremendously guilty about not sacrificing myself for Thomas the way I did for Emily.' She paused and, searching for words, said, 'It is as if I thought that women have no right to both have children and fulfil their own ambitions.'

Marcia's remarks seemed to touch a chord in Linda. Her face clouded, and she said in a subdued voice, 'I for one am always comparing myself to my mother. She had four kids – imagine that! – and yet was always so patient, so serene . . . I guess she was really proud to be a mother and homemaker.'

A pall had been cast over our small meeting. Several women looked pensive; others sighed and stirred restlessly. All of us were lost in thought. The conversation had exposed a collective raw nerve – maternal guilt. No matter what our individual choices, we all recognised that there are no easy ways of dumping society's extravagant expectations of how we should bear and rear our children. But why were all of us so passionately vested in being all-providing and all-encompassing mothers to our children? And why did we take direct personal responsibility for moulding perfect human beings? We were, after all, modern liberated women with other urgent goals to fill our lives. The explanation lay in our heritage. Not only did we carry the normal load of mothers – we loved our children, unreasonably and irrationally – but in addition, we had inherited (many of us unknowingly) the most powerful cult of motherhood this world has ever seen.[2]

The ultradomesticity of post-war America begat the ideal of complete motherhood. It is an ideal that haunts the consciousness of modern American women. Like Linda, many of my American contemporaries grew up during this era and tended to see motherhood fifties-style as the yardstick against which to judge their performance as mothers. It is also the standard against which US government policies are weighed. For this cult of motherhood convinced most politicians that children should be raised solely by their mothers, that there is no adequate substitute for mother love and mother care. For a generation, child-rearing experts declared that 'the worst natural mother is better in the long run than the best [day-care] mother'.[3] No wonder day care came to be seen as a third-rate alternative, suitable for the disadvantaged but not for 'normal' American families.

The odd thing is complete motherhood was a new idea in the late 1940s. The idea of devoting the better part of one's day to child care had seldom occurred to anyone. In every other culture throughout history, including America, mothers had always occupied themselves with other tasks and raised their children as a kind of parallel activity. In the 1930s mothers were even warned to stay away from their children and told to use day camps and nursery schools to foster independence. The conventional wisdom of pre-war America was that 'mother love is a dangerous instrument' liable to impede self-reliance in children.[4]

But fashions change, and with the new psychoanalytical perspective of the post-war period, child rearing became enshrined as the special responsibility of mothers. It was something only mothers could do and was more important than anything else they might do. Inspired by Sigmund Freud and Jean Piaget, a new post-war generation of child-rearing experts encouraged mothers to take responsibility for the psychological and cognitive development of the child and mould its total character and future potential. Any shortcoming in adult life was now seen as rooted in the failure of mothering during childhood. This was a remarkable view of child rearing, and it was to have serious repercussions on US government policy. How it became entrenched in post-war America is a fascinating tale.

Before the nineteenth century child-rearing practices the world over were dominated by the question of survival. Parents were much less involved in the lives of their children than today, largely because so few of these children survived infancy.

Three centuries ago, of every two babies born alive, only one was likely to be living on its first birthday. Evidence of the dreadful toll of death in childhood can be found in any seventeenth- or eighteenth-century churchyard. Take the colonial family of Cotton Mather. Cotton Mather had fourteen children. Seven Mather babies died soon after birth, one died at age two, and of the six who survived to adult life, five died in their twenties. In one epidemic of measles Cotton Mather lost his wife, a maid, and two daughters with resignation, but the death of a third daughter, little Jerusha, was almost too much for even this eighteenth-century Puritan to bear. 'Betwixt 9h and 10h at Night, my lovely Jerusha Expired. She was two years and about seven months old . . . I begg'd, I begg'd, that such a bitter cup, as the Death of that lovely child, might pass from me . . . Just before she died, she asked me to pray with her; which I did with distressed, but resigning Soul; and I gave her up unto the Lord. The Minute she died, she said, that she would go to Jesus Christ . . . Lord I am oppressed.'[5]

Although parents did grieve, often quite bitterly, losing one's children by death was so common that it fostered a resigned, even a detached attitude among parents, especially with regard to their younger children. In eighteenth-century France, Philippe Ariès reminds us, an infant who died was buried as casually as a pet cat or dog, for 'he was such an unimportant little thing . . . inadequately involved in life'.[6]

In England during this period similar attitudes held sway. In 1770 Hester Thrale, close friend of Dr Johnson and devoted mother of thirteen children, was extremely upset when one of her older children died but showed no grief over the deaths of her infants. Indeed, she took an instant dislike to one baby, saying that 'she is so very poor a creature I can scarce bear to look on her'. Later, when another newborn baby died, she commented, 'One cannot grieve after her much, and I have just now other things to think of.'[7] It is difficult to imagine a modern mother voicing such a sentiment.

If high rates of infant mortality engendered a detached attitude among parents in the pre-modern age, such detachment was further encouraged by the social and economic arrangements of the times. For example, up to the eighteenth century most children of wealthy parents were sent away to wet nurses until they were two or three years old. They then returned home to the care of servants and, at the age of seven, were often sent away again, either to serve apprenticeships or to attend school. Wet nurses ceased to be used in the early part of the last century, but servants and boarding schools severely limited contact between parents and children in middle- and upper-class circles until well into the twentieth century. It was not unusual for a professional middle-class household to have both a nanny and a nurserymaid. A conscientious nineteenth-century mother would supervise the care of her children, making sure that they ate wholesome food, dressed warmly in winter, behaved politely and said their prayers, but contact between mother and children was often restricted to an hour or less a day. Scrubbed and fed by Nanny and her helpers, a child would be allowed to sit in the parlour with Mother (and perhaps Father) for a short period at the end of the day. Occasionally an upper-class parent, fiercely determined to produce a genius, would devote innumerable hours trying to teach a small child to read Greek or to play Bach fugues on the piano, but these were rare and eccentric cases. Most affluent nineteenth-century mothers were content with a detached approach to child rearing.

Winston Churchill remembered his mother in the following terms: 'My mother always seemed to me a fairy princess: a radiant being possessed of limitless riches and power . . . She shone for me like the evening star. I loved her dearly – but at a distance. My nurse was my confidante.'[8] Churchill's mother was a beautiful upper-class socialite and, as was the custom in her circle at the end of the nineteenth century, saw very little of her son. However, servants were not peculiar to the upper classes, or indeed to Europe. Walter Lippmann, growing up in New York in the early years of this century, remembered his childhood as a time largely spent with servants and where contact with his mother was extremely limited.[9]

For working-class people of the eighteenth and nineteenth centuries, looking after children had to be a part-time activity because mothers were engaged, perforce, in arduous productive activity and expected their children to pitch in or, at the very least, not get in the way.

In pioneer families of the American frontier, 'for children of all ages, the daily work load was both physically demanding and time-consuming. For the younger ones [three to six years of age], there were the daily chores of carrying water buckets, gathering the buffalo chips and picking wild fruits. In later years they joined in the heavier work of plowing and planting, building fences and cabins, trapping small animals and helping about the house.'[10] In the tenements of the eastern cities a mother would park her small children in the corner of a crowded room while she stitched shirts for sale. Any child aged five or more would be expected to help out, either with household chores or in simple commercial tasks – match-making, for instance, was often done at home by small children on a piecework basis. Many children were sent to work in factories. Unfortunately, however, they tended to get sleepy in the afternoons and often 'mangled themselves in the machines'.[11]

As we enter the modern age, attitudes toward children change dramatically. The enormous medical advances of the late nineteenth and early twentieth centuries began to free parents from many of the health-related anxieties of the previous era. It was time to become more self-conscious about child rearing. The first modern school of thought on child-rearing practices emerged in the latter half of the nineteenth century and is associated with the names Luther Holt, Truby King and John Watson. These experts were to dominate the field of child rearing until the late 1930s. It comes as a shock to realise that their views of childhood and their recommendations to parents on how best to bring up children are as foreign to Dr Spock and the contemporary conventional wisdom as the thoughts of Dr Johnson's friend Mrs Thrale.

Luther Emmett Holt, a New York paediatrician, published his influential book *The Care and Feeding of Children* in 1894. Holt was obsessed with cleanliness – a sensible preoccupation in an age when childhood diseases could still end in death. Much of the book was concerned with the details of dealing with nipples and bottles and getting rid of germs. Breast-feeding was frowned upon as unscientific. Holt carried his concern for hygiene to the extreme of advising against mothers kissing their babies because of the dangers of transmitting tuberculosis, diphtheria, syphilis and other disease. Mothers were also discouraged from handling their babies in case they injured their spines or brains. Instead, they were to put them in playpens. 'A nursery fence two feet high, made to surround a mattress,' wrote Holt, 'makes an excellent box stall for the young animal.'[12]

The English equivalent of Holt was Truby King. He also believed passionately in proper hygiene and thought that raising babies in an environment as free from germs as possible was the most important aspect of caring for them. King paid little attention to mother love. To him a loving mother was no good to her infant if she infected him with lethal diseases.

Truby King worked out a scheme of rigidly regular four-hour feedings which became popular on both sides of the Atlantic. No baby was to be fed until the clock struck, no matter how much he cried. Most particularly babies were not to be fed at night. They had to learn to sleep at the proper times and not be allowed to manipulate and dominate their mothers by their demands. Regularity of bowel movements was seen as very important, and King advocated toilet training from the age of two months, aided by enemas if the baby did not perform. He advised against much physical contact between mother and child, particularly at bedtime.[13]

John B. Watson, who in America succeeded Holt as the most influential child-rearing expert of this period, was even more severe in his attitude toward maternal attachment. His major book, *Psychological Care of Infant and Child*, published in 1928, was dedicated to the first mother who brings up a happy child. He warned that doting mothers could retard the development of children, encumbering them with archaic values and constricting ties to the home. He maintained that excessive maternal affection rendered children incapable of assuming self-reliant positions in the adult world. '. . . remember, when you are tempted to pet your child that mother love is a dangerous instrument! An instrument which may inflict a never healing wound, a wound which may make infancy unhappy, adolescence a nightmare.'[14] Demonstrations of affection were therefore limited. 'If you must, kiss them once on the forehead when they say goodnight. Shake hands with them in the morning.'[15]

Watson's great complaint was that mothers were not sufficiently disciplined to keep away from their children for a large part of the day. 'I sometimes wish that we could live in a community of homes where each home is supplied with a well trained nurse so that we could have the babies fed and bathed each week by a different nurse . . . Somehow I can't help wishing that it were possible to rotate the mothers occasionally too.'[16] Most modern experts would disagree violently with such advice.

In more mundane matters Watson followed Holt and King in recommending feeding on a rigid schedule (and by bottle, not breast), early toilet training and such hardening techniques as moderate exposure to heat, cold and pain. The objective of these strict regimens was to foster the child's independence, which was then to be reinforced by the use of nursery schools and summer camps so that children could be emotionally weaned from their mothers.

It is easy to understand why this first modern school of child-rearing experts emphasised the dangers posed by germs and the importance of hygiene. By the turn of the century infant mortality was dramatically down but still significant enough to pose a real threat. Until the advent of antibiotics in the 1940s parents would have to devote some of their best energies to warding off infections and ensuring the physical health of their offspring. It is much harder to understand the rigid schedules, firm discipline and emotional distance advocated by this school of thought. These tenets are hard to come to terms with because they flout the spirit and purpose of all that modern mothers have been taught to believe in.

In the post-war world child-rearing theories underwent a revolutionary change. For mothers the pendulum swung from one extreme to another. In the thirties they were told to keep their distance and avoid harming the child with that dangerous instrument mother love. In the late forties the advice of the experts was the exact opposite. Now they were supposed to root the child in an all-encompassing maternal passion. As Erich Fromm put it in 1948, 'The child in these decisive first years of life [should have] the experience of his mother as the fountain of life, as an all-enveloping protective, nourishing power. Mother is food; she is love; she is warmth; she is earth. To be loved by her means to be alive, to be rooted, to be at home.'[17] Fromm clearly disagreed profoundly with Watson, Holt and King.

In the thirties, before Freudian enlightenment, mothers thought that they had done a good job if their children were healthy and well behaved. If a child also turned out to be dull and unimaginative that was generally blamed on genes or temperament, elements over which the mother happily claimed no control and for which she took no responsibility. In the post-war period child rearing became a much more demanding occupation, for 'Spock orientated mothers believed, deep in their hearts, that if they did their job well enough all of their children would be creative, intelligent, kind, generous, happy, brave, spontaneous, and good – each, of course, in his or her own special way'.[18]

Freud's contribution to the changing fashions in child rearing was his great emphasis on the importance of the maternal tie and of early childhood experience (particularly any traumatic childhood experience) on the development of the adult personality.[19] Freud's preoccupation with the oral, anal and phallic phases of psychological growth in the very first years of life and with such specific problems as anal retentiveness, penis envy, castration anxiety and oedipal conflict were seized upon by the post-war generation of child-rearing experts and translated into an impressive concern for mother–child separation, nursing, toilet training, sex-role identification and sibling rivalry. The fear was that if the early years were mishandled in any way, 'the child would be irretrievably fixated at that stage of abandonment and the child's character would carry with it a tiny spot of vulnerability for the rest of its life'.[20]

Spock, Fraiberg and others called upon mothers to expend a limitless amount of energy in protecting the child against a host of fears and anxieties which could, it was believed, produce deviant emotional growth and neurotic behaviour in the future. A single false step, a traumatic experience, might cause a child to develop insomnia, impotence or homosexuality later in life. The fact that between the trauma and the consequent neurosis could lie a seemingly normal childhood made the situation all the more unnerving. Like those long-incubating viruses that produce minor symptoms when they first enter the body and twenty years later result in multiple sclerosis, so parental miscalculations, misunderstandings, and mistakes might lead, after a long hiatus, to the most untoward consequences.

I have one extremely vivid memory of imagining the beginnings of neurotic behaviour in my then three-year-old daughter, Lisa.

The autumn and winter of 1981–2 had been hard, the family had moved to a new flat, and I had changed jobs. I liked my new position quite a lot, but the hours were fairly rigid, and the children had had to adjust to seeing less of me in the late afternoon and early evening than they had been used to.

In November Lisa started to twitch. The child did not seem to be aware of what she was doing, but every sixty seconds (I timed her) the left side of her face went into an involuntary slight spasm. Not wanting to give her a 'complex', I kept my mouth shut, hoping the twitching would just go away.

In December Lisa started to sniff. She didn't seem to have a cold; she just sniffed, about every sixty seconds, in between the twitches. I began to worry that these symptoms were the first signs of some deep neurosis. Something had gone wrong in Lisa's emotional development and the problem was leaking out in these twitching and sniffing symptoms. Perhaps we had been too authoritarian on the toilet-training front? Or maybe Lisa had failed to 'bond' with me and therefore was now having problems separating? I was certain that whatever the specific cause of these problems, it had something to do with my decision to continue in my career and not become a 'complete mother'. Aside from these large issues, there were also appearances to consider. Lisa had some important nursery school tests and interviews in January, and I very much wanted her to stop this behaviour by then. Besides, what would all the other mothers think? (Though I hated to admit it, I felt disapproved of by the non-working mothers of Lisa's friends and felt sure that this twitching and sniffing syndrome would be used as ammunition in the cause of putting down working mums.)

I plucked up my courage and tried talking to Lisa about her twitching and sniffing. Lisa did not appear to know what I was talking about, but she generally twitched and sniffed more rapidly after these conversations. Richard refused to take this family emergency at all seriously. Sometimes he said, 'Come on, Sylvia, don't let this thing get to you. Lisa's probably trying to get a little more attention, and if you stop attaching importance to it, she will give up. Just leave the kid alone.' Other times, when he found me stalking my twitching and sniffing daughter around the flat trying to pick up the scent of a neurosis or two, he would laugh uproariously – much to my chagrin. But then he had great trouble taking Freudian child development theorists seriously, and since he didn't take Lisa to school that year, he had never faced all those non-working mothers smirking at one's twitching and sniffing child.

By Christmas my more subtle energies were exhausted and I found that I had to clamp my mouth shut and sit on my hands in order to prevent myself yelling at or slapping Lisa as she twitched and sniffed her way through yet another family meal.

Lo and behold, the twitching and sniffing syndrome did go away later that winter (just after the nursery school tests!). One day Lisa just stopped. In retrospect, the family doctor blamed the symptoms on a low-grade upper-respiratory condition, Richard stuck to his attention-getting theory, and I secretly blamed it on myself. In my heart of hearts I suspected that those other mothers were right. It was a direct result of my new job. If I had not been working during those critical late-afternoon hours, if I had not taken this glamorous new job and 'put my career before my children', Lisa would never have developed such distressing symptoms. Of course, only I had thought Lisa's condition at all serious, but maternal guilt is such an extremely pervasive phenomenon that it is hard to avoid it, no matter what you do or don't do.

Three years and two children later I look back at this episode and have to concede that Richard had a point, it was pretty funny. But at the time I really believed that Lisa might have some major emotional problem. I had read enough Spock and Fraiberg to be nervous about any unusual behaviour and had a large enough store of job-related maternal guilt to be easy prey on the anxiety front.

Piaget did for cognitive skills what Freud had done for the emotional side of a child's life. In the 1920s and 1930s, Piaget developed a theory of cognitive growth which divided childhood into distinct developmental stages. The first two years of the infant's life, the period when language had not yet emerged, was described as the sensory motor period. From two to six years the child went through a pre-operational period, and from six to twelve years, a concrete operational period when he or she could begin to think logically and manipulate symbolically. Finally there was the formal operational period when all the characteristics of adult reasoning were potentially available to the adolescent.[21]

The concept of developmental stages lent itself to use – and considerable abuse – by post-war child-rearing experts. Authorities such as Burton White (whose sphere of influence was confined mainly to the United States) developed elaborate new tasks for mothers. There were ways of playing with, talking to, and encouraging baby so as to speed up the growth of cognitive skills and push him or her to the next stage of development. For example, a five-year-old who could be persuaded to perform concrete operations was said to have a mental age of six or seven. Mothers fuelled by the lure of turning their children into 'high-achieving' adults never questioned the benefit to the child of being ahead of his normal 'age-appropriate' stage of development. Never mind the conspicuous lack of evidence that child prodigies grow up into adult geniuses. (In fact, what evidence there is points the other way, that the great majority of precocious children do not fulfil their early promise.) Most European women were prepared to let their children take a chance, but thousands of American mothers, as Glenn Doman, chairman of the 'Institutes for the Achievement of Human Potential', rightly surmised, were willing to turn their best energies to the task of getting their child on the cognitive fast track. In 1975 he started intensive residential courses at his Better Baby Institute in Philadelphia. Lois Reed* was one of his students.

In the autumn of 1982, when her daughter, Julia, was nine months old, Lois Reed attended a seven-day course entitled 'How to Multiply Your Baby's Intelligence' at the Better Baby Institute in Philadelphia. She wanted to learn how to maximise her child's potential. Lois paid $500 tuition, plus the cost of her food and lodging.

During the morning sessions the chairman of the institute, Dr Glenn Doman, a kindly looking man with a white beard and glasses, lectured the eighty assembled mothers on the philosophy of the school. According to Doman, tiny children have limitless potential to learn. 'They can grow up speaking many tongues, fluently reading the most complex of languages, doing instant mathematics, swimming, riding horseback, painting in oils, playing the violin.' All of this by two or three, but *only if the mother provides enough love, joy, respect, and training.* Doman impressed on the mothers that if their babies did not get on to the fast track, it was their fault.

Other staff members then elaborated on the process of producing a 'Better Baby'. The mind of the young child was like the memory of a computer waiting to be programmed. It needed to be fed with data, and the earlier the input, the easier it was to enter. 'The ability to take in raw facts is an inverse function of age.' Stimulation should begin immediately after birth, by the mother's shining bright lights on and off into baby's eyes, clapping wooden blocks behind his head, and perhaps even putting a little mustard on his tongue. Once the baby had mastered this input – presumably by reacting – the next stage was to programme him to recognise shapes by holding huge black cards cut into triangles, circles, etc. between the light and his eyes. This training ensured that by the time he was a few months old he would be ready to learn the beginnings of reading. Although Lois had missed out on these two stages, it wasn't too late to save her baby's potential. By working especially hard and doing some catching-up exercises with Julia, she could move right on to the third stage – reading.

Teaching a baby to read involved the intensive use of flash cards with letters and simple words on them. If mothers conscientiously flashed cards in front of their child six times a day, it actually seemed possible to get most normal babies to read simple words (or at least go through the motions of reading them) by the time they were two years old. The afternoon sessions at the institute were devoted to technique and demonstration. To prove the efficacy of the institute's methods, properly trained one- and two-year-olds were brought into the auditorium to demonstrate their accomplishments.

Lois was dismayed by the sheer amount of time it seemed to take to produce a 'Better Baby'. If training a baby to read took six intensive sessions a day, and reading was but one of the several skills the institute deemed necessary to prepare your child for life, was a mother supposed to do nothing else with her life except devote herself to maximising her child's potential? And what of her daughter, Julia? Was it right and proper to bring Julia up to fulfil her potential if she was expected to turn around at the age of twenty-five or so and devote her best adult energies to *her* children? When Lois raised this question in class, Dr Doman quickly ruled it out of order and relegated her to the back row of the auditorium for the rest of the course. Only boys, apparently, are supposed to grow up to use their maximised potential in the outside world.

Thousands of mothers the length and breadth of America have attended the courses or bought the books and teaching kits of the Better Baby Institute and have religiously tried to improve their babies by sneaking up on them with scarlet flash cards bedecked with letters, dots and other 'pieces of information'. Some mothers attend these courses 'even before their child is conceived . . . so they'll be prepared to teach their infants math, reading, music and foreign languages with flashcards from birth'.[22] While it is not clear that these techniques have increased America's output of geniuses, they do seem to have added to American mothers' impressive load of maternal guilt and frustration.

Lois still feels that she let Julia down since she failed to teach her to read or do algebra by the age of two – or even five, for that matter. 'All those exercises made both of us irritable and anxious. I guess I couldn't put together enough joyful enthusiasm, and gradually I just gave the whole thing up.' Her inability to give her daughter that 'special edge of excellence' promised by the Better Baby Institute made Lois feel that she had failed in her maternal duties.[23]

Thus the theories of Freud and Piaget filtered down through Benjamin Spock, Burton White and the other post-war experts to leave the modern American mother with some weighty and time-consuming responsibilities. In his influential book *The First Three Years of Life*, White even inserts a graph purporting to show (scientifically) by what age mothers' arduous efforts at optimum child rearing would begin to show results. The typical onset of developmental divergence begins at nine months, and the well-developing child, spurred on by Mother, takes off on a special curve where he or she consistently outperforms his or her age group.[24] There is only one problem: there is no firm scientific evidence to support White's view that precocious nine-month-old babies will maintain their advantage throughout childhood and into adult life. According to Harvard psychologist Jerome Kagan, small differences in child-rearing techniques 'will have little predictive consequences for differences amongst [children] five or ten years hence'.[25] Factors such as a family's education, vocation, and income are much more powerful indicators of adult success. Despite this lack of evidence, any mother reading Burton White (as I did when Lisa was born) is left with an urgent sense that she has to work fast and hard.

Spock is perhaps the most disarming of the post-war experts. His advice is so down-to-earth, so practical, and he seems to be such a nice man! All of which is true, but Spock trained as a psychiatrist before becoming a paediatrician, and underlying the 666 pages of *Baby and Child Care* (in all three editions) are some rigorous Freudian assumptions about the role of the mother in child rearing. A mother is supposed to monitor her own behaviour so as to provide the proper environment for a child's 'self-realisation' through 'self-discovery' and 'self-motivated behaviour'. In fact, all the developmental tasks are now defined as mother work, for it is she who must preside over the teaching of bathroom protocol, restraint of aggression, and adjustment to peers. In toilet-training the child, Dr Spock instructs a mother to watch her toddler – if necessary for eighteen months – to see what stage of readiness he or she is in. Watching, considering whether or not to intervene, and determining the magnitude of insistence to use in guiding the child's potty behaviour are time-consuming and fraught with risk. For, as Spock points out:

[Toilet training is] actually the foundation for a lifelong preference for unsticky hands, for clean clothes, for a neat home, for an orderly way of doing business. It's from their toilet training that children get some of their feeling that one way of doing things is right and another way is not; this helps them to develop a sense of obligation, to become systematic people. So toilet training plays a part in the formation of a child's character and in building the basic trust between them and their parents.[26]

Selma Fraiberg in *The Magic Years* gives this classic Freudian theme even greater weight. She spends fifteen pages describing how a mother can go wrong potty-training her child. Elimination is vested with almost mystical significance. Fraiberg describes the child as regarding 'this act in the same way that an older child regards a gift to a loved person'.[27] To insensitively flush the faeces down the toilet is 'a strange way to accept an offering of such value'.[28] Moreover, the toilet itself has created quite new twentieth-century problems: 'This vitreous monster with its yawning jaws does not quite invite friendship or confidence at this age. The most superficial observation will reveal that it swallows up objects with a mighty roar, causes them to disappear in its secret depths, then rises thirstily for its next victim which might be – just anyone.'[29] Dealing with such a loaded scene is obviously a complex task, difficult to delegate to a baby-sitter. It is almost enough to make a working mother yearn for the simple discipline of Watson, who dealt with toilet training by recommending that at eight months a baby should be strapped on to a special toilet seat and left alone in the bathroom with the door closed for half an hour or so, however long it took before he or she performed.

The conventional wisdom of the early decades of this century was altogether easier on the mother. The advice of experts such as Holt and Watson trickled down to the general American population via a government department called the Children's Bureau, which began publishing a pamphlet called *Infant Care* in 1914. The early editions of *Infant Care* provoked thousands of letters from mothers requesting additional advice, and contrary to the traditions of the Washington bureaucracy, these letters were answered personally by the author of the original pamphlet, Mary West, and other staff members of the Children's Bureau. The tenor of the early editions of *Infant Care* as well as the responses to letters demonstrates that the convenience and needs of the mother were often put centre stage.

Infant Care, following the fashion of the day, touted strict scheduling, ignoring crying, and early toilet training and advised against rocking, tickling, or playing with infants. But *Infant Care* saw these rules as primarily protective of the mother: 'The care of a baby is readily reduced to a system ... Such a system is not only one of the greatest factors in keeping the baby well and in training him in a way which will be of value to him through life, but it also reduces the work of the mother to a minimum and provides for her certain assured periods of rest and recreation.'[30] For example, the use of a playpen was seen from the point of view not of the child but of the mother: thus 'an older child should be taught to sit on the floor or in his pen or crib during part of his waking hours, or he will be very likely to make too great demands upon his mother's strength'.[31] Mrs West comments sympathetically in one of her letters, 'No one who has not tried it realises how much nervous energy can be consumed in "minding" a baby who can creep or walk about, and who must be continually watched and diverted, and the mother who is taking the baby through this period of his life will need to conserve all her strength and not waste it in useless activity.'[32]

Contrast this with Burton White, who strongly urges mothers to do without playpens because 'there is no way of keeping most children from being bored'.[33] White sees everything from the child's point of view and has very strong feelings on the subject of playpens. 'To bore a child on a daily basis by the regular use of a playpen is a very poor child-rearing practice in terms of the child's educational needs.'[34] What is more, he extends the same principle to the use of cribs and high chairs. These prohibitions tend to guarantee that a mother has to creep around after her baby for the majority of the day.

Mrs West, the author of *Infant Care*, advocated a six o'clock bedtime. Again the main rationale is the convenience of the mother, for 'if you have not tried putting away your children at six o'clock, you have no idea what a relief it will be to you. It can be done, I have done it myself with three boys, and no mother who knows the satisfaction of having the care of her children cease before her evening meal, and the quiet comfort of a still household in the evening, would fail to immediately begin the training to make it possible.'[35] What mother would not respond to such advice! (When I discovered this passage in my research, I stopped and read it several times; it sounded like music to my modern ears. We are all so used to reading the child-centred contemporary advice which can make us feel either guilty or angry – depending on our level of confidence – but rarely soothes.)

Spock tells contemporary mothers that the central problem we should worry about at bedtime is making sure that it is 'agreeable and happy' for the child. 'Try not to rush going to bed no matter how much of a hurry you are in.' Don't 'turn it into an unpleasant duty', and above all, 'trust an infant to take what rest he needs'.[36] Not a word about how frayed a mother might be after a day of crawling around after her infant (or toiling away at her job).

Considering the developmental tasks given to the mother by post-war child-rearing experts, it is hardly surprising that these experts have heavily backed the notion that she stay out of the work force the better to perform her maternal duties.

For thirty years Spock (who is still the most widely read expert) told us that the children of working mothers may grow up neglected and maladjusted. Unless a mother absolutely must work, it makes no sense for her to 'pay other people to do a poorer job of bringing up [her] children'.[37] In the 1979 edition of *Baby and Child Care* Spock tries to adjust to modern times and to the fact that many mothers are now in the work force. He calls his babies she instead of he and inserts some language about women's liberation. But his heart is not in it. His preference is still that 'there will always be men and women who feel that the care of children and home is at least as important and soul satisfying as any other activity, and neither men nor women will feel the need to apologise for deciding to make that their main career'.[38] The very conditions he sets up for substitute care – continuity in the person of the caretaker for the first three years of life – would rule out a job for most women.

Paediatrician Berry Brazelton continues to come out against non-maternal care, putting forward the untestable argument that separation from the mother affects the child in ways 'that cannot be measured in observable behaviour',[39] and Selma Fraiberg stresses the dire consequences of maternal deprivation before a child is eighteen months old.[40] Burton White is even more emphatic. In 1981 he brought all his credentials to bear – as director of the Harvard Preschool Project – in a heavy-handed piece of advice to American mothers: 'For more than 20 years I've specialised in the study of successful child-raising . . . I've had the privilege of being able to compare the everyday experience of many children getting off to a fine start in life with those not so fortunate . . . I firmly believe that most children will get off to a better start in life when they spend the majority of their waking hours being cared for by their parents.' White goes further: 'Government . . . should resist the cries for free full time substitute care for babies for all who want it.'[41]

Interestingly enough, Burton White is so caught up in hostility toward working mothers that he does not devote any attention to maternity leave. Given his conviction that the first six months of life are absolutely critical and that the child 'has to be responded to intensely in this period',[42] you would think that he would urge the US government to guarantee a maternity leave for working women that lasted at least this long. Not so. White concentrates on advising mothers to stay out of the work force. As he told me in March 1983, 'I am not too interested in advocating maternity leave as this might encourage the mothers of young children to stay in the work force.'[43] Unfortunately, in the mid-1980s, 48 per cent of American mothers with children under twelve months old are already in the work force, and most of them work out of economic necessity. What these women need is decent maternity leave and high-quality child care, not another guilt trip.

Despite the enormous changes in society and the world economy since the 1950s, the popular child-rearing manuals on both sides of the Atlantic are still grounded in the assumptions and prescriptions of the post-war world. As a survey in the medical journal *Pediatrics* concludes: 'popular literature still regards the working mother as deviant'.[44] The early 1980s have seen a further flood of books on child rearing, and once again working mothers are either ignored, or segregated in a section on 'special problems'. For example, in 1984 the second most popular book on child rearing (after Spock) was *Babyhood* by the British writer Penelope Leach. In a thoughtful chapter on mother-infant attachment Leach makes absolutely no mention of the working mother.[45]

But despite all this hostility toward the working mother on the part of the child-rearing 'experts', the serious scholarship in the field casts doubt on the notion that working mothers raise less happy or less successful children. In a highly respected study Jerome Kagan, Richard B. Kearsley and Philip R. Zelazo find that 'attachment to the mother and rate of cognitive development . . . did not appear to be altered by day care . . . The assessments of language, memory, and perceptual analysis failed to reveal any obvious advantages or disadvantages to the day care experience . . . all the children preferred the mother to any other adult by a factor of 7.'[46] In an exhaustive review of the evidence, the psychologist Claire Etaugh finds that 'high quality non-maternal care does not seem to have adverse effects on the young child's maternal attachment, intellectual development or social-emotional behaviour'.[47]

It seems that young children can form as strong an attachment to a working parent as to a non-working one if the parent plays frequently with the child during the times they are together and provided that the substitute care arrangements are stable and stimulating. A major conclusion of the research in the field is that 'satisfied mothers – working or not – have the best adjusted children'.[48] Another finding in the maternal employment literature is that the children of working mothers perceive women as being more competent than do the children of non-working mothers. In a similar vein, the daughters of working women have higher aspirations for themselves than do the daughters of non-working women.[49] All of which makes intuitive sense; once one stops focusing on the first three years of life and takes a longer view and considers those other influences in later life, the role model a woman presents to her children becomes centrally important.

Policy makers need not be inhibited by Benjamin Spock (or Burton White for that matter); day care need not harm children. There are, of course, some things to avoid. Young children develop badly if they are physically neglected, if they have no continuity in people entrusted with their care, and if they are placed in care with such low adult-child ratios that they have no individual attention. But 'attendance at a day care centre should not in itself affect the child's development in serious ways, as long as the parents hold a positive attitude toward their children and the surrogate caretakers are nurturant, attentive and conscientious'.[50] In short, there is no evidence that begins to suggest that 'the worst natural mother is better in the long run than the best [day-care] mother'.[51]

The irony is that so little attention and so few resources have been devoted to day care in America that much of what exists is substandard. This tends to reinforce this nation's ideological bias against out-of-home care. 'A lot of what we have today in commercial day care [in the United States] is kennels,' says Dr Irving Lazar of Cornell University, 'and in a kennel there is no opportunity for learning.'[52] Dr Lazar is right. American parents do not want kennels for their children. Unfortunately, until the US government decides to subsidise child care on a substantial scale, millions of American children will be forced to spend their days in kennels. It is not that America doesn't know how to run high-quality day-care centres, for the United States has done more research on early-childhood development than any other country. It's just that America has decided not to allocate public resources to small children.

But how does America compare with the other industrial countries of Western Europe when it comes to its post-war cult of motherhood? In many European countries one can detect a similar swing in child-rearing fashions from the discipline and rigid schedules of the 1920s and 1930s to the psychological and developmental preoccupations of the post-war era. In Europe as well as in America this led to greater maternal involvement in child rearing (especially since this swing coincided with a decline in the availability of nannies and other household servants). However, there were significant countervailing trends in Europe which precluded the development of a cult of motherhood.

To begin with, in contrast with the American experience, most European nations did not undergo an extended baby boom in the post-war period. In 1955, for example, the US birthrate was running at 25 per 1,000 of the population, while in France the figure was 18.5; in Britain, 15.4; and in Germany, 15.7.[53] The lower European birthrate was accompanied by a steady rise in female employment. In 1950 only 37 per cent of American women were in the work force, compared with 44 per cent in Germany and 50 per cent in France.[54] This difference in work-force participation meant that European countries were forced to grapple much earlier with issues of maternity leave and substitute care, and mothers did not pick up so many responsibilities.

Secondly, America has always been more child-centred than Europe and therefore likely to provide the most fertile ground for a cult of motherhood. Children were scarce and therefore prized in that long-underpopulated country, and there is also a firmly entrenched regard for the importance of the individual. Indeed, 'Europeans have always felt that American parents paid far too much regard to their children's needs and far too little to the demands of adult social occasions.'[55]

Thirdly, there is a pronounced tendency for American parents to consider the child at least as important as themselves – perhaps potentially more important than they. An English anthropologist once said that whereas in other countries children were taught to look up to their parents as rather distinguished superior people whatever their objective place in the society, the remarkable thing about the United States is that parents will say to their child, 'If you don't do better than I've done, I won't think much of you.'[56]

This expectation of upward mobility goes along with two other distinctively American traits: geographic displacement and the lack of a firm class structure. In much of Europe, particularly conservative Catholic countries like France and Italy, parents absorb the goals and methods of child rearing from family traditions and from having grandparents nearby to advise and help them. These props are often lacking in America. Massive immigration and frequent moves (between cities and between regions in search of better economic opportunities) mean that American parents are often bringing up their children hundreds of miles away from relatives and in a socioeconomic context that may be quite different from that of their own parents. So they are much more likely to turn to professional advisers, books and new fashionable theories for the help they need. This obviously increases the impact of any new style in child rearing. In Italy I was impressed by the fact that bookshops in major cities carried very few manuals on child rearing. Italian mothers I interviewed relied mainly on family tradition.

Claudia* grew up in northern Italy, came to the US as a student, and married a New York businessman. She is now bringing up her children 'American style' and has an extremely clear sense of the difference between the cultures.

'In Italy young marrieds are supposed to have a good time, and it is perfectly OK to hand the baby over to relatives for large chunks of time. Some friends of mine, who live in Genoa, seem to go skiing or sailing most weekends. A grandmother and a spinster aunt live just around the corner and are delighted to take the children.' Claudia paused for a moment and then said disapprovingly, 'It is all very convenient for the parents, but it does mean that child-rearing practices remain dreadfully old-fashioned. You know I bought Sonia [the wife of the couple that lives in Genoa] a copy of Dr Spock's book when her second child was born, and I am sure that she hasn't even opened it. She says she doesn't like modern ideas, and I suppose that since the family are doing all the child care, she cannot turn around and tell them how to do it.'

I asked Claudia what she thought about traditional Italian methods of bringing up children. She confessed to a great deal of ambivalence. 'I suppose it has its good points. Children get a lot of affection from their relatives, they are allowed to stay up late, and in many ways childhood is very enjoyable in Italy; but really, attitudes about how to develop emotional maturity and cognitive skills are very primitive.' I asked Claudia to give me an example. After a little thought she said, 'A woman friend of mine runs a small business in Milan. She hired a nanny for her baby when he was three months old. When I saw her last summer, her child was about a year old, and she boasted to me that he was no trouble at all, that her nanny was able to leave him in his playpen all day long, and that he didn't bother anyone. Imagine,' said Claudia with a smile, 'an American middle-class mother boasting about such a thing. Why, here in America everyone knows that a child needs constant stimulation, and the last thing one should do is confine a child in a playpen all day long!' Claudia had read all the well-known American child-rearing manuals and had found Selma Fraiberg and Burton White particularly illuminating. As she put it, 'Fraiberg's book *Every Child's Birthright* convinced me that I should give up my career when Jonathon was born. It made me realise that no one could take my place.' Claudia paused and then added hesitantly, 'The odd thing is I would never have read those books had I stayed in Italy, and as a result, I wouldn't have given up my profession for my children.'[57]

In Britain the influence of American-style baby books has, perhaps, been felt more strongly than elsewhere in Europe. This is partly because the family structure in Britain is not as strong as it is in, say, Catholic France or Italy, which has meant that, particularly among the mobile middle classes, not everyone has had a willing grandmother just up the road who can drop in with a word of friendly advice. Therefore, the young British mother is more likely to go and buy a book on the subject than her French sister. Also, as Britain shares a common language with America, there are many more American child-care manuals published in this country than in the rest of Europe.

However, bombarded by, often conflicting, advice from the transatlantic child-care experts and a few closer to home, the modern British mother appears to be taking it all in her stride. In her refreshing book *How Not To Be A Perfect Mother*, writer and broadcaster Libby Purves cheerfully faces the fact that a busy working mother has neither the time nor the inclination to chase after a mischievous two-year-old all day, let alone indulge in some of the more esoteric exercises subscribed to by Glenn Doman. Instead, she suggests striking a balance between your own needs and those of the child, and sometimes letting your own needs come first — although she is also honest in saying that even this is not particularly easy to achieve, and the parental guilt does have an uneasy habit of creeping up on you:

Going off to work is all right; going out for pleasure feels terribly selfish. Yet the need for rough, physical, arm-swinging childfree exercise is overwhelming. A 'walk' with a buggy (shoulders rounded in defeat, little tripping steps) or with a dawdling two-year-old is not a real walk at all. It does not blow off any steam; it makes you tired in a snappish, unhealthy way. So does sitting in an office; the combination of both can drive you crazy.

So the occasional burst of private activity (or, if you prefer, private sloth) is worth planning for when you organise yourself back to work. This is a counsel of perfection; the balancing act between guilt at not hurrying home, and the irritation at not having any selfish pleasures is not one I have ever quite mastered.

I once took my 20-month-old son on a business trip to Plymouth, complete with Nanny, and we all shared a vast room at the Holiday Inn. What with the nanny lurching back in the small hours after a night out with half the navy, Nicholas getting overexcited about the bouncy beds, and room service forgetting to warm the milk for breakfast, it was all pretty intense. But the only thing none of us suffered from was guilt.[58]

In Britain, too, there is now a nationwide organisation for working mothers which produces its own 'child care manual'. *The Working Mother's Handbook* is full of practical advice about how best to juggle the demands of home and work, how to go about finding a childminder, what questions to ask when interviewing a girl for a job, how to deal with National Insurance etc. for your new nanny. At the back of the book there is a section devoted to working mothers' experiences. Take Jenine:

My key to surviving as a working mum, now I have a reliable childminder, is having a routine. Organisation doesn't come easily to me, but now our family has a weekday system things more or less run smoothly. Paul gets Amy up and dressed each morning while I prepare and give her breakfast. In the evening Paul gives Amy her tea, we play for an hour and then it's her bathtime and bed by 7.30 p.m. I never do any housework during the week apart from washing up and clearing away toys each evening. Now I have come to terms with the fact that I'm not a superwoman and I can't fit in everything I think I should do, I can enjoy my job during the day and Amy's and Paul's company the rest of the time.[59]

Jenine's routine is a 1980s version of the Truby King style of child care. She has allocated a sensible amount of time to each aspect of her life – work, the home, her family – and neither she nor her family appear to have suffered in any way. Nor does Jenine have a trace of guilt.

And so, British women today take the advice of the likes of Spock less seriously than their American counterparts, and are often more realistic about what they can achieve in a day only twenty-four hours long.

Whereas American post-war governments' child-care policies were deeply influenced by current thinking among child-care 'experts', in Europe a very different policy climate reigned. For example, in the late forties France developed a whole range of benefits and services to support the family. A family allowance system was instituted, infant nurseries (crèches) were publicly subsidised for the first time, and the network of public nursery schools (*écoles maternelles*) was greatly expanded. By the 1950s most French three- to five-year-olds were enrolled in these *écoles maternelles*.[60] An explicit goal of these family support policies was that mothers be free to choose between staying at home or working in the outside world.

Contrast this with America, where the belief that mothers should stay at home and look after their own children reverberates through post-war policy. In 1960, at the beginning of the Kennedy administration, a conference was convened at the White House to consider services to working mothers and children. The main recommendations of this conference were:

– that to maintain the important relationship of infant and mother, children under 3 should remain in their own homes unless there are pressing social or economic reasons for care away from home.
– that social casework and other counselling services be available both before and during employment of the mother, to help parents decide wisely whether her employment will contribute more to family welfare than her presence in the home.[61]

These recommendations could have been taken directly from Spock. In *Baby and Child Care* he says, 'If a mother realises clearly how vital this kind of care is to a small child it may make it easier to decide that the extra money she may earn . . . is not so important after all.'[62] Needless to say, this conference did not spur much action on the public child-care front. There was a small federal appropriation for day care in 1962 ($4 million), but it was cut out of the budget in 1965.[63]

By 1971 a third of all pre-school children had mothers in the US labour force, and Congress did pass the Comprehensive Child Development Bill (sponsored by Senator Walter Mondale and Representative John Brademas) in December of that year. It was promptly vetoed by Nixon. Nixon took a strong ideological stance. He talked emotionally about his desire to 'cement the family in its rightful position as the keystone of our civilisation'[64] and stated categorically that 'good public policy requires that we enhance rather than diminish both parental authority and parental involvement with children – particularly in those early years when social attitudes and a conscience are formed'.[65]

According to Nixon, it was OK to have day care 'for the children of the poor so that their parents can leave the welfare rolls', but it was 'unacceptable to encourage or support middle-class mothers who leave the home'.[66] Nixon seemed not to know – or to care – that a third of these mothers had already left home for the workplace, and most of these women were propelled by economic pressures. His veto did not resurrect motherhood 'fifties-style'. It merely left 'thousands of children with no care and hundreds of thousands of others in inadequate and sometimes even destructive care'.[67]

Nixon couched his 1971 veto in such strong ideological language that the Comprehensive Child Development Bill could not be revived; he had succeeded in re-establishing day care as an un-American activity. A scaled-down version of the bill was introduced – again by Mondale and Brademas – in 1975, but no action was taken by either the Senate or the House.

In 1983, at the time of my interview with Faith Whittlesey at the White House, half of all pre-school children had mothers in the work force, yet despite this trend line, Whittlesey assured me that Ronald Reagan was confident that once the economy picked up, 'all those women can go home and look after their own children in the way they did when I was growing up'.[68] As if to encourage this return to complete motherhood, the Reagan administration has been careful to cut back even further America's very modest commitment to public child care: funds which provide child-care subsidies to poor families have been cut by 21 per cent since 1980.

In some of its aspects the culture of America in the 1950s seems strange but distant. A re-run of *I Love Lucy* is not threatening because most of us recognise the styles and values of the show as a relic from another age. Not so when we come to fifties attitudes toward motherhood and child rearing. The cult of motherhood is alive and well and living in America; standards of parenthood in the United States are still set by the 'smother love' of the 1950s. Images of the complete, all-providing mother remain powerful enough to furnish working American women with a bottomless pit of maternal guilt. It was this guilt that reverberated around my local play group on innumerable Friday afternoons.

My children were born in 1977, 1980, and 1984, and I have been an active consumer of child-rearing manuals for the better part of the last decade. Every few years I make the dreary round and discover that the most recent edition of Spock, Brazelton and White, and the new best-sellers by Leach and Salk, continue to pretend either that mothers don't work (Leach), or that mothers can deal with their work commitments during a baby's nap time (White). The overwhelming message remains: Mothers should devote themselves to their children for the first three years of life, mothers are responsible for developing a child's total potential, and full-time work is incompatible with good mothering. The fifties lure is held out to the eighties mother: 'that with attentiveness, emotional vigilance and her uninterrupted presence she can provide an environment from which a superior individual will emerge'.[69] As Nancy Weiss has so aptly put it, 'child rearing manuals might [well] be renamed mother rearing tracts'.[70]

The advice of the child-rearing 'experts' is irresponsible and counter-productive in the modern world. It is irresponsible because there is no evidence that supports the notion that mother-intensive child-rearing techniques constitute the only good way of bringing up children. And it is counterproductive because it impedes the development of sensible child-care policies, particularly in America. The majority of mothers work, and the misguided notion that governments cannot and should not help provide a substitute for mother love and mother care has prevented the United States from creating high-quality day-care facilities. As a result, millions of children spend their waking hours in 'kennels', and their mothers (and fathers) are subjected to high levels of strain and stress. The glorification of the fifties mother and the fifties approach to mothering helps explain why child-centred America can be so neglectful toward children.

One more question needs to be answered. If modern Americans can put Doris Day and Lucille Ball in perspective and recognise that being a dizzy blonde or a nincompoop is not going to get one very far in the 1980s, why can't they do the same with Benjamin Spock and Burton White? After all, their values and methods are equally at cross-purposes with the needs of America in the 1980s.

When Adam was born in the spring of 1984, I picked up Burton White's *The First Three Years of Life* and felt my anxiety level rise as I read, once again, of all the tasks I should be engaged in to give my son a head start in life. I had a little perspective but clearly not enough. (Adam was, after all, my third child, and I had done all this research on child rearing and knew that my grandparents had followed the advice of Truby King. Consequently, my parents had received lots of discipline but little maternal attention. They had turned out OK; why shouldn't my kids?) But somehow I couldn't put the cult of motherhood into the same distant, unthreatening perspective as Doris Day and fifties ideas of femininity.

This is because the modern women's movement has helped us change our image of women – particularly of women as workers – but has failed to deal with motherhood. As we saw in Chapter Seven, the American women's movement has alternatively ignored or reviled mothers, which has not put feminists in a good position to either understand or come to grips with the cult of motherhood. True, the movement has been concerned with issues such as regaining control over the birth process and raising children in a non-sexist way. But this feminist agenda has served to add to the long list of maternal responsibilities rather than lighten the load.

This failure of the American women's movement to connect with motherhood and family has had some extremely serious repercussions. It has made modern American mothers vulnerable to the expectations of Spock and

White because they are not equipped with an alternative vision of how to mother. Feminism has given women alternatives to Doris Day. Whether one's tastes run to Geraldine Ferraro or Jane Fonda, most of us understand that nowadays it is good to be an accomplished, independent woman. But on the mothering front American women have merely added to the burdens of the fifties. As one eminent New York obstetrician put it, 'Modern superwomen take it for granted that they can hold down a job as vice-president of Chase Manhattan Bank, give birth naturally, and breastfeed. Few realise before the fact that this is an impossible set of demands.'[71]

Had coming to terms with motherhood been a central task of American feminism, the women's movement might have cut the overblown fifties vision of mothering down to size. Women might also have acquired some concrete help in discharging maternal responsibilities. For the failure of the women's movement to deal with motherhood left a vacuum in public policy which was filled by traditionalists. These men (and women) are all too comfortable with the fifties notion of complete motherhood and find it easy to stick their heads in the sand and pretend that maternity leave or child care aren't necessary. They glorify 'Mom and apple pie' and believe that it is 'unacceptable to encourage or support middle-class mothers who leave the home'.[72] For we should not underestimate the powerful hold the decade of the fifties has on the American imagination. Many mainstream Americans – not just Jesse Helms and Phyllis Schlafly – would like nothing better than to return to that golden age. Their vision is, of course, a nostalgic vision and has little to do with modern America, yet it has informed government policies on the child-care front. The women's movement, which should have been the countervailing force, producing policies which more nearly fitted the needs of contemporary families, was busy on other fronts. And because feminists abdicated their rights to this important territory, family policy in America has become the preserve of nostalgic traditionalists.

Of course, the real victims of the lack of state-aided child care and job-protected maternity leave are working-class women and their children. A vice-president of Chase Manhattan Bank might have a rough time of it when she attempts to breast-feed without missing a beat on the work front, but Chase Manhattan has a decent maternity policy (decent, that is, by American standards), and the odds are she can afford to pay the market rate for a full-time nanny. For fast-food waitresses and shop assistants, the consequences of a lack of support policies are more severe. Most of them have no rights to maternity leave, and they can't afford adequate child care. Tell them that America is a nation that venerates mothers and children, and they will tell you a different tale.

Revolt and Reaction

11. The Unravelling of the Fifties

In the spring of 1968, while I was a graduate student at Harvard, I attended a two-day conference in San Francisco. On my way back to Cambridge, Massachusetts, I met Nancy Barrett.* Her life story throws into sharp relief the painful undoing of the fifties.

I had left the conference a few hours later than expected and, as a result, missed my flight to Boston. The next direct flight was full, so eager to get back before the weekend, I booked myself onto a plane to Chicago which had a connecting flight to Boston. Once aboard, I had settled down with a pile of conference papers, intending to do a little serious reading, when I realised that the woman sitting next to me was quietly crying. She was a pretty blonde woman of about forty. In her fresh spring suit and matching accessories she looked well groomed enough to have stepped straight out of the pages of *Good Housekeeping*. At first I thought that she was merely shedding a tear or two on account of saying good-bye to her husband or children at the airport. But as time went on, the discreet, ladylike sobs became more desperate, and small moans of misery began to escape the damp wads of Kleenex she had hidden behind. I offered her a handkerchief and made sympathetic noises. In return she began to confide in me. To begin with, she talked mostly to let out some of her pain, but after a while she came to see me as a potential ally, a sympathetic member of a generation that she found alien and damaging.

Nancy Barrett was returning from a week in San Francisco, where she had been visiting her three children, all of whom had dropped out of school and were living in the counter-cultural mecca of Haight-Ashbury. Her eldest child, Franny, had dropped out of college when she was nineteen; her two sons, Mark and Robert, aged sixteen and seventeen respectively, had recently dropped out of high school. All were into drugs and chic revolutionary movements. Nancy was particularly worried about Franny, who she thought was being exploited by the 'hip' man she was living with. As Nancy put it

191

rather bitterly, 'In the last year Franny has had two illegal abortions, at least one of them dangerously late. She had to come to her parents for the money to pay for them because her groovy man wasn't into responsibility.' These thoughts occasioned a fresh outburst of weeping, and it soon transpired that Nancy's problems went beyond the countercultural rebellion staged by her children.

As Nancy saw it, her entire world – the safe, predictable world of the 1950s – was coming down about her ears. In her teens Nancy had been an exemplary student and a talented violinist, but as was the fashion in the post-war period, she had married while still at college. She had then left college to take a clerical job in order to help pay for her husband, John, to go through medical school.

The years when the children were little had been tough. John's housemanship had been followed by military service and a series of jobs in teaching hospitals up and down the east coast. They had little money and moved, on average, once every eighteen months. Since John worked long, hard hours on the job, Nancy had pretty well managed the domestic scene and brought up the children on her own. Eight years ago they were finally able to reap the rewards of their hardworking partnership. John obtained a prestigious appointment at Northwestern University and started a lucrative private practice, while Nancy settled into a gracious home in the suburbs. She took up tennis, became active in the PTA, and even started playing the violin in local amateur groups.

But the suburban idyll was soon shattered. First came the rebellion of the children. Somehow, somewhere, all three kids had learned to despise their parents. They acquired weird friends, wore their hair long and dirty, were abusive to adults, smoked pot, played truant from school, allowed their school work to slip out of sight, and finally absconded to Haight-Ashbury. John's reaction had been one of disgust and disillusionment. 'Why have I striven all these years to be a good provider if all I get is ingratitude!' was his oft-repeated refrain. According to Nancy, John was now thoroughly alienated from the children. He had refused recent requests for money from both Franny and the boys and did not want to see any of them until they 'shaped up'.

Nancy, on the other hand, was still trying to bridge the gulf between the generations. She started to cry again. 'When I see how vulnerable, how bewildered my kids are, and when I read about teenagers dying from drug overdoses, I feel such anguish I have to try to help them.' It turned out that Nancy had not been visiting her children in Haight-Ashbury, but had gone, uninvited, to try to bring them home. She had pretended to her husband that she was visiting her sister and her brother-in-law. John would have prevented her from going had he known that she was going to try to see the 'ingrates' (he could easily do that since she didn't have any money of her own).

Nancy had succeeded in tracking down Franny and Mark and had talked to them – to no avail. Fran had told her that she had no intention of becoming a plastic, sanitised suburbanite like her mother, and Mark had been too stoned to say anything coherent at all. As for Robert, she had not even been able to find him, and she was incredibly anxious because one of his friends had told her that he was in Mexico dealing drugs. 'My poor baby, for all I know he might be dead or in some Mexican jail.'

If Nancy's problems had started with the defection of her children, the current crisis centred on her husband. His disillusionment with family life ran so deep that in recent months he had had at least three affairs, all with much younger women. Two were graduate students; the other was a secretary at the university. John had recently bought himself an Alfa Romeo sports car and had taken to reading *Playboy* and wearing bell-bottomed jeans. Nancy was terrified that he was going to ask her for a divorce. That prospect truly frightened her. As she put it, 'The thing is, I have no skills. All I can do is give violin lessons to little kids, and what kind of income does that bring in? Maybe a thousand dollars a year!'

By the time the plane landed at O'Hare Airport in Chicago Nancy and I were enthralled with each other. I was fascinated by her story. She was tremendously excited at having found a member of the sixties generation who was willing to listen and even to sympathise with her side of the story. Nancy impulsively invited me to spend the weekend at her home, and instead of getting my connecting flight to Boston, I found myself shaking hands with a rather startled John Barrett and being driven in a large, luxurious car to Evanston. Conversation was strained. Nancy had put on fresh make-up just before we landed, and with her husband she was perky and bright, full of tales of her sister's new house and her brother-in-law's new job. John was courteous enough but quite distant. As soon as he had unloaded the luggage and fixed the drinks, he disappeared to his study 'to catch up on some work'.

My weekend in Evanston was full of strange and oddly moving experiences. I still remember some of the scenes. I had cocktails with Nancy on the fortieth floor of some new skyscraper in the Chicago Loop and saw the streets below us fill with smoke and angry lurching shadows as blacks reacted with violence to the news of Martin Luther King's assassination. That particular evening the rioting became so ugly that the National Guard was called out and a curfew was imposed in the downtown area. Somehow these scenes of violence and frustration seemed a fitting backdrop to our talk, which centred on the clash between values and between generations.

That night Nancy, talked out and exhausted, went to bed early. I, on the other hand, was far from sleepy; my imagination had been working overtime. About midnight I went down to the Barretts' kitchen and was making myself some tea when I was startled out of my wits by a hand on my shoulder. It was John Barrett. He now wanted to talk, to pour out to me his side of the story. No one had ever understood how hard it was to make it in his profession and how little psychological support he had ever received from his wife or children. All they had ever understood was 'how to spend my money'. I can remember wanting to listen and understand better where this troubled and isolated man was coming from. But he touched me again and muttered something about the sexual revolution, and I knew the time had come to beat a hasty retreat. Clutching a teacup in my hand, I muttered good night and backed up the stairs to my room.

That next week, when I got home, I sent Nancy Barrett some flowers – a token of my appreciation for her hospitality and her trust. She called me to say thank you and to tell me that she had decided to enrol for a master's degree in education. She was preparing herself for a belated teaching career and a lonely middle age. She made one bitter comment: 'Given my age, I guess teaching is the best thing I can do, but I will never earn even a quarter of John's salary.'

Nancy Barrett's story contains many of the ingredients of post-war American social history. It conjures up the extremely divided world of the 1950s, when men and women led such separate lives. Nancy kept house and reared the children while John clambered up the slippery pole of career success. Nancy's life story also runs full tilt into the counter-cultural explosion of the mid-sixties. It was a time when many young people rejected the lifestyles of their parents and dropped out of the system. By moving to Haight-Ashbury and taking up drugs and chic radical causes, Franny, Mark and Robert were merely doing the same as hundreds of thousands of their contemporaries.

By the time I met Nancy in the late sixties, she and her husband were themselves poised on the edge of major changes to their lives. Her husband was ready to kick over the traces. He had had his fill of life in the work harness, bringing home the bacon for a bunch of ungrateful children. He was ready to spend money on himself and experiment with (sexually liberated) younger women. After all, his children were reaping the rewards of the sexual revolution. Why shouldn't he?

Nancy herself was beginning to face a very different future from that which she either wanted or expected. She did go ahead with her post-graduate course, and in the autumn of 1968 John left her, taking off into the sunset with one of his post-graduate students. Nancy's experience was not unusual. The American divorce rate doubled between 1965 and 1975, and millions of 'displaced homemakers' became downwardly mobile as they struggled to earn some sort of a living in their middle years. I was last in touch with Nancy in 1970. I called her from O'Hare Airport; I was changing planes again and had thirty minutes to spare. The news was not good. She had not seen her children recently. Franny and Robert had joined a commune in New Mexico, and Mark was in India, where he had linked up with some religious sect. John had ceased to pay alimony, and the lawyers could not track him down. Nancy was deeply in debt and, although she had qualified as a teacher, she had not yet found a job. The only bright spot on the horizon was that she had just joined a consciousness-raising group and was feeling good about having found some supportive women.

Why has post-war America been so marked by fierce clashes between the generations and violent battles between the sexes – more so than any other country in the Western world? A large part of the explanation lies in the cosy and oppressive world of post-war America. For the fifties succeeded in defining men and women in an exceedingly narrow way, and both sexes expended a great deal of energy in a struggle to break loose and better fulfil their individual identities.

It is often not fully understood how aberrant American society was during those formative post-war years. In the late forties and fifties Americans developed a type of exaggerated role playing that was deeply at odds with history. As described in earlier chapters of this book, the United States has a long tradition of independence and equality, and Americans, both men and women, have cherished a reputation for strength. But during this post-war period relationships between the sexes became deeply distorted, and America is still suffering the consequences of this distortion, for many of the subsequent clashes and battles can be explained as waves of reaction to what was a profoundly artificial social scene.

America in the fifties was also out of step with other advanced democracies. The courtship rituals, the role of the housewife and the role of the breadwinner all seem to have been more intricately wrought – and more onerous – than in other Western nations. As David Bouchier has put it, 'the baroque elaboration of the full-blown American suburban life' was outside the experience of Europeans.[1]

When I was growing up in a backward corner of South Wales in the fifties, tales and images of the strangely elaborate and exotic roles played by American men and women drifted across the Atlantic – via television, films and novels. The courtship rituals seemed to start early. The thought of having a boyfriend at the age of twelve ('mere children,' our parents would mutter) and pink tulle gowns and tuxedos to school dances (just like royalty!) made us British teenagers very discontent as we struggled into our short white socks and bottle-green uniforms and dragged off to our single-sex schools.

As an undergraduate at Cambridge in the mid-1960s I knew a few American men. I remember thinking that they seemed to spend a lot of time running around cars opening doors for able-bodied young women, and most were distressingly eager to spend lots of money on girls they hardly knew. But then I told myself that only ultra-polite and super-rich American men ever strayed into British universities.

In the late sixties, when I arrived in Cambridge, Massachusetts, as a post-graduate student at Harvard, I confronted the natives on their own territory and discovered that many of these exaggerated impressions held true at close quarters. American men and women were engaged in elaborate and antagonistic courtship rituals. They ranged up in opposing camps, and their social life consisted of carefully orchestrated forays into enemy territory, where you were supposed to win points and become 'popular'. As an outsider I caused great confusion by unintentionally breaking the rules. Simple gestures like inviting a man to share some concert tickets, or offering to meet a 'date' at a restaurant instead of being picked up, were capable of triggering panic in a well-brought-up member of the opposite sex. It took me a long time to realise that 'dating' was not primarily about romantic love and need not entail friendship. Contrary to conventional wisdom, the spirit of courtship 'American-style' was that of an adversarial business relationship, and it was imperative for the more hungry player (the woman) to 'know the score' and 'cut the best deal'.

Barbara Levine,* a university professor who went to college in the late fifties, sums up the spirit of the age: 'The boy was your enemy; you "negotiated" all the time. Even if you didn't want him, you couldn't afford to antagonise him; he might say bad things about you that (true or not) might lower your status in the marriage market. But even if you did like him, you had to watch your step and make sure you didn't give him anything physically before it was "proper" to do so, because that would downgrade your status not only with him but with other men. While he might not be able to ruin your chances for marriage totally, by gossiping he could considerably narrow your pool of "availables" – i.e. the nice, bright, *serious* boys (the ones who went to medical school and so on) who would earn good salaries and be able to support you in style. These boys wouldn't want you if you had a tarnished reputation.

'Virginity was the *big thing*. If you didn't have that to offer a potential marriage partner, you didn't have any marbles to play with. I remember this girl who had slept with a boy and then married him. We all were shocked. We thought it was great but couldn't understand why he would marry her once he had slept with her. After all, he'd got *it* – her virginity – without having to "pay" for it.

'Even when the two of you were going steady, you were still in an adversary relationship. He was supposed to spend money on you, and you were supposed to respond physically in certain ritualistic ways. The first signal that you found him acceptable was when you let him hold your hand. On the first date, no kiss ever. But if you didn't let him kiss you on the third date, that was usually a signal for him to give up, though a really popular girl could make the guy come back for four or even five dates without even kissing him. It was as if you got points for holding out and making him come back again and again. You were supposed to try to make him desire you like crazy, but you yourself weren't supposed to be affected by all this because after all, you were "innocent". You were merely displaying the wares that would be available to Mr Right for the "best offer" marriage.

'How could you tell who was where physically in the sexual sweepstakes? Fraternity pins were one clue. Most of those pins were in two parts, with one part dangling from the other, and the girl would always wear the pin on the tip of one breast, so the dangling part really jiggled all the time. If you were sporting an engagement ring, slightly heavier petting was allowed – i.e. below the belt. But no bride-to-be was supposed to "go all the way".

'To maintain your status in the marriage market, you *had* to be busy Saturday night; it was proof of your desirability. If you weren't, you hid out in your room at the dorm. One girl I knew even put out her light and just listened to the radio in the dark all evening so that no one would know she didn't have a date. If you stayed at home by choice, you were considered a *freak*. It didn't matter that you would have preferred to settle down with a good book that night, or you just weren't in the mood or didn't like the guy who asked you out. You went.

'When I was in my last year at college and still unattached, my parents absolutely panicked. I was obviously going to be an old maid if I didn't get married by the time I graduated. I had an incredible rash of blind dates that year; even the rabbi fixed me up once. One Saturday night, when I was still living at home, I had this blind date who came all the way out to our house. He had a car. We drove back to New York and had dinner and went to the theatre. Then he drove me all the way back home again. Naturally I refused to kiss him good night. My brother had exercised his male prerogative and spent the entire evening at home reading. When I came inside, the two of us sat down and, for a laugh, started to figure out exactly how much this poor guy had spent on me: the cost of theatre tickets, the dinner at an expensive restaurant, the parking. It came to quite an impressive sum.

'Naturally, once you did manage to marry someone, you were supposed to be as devoted to his welfare as you previously had been to "landing" him. After all, he was your breadwinner.'[2]

The elaborate role playing of the fifties was fundamentally at odds with the egalitarian roots of American culture. Precisely because of this, it provoked fierce waves of reaction as both men and women sought to escape the confines of this rigid and artificial era.

Wifely duties, Norman Rockwell, 1960
(courtesy of the estate of Norman Rockwell)

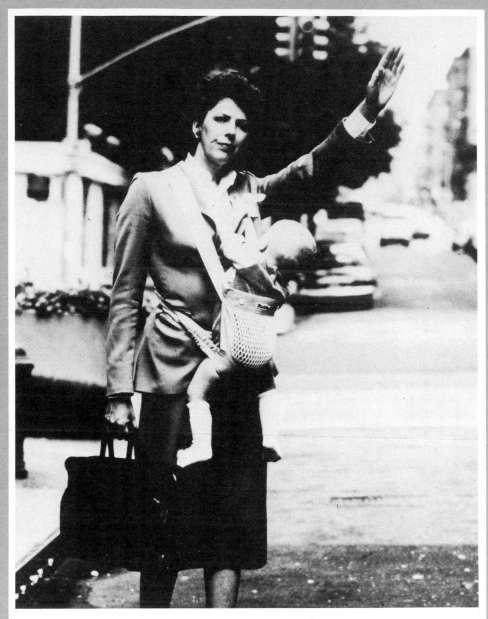

Superwoman, eighties-style
(copyright by Steve McCurry)

Getting a head start in life: an infant being introduced to Glenn Doman's
methods at the Better Baby Institute, 1983

(courtesy of the Institute for the Achievement of Human Potential)

GROWING PAINS

"My God! Ethel, he's shrunk!"

"I'm worried about him, Paul. He doesn't <u>listen</u> to his cereal any more."

"There's nothing in Dr. Spock about it."

"Dont call me, I'll call you."

Fun at the expense of Dr Spock, *Punch*, August 1960
(*courtesy of* Punch)

12. The Male Rebellion

American men who had lived and worked through the fifties came to feel oppressed by their role as breadwinner, and at least some of them tried to escape the narrow confines of a life dominated by the need to earn the money to buy the goodies to support wife and children. Like Peter Pan, they decided that the life of a grown man contained precious little fun:

PETER: Would you send me to school?
MRS DARLING: Yes.
PETER: And then to an office?
MRS DARLING: I suppose so.
PETER: Soon I should be a man.
MRS DARLING: Very soon.

'I don't want to go to school and learn solemn things,' he told her passionately. 'I don't want to be a man. O Wendy's Mother, if I was to wake up and feel there was a beard!'

'Peter, said Wendy the comforter, 'I should love you in a beard'; and Mrs Darling stretched out her arms to him, but he repulsed her.

PETER: Keep back, lady, no one is going to catch me and make me a man. I want always to be a little boy and have fun.[1]

American literature is full of tarnished images of male success. Titles such as *The Hucksters*, *The Gilded Hearse* and *Death of a Salesman* speak for themselves. As C. Wright Mills saw it, in American plays and novels men are often portrayed as external success stories but underneath they are 'ulcerated people of uneasy conscience, miserably at war with their tormented self'.[2] Part of the problem lies in the stifling nature of most jobs. Biff in *Death of a Salesman* (1949) gives vent to this typically male complaint: '. . . it's a measly manner of existence. To get on that subway on the hot mornings in summer. To devote your whole life to keeping stock or making phone calls, or selling or buying. To suffer fifty weeks of the year for the sake of a two-week vacation, when all you really desire is to be outdoors with your shirt off.'[3]

199

Modern American literature also tells of a double standard. Men slave away, often under great pressure, while their wives and children enjoy the 'good life'. In Herman Wouk's novel *Marjorie Morningstar*, published in 1955, the father stays at his job in Manhattan during August while his wife and daughter leave to stay at the Prado, a luxurious resort hotel on Long Island:

Mr Morgenstern was remaining in the city; the summer was his busiest season. They [his wife and daughter] had stopped briefly in his office in the garment district to pick up some cash and Marjorie had all but fainted in the windowless little office smelling so strongly of ink, stale coffee and the peculiar dust of the feathers and straws lying baled in the shop. Mr Morgenstern, in a gray tie and coat despite the killing heat, with a face almost as gray wished them a pleasant time.[4]

They drove out to the Prado, which 'had smooth green lawns, a white crushed-stone driveway, broad terraces, red clay tennis courts crisscrossed with new whitewash, and a huge blue swimming pool full of bronzed young people diving, splashing and laughing'.[5]

If breadwinning had its down side, the male role had other attributes which were equally limiting. Warren Farrell in *The Liberated Man* describes the emotional and sexual straitjacket of his fifties generation. Men were supposed to be invulnerable and to have great psychological strength; they suppressed their fears and controlled their emotions. They were expected to know all the answers; they never sought help and were tough and independent. They had ambition and were physically and sexually aggressive. Above all, they were in control, in sexual relations and in all relations. They initiated sex and got what they wanted when they wanted it. Farrell remembers in graphic detail his own initiation into male sexual values: 'The circle jerk – that's one of my first memories. We all stood around in a circle and told stories about girls or rubbed our penises until we got hard-ons. Then we ejaculated. The purpose was to see who could ejaculate the farthest. The guy whose sperm went the farthest was "the biggest man". He was the one who could really "give it to some chick". The guy who couldn't produce or who had a dinky ejaculation – well, we sort of laughed at him.'[6]

These pressures – to succeed, to perform, to control – in the financial and sexual arenas have conditioned men's lives for centuries. Why did these pressures become particularly acute in post-war America? Part of the answer lies in the fact that American men of the fifties were under a special strain and faced a unique set of disappointments.

By the early fifties the consumer society was in full swing, creating a treadmill of relentless money pressures. As Sloan Wilson, author of *The Man in the Gray Flannel Suit*, puts it, 'For almost all of us the scramble for the buck, if not morally uplifting, was pressingly necessary, for there were never enough dollars to raise a family, to build the kind of house which filled our dreams – or at least those of our wives.'[7]

The men and women of fifties America had looked forward to material abundance for so long. The extended agony of the Great Depression and the Second World War had been made slightly more bearable by visions of the good life that was to follow. And in America the post-war years did bring incredible prosperity. The economy grew at an unprecedentedly high rate; between 1945 and 1955 the GNP more than doubled. But an abundance of well-paid jobs, the house of one's dreams, the latest model of car, and an elaborate set of household appliances failed to fill the souls of men with satisfaction and contentment. This array of goods merely whetted the appetite for a bigger and better lifestyle. The whole population moved 'endlessly and breathlessly up one long, unbroken, incline of acquisition . . . from every point on the unbroken incline one can see others with more than one has oneself'.[8]

Many American men felt they had been 'had'. The long-heralded era of widespread and considerable affluence failed to produce fulfilment. For two decades men had yearned for material abundance, had looked forward to being 'good providers' and to proving their manhood in the marketplace. But the dream was not what it had been cracked up to be. The rapidly expanding economy of the fifties and sixties used up men, and uninhibited consumerism created an exhausting treadmill. As Charles A. Reich describes it in *The Greening of America*, the end result was 'a hollow man'.[9] The goals of the era – status, promotion, institutional approval, and a correct image for the outside world – were hollow in terms of personal satisfaction. Men worked under terrible stress, which prevented them from finding more worthwhile aims and drove them to ulcers, heart attacks and the psychiatrist's couch. In fifties America '. . . freedom came to mean consumer freedom . . . freedom to buy anything and go anywhere. For work, on the other hand, there was no longer any concept of freedom at all.'[10]

In frustration and anger, disillusioned men began to lash out. One target was the suburbs, for the massive post-war migration to suburbia had produced the daily commute and increased the price men had to pay for career success. As one commuter of the period put it, 'I soon came to detest a way of life which required me to travel almost a hundred miles a day.'[11] The magazine headlines of the period point to serious male discontent with suburban lifestyles: 'Life and Love in the Split Level Slums', 'The Crab Grass Roots of Suburbia', and 'On the 5:19 to Ulcerville'.[12]

In *The Crack in the Picture Window*, a best seller across America, John Keats invents an imaginary couple who move first to Rolling Knolls and then to Maryland Dell. Keats describes these communities as comprising 'row on row of identical boxes spreading like gangrene' through the countryside.[13] The family featured in his novel contracts money ills, is weakened by Dad's long commute to the city, and finally collapses into a permissive child-centred matriarchy.

But although suburban living came in for some harsh criticism, it was generally thought to be a symptom rather than a cause of the problem. The prime cause of male discontent was seen as the parasitic woman of the 'feminine mystique' and her ever-increasing brood of children. After all, most American men sought out the spacious houses and good schools of the suburbs not for themselves but for their wives and children.

The family responsibilities of fifties men were heavy. The most common age of marriage for men was twenty-three – an all-time low. And men had, on average, 2.8 children – a twentieth-century record for the United States. For the first time in history these children needed to be supported till their early twenties as college became an expected component of middle-class education.

The ethos of the day demanded, in no uncertain terms, that men grow up, marry, and support their families. The individual who deviated was a social outcast. As Philip Roth points out in *My Life as a Man*, for those 'young men who reached maturity in the fifties . . . there was considerable moral prestige in taking a wife'.[14] Not only that, men could not afford to scoff at marriage because if they did, they laid themselves open to the charge of 'immaturity', if not 'latent' or blatant 'homosexuality'.[15] During this period nothing was more frightening to an Establishment man.

Fifties men lived by onerous rules. According to Morris Dickstein, they belonged to 'a generation that willed itself from childhood directly into adulthood'.[16] They spent their late teens and early twenties getting on the slippery rungs of the career ladder. They then quickly found a wife, bought a house, and started a family. The next forty years were spent trying to fill a bottomless pit of demands emanating from wife and kids. It wasn't just a question of food, clothing and shelter; a second car, elaborate dental work, skiing holidays and country-club membership – all became standard features of American middle-class family life in this affluent decade. The male workhorse died in harness in his sixties, a good seven or eight years before his idle wife. Practising home-maintenance skills in the basement, or cooking frankfurters in the back yard on Saturday night, hardly seemed compensation enough for a life of unremitting toil.

A few dissidents dreamed of becoming great artists or writers, of chucking it all in and absconding to Paris. Frank Wheeler, the protagonist in Richard Yates's novel *Revolutionary Road*, 'was among the few who bucked the current'.[17] Despite the fact that he was a low-level bureaucrat at Knox Business Machines, he persisted in dreaming of a career somewhere in the humanities that would involve his early and permanent withdrawal to Europe, which Wheeler saw as the only part of the world worth living in. To his chagrin this self-styled 'intense, nicotine-stained, Jean-Paul-Sartre sort of man'[18] ended up like everyone else in the suburbs, where he had moved to produce a better life for his wife and children.

The happy housewives of the 1950s may have been bored out of their skulls and popping Valium, but disgruntled men of the period often saw these same wives as leeches sucking the lifeblood of their hardworking husbands. Men were developing a growing aversion to 'the feminine millstones hanging around their necks'.[19] Consider the Texas housewife described, perfectly seriously, in a magazine of the period:

Janice Crabtree lives in a handsome, pink brick ranch house on the best and newest street in Grapevine, Texas. She is a comely young woman of 34 with wavy blue black hair and very even white teeth. Even at this hour in the morning – it is barely 9 o'clock – she is wearing rouge, powder and lipstick, and her summer dress is immaculately fresh. The somber chords of Beethoven's Fifth Symphony crash majestically from the phonograph as she sits serenely enjoying a fourth cup of coffee.

'Friends seem continually amazed at me,' says Janice. 'By 8.30 a.m., when my youngest goes to school, my whole house is clean and neat and I am dressed for the day. I am free to play bridge, attend club meetings or stay home and read, listen to Beethoven and just plain loaf.'

How does she do it? According to husband Billie, every morning at 7 a.m. she hits the housework like 'greased lightning'.

Hurrying through the house in her pajamas and robe, she makes four beds in quick, step-saving motions and hangs up night clothes. She wipes the bathtubs and washbowls and straightens the towels. Then she may run a dustcloth over the grand piano or pick up some crumbs with the vacuum. By 8 a.m. she is done.

Mornings she is having bridge at her house are the busiest, for then Janice must get out the tables, cards, tallies, put up fresh coffee and prepare lunch. During the winter months she may play as often as four days a week from 9.30 a.m. to 3 p.m. Janice is careful always to be home before her sons return from school in the late afternoon.

'Sometimes I feel I'm too passive, too content,' remarks Janice, fondly regarding the bracelet of large family diamonds she wears. 'But I'm grateful for my blessings . . . for my good health and faith in God and such material possessions as two cars, two TVs and two fireplaces.'

Her favorite possession is her four-poster spool bed with a pink taffeta canopy. 'I feel just like Queen Elizabeth sleeping in that bed,' she says happily. Since her husband snores he sleeps in an adjoining room.[20]

If you were a breadwinner sick of the relentless pressures of corporate life or fed up with the dreary monotony of the assembly line, such a portrait might make your blood boil. After all, you were footing the bill for this leisured existence, for the pink-brick ranch house, the four-poster spool bed and the two fireplaces, and you were the one relegated to the spare bed.

A male revolt against the breadwinning role began to gather momentum in the fifties. Male magazines ran bitter articles about how the male sex was being held to ransom by predatory women, like this article by Bob Norman in a 1953 issue of *Playboy*, which captures the 'we've all been had' spirit of the period:

A young couple gets married. They're in love, or think they are, but for one reason or another marriage doesn't work. Maybe it's the guy's fault; maybe it's the girl's. Could be neither one is to blame – just two nice people who aren't really suited for one another.

You might assume that having discovered their mistake, a couple could successfully call it quits, no strings attached, and try to find happiness elsewhere. 'Tain't so.

When the time comes for going their separate ways, the young lady may, if she is so inclined, stick her ex-spouse for a healthy chunk of his earnings from that day forward, for the rest of his unnatural life . . . The marriage has ended. The unhappy stag is entitled to none of the privileges of a husband, but he's expected to pay for them as if he were.

It doesn't matter who is to blame for the marriage going on the rocks. The wife may be a trollop with the disconcerting habit of crawling in and out of bed with the husband's friends. She may be a spendthrift whose expensive tastes he cannot afford. No matter. When the judge grants the divorce, he will also grant the little missus a healthy stipend for future escapades and extravagances.

Nor is modern alimony merely a matter of principle. For many men it is a serious question of economic survival.

A young TV director was overpowered by a 37″ 25″ 37″ brunette early in his career and happily exchanged the vows that were to guarantee a lifetime of marital bliss. Five years later his 37″ 30″ 37″ wife sued for divorce. In claiming her severance pay, she explained that she had inspired her husband, contributing nightly to whatever success he now enjoyed.

The judge listened to this tender American love story and ordered the defendant to fork over 50 per cent of his present salary – plus 50 per cent of whatever he earned in the future. The man was professionally whipped.[21]

A small group of men did more than complain about their domestic burdens. Toward the end of the decade, the beats and their imitators, the beatniks, staged a more thorough-going revolt. Led by such colourful personalities as Jack Kerouac and Allen Ginsberg, these movements flourished in a twilight world of poetry, jazz, drugs and violence. The beats spurned steady work as well as family responsibilities, but because they remained a minuscule minority, mainstream society was shocked rather than threatened by their antics.

A much bigger wave of rebellion hit in the mid-sixties as the counter-cultural revolution swept through America. In mid-decade hundreds of thousands of young people rejected the values and lifestyles of their parents. Some dropped out of school, grew their hair, donned flowing, funky costumes, and moved to Haight-Ashbury or the East Village, where they shared crash pads and dealt drugs. By 1967 as many as 75,000 young people were living in the Haight-Ashbury psychedelic community.[22] Others, more idealistic, went on freedom marches in the South, protested against American involvement in the Vietnam War, or joined the Peace Corps. Most were middle-class kids who professed to despise the conformist, constrained and sanitised lives of their suburban parents. Like Nancy Barrett's three children they wanted to be free – from the panoply of consumer goods and from family commitments.

A major reason the counter-cultural rebellion came to involve so many people was the Vietnam War. Close to three million American men fought in the debilitating failure that was Vietnam and 100 million more watched the war on television. Every evening, before dinner, one was treated, in full colour, to the spectacle of malnourished peasants being pounded by the technological might of an ugly and impotent America. One way of coping with the gratuitous brutality and the impending military defeat – not to mention the danger of being drafted to fight this war – was to reject the whole set of Establishment values that had created the war in the first place. Cold-war militarism, the capitalist system, aggressive masculinity, marriage, monogamy, the nuclear family and suburban existence – all got lumped together by the angry young men of the sixties as being part of a value system that had failed them. The rebellion deepened and spread in 1967, when President Lyndon Johnson extended the draft to students. Privileged youths were particularly loath to fight in this vain and inglorious war. Who needed to die in the jungles of South-east Asia? Even your countrymen would not consider you a hero. In October 1967 several hundred thousand young rebels marched on the Pentagon in a mammoth anti-war demonstration. Norman Mailer called them the Armies of the Night. In a haze of marijuana and tear gas they attached flowers to the bayonets of the military police and vowed to make love, not war.

The issues that galvanised the hippies of the counter-culture – consumerism, commitments, the draft – were predominantly male issues. The tensions of climbing the career ladder, the pressures of being the family breadwinner, the dangers of fighting the war in Vietnam were, in the main, male problems, and men had a lot to gain by denying their legitimacy. Of course there were women around and about the counter-culture, but they were treated as camp followers, not as equals. 'Liberated men needed groovy chicks who could swing with their new life style',[23] but God forbid that the chick got it into her head to demand an equal role in the rebellion or some old-fashioned personal commitment. If she did, she was 'uptight', 'screwed-up', or, worse still, a 'real bring-down'. A chick was expected to stuff envelopes and operate the mimeograph machine for the movement, and to take birth control pills and go for VD check-ups so that she didn't become a drag on her old man.

The youthful male rebels of the sixties seemed to reject the 'straight' values of the previous decade in a highly selective way. They ruled out conventional fifties expectations of career success, marriage and family, but retained the equally conventional notion that women should be subservient to men. Stokely Carmichael accurately reflected the spirit of the sixties rebellion in his famous remark, 'The only position for women in SNCC [Student Non-violent Coordinating Committee] is – prone.'[24] Even the songs of the period were 'full of sardonic put downs of women'.[25] A Mick Jagger song, 'Under My Thumb', is a case in point: 'Under my thumb the girl who once had me down / Under my thumb the girl who once pushed me around.'[26]

As the chicks became older and wiser, they realised that they had been had. As Marge Piercy described in her 1969 exposé of sex and politics in the counter-culture: 'A man can bring a woman into an organisation by sleeping with her and remove her by ceasing to do so. A man can purge a woman for no other reason than he has tired of her, knocked her up, or is after someone else: and that purge is accepted without a ripple.'[27] Robin Morgan, a sister feminist, wrote in 1970, 'We have met the enemy and he's our friend . . . It hurts to understand that at Woodstock or Altamount a woman could be declared uptight or a poor sport if she didn't want to be raped.'[28] She described a young male revolutionary 'supposedly dedicated to building a new, free social order' turn round and absent-mindedly order his 'chick' to 'shut up and make supper or wash his socks'.[29]

The sexual revolution of the American counter-culture was decidedly lopsided: it boasted a single standard, but the burdens of free sex were very unequally distributed. The women of the sixties increasingly found themselves 'traded, gang-banged, collected, collectivised, objectified, and turned into the hot stuff of pornography'.[30] One embittered feminist described it as a sexual revolution that did not free women. Its purpose was 'to free men to use women without bourgeois constraints'.[31] Needless to say, the easiest way for a woman to become a victim of this new sexual code was – to become pregnant. In the mid- and late sixties abortion was still illegal in America, and the flower girls found that they 'did not want to claw out their own insides or pay someone else to do it'.[32] But the alternative – to bear and raise a child without a husband or a home – did not look very appealing either.

Women were both the idealists and the victims of the counter-culture. They promoted noble causes and laid to one side their own self-interest. They opposed the Vietnam War, although their own lives, unlike the men's, were not at stake. They learned to despise the consumer culture, the rat race and the traditional family, yet this rebellion imperilled their own security and that of their children. And they joined in a sexual revolution which left them dangerously vulnerable. For a while the free-floating idealism and the soft, androgenous imagery that characterised this period obscured the fact that the counter-culture had an exclusively male agenda. But by the late sixties women had had their fill of noble male causes and left the men in droves to form their own autonomous women's movement.

But the women's movement only sped up the male rebellion. New antagonism between the sexes was triggered by the fact that radical feminists saw men as Enemy Number One. As the Redstocking Manifesto puts it, '*All men* receive economic, sexual and psychological benefits from male supremacy. *All men* have oppressed women.'[33] Men did not like being described as oppressors – or male chauvinistic pigs, for that matter. Most were still hard at work earning a crust and resented the attacks of feminists. Herb Goldberg in his book *The Hazards of being Male* records the bitter comments of a 57-year-old college professor: 'The famous male chauvinistic pigs who neglect their wives, underpay their women employees and rule the world – are literally slaves. They're out there picking the cotton, sweating, swearing, taking lashes from the boss, working 50 hours a week to support themselves and the plantation, only then to come home to do another 20 hours a week rinsing dishes, toting trash bags, writing checks and acting as butlers at the parties.'[34]

If the rhetoric of the women's movement increased male disaffection, the practical effect of the movement was to facilitate the escape of the disaffected male. For women's liberation supported women in their attempts to work and become self-sufficient; it also encouraged wives to leave unhappy marriages. Both of these trends increased male freedom. In his book *The Liberated Man* Warren Farrell lists a multitude of reasons why men should welcome the women's movement. Many of his reasons hinge on the increased economic and emotional independence of liberated women.[35] He sees this independence as allowing men greater freedom to pursue their own goals. Karen De Crow, a former president of NOW, could not have agreed more. 'Men are not money machines put on this earth to fight wars and support women and children,'[36] she declared flatly.

The net result of these waves of rebellion is a generation of Americans that contains a significant proportion of men who successfully avoid the heavy family responsibilities of the 1950s. A 1979 survey of the values and goals of American males tells us about these new men. For starters, a large and increasing proportion are narcissistic – that is, they are 'individualistic, self-centered and pleasure-orientated in their approach to life'. The study finds that one of the main distinguishing characteristics of this 'new' man is that he believes in the family of 'limited liability'. In concrete terms, this means that he seeks out an independent mate who is capable of supporting herself, that he prefers a small family, and that he would contemplate divorce if the quality of a marriage deteriorated. Specifically he 'would not remain in an unsuccessful marriage for the sake of the children'. These men are not deviant in other aspects of life; they hold jobs, earn and spend money, and are 'effective participants in the system'.[37]

Psychiatrists confirm the advent of the narcissistic man. Dan Kiley, psychiatrist and author of *The Peter Pan Syndrome: Men Who Have Never Grown Up*, reports that his private practice is increasingly peopled with young men who cannot make personal commitments, who refuse to come of age. 'Narcissism locks them inside themselves . . . [and] temper tantrums are disguised as manly assertion. They take love for granted, never learning how to give it in return. They pretend to be grown up but actually behave like spoiled children.'[38] In other words, they behave just like Peter Pan.

Paul Johnson* is a 34-year-old musician who lives and works in Boston. He teaches in a private school, gives private piano lessons, and has a modest career as a concert pianist. All this adds up to a sixty- to eighty-hour week. Paul is a good-looking, gregarious man who enjoys being single. He says reflectively, 'I am very glad I got away from the whole concept of commitment. Ten years ago I almost married a college classmate. Luckily the engagement fell through. Now I am not sure that I will ever choose to tie myself to one person.' In his free time Paul practises the piano, collects rare books, and takes sailing lessons. His savings are earmarked for a boat he plans to buy this coming summer. I asked Paul how children fitted into his life. He thought about the question for a few minutes and then said, 'I like children, and I know I am good with them; but you know, I work with kids all day long, and I am not at all sure I want to come home to them in the evening. I don't think that I will be having children.' Paul hesitated and then added, 'A lot of single women I know in their mid-thirties desperately want a baby, and without wanting to sound callous' – Paul smiled charmingly – 'I have little patience with the problems that revolve around women's biological clock. Quite frankly I prefer to go out with women in their twenties. They aren't so uptight about having kids.'[39]

These new men are impressively different from the commuting family men of the fifties. Over the course of the last thirty years social values in America have changed so as to permit men more freedom. The sexual revolution snapped the link between sex and marriage. Amendments to the divorce laws (no-fault and equitable distribution) paved the way for simpler, less cumbersome legal procedures and weakened the rationale for alimony – all of which made divorce a much less expensive proposition. Feminists encouraged men to get off the hook. As Betty Friedan pointed out, 'Perhaps men may live longer in

America when women carry more of the burden of the battle with the world, instead of being a burden themselves.'[40] And finally, millions of women entered the job market and took up (badly) paid work, which lessened female dependence and facilitated divorce. All these changes permitted the new men of eighties America to realise the family of limited liability, and, as we saw in Chapter Two, it is the women and children who suffer. Divorce is a painful and miserable business for all concerned, but while the living standards of the average divorced American man rise after the marriage has ended, those of divorced women go quite dramatically down and, as we also saw in Chapter Two, a divorced American male is more likely to cough up on his car repayments than any child-support dues. In short, the vast majority of divorced women in America are expected to support themselves, *and* they are increasingly left with complete financial and physical responsibility for the children of divorce.

But this does not mean that men are without their grievances. If mothers get custody of the children in 90 per cent of all divorces, it still means that thousands of children end up with their fathers. If alimony is only paid in 5 to 10 per cent of divorces, it still means that thousands of men feel ripped off. In short, America is a big enough country for 5 or 10 per cent to be a large number of people capable of making a lot of noise.

'New' men look least good on the fatherhood front, and once again it is a conspicuous minority that distorts the overall picture. A few modern fathers have got into nurturing. Like Dustin Hoffman in *Kramer vs. Kramer*, they deal with nightmares, meet the kids from school, cook dinner, and sometimes even put parenthood ahead of career. I am married to such a man, so I know that they exist. However, for many new men being a father is largely a verbal accomplishment. They take natural childbirth classes; talk with great eloquence at dinner parties about bonding, separation anxiety and role models; and quite convince themselves that they are great fathers. When push comes to shove, they are often missing. Only a third of American men will pay up the child support in the event of divorce, and on a daily basis the division of labour remains the traditional one. It is the mother who makes up the school lunches, buys the present for the birthday party, wipes up the vomit, and stays at home with the sick child. Parenthood mostly involves hard, relentless work and the willingness to be there when needed. Most new American men do not arrange their priorities that way. As Donald Bell puts it in *Being a Man*, 'For many adult males there persists a gnawing sense that we have more important things to accomplish than to be stuck changing diapers, feeding a drooling infant, or arranging for playmates or babysitters . . . childcare tends to turn the adult mind to mush [and] since contemporary middle-class men work mainly with their minds, we can ill afford to allow our minds to become mushy.'[41] What of women? I suppose it's all right if their minds turn to mush!

In June 1984 it was the end of term for my stepdaughter Shira and the rest of her class. There was a simple ceremony, and her class was allowed to choose one song. It chose 'Cat's in the Cradle' by Harry Chapin:

> My child arrived just the other day;
> he came to the world in the usual way.
> But there were planes to catch and bills to pay;
> he learnt to walk while I was away.
> And he was talkin' 'fore I knew it,
> and as he grew he'd say,
> 'I'm gonna be like you, Dad,
> you know I'm gonna be like you.'
>
> CHORUS
> And the cat's in the cradle and the silver spoon,
> little boy blue and the man in the moon.
> 'When you comin' home, Dad?'
> 'I don't know when,
> but we'll get together then;
> you know we'll have a good time then.'
>
> My son turned ten just the other day;
> he said, 'Thanks for the ball, Dad, now come on let's play.
> Can you teach me to throw?' I said, 'Not today,
> I got a lot to do.' He said, 'That's OK.'
> And he walked away, but his smile never dimmed, it said,
> 'I'm gonna be like him, yeah,
> you know I'm gonna be like him.'
>
> CHORUS
> And the cat's in the cradle and the silver spoon,
> little boy blue and the man in the moon.
> 'When you coming home, Dad?'
> 'I don't know when,
> but we'll get together then;
> you know we'll have a good time then.'
>
> He came home from college just the other day;
> so much like a man I just had to say,
> 'Son, I'm proud of you, can you sit for a while?'

He shook his head and he said with a smile,
'What I'd really like, Dad, is to borrow the car keys;
see you later, can I have them please?'

CHORUS
And the cat's in the cradle and the silver spoon,
little boy blue and the man in the moon.
'When you coming home, son?'
'I don't know when,
but we'll get together then, Dad,
you know we'll have a good time then.'

I've long since retired, my son's moved away;
I called him up just the other day.
I said, 'I'd like to see you if you don't mind.'
He said, 'I'd love to, Dad, if I can find the time.
You see, my new job's a hassle and the kids have the flu,
But it's sure nice talkin' to you, Dad,
it's been sure nice talkin' to you.'
And as I hung up the phone, it occurred to me,
he'd grown up just like me;
my boy was just like me.

CHORUS
And the cat's in the cradle and the silver spoon,
little boy blue and the man in the moon.
'When you comin' home, son?'
'I don't know when,
but we'll get together then, Dad,
we're gonna have a good time then.'[42]

It seems that America's twelve-year-olds are not convinced that much fathering is going on in the United States today.

13. Contemporary Women in America: Two Hostile Camps

The feminist revival in America in the late sixties drew its energy from two sources. It was a rebellion against the ultradomestic, stultifying world of the 1950s, and it was a revolt against the male-centred counter-culture. The women who had been radical in counter-cultural terms now became radical in feminist terms. They were through with being menial servants and unpaid prostitutes to left-wing men and through with chic male causes. From now on they sought succour and support from their own sex. As we saw in Chapter Seven, by the early 1970s this radical segment of the women's movement was strongly man-hating.

But the ex-housewives didn't feel too sympathetically disposed toward men either. Marilyn French in *The Women's Room* describes her reaction: 'My feelings about men are the result of my experience. I have little sympathy for them. Like a Jew just released from Dachau, I watch the handsome young Nazi soldier fall writhing to the ground with a bullet in his stomach and I look briefly and walk on. I don't even need to shrug. I simply don't care. What he was, as a person, I mean, what his shames and yearnings were, simply don't matter. It is too late for me to care.'[1]

Disillusioned housewives felt justified in ignoring men because of an urgent need to deal with their own problems. They felt that they had been ripped off and put down. It was hard to feel good about what had been their main activity – looking after the home. Despite all that heartwarming rhetoric about 'Mom and apple pie', it was by now an open secret that large segments of American society thoroughly despised women who stayed at home. These women believed that they had vested their best energies and their prime years in a socially devalued role. In one Labor Department ranking of jobs according to complexity of skills required, looking after home and family got the same ranking as parking lot attendant and was ranked below marine mammal handler.[2] How could these women derive much self-esteem from a role that society thought so little of?

Many of these women looked back at the years spent at home and were bitter. It had been so arduous and so little understood, let alone appreciated, by husband and children. In retrospect they resented all that household drudgery, they regretted that they had sunk quantities of precious energy into 'his' career, and they were horrified to discover that even their sexuality had been distorted to serve male needs. These grievances were to become potent sources of feminist anger.

Take housework. Janice Crabtree, with her four-poster spool bed and two fireplaces, seems to have been the exception rather than the rule. In 1953 sociologist Mirra Komarovsky found that a day in the life of a 'typical' American housewife was something like this:

I get up at 6 a.m. and put up coffee and cereal for breakfast and go down to the basement to put clothes into the washing machine. When I come up I dress Teddy ($1\frac{1}{2}$) and put him in his chair. Then I dress Jim ($3\frac{1}{2}$) and serve breakfast to him and to my husband and feed Teddy.

While my husband looks after the children I go down to get the clothes out of the machine and hang them on the line. Then I come up and have my own breakfast after my husband leaves. From then on the day is as follows: breakfast dishes, clean up kitchen. Make beds, clean the apartment. Wipe up bathroom and kitchen floor. Get lunch vegetables ready and put potatoes on to bake for lunch. Dress both children in outdoor clothes. Do my food shopping and stay out with children until 12. Return and undress children, wash them up for lunch, feed Teddy and put him to nap. Make own lunch, wash dishes, straighten up kitchen. Put Jim to rest. Between 1 and 2.30, depending on the day of the week, ironing, thorough cleaning of one room, weekend cooking and baking etc.; 3 p.m. give children juice or milk, put outdoor clothes on. Out to park; 4.30 back. Give children their baths. Prepare their supper and help put them to bed. Make dinner for husband and myself. After dinner, dishes and cleaning up. After 8 p.m. often more ironing, especially on the days when I cleaned in the afternoon. There is mending to be done; 9 p.m. fall asleep in the living room over a newspaper or listening to the sound of the radio; 10 p.m. have a snack of something with my husband and go to bed.

I read this account to my husband and he said that it sounded too peaceful, that the children seem to keep out of the way too much. I haven't conveyed to you all the strain of being constantly with the children for twelve hours a day, day in day out.

I wouldn't call myself a contented housewife. I find it hard to be so tied down . . . I have sometimes the feeling of being imprisoned.

Besides, I find my life dull. I described my day to you. It isn't just one day

– it is every day. Believe me there is not enough stimulation in the incessant dishwashing, picking up, ironing, folding diapers, dressing and undressing the kids, making beds day in and day out. My social life with the other mothers on the park benches is depressing. I cannot get them away from the same old talk. They have nothing fresh to give me because they, too, are up to their necks in the same routine . . . I think there must be something wrong with this set-up.[3]

But this wasn't the whole picture. Fifties women in America pumped an extraordinary amount of energy into the emotional and cognitive development of their children and into supporting their husbands' careers, efforts which went well beyond the physical care of home and family.

It was the era not of the dual-career family but of the two-person career. The competitive pressures of the male work world created great tensions, which the wife was supposed to offset by providing elaborate emotional support. William H. Whyte, Jr., describes how a wife was meant to liberate her husband's total energy for the job. She must maintain their home as an island of tranquillity, and herself act as 'sounding board', 'refuelling station', and 'wailing wall'.[4] Philip Slater writes of the 'opiate role' played by wives. Men are daily buffeted by the economic structures they have created, and they tend 'to use their wives as opiates to soften the impact of the forces they have set into motion against themselves'.[5] In 1956 Sloan Wilson in an article for the *New York Times Magazine* describe the male executive as being totally dependent on his spouse: 'Without a capable wife to screen his speaking and social engagements, keep track of his personal finances, run his house and take care of his children, he would have been "lost". Modern man needs an old-fashioned woman around the house.'[6]

One of the most draining of the support roles was that of moving. The expectation was that if a husband's career could be enhanced by relocating, the whole family upped sticks and moved, no matter what this meant in terms of loss and disruption – and studies show that moving produces almost as much strain as the death of a spouse.

Wives were often expected to settle into new homes, build new friendships, and launch their children into new schools every few months. In the late fifties one out of every five American families was changing homes at the rate of once a year. As *McCall's* put it, 'Each year a quarter of a million corporate families crisscross the country in a frantic relocation tango.'[7] This rate of change was not to slow down until the mid-seventies, when working wives began to resist repeated moves, and their husbands began to balk at corporate policies that produced this relocation tango. Women seem to have borne the brunt of all this shifting around. After all, the husbands generally stayed within the same corporate culture, while their wives were forced to start from scratch in strange communities. One study reported that 'some women in their 30s have lived in 16 different communities since they married; a few have even moved four times in a single year ... Often they become defeated people ... chronically depressed, addicted to alcohol.'[8]

It is interesting to note that European societies have not experienced this frantic mobility. A recent study shows that 70 per cent of West Germans live within five miles of their birthplaces.[9] Similar statistics could be found for many other European countries. Even in Britain, families have not had to move so far nor so frequently as in America. Only in America has geographic mobility played such a disruptive role in the lives of women and their families.

On the sexual front, disillusioned American housewives felt that they had been taken for a ride. In retrospect, the pop psychology that flourished in the fifties and early sixties seemed guaranteed to stunt women's lives. As we saw in earlier chapters, many of the attitudes of this period rested on Freudian theory. Freud was convinced that all females suffered from penis envy. As a result, little girls came to perceive themselves as mutilated boys, a trauma the resolution of which could take the neurotic form of seeking for the lost penis through an imitation of masculine activity (to wit, pursuing a career) or take the proper form of translating the wish for a penis into the wish for a child. This notion had all sorts of ramifications for the relations between women and men. For example, Freudian theorists decreed that true sexuality for a woman resided in her capacity for a vaginal orgasm as the vagina was seen as the only authentic female organ of erotic sensation and release. The clitoris, on the other hand, was seen as a hidden vestige of (or shrunken surrogate for) the penis. In short, it was the instrument of arrested childish narcissism.

The end result was that in the 1950s, orgasm was presented to women in a hierarchy of virtue and achievement. A clitoral orgasm was a 'bad' unwomanly experience, while the vaginal orgasm was not only 'good', but constituted the only full testament to womanhood. One need hardly point out that the good orgasm was dependent on an erect penis, and a woman could achieve sexual satisfaction only as a concomitant of a man's seeking his. A clitoral orgasm was judged to be of no account because it was 'unfunctional, gratuitous, masturbatory, required no penis and led to no possibility of conception'.[10] The superiority of the vaginal over the clitoral orgasm was proclaimed in novels, Broadway plays and popular magazines as well as by psychologists and marriage counsellors. Clitoral women were deemed immature, neurotic, bitchy, and masculine; women who had vaginal orgasms were maternal, feminine, mature, and normal. Although frigidity should technically be defined as total inability to achieve orgasm, the Freudian experts of this era preferred to define it as an inability to achieve vaginal orgasm – a definition which proclaimed three-quarters of all adult women frigid failures.

In 1966 Dr William H. Masters and Mrs Virginia E. Johnson published *Human Sexual Response*, a massive clinical study of the physiology of sex. Their main conclusion was that the dichotomy between vaginal and clitoral orgasms is entirely false. 'Anatomically, all orgasms are centred in the clitoris, whether they result from direct manual pressure applied to the clitoris, indirect pressure resulting from the thrusting of the penis during intercourse, or generalised sexual stimulation of other erogenous zones like the breasts.'[11]

So much for Freud. Scientists had discovered (rather belatedly) that the noble womanly vagina was inert and nerveless, while the subversive clitoris was the true site of female erotic pleasure. But this discovery was a little late for fifties women who had wasted years trying to achieve authentic vaginal orgasms. Many were enraged. They saw that even their sexuality had been 'defined by men to benefit men'.[12] They realised that they had been conned into making the vaginal orgasm a status symbol in a male-dictated system of values. For women had persuaded themselves that a preference for clitoral orgasm was ignominious, a source of secret shame. This internalisation is amply demonstrated in the novels of the period. Mary McCarthy and Doris Lessing wrote about orgasm in much the same way as D. H. Lawrence and Ernest Hemingway, and even Simone de Beauvoir is an unreconstructed Freudian in this matter. In *The Second Sex* she refers to vaginal orgasm as the only 'normal satisfaction'.[13]

Thus the decade of the 1960s saw the emergence of two types of bruised and bitter women in American society. A group of young women, burned by their experiences in the counterculture, 'and without firm roots in family or career, gave vent to their rage in the rhetoric of sexual politics'.[14] They became radical feminists. Older women had a different grievance. Many of them were disillusioned wives or ex-wives, and at least some of them were 'displaced homemakers'. Their prime had coincided with the fifties, and they had used up their youth on home and family – some with precious little to show for it. As Nancy Barrett found out, your children could just drop out of sight and you could lose your husband to a younger playmate. Most of these ex-housewives headed off into the job market, where they had indifferent luck, and some of them joined NOW and became mainstream feminists.

In view of this history, it comes as no surprise that some of the best energies of modern American feminism have gone into avoiding the whole family set-up. Radical feminists became passionate in their pursuit of self-sufficiency, and many tried to build a life without men. Mainstream feminists, on the other hand, have concentrated on cloning the male competitive model in the marketplace, which they see as more reliable than family life as a source of long-term satisfaction. Both factions have ignored children.

But a large group of American women see all feminists (radical or main-stream) as destructive elements in society. These are the traditional women of Middle America, who by the early seventies were hanging on by their fingernails to the American Dream. In the main they had a simple ambition: they wanted to be able to continue their lives as wives and mothers.

These women knew that they were living in treacherous times. The divorce rate, which had been inching upward, suddenly doubled in the decade between 1965 and 1975. Breadwinners were rapidly becoming an endangered species, at least over the long term. Traditionalists blamed the breakdown of the family on a variety of factors: no-fault divorce laws, legal abortion, gay rights, and permissive child-rearing practices. But mostly they blamed those 'women libbers': 'Women's liberation wants to liberate us from the very institution that is most indispensable to overcoming our present social crisis: the family. They want to make marriage more open, more flexible, revocable at a time when it is already opening up all over the country and spewing forth swarms of delinquents and neurotics.'[15] Women's liberation was seen as 'relieving men of their responsibility as head of the family. That makes it easier for a man to walk out' on his wife and children.[16]

Traditional women were and are deeply suspicious of the package we call the sexual revolution. They know that in the past women were valued for sex and reproduction, and they believe that wives should hang on to their monopoly on legitimate sex for the very simple reason that it enhances their value. Their abhorrence of abortion stems from religion, but it also stems from crude self-interest. They see the fear of pregnancy as a powerful brake on sexual freedom and pregnancy itself as the ultimate sanction – the only consequence of sex that makes men accountable to women for what men do to women. In Andrea Dworkin's words, 'they use sex and babies to stay valuable because they need a home, food, clothing'.[17]

Traditional women are thus convinced that sexual freedom and legal abortion bring with them an increase in female vulnerability. The 1960s did not pass them by. They learned from what they saw, and what they mainly saw was the sexual exploitation of woman. To them the new morality is a cheat and a thief. As Phyllis Schlafly points out, 'It robs the woman of her virtue, her youth, her beauty and her love – for nothing, just nothing.'[18] At least under the traditional rules a woman would get a husband in exchange for sex and looking after the home, a breadwinning husband who would support her 'until death us do part'.

In the political sphere in America these women have a strong voice. Their goal is to turn the clock back, to return to the simple social order of yesteryear, in which women were guaranteed the basic protections of shelter, support and love. They wage campaigns against legal abortion, no-fault divorce, and gay rights; they attempt to prevent passage of the ERA; and they advocate school prayers. All this political activity is meant to bolster the old-fashioned family-centred props of women's lives.

In the personal sphere these traditional women devote a great deal of effort to techniques that will make them better loved and more secure. Marabel Morgan in her book *The Total Woman* promises that it is possible 'for almost any wife to have her husband absolutely adore her in just a few weeks' time'.[19] The trick is to cater to a man's special quirks, whether it be in 'salads, sex or sports'[20] and to improve her 'curb appeal'. Morgan goes to some lengths to explain the relevance of curb appeal – the term American real estate agents use to describe the outer shell of a house. She feels that all wives should ask themselves the tough question, 'Is your curb appeal this week what it was five years ago?'[21] She reminds them, 'Before a man can care about who a woman is, he must first get past the visual barrier of how a woman looks.'[22]

Much of Morgan's advice on how to improve one's curb appeal is exceedingly concrete. When hubby comes home, 'waltz to the door in a cloud of powder and cologne'.[23] She tells how 'for an experiment I put on pink baby doll pajamas and white boots after a bubble bath . . . When I opened the door that night to greet Charlie, I was unprepared for his reaction. My quiet, reserved, non-excitable husband took one look, dropped his briefcase on the doorstep, and chased me around the dining-room table.'[24]

The reward for developing one's curb appeal is not just love and kisses. Total women also get loaded up with presents from their appreciative husbands. Said one graduate of Morgan's 'Total Woman' course, 'He began to bring me gifts. One afternoon he called to find out if I'd be home at 3 o'clock. I couldn't imagine what was coming and I was stunned to see a truck pull up with a new refrigerator and freezer. I had nagged for a new one for years and for years he had refused.'[25]

If the man in your life fails to come up with the goods, traditionalists offer women the love of Jesus, who is portrayed as the beautiful brother, the compassionate friend, and the perfect healer of sorrow and resentment – in short, the man who will never fail you.

In *The Gift of Inner Healing* Ruth Carter Stapleton advises a young woman who is in a desperately unhappy marriage, 'Try to spend a little time each day visualising Jesus coming in the door from work. Then see yourself walking up to Him, embracing Him. Say to Jesus, "It's good to have you home, Nick."'[26] Stapleton used this technique herself with great success. Her own marriage at age nineteen (to Nick) had been desperately unhappy. After the birth of her fourth child she attempted suicide by jumping from a moving car. Shortly afterward she found peace by surrendering to Jesus.

Anita Bryant appears to have spent a good part of her life on her knees begging Jesus to help her love her husband, Bob Green. She writes candidly of her near-constant struggle. Green's demands – which ranged from enshrining her as the spokeswoman of anti-homosexual bigotry to doing all the child care for four children – were endurable only because Bryant took Jesus as her real husband. As Bryant describes in *Bless This House*, 'Only as I practice yielding to Jesus can I learn to submit, as the Bible instructs me, to the loving leadership of my husband. Only the power of Christ can enable a woman like me to become submissive in the Lord.'[27]

This right-wing school of thought displays a type of bleak realism. Traditional women are not dumb Barbie dolls. They are essentially correct when they say that they are worth more in the house than outside it. A wife is still 'given' more money by her husband than she herself could earn at a job. All women need do is look around them to realise that work for wages outside the home does not effectively free women because of the undervaluation of their work. As we saw in Chapter Three, many American women cannot earn enough money (while working full time) to lift themselves out of poverty. Many housewives 'do not buy the argument that work outside the home makes women sexually and economically independent of men. They see that the streets are cold, and that the women on them are tired, sick and bruised.'[28] Women are paid too little in the work force. And many traditional American women are clear-sighted enough to know it.

At bottom these traditional women see feminists as traitors and fools. They are traitors because they undermine the traditional family-support systems for other women and their children. And they are fools because they do not seem to understand that there is no point in alienating men. Most women want children, and most women have no alternative to marriage if they want decent lives for themselves and their children. Traditionalists see feminists as out of touch with reality. Only élite East Coast 'libbers' would be foolish enough to imagine that independence can be found in the job market, a truth that Nora Ephron discovered in *Heartburn*. 'Wives went out into the world free at last, single again and discovered the horrible truth: that they were sellers in a buyer's market and that the major concrete achievement of the women's movement in the 1970s was the Dutch Treat.'[29]

The other day I received through the mail a document prepared by some of these right-wing women. They called themselves the Concerned Women for America, and their pamphlet was entitled *To Manipulate a Housewife*.[30] It comprised a collection of quotes from prominent feminists:

Dr Mary Jo Bane: 'It [divorce] makes for better family life ... Divorce improves the quality of marriage.'

Gloria Steinem: 'By the year 2000 we will, I hope, raise our children to believe in human potential, not God ...'

Betty Friedan: 'The ERA has become both a symbol and substance for the whole of the modern women's movement for equality ... I am convinced if we lose this struggle we will have little hope in our own lifetime of saving our right to abortion ...'

And from a publication of the movement entitled *Women's Liberation, Notes from the Second Year:* 'We must destroy love ... Love promotes vulnerability, dependence, possessiveness, susceptibility to pain, and prevents the full development of woman's human potential by directing all her energies outward in the interest of others.'

The Concerned Women for America felt so threatened and betrayed by feminists that they printed a selection of quotes from the movement in order to warn other women of the powerful destructive force of feminism. They obviously believe that nothing explains their anti-ERA case better than a few statements from the pro-ERA feminist camp. In her brief introduction to the quotes which constitute *To Manipulate a Housewife*, Beverly Lahaye (described as author, lecturer, mother, and pastor's wife) writes, 'Before you and I decide about ERA let us consider from what motivation it was born.'[31]

Thus in America in the mid-1980s two opposing movements seek to represent women in a hostile and insecure world: the feminist movement (pro-ERA) and the anti-feminist movement (STOP ERA). As a woman you must either go out and compete as a male clone in an unequal job market, or you must attempt to bind men more tightly to you in an era when family bonds have become increasingly thin and fragile. For, fighting the ERA or banning abortion may slow the pace of change, but there is no effective way of putting the clock back and re-creating the values and lifestyles of the fifties. It's a little like trying to unscramble an egg. The attitudes and beliefs of the American people – toward sex, toward the family – have permanently shifted. Men, and at least some women, have grown to depend on their new freedoms and are unlikely to give them up. In short, there is a depressing futility to much of right-wing strategy.

While the right-wingers have been urging women to stay at home when the vast majority of American women cannot afford to do so, even if they wanted to, the modern feminist movement has told them to get out into the work place and take what is rightfully theirs. Caught in the middle are the 'displaced homemakers', whose sense of security in the home has been swept from under them, and women with small children who feel torn between their careers and the needs of their families and are not receiving adequate help from governments or husbands to enable them to juggle the two without sacrificing either or both. One thing seems sure: neither the feminist movement nor the anti-feminist movement has yet had much success in improving women's economic security in America today, at work or in the home.

·P·A·R·T· ·F·I·V·E·

Political Possibilities

14. What Can Trade Unions Do for Women?

Jane Brenner* lives in Oakland, California. She is a flight attendant with Pan American Airlines, a job she has held – with one interruption – for seventeen years. Her basic salary is $22,000 a year, but with overtime she can sometimes earn as much as $29,000. Jane is divorced and has a fourteen-year-old daughter.

Jane and I had breakfast together in the spring of 1985. We talked about her life, her job, and her union. In America unions are seen largely as an irrelevancy to everyday life. There are few closed shops, people working in industry do not belong to a union as a matter of course, and unions are not a central feature of public life. So I was rather surprised when Jane brought up the subject of her union. However, as she put it, 'The union has really come through for me. It has given me a much better deal on the job, and it has provided real security. Since my divorce [six years ago] this has been particularly important to me. You see, I wasn't entitled to any alimony, and my ex-husband pays only a hundred dollars a month in child support – despite the fact I was awarded two hundred and twenty-five dollars. All this means I am pretty much on my own financially.' Jane hesitated and added rather defiantly, 'I know it sounds kind of crazy, but my union has watched out for me and protected me. It has been like a father.'

I hastened to assure Jane that her point of view did not strike me as odd. When I told her that in Europe no one thinks it the slightest bit strange to belong to a union and that most people, including the highly educated, look to their unions for a basic set of rights and benefits, Jane relaxed and said with a small smile, 'I am so used to getting these hostile looks when I say that my union is important to me, it's as though I had confessed to some subversive activity.'

Jane's history is as follows. She joined Pan Am as a flight attendant in 1968. At that time the Transport Workers Union (TWU) represented most of the

Pan Am employees. Jane does not remember the TWU as being particularly helpful. For example, when she became pregnant in 1971, she was immediately fired (airline policy in the early 1970s). A group of flight attendants brought a class action suit against the airline industry, but although they eventually won the suit and established their right to keep their jobs through pregnancy, the TWU was not particularly interested in this fight and did not get too involved. Jane was reinstated in her job in 1973, and several years later a new union was formed by the flight attendants at Pan Am. According to Jane, this new union – the Independent Union of Flight Attendants – has done a terrific job.

'They get us big pay increases, but that isn't all. They understand that the conditions of work are at least as important as the rate of pay. I guess it's because the new union leaders are mostly women, and they have faced the problems involved in holding down a job and looking after a family. For example, if you have kids, it's important to be able to plan ahead so that you can arrange child care. Before this new union the airline could break your line whenever they wanted to – that is, they could tell you in London that you had an extra flight to Frankfurt and wouldn't be going home for another forty-eight hours. They can't do that any longer without paying a big penalty, and as a result, I now know my schedule ahead of time. The union has also won other rights. For instance, on long trips flight attendants are now entitled to rest seats or bunk beds, and if the aircraft is understaffed, they are entitled to overtime. All this makes for a much better job. The TWU never tapped these issues. The leadership of that union was composed of older men, and they couldn't get inside our skins and figure out what was important to us.'

I asked Jane what kinds of benefits were now available for pregnancy and childbirth. Her eyes lit up, and she said enthusiastically, 'You're not going to believe this, but most women I know get at least nine months, and they can arrange it so that about half that time is paid.' I looked at Jane in disbelief. I was simply not used to interviewing American women who had good news to report on the maternity leave front. So I asked Jane to explain how these, by American standards, incredibly generous policies came into being.

'Pan Am employees get six to eight weeks' paid disability leave for childbirth. On top of this our union contract gives us the right to accrue sick leave at the rate of two and a half days per month and use it as supplemental maternity leave. Most women who have been in the job a while can accumulate several extra months of paid leave this way. And what is more,' said Jane, taking a deep breath, 'if you can get a doctor's note saying that you need more time to recover from the birth or to breastfeed, the union will stand up for you and get you a job-protected leave of absence for another three to six months.' Jane paused and then said more reflectively, 'You see, the union can bargain for things an individual would never get on his or her own.

Imagine marching into the personnel office at the end of a four-month leave and asking for another few months off! You would most likely be fired. No matter how many doctor's notes you had, it wouldn't do you any good.'

Jane had one last thought: 'No one expects flight attendants to join a union. Most of us are college-educated, and many of us are nurturing, feminine women; we just don't fit the union stereotype of militant blue-collar workers. But despite our glamorous image, we don't work for pin money. These days we work for the same reason men work – we need to support ourselves and our children – and earning a good wage and getting decent working conditions have to be top priorities. If the union helps us achieve these things, of course we will become loyal members of the union.'[1]

It seems an obvious alliance – that between trade unions and working women. To put it baldly, they need each other. Women need better pay and better working conditions, and unions can help them fight for these things; unions need more members, and women are potential candidates because they comprise the fastest-growing segment of the work force – in America and in Europe.

Women continue to confront major obstacles in the work place. They bear the burden of a double work load, at home and on the job; they are segregated in low-wage jobs (which carry meagre benefits); and in every country in the Western world earn less than men – regardless of occupation. In short, they are at the end of the line when goodies are handed out.

As individual workers most women are powerless because they have few skills and little market power. A waitress, an office cleaner or an air hostess is dispensable and easily replaced. It therefore makes sense that women workers should band together and use their collective strength to raise wages and improve working conditions. Threatening to shut down a plant or to paralyse a bureaucracy by striking is one of the few ways unskilled workers can produce leverage over management and win a better deal on the job. The fact that, in America, unionised women workers earn, on average, 30 per cent more than non-unionised women workers speaks for itself.[2] Collectively women workers do better.

For more than a century this is what trade unionism has been about. Workers who are individually weak and disadvantaged join forces to improve their earning power and conditions of work. It is a practice which has been successfully followed by male workers in every industrial country, but curiously not one which women have used to nearly the same degree – especially in America. For Jane Brenner is the exception rather than the rule. Only 14 per cent of working women in the United States belong to unions,[3] as opposed to 40 per cent in Britain and a full 70 per cent in Sweden.[4]

227

Dana Stark's* experience is typical of the other 86 per cent of American women workers. Dana is in her early thirties and is married to a postal worker. She has two sons, aged six years and twelve months, and she works as a kindergarten teacher in a private school in Boston. She does not belong to a union. Ever since her first child was born, Dana has found it a continuous struggle to both hold down a job and raise her children.

In the autumn of 1982, when her second child was born, Dana ran into some particularly severe problems. It all started when she took a three-month leave of absence in the wake of the birth. She had verbal assurances that her job would be kept open for her, and she had also been told that six to eight weeks of this period would be covered by disability insurance – the only method of receiving some sort of maternity benefit in the United States. Both things turned out not to be true. When she reported back for work in January 1983, she discovered that all the school would offer her was a part-time job at half her former salary. Her old job had been filled. Dana said, 'It was a real shock to be treated so badly. I thought I had such a good relationship with the head of the school that I had neglected to obtain anything in writing.' As for the disability insurance, which has to be claimed from a private insurance company, it just failed to come through. When I interviewed her in the autumn of 1983, Dana had yet to be paid for the weeks she had been out of work. She had filed her claim five or six times, but nothing happened. As she put it, 'I think the insurance company is just waiting for me to give up.'

Reflecting on her recent experiences, Dana told me, 'It's very hard fighting big bureaucracies on your own, especially if you have just had a child and are up to your eyeballs in sleepless nights and dirty diapers. I really needed some protection this last year, someone to help me deal with the insurance company, someone to help me get my full-time job back at the school.' Dana needs a union.[5]

If women need unions, unions need new members. Over the past decade trade unions in the United States have suffered massive membership losses in the industrial sector of the economy, their traditional power base. Fierce foreign competition has spurred many companies to shift production to low-wage countries. This, coupled with a severe recession, has resulted in exceptionally high levels of unemployment, especially in manufacturing industry. The AFL-CIO lost 2.7 million members between 1980 and 1984, even though employment in the United States rose by 3.8 million during this period.[6] If trade unions in America want to avoid becoming just a part of urban folklore, they must move into non-traditional areas and recruit workers in the fast-growing financial and service sectors. Since more than two-thirds of new jobs in these sectors are now going to women, this means that unions need to make themselves attractive to American women.

Some unions are seizing this opportunity. The American Federation of State, County and Municipal Employees (AFSCME), for example, which sees itself as 'a leading advocate for the rights of women workers',[7] and declares in its promotional literature that 'the battleground for women's rights is the workplace',[8] has been concerned with work and family issues for a decade now. In a country where no one has statutory entitlement to maternity leave, AFSCME's New York area branch has negotiated child-care leaves for both mothers and fathers in many of its contracts. The leave, at the time of birth or adoption of a child, is unpaid but fully job-protected for a period of four years for a first child and three years for each subsequent child. The union has also actively pursued flexitime.

Many of AFSCME's women members are segregated into traditional low-paid areas; indeed, half of them work in clerical jobs. And to help these workers improve their earning power, AFSCME has become a vigorous proponent of the principle of equal pay for jobs of comparable value. As we saw in Chapter Three, the argument is that women have been segregated into jobs on the basis of sex and as a result are paid less than employees in male jobs which require an equivalent amount of skill, effort, and responsibility. The strategy is to conduct job evaluations, measure the intrinsic value of different jobs, and come up with a numerical rating for each. If a secretary is rated the same as a caretaker, then a secretary should be paid the same as a caretaker.

In July 1981 the San Jose branch of AFSCME representing municipal workers in the city went on strike for nine days over the issue of pay equity for its women workers. The strike was settled when the city agreed to provide $1.5 million for pay equity adjustments of 5 to 15 per cent over two years for more than sixty female-dominated job classifications. These increases were in addition to the 15 per cent pay raise negotiated for all union members over the two-year contract.[9]

Unions are a natural vehicle for combating discrimination through occupational segregation. Attempting to prove that secretaries, nurses or social workers are systematically underpaid is an arduous and expensive process. It often involves underwriting the costs of job evaluation studies, negotiating collective-bargaining agreements that include equitable wage increases, filing litigation against employers, and educating employees through meetings and publications. Few individuals could begin to bear the costs of such processes.

Despite the enthusiasm displayed by Jane Brenner and individual unions such as AFSCME, there are some powerful obstacles in the way of an attempt by organised labour in America to forge an across-the-board alliance with women workers.

First there is the historical legacy. Unions in America have a history of either ignoring or being hostile to women workers. From the beginning of the labour movement in the mid nineteenth century the focus was on the white male breadwinner; women were regarded as second-class workers. They were excluded from all but two of the thirty national unions formed during the 1863–73 period, and discrimination worsened under the influence of the American Federation of Labor (AFL), founded in 1886 by Samuel Gompers. Gompers created the AFL as a vehicle to organise skilled workers on the basis of craft. This automatically kept out women, who were clustered in unskilled and less prestigious work. But the AFL's antagonism to women ran deeper than this.

According to historian William Chafe, the AFL was hostile to women workers on pragmatic grounds.[10] The transient, impermanent, and unskilled nature of most women's work made organising women workers a difficult and time-consuming process, and in the end the gains would be small. The AFL thought that its energies were better invested in male workers, who, if the efforts of the union were successful, would earn enough to support entire families. The goal of achieving a 'family wage' for the working man was touted loudly and continuously by the AFL, despite the fact that many women also needed a decent wage (more than 90 per cent of working women in America at the turn of the century were single, and many of them belonged to families that were in no fit state to support them).

Trade union pragmatism on the subject of working women was embedded in an overall conservative philosophy. The AFL believed in a bread-and-butter labour movement, the goal of which was to protect the wages, skills and status of the native-born craftsmen who formed the élite of the American working class. This philosophy stood in sharp contrast with the radical socialism espoused by less influential workers' organisations such as the Industrial Workers of the World (IWW). The conservatism of the AFL spilled over into its stance on women workers. Gompers spelt out his organisation's view of women in the work force: 'We stand for the principle that it is wrong to permit any member of the female sex of our country to be forced to work, as we believe that the man should be provided with a fair wage in order to keep his female relatives from going to work. The man is the provider and should receive enough for his labor to give his family a respectable living.'[11] The AFL's hostility toward organising women had predictable results: in 1908 women represented a mere 2.9 per cent of union members in the United States.[12]

In response to this exclusion from the male unions American women formed their own organisations. The WTUL (Women's Trade Union League) was founded in 1903. Led by a national policy-making unit and supported by local leagues in cities such as New York, Boston, Chicago and St Louis, the

WTUL provided money, publicity, tactical advice and political support for women attempting to unionise themselves at work. The league demonstrated its success in the 1909–10 strike of women in the New York garment industry, which resulted in better working conditions for women in this sector of the economy.

Despite this encouraging beginning, the WTUL soon became bogged down in tensions with the AFL, and by 1915 the WTUL had turned away from the direct organisation of workers. From then on it sought to solve the problems of women at work by lobbying government offices for changes via the legislative process. By the 1920s the WTUL was almost exclusively geared towards protective legislation. As we saw in Chapter Eight, its sponsorship of protective legislation put it at odds with the dominant feminist groups of the day. Organisations such as the National Woman's Party were interested in equal rights, not in special treatment.

The late 1920s and early 1930s were a difficult time for organised labour in America, and in these chaotic years unions increasingly concentrated their energies on protecting their male workers. However, in the mid-1930s things started to look up and in 1936–9 the CIO (Congress of Industrial Organisations – a sort of TUC) went on a massive recruitment drive of women, as a result of which a significant number joined the labour movement. For the first time large numbers of women workers won the right to adequate pay, holidays and fringe benefits. But even the CIO did not treat women equally and in male-dominated industries many union contracts featured unequal pay scales for men and women. During the Second World War some unions did fight for equal pay for women, but generally only for women who took over men's jobs, the main goal being to preserve high pay rates for the men who would be reclaiming their jobs after the war.

In the post-war era the CIO continued to have some success in organising women. But in general, modern American unions have failed to become a primary vehicle for solving the problems of women workers. In the 1980s only 14 per cent of women workers belong to unions (compared with 23 per cent of male workers), and women constitute only 28 per cent of union membership despite the fact that they now make up 45 per cent of the total United States work force.[13]

The historical antagonism to women workers and bias towards the male breadwinner spills over into the modern American labour movement.

Lisa Gorden* is twenty-seven years old and has worked for the phone company since she was sixteen. She started out as an operator but about four years ago was promoted and is now a communications technician. She earns approximately $35,000 a year, and as Lisa says, 'That's not bad for a working woman.' Ever since she started work, she has been a member of the

231

Communications Workers of America (CWA). Indeed, for a couple of years in her early twenties she was a shop steward in this union.

Lisa was married in 1982 and gave birth to a daughter in May 1984. Before her baby was born, Lisa knew she would return to work. Her husband works nights as a security guard and is not well paid; Lisa's salary represents 65 per cent of total family income. They could not make ends meet on her husband's salary alone. Besides, she feels she has put in a lot of time at the phone company and she would never be able to find another job as well paid.

Before her daughter was born, she did not anticipate any difficulty. She would take the six-month maternity leave she was guaranteed in her union contract (six weeks at full pay, the rest unpaid but with a job guarantee) and then leave her daughter with a baby-sitter while she went back to work.

The first week back at work Lisa realised that the baby-sitter she had lined up (an unemployed teenager) was not going to work out. The sitter couldn't handle the baby and kept calling Lisa at work. Lisa didn't know what to do. She couldn't just go home and get her baby; she was afraid of losing her job. As it turned out, she spent a good part of that week crumpled up in the ladies' toilet crying. But at least she punched the time clock, and no one could say she wasn't putting in the hours.

Lisa finally found a member of her family (her husband's cousin) to look after her daughter. But the cousin lives far away, and Lisa has to get up at 5.30 a.m. and take her daughter there by bus before taking the train to work. Often either the bus or the train is late, and by the time Lisa gets to her office she's 'all wound up and in a foul mood'.

Lisa knows what she needs: on-site child care. Failing that, she would settle for part-time work or a job-sharing arrangement.

Despite her previous union involvement (or perhaps because of it!), Lisa has not taken her problems to the union. 'I know that they are totally uninterested in providing child care. The official CWA position is that child care should be a government responsibility. Fat lot of good that does me. As for part-time work and job sharing, they are not strong advocates of either one. You see, the union is still oriented toward men with stay-at-home wives, and these men don't want job sharing. In fact, they find the whole concept threatening.' Lisa paused and then said thoughtfully, 'I guess that by catering to the male head of household, the union did become pretty good at negotiating high wages, but this same orientation gets in the way of helping women workers deal with family demands.' (One fact seems to support Lisa in her contention that the CWA continues to gear itself toward the male breadwinner: the union is still led by men. As of early 1985 only one out of a 23-member executive board was a woman.)

I asked Lisa one last question. Did she think that the American women's movement had helped people like her? Lisa hesitated before answering. 'That's a hard question,' she said. 'You see, the goals of the feminists are great, we all want to be equal, but I can't think of anything concrete they have accomplished for working women like me. I wish they had spent less time on ERA and more on child care. Access to high-quality day care – now that is something that would really make a difference.' She paused and then added, 'I guess those women libbers can mostly afford private baby-sitters and don't realise how hard it is for ordinary families.'[14]

If unions in America are handicapped by their historical orientation towards the male breadwinner, they are also inhibited by their declining strength and by their political unpopularity.

In 1945, 35 per cent of employed wage and salary workers in America belonged to unions. By the mid-1980s this figure had dropped to 19 per cent.[15] An important contributing factor in the recent decline was the 1981–2 recession because 'unemployment hit hardest in industries where unions were strong, but, to date, the recovery has been most vigorous in industries and occupations that typically have low levels of unionisation'.[16]

For union membership in the United States is concentrated in declining sectors of the economy. In mining, construction and manufacturing more than 30 per cent of all workers are unionised[17] – low by British standards, but high by American standards, where there are few closed shops. However, because of fierce foreign competition, this so-called sunset segment of the American economy suffered a net employment loss of 800,000 jobs between 1980 and 1984.[18] Most unions in this sector have their backs to the wall and spend their best energies keeping as many of their members as possible in work. By and large, industrial unions have failed to move aggressively into growth areas of the American economy.

In addition to the problems posed by its declining industrial base, organised labour in America is, as in Britain, currently operating in a hostile political environment. This was signalled early on in the Reagan administration when 12,000 striking air traffic controllers were fired and their union was decertified – that is, its official licence to operate as a union was taken away. As the political influence of the American trade union movement reaches a new low, so, too, does the appeal of the movement to the average American worker. As one UAW (United Auto Workers) member put it, 'The unions don't work for our interest. They are just another power structure. Uncle Sam takes our taxes, and the union takes our dues. Neither does anything for us.'[19]

All these factors argue for a change in focus. If American unions are to recoup their strength, they have to shift gears. They have to move away from their historical identification with the male breadwinner and the industrial sector and become relevant to women workers in service-sector employment. For the American labour market is undergoing massive change. In the 1980–84 period, when 800,000 jobs were lost in the industrial sector of the economy, employment in services grew by 5 million as health care, business services, finance and insurance expanded rapidly. More than 3 million of these jobs went to women.[20] These new recruits to the American work force have a long list of unmet needs.

In Europe, the commitment of trade unions to working women has varied from country to country. However, on the whole they have organised a much larger proportion of the female work force than in America, providing women with a standard set of benefits and protections – a better wage, job security, health and retirement benefits. Unions in Europe have also been successful in fighting for items that are of particular concern to women workers: subsidised day care, generous maternity and parental leave, better conditions for part-time work, and pay equity (narrowing the gap between male and female earnings). Sometimes unions have included these items in their contract negotiations; sometimes they have prevailed on government to provide these benefits to the population at large.

Marie Norstrom is thirty-six years old. She is a blue-collar assembly-line worker at an aerodynamics plant in Stockholm, Sweden. Altogether she has worked there for fifteen years. Her husband and her ex-husband both work in the same plant.

She has two sons, a ten-year-old from her first marriage and a three-year-old from her present marriage. She works part time (seven hours a day instead of eight) and will be allowed to keep this part-time schedule until her youngest child is eight. This is important because otherwise she would have to leave for work too early to drop off the youngest at the childminder on her way to work. She takes him to the childminder at 7.30 a.m. and starts work at 8 a.m. Her husband, who is a foreman at the plant, starts work at 7 a.m., as would she if she worked full time. The older boy goes to school by himself. In the afternoons he goes to the same childminder as the younger child. This woman also looks after three other children. Marie and her husband pay an income-adjusted fee for family day care; it amounts to 10 per cent of Marie's salary. They pay the city government, and the city pays the childminder directly. The childminder has a good income from her job and runs a comfortable home with lots of special equipment for the children. Marie is very satisfied with the care her children receive.

When her first child was born, maternity leave was not an issue because

Marie was not working. When her younger son was born, she took nine months off at full pay and one additional month at reduced pay. After the tenth month she went back to work and the baby was placed in the care of the same childminder who cares for him now. Marie is also entitled to leave from work to care for her children if they are sick. Over the past year she has taken twenty-three days for this purpose.

Marie feels very satisfied with her life. She says that even if she didn't need to work, she would work. Because of her divorce, she is aware of how important it is for women to be economically independent. Her one wish would be for a larger flat, but they are hard to find and very expensive. Her flat is clean and modestly furnished, but small. There are three rooms plus a kitchen and bathroom. Each boy has his own room, and Marie and her husband sleep in the living-room.

I asked Marie if she belonged to a union. She looked at me in surprise. 'Of course,' she said. 'In Sweden almost everyone belongs to a union.' I then asked her if the union provided important benefits. Marie thought for a moment and then said, 'Fifteen years ago workers – particularly women – had to fight hard to get decent wages and decent conditions of work. They mostly fought for these things through the LO [workers' federation]. I remember the women in my union fighting very hard to get union support for day care. Most of these battles were won, and eventually the government passed laws that gave working people a whole range of benefits and services. These days we don't need the union to fight for parental leave because now it is available to everyone.' Marie paused and then added, 'Most of us take these benefits for granted.'[21]

Sweden is an example of a country where trade unions have done much to improve the economic conditions of women's lives. The work-force participation rate and the union membership rate for women are among the highest in the world. Of working-age women, 65 per cent are in the work force, and women constitute 45 per cent of the work force. Of these women workers, 70 per cent are unionised, a figure that rises to 90 per cent among manual workers.[22]

The early history of trade unions in Sweden is similar to that of other Western countries. They grew up in the late nineteenth century, and the early days of the movement were marked by sex-segregated unions and separate and lower pay scales for women workers.

In the 1940s the LO and the SAF (the employers' federation) began to work together. In 1948 a joint LO–SAF committee was formed to investigate women's pay, and in 1951 a joint LO–SAF Women's Labour Council was formed. The council supported ways to get women into the work force and advocated higher wages, part-time work and subsidised child care. But not too much happened until the labour shortages that accompanied the economic expansion of the early 1960s. Other European countries solved the labour shortage through guest worker schemes, but the LO strongly opposed this option, stating that it would 'slow down the trend towards greater equality for women in the job market . . . which is taking place too slowly in any case'.[23] To encourage women to join the work force, the LO supported policies designed to reduce women's double burden in the home and in the work place. Subsidised day care, extensive maternity leave and the right to part-time work for mothers with young children were part of this initiative.

The single most important initiative for women workers was the solidarity wage strategy adopted in agreements between the LO and the SAF in the mid-1960s. The first step in this plan was the phasing out of separate pay scales for women, and further steps included raising the wages of low-paid workers and of workers within low-wage industries. Women benefited disproportionately from the solidarity wage strategy since they were concentrated in low-paid jobs and industries. The wage gap between women and men in manual occupations narrowed from 30 per cent in 1959 to 7 per cent in 1981.[24]

In the late 1960s Swedish attitudes underwent a further change, and a concern for women's rights was replaced by a concern for gender equality. The trade unions and the Social Democratic Party began to realise that true equality would require changes in the social role played by men. In keeping with this new thinking, the unions abolished their women's councils toward the end of the decade and replaced them with family councils. Meanwhile, the Social Democratic Party launched a programme to achieve equal status for men and women in work and family life. It included legislation to enforce non-discrimination in hiring, promotion and wage determination; parental leave at the time of childbirth (for women and men); separate taxation for married couples; and training programmes for men and women entering non-traditional fields. The LO remains sceptical of the effectiveness of legislation and has insisted on keeping wages, hiring and promotion practices within the sphere of collective bargaining.

Italy is another example of a country where unions have helped upgrade the economic position of women.

The modern Italian labour movement emerged after the Second World War with the formation of three major union confederations: the CGIL (dominated by the Communists), the CSIL (dominated by the Catholics), and the UIL (dominated by the Social Democrats). All three union confederations and their affiliated unions had women's commissions. It was through these commissions that union policies toward women workers were formulated.[25] In 1946 the CGIL and the employers' federation signed an agreement on maternity leave. The provisions of the leave were improved upon four years later, when national legislation, proposed by the CGIL, was passed. This legislation provided for a compulsory leave from work at 80 per cent of normal wages for three months prior to, and two months following, childbirth. It also required employers to allow work breaks for breast-feeding for the first year of a child's life, and made it the employer's responsibility to provide special nursery space for this purpose. In addition, it became illegal to fire a woman while she was pregnant or for a full year following childbirth. In 1971 this legislation was expanded to include health care benefits and a six-month additional, partially paid, maternity leave. Over the last ten years the unions have been involved in the successful effort to establish subsidised day care, and they have been strong advocates of the Family Charter described in Chapter Six.

On the wages front Italian unions, like Swedish unions, have been concerned with upgrading the weakest elements in the work force. They supported the 1960 legislation on equal pay for women, but they have also fought to raise the wages of the lowest-paid workers by pushing for flat-rate wage increases. Since women predominate in low-paid work, this has had the effect of narrowing differentials between men and women. Between 1962 and 1980 women's wages in the industrial sector rose from 70 per cent of men's earnings to 84 per cent.[26]

Article 37 of the Italian Constitution endorses equality between men and women as regards work and wages as long as the conditions of work do not endanger 'women's essential family and maternal roles'.[27] This wording was the result of a compromise among the political parties, the trade unions and the Catholic Church. The modern Italian state tries to promote both equality of opportunity and a strong family life. It sees the need for equal rights in the sphere of work and social benefits to ease the family responsibilities of working women.

In both Sweden and Italy trade unions have significantly improved the lot of women workers. In Britain, unfortunately, the trade union movement has been conspicuously less enthusiastic in its pursuit of women's economic rights.

Cathy Holdern is thirty-two years old, teaches in a primary school in Oxford, England, and is an active member of a union – the National Union of Teachers (NUT). She is also the mother of a ten-month-old daughter. When she gave birth, she was entitled to a six-month, job-protected maternity leave – the first month at full pay, the next two weeks at nine-tenths pay, the following three months at half pay, and one and a half months at no pay. Cathy and her husband could not manage without her salary, so after four and a half months she returned to work, leaving her daughter with a childminder, whose services cost about half of Cathy's salary.

Cathy has mixed feelings about how much her union has helped her cope with her new responsibilities. 'The union did negotiate a better maternity leave than I would have been entitled to under the Employment Protection Act, but progress on other fronts has been minimal.' For example, Cathy would prefer to put her child in an on-site nursery, but when she tried to drum up support for this idea within the union, she failed to get any response from her male colleagues. She finds that the problem of stirring up interest in child care is compounded by the difficulties she now faces in attending union meetings – a problem that most working mothers have to contend with. 'Local meetings are held at 4.15, and since babies and young children are allowed to come along, I can attend these, but regional and national meetings are another story. These are invariably held in the evenings or at weekends, and there are no arrangements for baby-sitting, so there is no way I can go.' Partly as a result of this, the leadership of Cathy's union remains predominantly male – despite the fact that 70 per cent of its members are women.

Cathy sees herself as a feminist and has been active in a wide array of feminist causes and organisations. Her considered judgement is that the lack of affordable, high-quality child care is the major obstacle preventing women from achieving equality in the British job market. She told me rather bitterly, 'It's the old story: women get penalised for having children, and men get promoted for having children to support. Child care is society's responsibility, but this will come about only if individual women band together and fight for it. The labour movement is a good place to start, although not much has happened yet.'[28]

Cathy Holdern is right: British unions have made little headway on the child-care front. There are certainly more child-care facilities available to the average British worker than to her American counterpart, even if they fall far short of needs. However, compared with the rest of Europe, the British working mother fares badly. The unions have failed to persuade government to provide day care and pre-school nurseries for the children of working parents, and have done little to subsidise child care directly.

Over the years, the TUC has paid considerable lip service to women's issues. Directly after the First World War it established a women's division and in 1931 the first conference of unions enrolling women was held. A permanent Women's Advisory Committee was set up; however, this committee was only 'advisory', without decision-making or executive powers. Throughout the thirties women who belonged to unions held 'women's jobs' that were designated as such, and were paid at 'women's' (i.e. lower) rates of pay. Women were never really accepted as full union members by their male colleagues, but were organised into special sections. They paid a reduced membership fee but received reduced benefits.

It was not until the 1950s that British women workers really began to fight for equal pay. The first struggle was fought by women civil servants, supported by their unions, and they did not achieve equal pay until 1961. By the mid-1960s teachers and many professional women had won equal pay concessions, but the *right* to equal pay was not guaranteed to the rest of the female work force until the Equal Pay Act was passed in 1970, after receiving the belated support of the union movement. The Equal Pay Act was followed by the Sex Discrimination Act in 1975, both of which came into force in 1976.

However, since the passage of the Equal Pay Act, there has been less progress in narrowing the gap between men's and women's earnings than had been hoped for. This is partly because of the less-than-forceful language of the final act, and partly because many employers can circumvent the requirements by restructuring their work force or by re-evaluating jobs, and the enforcement mechanisms are inadequate. Also, with legislation, as opposed to collective bargaining, it is often up to the individual woman to bring a discrimination suit against an employer, which is a daunting process for most people. Since 1972, women's earnings compared to men's have increased from 59.5 per cent to 68.9 per cent, but since 1976, the year the Equal Pay Act went into effect, the pay differential has remained static. Most recently, British unions have pushed employers and the government to move towards equal pay for work of equal value. For example, in early 1985 SOGAT (Society of Graphical and Allied Trades), one of the few unions actually led by a woman, Brenda Dean, used the threat of an equal value lawsuit to close the wage gap between jobs held mostly by women and those held mostly by men.[29]

The TUC has campaigned more effectively in the area of statutory maternity leave. In 1975 the Employment Protection Act gave women – for the first time – statutory protection against job loss through pregnancy and childbirth. The benefits granted were less far-reaching than the provision the TUC had lobbied for; however, many unions have been successful in negotiating for better protection with individual employers. In theory, the TUC officially supports comprehensive and universal child care and nursery schooling for all children, but in practice it has done little in the way of pursuing this policy.

British unions have been highly successful in their recruitment of women workers – no mean accomplishment in view of the stagnant economy and high rates of unemployment. Between 1971 and 1981 there was a 50 per cent increase in the number of women in trade unions; indeed, a full 40 per cent of women workers now belong to a union.[30] It is therefore crucial to the unions, now that women make up an increasingly large percentage of their members, that they address very seriously the concerns of women workers. The TUC is cautiously optimistic, pointing to:

obvious improvements in the attitude of unions to women members and action has been taken in particular on the inclusion of equality clauses in collective agreements, the provision of child-care facilities, women's conferences and training schools, and especially, the establishment of advisory committees on equal opportunities at national and local level.

However, although improvements can be seen there is certainly no room for complacency.[31]

Like Britain, trade unions in France have a mixed track record when it comes to women workers, but there are some early examples of constructive action. The *Accords Matignon* negotiated in 1936 was an agreement between the government and the unions to establish a code of work regulations for the treatment of pregnant women and the equalisation of women's wages with men's. The laws established maternity leave for women workers and guaranteed benefits and job security. They reflected the unions' and the government's shared belief that motherhood was 'a social function, similar to military service for men, that had to be financially supported by the whole community'.[32] The *Accords* guaranteed maternity benefits to housewives as well as workers, thus gaining the support of conservatives and Catholics. The 1936 union–government agreement had a significant effect on women's wages. Until 1935 women had earned half men's wages; after the agreement the gap narrowed by 15 per cent.[33]

Most recently, the unions have given their guarded approval to what has come to be known as the Rondy law (after Yvette Rondy, Minister for Women's Rights), passed in 1982, in which positive discrimination towards women has been introduced for the first time in France; the law also sets up the legal framework through which women can exercise their rights. However, women's committees in some unions have been encountering difficulties with their male colleagues, and others are even having their existence questioned. It remains to be seen how serious French trade unions are in their pursuit of women's rights.

There are some obvious differences between the labour movements in the United States and in Europe. In many Western European countries trade unions hold a legitimate and powerful position in the overall structure of society. Today 53 per cent of all workers are unionised in Britain; 60 per cent in Italy; 25 per cent in France; 70 per cent in Sweden; and 42 per cent in West Germany,[34] as compared with the United States, where only 19 per cent of the work force belongs to trade unions.[35] Cathy Holdern might be critical of her union, but one should not lose sight of the fact that some protection is better than none. At least 40 per cent of British working women have better maternity leave and better job protection because they belong to unions, while only 14 per cent of American working women have these advantages.

The greater strength of the labour movement in Europe is a result of the deeply ingrained class structure of most European countries, the socialist tradition that runs through their histories, and the strong alliances most trade unions have with the established political parties. Unions in Europe exert their power differently – through strikes in Britain and Italy, and through co-determination and co-operation in Germany, France and Sweden. However, in all these countries trade unions do have tremendous power to exert. Their power may be modified in times of recession, but it is not fundamentally questioned.

The greater strength and legitimacy of trade unions in Europe have enabled them to do more for working women. They have supported 'protective' or gender-specific social legislation that has led to extensive rights and benefits for working women at the time of pregnancy and childbirth. And they have successfully narrowed the gap between male and female earnings by working to raise the wages of the lowest-paid workers in the work force.

But it is not just that European trade unions have greater power than their American counterparts; the specifics of their political agendas owe much to the goals and strategy of social feminism. As we saw in Chapter Seven, European social feminists, unlike American feminists, chose not to form their own separatist organisations. Instead, they decided to work through political parties and trade unions to obtain concrete benefits for women. Relatively less concerned with formal equality, they openly pressed for special support structures that would help women bear their double burden in the home and on the job. When Marie Norstrom talked about Swedish women's successfully pressuring the union to support day care, she was describing social feminism in action.

Contrast this with the United States, where protective or special legislation for women workers has always attracted the vehement opposition of feminists. This is a result of the American preoccupation with equal rights, but it also flows from the élitism of the feminist organisations. In the 1920s it was difficult for the upper-middle-class supporters of Alice Paul's National Woman's Party to grasp that ordinary working women might need protection and support. And in the 1980s it is hard for Yuppies on the fast track – the constituency of NOW – to see that bank clerks or nursery-school teachers need maternity leave, even though such leave discriminates against men. Lisa Gorden is right when she accuses the American women's movement of being out of touch with the reality of working-class life.

American trade unions also have to decide whether they will continue as before, fighting for the needs of male breadwinners in declining industries, or whether they will follow a new path and respond to the massive increase of women workers in the service and new technology sectors of the American economy, and so turn their resources to furthering the cause of women in the work place.

Some union leaders voice great optimism; they do see trade unions forging a valuable alliance with working women. Joyce Miller, a vice-president with the Amalgamated Clothing and Textile Workers Union, says with quiet confidence, 'We in the labor movement know the fastest way for women to gain economic equality is to join a union',[36] while a senior officer at the Communications Workers of America told me that 'pushing for women and women's issues would definitely be a way of getting us [labor] out of a hole'.[37] And it is clear that some unions in the United States – especially those, like AFSCME, that are based in the expanding service section – have begun to address these issues. However, it must be said that most unions and most union leaders have not shifted gears. One fact speaks for itself: between 1980 and 1984, years when service-sector jobs increased by 5 million in the United States, the number of service-sector employees belonging to unions fell by 700,000.[38] Despite valiant attempts by AFSCME and other unions spearheading change, the American labour movement has actually lost ground in the most dynamic segment of the economy. It seems that most unions are too busy fighting rearguard actions in declining industries to see even their own self-interest. For the American labour movement is fighting for its life and can no longer afford the luxury of concentrating on male industrial workers. Industry is a declining segment of the American economy, and men are a declining proportion of the work force. In 1984 for the first time white men did not represent a majority of the American work force.[39]

One thing seems sure: trade unions are much more likely to take up the cause of women workers if feminist leaders encourage them to do so. Feminists can help unions broaden their appeal because they can help reach out to women in offices, banks and shops. These women tend to associate unions with factories and like to identify themselves as middle-class. But, as Jane Brenner found out, even college-educated women in America can learn to value the protections and benefits conferred by trade union membership.

To date union leaders and feminist leaders in America have had different sets of priorities. While feminists have been separatist and élitist in orientation, unions have been dominated by men and male concerns. Moreover, the feminist focus on legal equality has been inconsistent with bargaining for special benefits to meet the needs of working women.

As Europe, and in particular Sweden, has shown, feminists and trade unionists can work hand in hand to achieve concrete objectives on behalf of working women. If America were to take the same course, trade unionism and feminism in the United States would also reap the benefits, for they would take on a new relevance and a new vitality in a country where both movements have lost much credibility with ordinary working people.

A final note. Shortly after inteviewing Jane Brenner, I came across a newspaper account of a new agreement between Pan Am and its flight attendants. The *New York Times* announced: 'The Independent Union of Flight Attendants . . . agreed to major concessions to Pan Am, including more flexible work rules and starting pay for new attendants that is 37 per cent lower than the pay at which current attendants started.'[40] My heart sank. Jane's confidence in her union had been contagious; I did not want to know that this confidence had been misplaced. I read the rest of the article and was somewhat cheered to learn that flight attendants currently employed by the airline would receive a wage increase of 21.5 per cent over a three-year period, and at least some of their protective work rules would be maintained.

The moral of this story is that when the going gets rough – and since deregulation the going has been very rough in the American airline industry – workers need union protection more than ever. I talked to Jane about the new agreement, and she is convinced that without her union she would have lost her job. As she put it, 'Why not get rid of expensive older workers and bring in 21-year-olds at a much cheaper rate? After all, there are no skills in this business. A 21-year-old can serve drinks as well as I can . . . The only reason I am still around is that the union fought for our jobs real hard . . . and they even got us a raise.'[41]

15. The Establishment Gropes for an Answer

Many of us have opinions on what policies government (or private employers) ought to take up in order to help women. I, in particular, have well-developed opinions on what should happen in America. I have thought about this topic a great deal over the last three to four years.

But strong opinions or even well-informed opinions do not, on their own, produce change. I decided that if I were to come up with a plan of action that carried any conviction, if I were to avoid building castles in the sky, I would have to engage the energies of people close to the centres of power. So I decided to turn directly to some major players in the American economy.

Since 1981 I have been director of the Economic Policy Council (EPC) of the United Nations Association, a powerful private-sector think-tank made up of business leaders, labour leaders, economists, educationalists and policy analysts.[1] Each year the council launches two study panels each of which explores a major economic problem and comes to a set of policy recommendations. I persuaded the EPC that family life in America was in the midst of revolutionary change and that this was throwing off problems that had major economic as well as social implications. In 1983 we set up a policy panel chaired by Alice Ilchman (president, Sarah Lawrence College) and John Sweeney (president, the Service Employees International Union), and funded by the Ford and Rockefeller foundations. Its mission was to investigate the problems facing working women in America and to recommend policy measures that would help resolve these problems. Members of the panel included former President Gerald Ford, Steven Ross (chairman of Warner Communications), Katharine Graham (chairman, the Washington Post Company) and the prominent feminist leader Betty Friedan. What follows is an object lesson in how a powerful segment of the American Establishment views issues of family and working women.

Trouble started almost immediately when I began to invite EPC members to join the panel – absolutely standard procedure once the chairpersons and funding are in place. I had always known that it would be important to include a large contingent of prominent men in this work. All too often issues such as child care and parental leave are treated as women's problems, and most committees and panels on these subjects feature women sitting around talking to the converted. If I was interested in the view of the Establishment, or if I was interested in making an impact on those in a position to do something, my panel had to speak for and to male leaders.

To begin with, I did not envisage a problem in getting my male membership involved. In 1983 the Economic Policy Council had approximately 100 members, and since these members were from the topmost ranks of business, academia and organised labour, very few of them were women. Quite aside from counting on the numerical dominance of men within the Economic Policy Council, the staff had done careful groundwork for this panel and we all thought the stage was set for enthusiastic male participation. The project was developed in such a way as to stress: the importance of bolstering the family; the parental burdens faced by fathers as well as by mothers; the price paid by children for America's lack of family support systems; and the desirability of investing in the next generation. The hidden agenda was, of course, the need to convince mainstream Establishment men that these problems go way beyond women's rights and the politics of liberation. Conservatives have an interest in keeping the family healthy and strong, and most businessmen can see the point in investing in human resources.

But when I attempted to convene my panel in the spring and summer of 1983, I got a rude awakening. Most of my distinguished male members were simply not interested; they either yawned or raised their eyebrows when I insisted on explaining to them why they should get involved. After listening to my pitch, one eminent banker looked embarrassed and told me rather lamely that he was not 'up to speed' in this area, and couldn't he join one of our other panels? I should point out that these men were not, in general, shrinking violets and had no problem in speaking out on Japanese defence policy or Third World debt, even when they had no expertise in the area. Somehow issues like maternity leave and child care made them very nervous. But it was not just nerves; I could have overcome an attack of nerves. When pushed, they revealed another reason behind their reluctance to get involved: family policy simply had no standing in their world. Being involved in this project would get them no Brownie points in boardrooms or at cocktail parties. It seemed clear that while they might sacrifice precious time getting 'up to speed' on Japanese defence policy, they were not prepared to do so for 'women's stuff' – as one member called it.

If the male reaction was bad, the female reaction was even more difficult to take. I discovered that most of my distinguished women members weren't interested either. I remember feeling almost numb when one woman, a senior vice-president at a major manufacturing corporation, excused herself on the ground that she could not afford to become identified with this panel. She explained, 'It has taken me fifteen years to get a hard-nosed reputation, and I just daren't risk it. If I were to get involved in these messy women's issues, it could do me a lot of harm in the company.' She was a kind woman and followed this up with a piece of personal advice: 'You know, if I were you, I would drop this whole project. You are an economist who has had enough sense to build a career in serious fields such as development economics. Why risk all that by getting everyone's back up?' The most depressing thing about her response was that I knew enough about her personal history to understand that she herself had encountered difficulties in bearing children mid-career. If she wouldn't take these issues seriously, who would?

Another corporate woman did allow herself to be persuaded to join the panel but halfway through the project threatened to resign because I would not take child care off the agenda. Needless to say, we had always planned to spend at least two panel sessions on the critical problem of child care. Imagine, then, my surprise when this top-ranking woman executive called, just before the first child-care meeting, and tried to derail it. 'I don't know what child care has to do with the employment problems of women,' she said militantly. 'If a woman chooses to have children, then she should deal with the consequences.' I opened my mouth, intending to explain how children were a social as well as an individual responsibility. But then I closed it again. I didn't know how to combat such entrenched hostility toward working mothers. This particular corporate woman was in her fifties and childless. I suspected that she had mixed in with her policy perspective a great deal of bitterness and resentment.

A word on feminist participation in my family policy panel. I never thought it appropriate to involve a large contingent from the women's movement. The EPC was, after all, a labour–management group and our task was to work with business and trade union leaders. Despite this constraint, I did try to involve two influential feminists. I thought they could help us by bringing information and experience to our deliberations, and we could help them by providing a policy agenda for working women that stood a chance of being supported by the Establishment. I was wrong in supposing I could produce this kind of collaboration. One of my two hand-picked feminists (chosen because she claimed to care about the plight of families and children) did not participate at all. After accepting the invitation to join the group she failed to turn up at any meeting, and subsequently declined to comment on a draft of the report. My other feminist came to the first meeting, left a little early, and quite soon after resigned from the panel. She told a staff member that the issues we were discussing lay outside her field of interest. All of which confirmed me in my view that family policy hardly figures in American feminists' scheme of things.

Disillusioned but determined, I went to work recruiting new members to strengthen the panel. Slowly and painfully I was able to find concerned individuals. I wrote innumerable letters: to senior executives of corporations that have innovative policies in this area; to labour leaders who are beginning to think of these issues. Over the course of the next two months I talked myself hoarse over countless breakfasts and lunches trying to convince busy executives to devote their precious time to this project. Finally, by the winter of 1983, I was able to put together an eminent group of individuals, and we officially launched the panel in January 1984.

The hardest part was accomplished, but the panel had recurrent difficulties in hanging on to the loyalties of its members. A disappointing number of panellists failed to show up at sessions, and some resigned when they discovered (with the appropriate expressions of surprise) that their diaries did not allow them to honour this particular commitment. Every few sessions it seemed necessary to recruit new members so as to fill gaps and keep the panel up to strength. Sometimes Alice Ilchman (president of Sarah Lawrence College), an extremely responsible participant herself, started a meeting by scanning the room to see if she recognised anyone. She often quipped that I was so good at getting new bodies on board that this panel had a good chance of rotating through the entire corporate community! But despite a certain amount of gallows humour, we all got tired of working with a revolving door.

Even those panel members who stayed with us found that their attention easily strayed into more 'serious' fields. On one occasion, in September 1984, when three panels of the EPC were meeting in the same place at the same time, one woman member just walked out of our session after sitting through five minutes of a presentation on parental leave and crossed the hall to join a discussion on finance.

Things reached a new low in October 1984, when John Sweeney, head of the Service Employees International Union, offered to resign as co-chair of the panel. As he told me over the phone, he continued to believe in the importance of the subject matter, and he wanted to commend me on how well I had run the panel to date, but since he had missed one or two meetings, he felt that he should not continue in the chair. Knowing that the project would totally disintegrate if he resigned, I put all my persuasive skills to work, and eventually Sweeney agreed to stay on. To his credit he then shouldered more responsibility for the remaining lifespan of the project. But it was a depressing episode and pointed to the real difficulties even enlightened trade union leaders in America have in taking these issues seriously. Sweeney is, after all, the head of a union that is 70 per cent female, a union which is aggressively trying to organise women in the fast-expanding service area of the American economy. If he cannot see the logic of developing policies that address the concerns of working parents, what trade union leader would?

The entire staff of the EPC worked very hard at keeping things going. We pumped all our panel members – new and old – full of working papers, fact sheets, transcripts, and clippings. We brought in powerful speakers from Europe – cabinet ministers and famous scholars. We even scheduled special briefing sessions for panel members who couldn't make regular meetings but showed some interest in what had gone on. The EPC staff was committed to the project, as was a tiny core group within the panel; Alice Ilchman and Sheila Kamerman (professor of social work, Columbia University) stand out as being particularly loyal and hard-working. We would not allow it to die, so the panel did, in fact, limp along.

Despite all these problems, over the course of the eighteen months or so of the panel's existence some new light was shed on family policy in America.

Of all the European case studies that were explored by the panel, the one that members found most appealing was that of France. They liked the conservatism of French family policy, the fact that it is designed to strengthen traditional family ties (e.g. by providing pre-school nursery schools for the children of at-home mothers) as well as dealing with the casualties of the modern age (e.g. by providing benefits for single parents). They were impressed by the national consensus that the French have managed to build around family policy and by the fact that the Catholic Church and right-wing political groups join with trade unions and the Socialist party to support such measures as child allowances and generous maternity benefits. Finally, they liked the French vision of things, which regards motherhood as 'a social function similar to military service for men, that had to be financially supported by the whole community'. One panel member remembered that twenty years ago, when he did National Guard duty, he had no trouble getting a six-month paid leave from his job as a junior executive with a Madison Avenue advertising firm. He told the panel that giving a child a good start in life was probably just as important to the nation as a tour of military duty.

Visiting French experts, in their turn, were somewhat stunned by the almost total lack of family support systems in the United States. Olga Baudelot, a well-known French scholar, came to talk to the panel about French policies toward children. At the end of her session she asked as many questions as she answered. 'If only 40 per cent of working women have any right to maternity leave, how on earth do the others manage?' she asked in shocked tones. A little later she asked, 'But why don't you women just scream and shout until the politicians produce maternity leave and child care?' To illustrate her point, Baudelot told the story of how in 1982, Jacques Chirac, then Conservative mayor of Paris, was brow-beaten by militant groups of working women into expanding the crèche system so as to provide many more places for infants and toddlers. In her words, 'Chirac would have been voted out of office if he hadn't caved in to these demands.'

I didn't have any good answers for Baudelot, but her questions did make me realise how backward – and barbaric – these areas of American social policy seem to most Europeans. One of Baudelot's more telling questions was: 'Why have issues such as child care become so politicised in the United States? Why, in France presidents as far apart in their political philosophy as Charles de Gaulle and François Mitterrand have had no trouble in providing support systems for children. How can prenatal care, family allowances, or nursery school be issues that belong to either the right or the left?'

Baudelot is, of course, right. America has succeeded in politicising these issues so thoroughly that it takes a brave candidate for public office to even mention the words 'child care' for fear of running into vast quantities of political abuse.

Another distinguished visitor, Anna-Greta Leijon, the Swedish minister of labour, also asked a lot of questions. 'What really puzzles me is that the far right seems to be the only group that even talks about family policy in the United States. Why is this so?' was one of her queries. To illustrate her point, she gave the example of that well-known arbiter of the nation's morals Senator Jesse Helms, whose 1981 family protection bill sought to get rid of sex education, eliminate birth control information, and repeal federal wife and child abuse laws in the name of supporting the family. Leijon had a great deal of trouble in seeing this right-wing proposal as answering the desperate need of American families for concrete benefits and services. One reason she agreed to come and speak to the EPC's family policy panel was that she was hopeful that a mainstream group was beginning to think sensibly about these issues.

There were, and are, no easy answers to Baudelot's or Leijon's questions. Comprehending the politicisation of child care in the United States entails coming to terms with the 1950s, a decade which was so different in Europe and America. In France the 1950s were a time when free public nursery schools came to be regarded as a given; while in Sweden these years featured a joint LO–SAF Women's Labour Council that supported higher wages for women, part-time work and child care. In America, on the other hand, it was the decade of complete motherhood, when putting your child in group care was seen as a subversive act.

*

Another by-product of the family policy panel was that I came to understand anew the irrelevancy of the ERA. I did not expect the ERA to be a useful policy tool in obtaining maternity leave or child care for working women. As we have seen, equal rights are often a stumbling block in the way of special benefits and services for women. However, I did think that the ERA might be an important item on the agenda when we talked about pay equity. But although the panel deliberated long and hard over how to close the gap between male and female wages, the ERA never came up. We had an important session on pay equity with our corporate members centre stage, and we had an important session on pay equity with our union members centre stage. We argued the issue of comparable worth *ad nauseam* with our pro-free-market corporate members, and we invited economists from both the left and the right of the discipline to advise us on this topic. But over the course of the months we debated this critically important issue no one mentioned the ERA. It is not as though we had ruled the ERA out of bounds because it was too contentious; most people on the panel had political positions that supported the ERA. Rather, it just didn't come up as a policy measure relevant to obtaining a better economic deal for American women.

By the summer of 1985 the EPC's family policy panel had a tentative list of recommendations covering six areas: pay equity, maternity and parental leave, maternal and child health, flexible work schedules, pre-school and early childhood education and child care. In the sphere of pay equity, the panel recommended collective bargaining and stricter enforcement of existing legislation and job evaluation as ways of creating a better balance between male and female wages, pointing out the long-term benefits to the country of women in low-paid jobs raising themselves above the poverty line. On maternity and parental leave, the panel made a very modest set of proposals by European standards, which included six to eight weeks' maternity leave, partially paid, with a job-back guarantee at the end of it, and unpaid leave for either parent to look after the child up to six months after the birth. The panel also recommended that pregnant women and children be given priority health coverage. On the work front the group suggested, among other things, more flexible work hours and the encouragement of job-sharing and part-time schemes for women with young children. As regards pre-school care and primary education, the panel recommended that pre-school nurseries be made available on a voluntary basis to 3-, 4- and 5-year-olds, that the school day should be lengthened in order to serve important educational and child-care objectives, and that school facilities should be used for before- and after-school programmes. The realists in the group did not think we could hope for very much on public spending on child care in times of government cutbacks, but recommended that at least those funds which had previously been made available for child care for the very poor, but which had since been cut by the Reagan administration, should be restored or even expanded. Finally, the panel suggested that trade unions, community groups and large companies should be encouraged to develop child-care services, either on their own or with the local community.

These recommendations constitute, in my view, a realistic list of what might be done in contemporary America. But, given the rocky history of the EPC's family policy panel, it is hard to get too excited about these recommendations. I now think that working out what should be done is not the problem. Any group of intelligent people is capable of doing this. Family policy is not an obscure area. It does not need detailed technical analysis, for the facts are clear and they speak for themselves. What is conspicuously lacking is any sense that this is an important policy area in American public life worthy of serious attention. Until the Establishment makes this commitment, there will be no action.

I found the experience of directing the family policy panel profoundly disturbing, even radicalising. The panel was the eighth I had directed at the Economic Policy Council, and before I took on this project, I saw myself as an old hand at running policy panels. But none of my previous experience had prepared me for the difficulties I encountered with this one. And it isn't because the EPC generally took on straightforward topics or made a habit of working only with easy personalities – we had tackled head-on notoriously difficult topics like immigration control and the International Monetary Fund, and managed to reach a consensus among a very broad range of interests from commercial bankers to trade union leaders. Yet the family policy panel failed to generate loyalty from most of its members despite all the energy I pumped into it. It is true, we have recommendations and we published a report, but on the important level of involvement of panel members the project failed.

I have often tried to explain why this happened and find it tough going. You see, my panel members are not just powerful people; they are concerned citizens who often devote time, energy, and resources to worthy causes. The very fact that they are members of the EPC speaks for itself. These men and women are willing to spend time on public policy questions; they cannot be accused of having narrow, selfish attitudes. Yet they could not work up any real enthusiasm for this topic, which touched them in more important ways than any other. What business leader should not be concerned about how to hang on to his or her best female managers and avoid the risk of losing them when they are forced – by an unyielding work place – to choose between a career and a family? What trade union leader should not be addressing the concerns of women workers as the labour movement struggles for survival in an age when most new jobs are going to women? But the case is stronger than this. Business executives and trade union leaders are also husbands and fathers, wives and mothers and have first-hand experience of the need for better policies. It is truly hard to explain why these powerful people were much less interested in family policy than in immigration reform or the International Monetary Fund.

I reluctantly came to the conclusion that my panel members did not warm to these issues for all the reasons explained in this book. Many men on the panel had been moulded by the fifties and at some level believed that children should be looked after by their mothers and that child care is not an appropriate sphere for government action. The career women on the panel were resistant to the idea that working women might need special benefits in the work place; they had absorbed the feminist message of the 1970s, which was that if women wanted equal opportunities they should behave exactly like men. And the trade unionists had risen to power fighting for a family wage for family men; they had not yet adjusted to the labour market realities of the 1980s. For one reason or another these enlightened men and women maintained a residual hostility toward working mothers. When forced to confront the facts, they did manage to draw up a rather obvious programme of reform. But their hearts were not in it.

It is, of course, infuriating to think through the consequences of continuing to neglect these issues. Over the last few years women and children have fallen below the poverty line in America at a frighteningly rapid rate. During the Reagan years 3 million more children and 4 million more women have slithered into poverty. This is not a record to be proud of. But national pride is not the only thing at stake. America pays a double price for its failure to provide support structures for today's families. The country sacrifices efficiency. For money spent on day care and nursery schools is not money down the drain. Investment in our human resources actually saves money in the long run. As Albert Shanker, president of the American Federation of Teachers, said in his testimony before Congress, 'The nation goes on year after year spending excessive time, money and effort on the problems of juvenile delinquency and crime. We are looking in the wrong place for solutions to problems resulting from a generation of children growing up without proper supervision.'[2]

The nation also sacrifices its humanity. Millions of women workers in America have no right to job-protected maternity leave and many of these women can't just chuck in their jobs when they have children; they need to continue working. They end up in the position of Gail Tobias, who, as described in Chapter Three, went back to work two and a half weeks after giving birth by caesarean section. As Gail told me in an interview, 'I don't know how I lived through those first weeks back at work. I was exhausted and in pain from the surgery. I could hardly drag myself around. The worst thing was the lack of sleep. Annie woke to be fed at least three times a night, and by midday I was ready to kill for sleep. But somehow I had to work – and to smile and pretend to my boss that I didn't have a family care in the world.' Gail Tobias is not a masochist. The only reason she did these things to herself and to her child was to keep her job. America is alone in the civilised world in making it so difficult for women to bear children while working.

16. Epilogue: Voices from the Post-Feminist Generation

In the autumn of 1984, as I approached the end of my labours on this book, I decided to test my ideas against the sensibilities of today's young women. By this time I had directed a policy panel, analysed large quantities of data, and interviewed hundreds of workers, mothers and government officials. But I wanted to know the reactions of a group that I knew and thoroughly understood. So I turned to my ex-students.

How had the young women I had taught at Barnard College come out of the pressure cauldron of the 1970s? How are they coping with the expectations of the 1980s? Do they see themselves as being 'squeezed between the devil and the deep blue sea'? Or do they feel that they can have it all – career success, marriage, and children? I also wanted to probe on other fronts. What do these women think of motherhood? Where do they look for role models? How do they relate to the men in their lives? And what do they think of the women's movement? In other words, I wanted to share the thoughts and feelings of a group that includes some of the best-educated and privileged women of this post-feminist generation in America.

In September 1984 I staged a reunion for the women I had taught at Barnard College during the years 1974–81. I invited all those whom I had known well – some fifty students in all. I was able to track down thirty-five of this group of fifty. Seventeen came to a reunion at my home, eight met me for lunch or talked to me on the phone, and ten filled out questionnaires. With the exception of five students who had come to me for career advice shortly after graduating, I had not seen or heard of these women since they left Barnard College.

At 8 p.m. on 21 September 1984, my apartment filled with excited young women greeting long-lost classmates. They ranged in age from twenty-three to thirty-three, and half were married. Some were self-consciously businesslike in

254

skirted suits, little string ties and cropped hair. But even the more feminine members of the group, in elegant dresses and clever make-up, carried bulging briefcases. Most of them had come straight from work, two brought spouses, and one woman was conspicuously pregnant. After an hour of eating, drinking, gossiping and cuddling my children (my third child, Adam, was just five months old and particularly popular, despite a tendency to dribble down silk blouses) the serious business of the evening began. We sat around in a big circle, and after some encouragement (I, after all, was an old hand at conducting seminars) everyone started to talk. The first topic these women gravitated towards was how to combine careers with children (a rather surprising choice, for although one of these women was pregnant, *none* had yet had children).

Marion,* aged twenty-four, class of '81, one of the most able students of her year, now holds an entry-level position at an investment banking firm, a job she took after completing a master's degree in economics. Marion likes her work and looks forward to building a career in international finance. Marion is getting married in the spring, and her one great worry is: 'Can I make room in this career for children?' She recognises that she has chosen a very time-consuming profession: 'Ten to twelve hours a day plus a lot of travel. Not only does my job require me to travel abroad ten days of each month, but I have a ninety-minute commute, which means that I never get home until eight in the evening.' Marion particularly regrets that there are no role models in her field. 'In my firm there are a hundred partners, only three of them are women, and none of these are in my department, so I don't know them.' In the larger financial world Marion has found some women, 'but if they are married, they tend to be childless'.

Marion does not see herself attempting to have children for at least five years, yet, as she freely admits, 'it is a question I think about a lot'. Her great hope is that by then 'I will be in control of my career and have much more ability to dictate my terms to it.'

At this point Marion was interrupted by Laura,* aged twenty-nine, class of '77, who said quietly but with conviction, 'It's not as easy as that. Things don't resolve themselves. In some ways the choices get harder.

'My situation is typical. I'll be thirty in July and am beginning to feel enormous pressure to have a child. I read somewhere that infertility problems begin to mount in your early thirties, and I would very much like to avoid that kind of trouble. Besides, I've been married for seven years, and both of us want a child quite badly. The other day Michael told me that he "needed" a child. Yet I cannot decide how to reconcile a family with my work. The basic problem is that my career cannot be put on hold for a few years. If I were to take time out, there would be no way of picking up the threads two or three years down the line.'

Everyone in the room was listening very closely to Laura. She was seen by her classmates as an immensely efficient woman thoroughly in control of her life. If she was encountering problems, they were surely significant ones. Marion pushed Laura to be more explicit. 'I don't understand. I thought it was OK to slow down once your career was established.'

Laura decided to tell of her experience in some detail, and as she talked, her voice rose and became filled with emotion. Clearly her dilemma was causing considerable pain.

'Professional careers do not become easier or plateau out in your late twenties or early thirties. At these critical early stages there is always *the next step*. I work in a commercial bank. When I started seven years ago, my first goal was to become an officer. Then I wanted to become a higher-level officer, then assistant vice-president. And now I am waiting for my vice-presidency.

'I put in twelve- to fourteen-hour days. I have taken only four sick days in seven years, and I have earned my medals; but that does not mean that I can relax a whole lot now. There just isn't much flexibility in my career. Citibank thinks it has a decent maternity policy – three months' leave – but the kid is not even sleeping through the night by then. The bank will not tolerate part-time work or flexitime and has no child-care facilities. Besides, as soon as you get pregnant, people at work start viewing you differently. They assume your priorities have changed and you will have less energy for your job.

'We bought a house in the suburbs a year and a half ago, and since my husband wants to be a neurosurgeon and has four years of specialised training in front of him, there is no way we could keep the house if I stopped work.

'So, you see, despite the fact that I have launched my career, delayed child-bearing, and done all the things I was supposed to do, I face some very tough choices.

'When we have a child, I can do one of three things. I can continue my career by hiring enough help for full-time coverage at home. I have costed it out; it would cost twenty thousand dollars a year. The snag is I would have to resign myself to seeing my baby only an hour or two a day. Or I can opt out of my banking career and work part time for my father (who has a small business). This way I can make enough money to pay the mortgage and still have time to see my child and manage the house. Or, finally, we could sell the house, move into an apartment, and I can take time out of the work force and become a traditional housewife.

'All three options entail huge costs for me. I can already visualise the massive guilt I would feel if I took option number one. I had a very traditional upbringing, and an important part of me believes that mothers should be with their children. I have nightmares about my child forgetting that I am its mother, preferring the nanny to me. I can deal with hard work and crazy

256

hours, I would even get up at 5 a.m. to spend some time with my child, but can I cope with the guilt? I don't think so.

'Option number two would kill my career – at least any ambitious version of my career. If I took even a few years out of banking, there is no way I could get back on the fast track in my mid or late thirties. In other words, if I opted to work part time for my father, I would have to permanently lower my expectations of money, status and power.

'Option number three is the least attractive to me. I would not like losing the house; I have worked hard for my creature comforts and value them. But more than that, if I were to stay at home all day, I would more than likely go crazy. I thrive on stimulus and love my work. I am now a fully developed person and cannot change my personality or temperament because it's convenient to do so.'

Laura's painful choices seem not to be shared by her husband. When asked, Laura stressed that Michael very much wanted children and could maybe pick up 30 per cent of the child-care and 10 per cent of the household responsibilities if she continued in her high-pressure career, 'but his schedule is worse than mine, so he could not do more'. Obviously Michael's decision to take on four years' extra training in order to become a neurosurgeon had not been influenced by child-raising considerations. Laura had not even considered that he might modify his career aspirations in order to help raise a child, and this was despite the fact that she earned considerably more than he did.

By the time Laura finished her story a rather sombre mood had gathered in the room. Laura tried to lighten things up by saying rather jokingly to the pregnant woman sitting next to her, 'All my views are in the realm of speculation. Debbie is really facing these problems and probably has come up with all kinds of solutions.'

Debbie,* class of '80 and an associate editor at a top women's magazine, was six months pregnant. She tried to rise to the challenge that had been thrown her and said with some irony, 'I wish I did have some solutions, but in many ways my options are more limited than Laura's. You see we face a Catch Twenty-two situation. Both John and I work in low-paying fields, so I need to earn money for us to survive. And I mean, survive. We rent a small apartment in Brooklyn, we don't own a car, yet we barely get by on our two salaries. Despite this need to earn money, which will become more acute when we have a child, it will be impossible for me to keep my job. My maternity benefits are far from good – four weeks of partially paid leave before the birth and four weeks afterwards. But even if I could cope with so little time off, full-time high-quality child care would consume all my salary. So my solution (if you can call it that) is to leave my job after the birth of my child and become a freelance writer. This way I can do a large part of the child care myself and continue to earn at least some money.

'But it's scary. I'm afraid of becoming isolated and unproductive – at home all day with a tiny child. And I'm afraid that John and I will lose the equality we have so carefully built up. If he begins to earn much more than I, it will obviously be difficult to maintain an equal division of household tasks, and I think I will become resentful if I end up with all the cooking and cleaning.'

Debbie paused and then added reflectively, 'You know, there are a lot of women on the creative, editorial side of the company [the Hearst organisation, which owns several magazines including the one Debbie works for], but in management, upper management, I don't think there is one woman, and it is in management that the high salaries are. Even Helen Gurley Brown [highly influential editor of American *Cosmopolitan*] has no clout; she is not even on the board. All these women's magazines are supposedly setting up role models for women, but good role models don't exist at the source.'

Debbie had one final comment: 'This past summer I have been troubled by the fact that I could not work up much enthusiasm for Geraldine Ferraro. Somehow I felt guilty about not giving her more support. I think the problem is that her life has been so unreal. She took thirteen years off to have her children and then was able to jump back into the work force and get back on track as a lawyer and a politician. I guess I don't believe that you can do that unless you are married to a wealthy man and have great political connections. Most of us need to earn money in order to survive, and many of us are in competitive professions, where it just isn't possible to take a few years off to have a family, let alone thirteen years off. Ferraro talks a lot about her hard life, but she really hasn't faced the toughest issue – rearing children and building a career at one and the same time. I suppose that makes it hard for me to see her as a role model.' Debbie stopped and said with a small smile, 'But that won't stop me voting for the Mondale-Ferraro ticket. Reagan has been a disaster for women.'

Role models – whether these women perceived them to be there, how appropriate they are – was another important theme of the evening. Kathryn,* twenty-five, class of '81, currently in her second year of law school, described the two most important role models in her life: 'My mother is a typical fifties woman. She was well educated and worked before she was married yet chose to take eighteen years out of the labour force to rear three children. She is a practical, personable woman and has tremendous energy. During her years as a housewife she was always involved in volunteer work in the community, frequently holding positions of considerable influence such as being president of the school board. As a child I remember her writing proposals, reports and budgets, but I also remember that she was a great mum. She was always there when I came home from school, and she baked bread, sewed Halloween costumes, took me to ballet lessons and showed up at school events like all the other surburban mothers.

'In addition to bringing up us kids and doing all this community work, my mother was a corporation wife. She devoted huge amounts of energy to holding dinner parties, travelling to conferences, remembering people from the past, and in general keeping up the personal contacts so important to my father's business life.

'But in her middle years my mother has encountered difficulties. She went out and got a teaching job when my youngest sister left for college, but two years ago she was made redundant when the numbers of children going to school dropped in our area. She says that volunteer work no longer satisfies her, that she is now old enough to appreciate an income of her own and some professional status. She feels this especially acutely since we kids are gone and my father is at the peak of his career, with all kinds of invitations to be the guest of honour here and the featured speaker there.

'When I look at my mother's life and contemplate my own future, I am torn between contempt (did I say contempt? I am not sure I should use such a strong word!) for her lack of a career that transcended family life and admiration for her ability to do so many things well. I know that if I want to be a person with an exciting and challenging career, I can't be the person my mother was – someone who was always there for her children, who devoted much of her life to helping other people, who did not measure her time and energy in terms of paid work. But seeing her frustrated attempts to build a working life in her fifties, I think I will try not to sacrifice career for family in the extreme way she did.'

Kathryn's alternative role model is Lauren Siegel* – a successful woman lawyer in her late thirties. Lauren is a friend of Kathryn's family and is also a former employer; Kathryn worked for her two summers ago. Kathryn sees Lauren Siegel as 'a typical product of the 1970s. Just fifteen years older than me, she is a high-powered lawyer, a partner in a prestigious firm, and well respected by her colleagues. But her personal life is a shambles. She works tremendously long hours and is always travelling. She is divorced, with a twelve-year-old son who recently chose to move from her house to his father's. She clearly has had problems coping with being a parent. Often she would call on my mother to help out; if her son were sick or alone in the afternoons, he would come to our house, where my mother would look after him. She also felt the pressure of raising a child alone – for example, creating appropriate after-school activities when she was hardly ever there. It seems to me she always expressed considerable relief when her son went off to camp for the summer.

'She has recently been seeing a divorced man who also has children, and their life together is almost a caricature of the modern dilemma. He has joint custody, and until recently she had full custody. They are continually balancing the children's activities with busy work schedules and never seem to have time alone. In any case, she always seems very wired up, somewhat tense, and often looks to my parents for advice and support. I can't say that I find her lifestyle very appealing; the money, status and responsibility of her job don't seem worth the screwed-up family life she has, although I am well aware that one didn't necessarily cause the other.

'I would like to choose what I like from my mother's life and from Lauren's life and combine them. But I fear that these two goals – a high-powered career and a rich family life – conflict with each other. I worry a good deal about how to make these goals merge and become less of a fantasy and more of a reality.'

When Kathryn finished, the room was full of glum faces. No one jumped in to reassure her or to say, 'My mother has achieved both goals.' One woman did mutter something to the effect that her mother had recently gone through a divorce at the age of fifty-five and was a really sad example of being ditched in middle age. However, she did not want to talk about her mother; perhaps it was too painful! She was eager to get back to discussing her life.

The topic I pushed hardest to talk about was the women's movement. It did not come up spontaneously, it seemed peripheral to these women's lives, yet I was interested in whether it had influenced these women, and if so, how.

Jackie,* aged thirty-three, class of '75, was at Barnard during the time when a fairly militant brand of feminism was sweeping the campus. She tried to remember how it affected her.

'You know, back then I had a steady boyfriend and liked clothes and dances. I just didn't have anything in common with the women in the movement. All I saw was the dirty jeans and the hairy legs, and all they saw was a prim young lady. I guess we just couldn't communicate. It's odd to think that, despite appearances, we probably shared certain values. I have always felt as able and as capable as a man, and that's the kind of thing the movement has tried to promote.

'The thing that really turned me off was the tremendous hostility towards men, family and children, as though you couldn't be a feminist unless you gave up all the good parts of being female. Remember all those weird groups like WITCH and SCUM and the time one of them tried to castrate Andy Warhol? I never did work out where all that anti-men sentiment came from.'

Jane,* twenty-four, class of '82, jumped in eagerly, 'It's a great pity the radicals have dominated the movement to the extent they have because it has alienated a lot of mainstream support. Just before I graduated from Barnard in

May 1982, there was this huge uproar because the Women's Center had published a diary of sexual options open to women which featured some very graphic pictures of naked women. The diary was published just before Barnard's annual 'The Scholar and the Feminist' conference, and the Helena Rubinstein Foundation withdrew its funding for this conference because of the controversy surrounding the diary. I remember being very fed up that the radical feminists had undermined the conference, which is a first-class event with national standing.

'Barnard tries to prepare women for being successful in the world, and I feel that the college really strengthened me in terms of skills and self-confidence. But somehow the women's movement on campus never seemed to address the concerns of us mainstream types; it was always off into some fringe issue. Why, in my last year the Women's Center was more likely to run a talk on matriarchy in Finland than on parenthood and careers.' There were assenting smiles all around the room. Jane had obviously hit a nerve.

Laura offered this comment on the movement: 'You know, when I was at Barnard, the activists at the Women's Center were mainly into sexual freedom and abortion rights. I remember that if you were having trouble deciding whether or not to have an abortion, or if you were trying to figure out which was the best place to have one, there was this hot line you could call for advice. I am sure that kind of help was very much needed. But now here I am facing the problems involved in trying to have a child and the movement couldn't be less interested; there is no feminist support network for women like me. It's time the movement concentrated on helping women have children.' Laura paused for a moment and then said rather self-consciously, 'I'm pro-choice and all that, but now I'm approaching thirty. For me the right to have a child is more important than the right not to have one.' Laura paused and then laughed ruefully. 'One thing I will say for the movement: it helped raise the ambitions of women like me. Without this burning desire to have a career, to do something with our lives, none of us would be facing these crummy choices.'

Kathryn volunteered one last thought on the movement: 'One thing I often resent is the way women's liberation has increased the expectations of men. Last summer I worked for this big Washington law firm, and in August the firm threw a big party – an elaborate dinner dance at the Hay-Adams Hotel. I remember thinking that twenty years ago it would have been *de rigueur* for every young male lawyer in the firm to arrive with a stunning blonde on his arm. But last summer there was even greater cachet in turning up with a high-achieving woman. All those young male lawyers tried to adorn themselves with a doctor or, at the very least, another lawyer. The only catch was that these Yuppie women had to look every bit as glamorous as the stunning blondes of the past. I found it depressing. It's as though men now expect women to be beautiful traditional women and hard-bitten professionals. I can't see how anyone does it over the long haul.'

An important theme of the evening was the angst associated with being single and childless in your thirties (the condition of a quarter of the women in the room). Elizabeth,* class of '75, at thirty-two was one of the older women at the reunion. With her long blonde hair and aristocratic good looks she has always reminded me of Meryl Streep. For the last several years Elizabeth has worked as a fund raiser for a large non-profitmaking organisation. She lives in a house she owns in Old Greenwich, Connecticut.

'I have a pleasant life. I earn a good salary without having to work crazy hours. I have a five-minute journey to my office, and my work hours are 8.30 to 4.30. In the summertime I get out of the office at 3.15 on Fridays and can be on the tennis court at four. But my personal life is drying up. There are dozens of us single women in the suburbs, but most of the good men I know are married. The few who are divorced seem to be exclusively interested in twenty-year-old kids.' Elizabeth paused and said with humour, 'Some weekends the most I have to look forward to is working on my cellulite at the health club!

'Last night I woke up in the middle of the night to go to the bathroom. As I padded around my empty house at 2 a.m. and thought about today's reunion, I wondered what I will do if I am alone and childless when I am forty-five. It gave me the shivers, imagining myself dealing with having missed out on children, knowing that I would never have a child. It would seem like such a chasm, such an unfillable gap in my life. I don't know how much of this need is social conditioning and how much is individual desire, but I do know that I will never see my life as being complete unless I have a child.' Elizabeth thought for a while and then said pensively, 'So many of my career choices have been conditioned by my wish to create good conditions for a family. You see, an important reason I took this job was that it had great hours and meant I could live in a house with a yard. I know it sounds a little weird, considering I am not even married.'

Elizabeth looked over at Laura and Debbie and said rather apologetically, 'Listening to you both describing your problems in reconciling career and children, I felt this great ground swell of jealousy. I would give anything to be dealing with that particular dilemma. I guess I will give myself another three years, and if I haven't found Mr Right by then, I will consider having a child on my own.'

The whole room was still as Elizabeth said these words. Her anguish was palpable, yet she was only thirty-two. Theoretically she had another ten years before this sense of loss need seem real. But the single women in the room could clearly understand Elizabeth's feelings. Sonia* broke the silence. She is a contemporary of Elizabeth's, newly divorced and childless; she has recently been promoted to vice-president at a high-tech firm in Boston.

'It's so sad that we feel such time pressure. It's as if women have to succeed on three fronts by the time they are thirty-five or else resign themselves to huge holes in their lives. If your career is not well developed by this point, you might as well give up since in most professions you have to be halfway up the ladder by your mid-thirties. But somehow or other you have to find the time and energy to pick up a husband and a child while you are in the throes of establishing a career, for both these projects become increasingly difficult as you move through your thirties. Men have much more flexibility, for time is on their side. If he wants to, a man can devote his twenties and thirties to his career and defer having a family until his forties, when he can still pick and choose from a whole selection of younger women. And a man in his fifties can still have children.' Sonia paused and then said hesitantly, 'In today's world men and women have roughly the same goals, but a woman has less time to put together what she needs and, I guess, runs a bigger chance of failure.'

Sonia offered one last bleak comment. 'You know, I had an abortion four years ago, when I was twenty-eight. Jim and I had just got married, and I was in the middle of a very tough career change. It just wasn't a convenient time to have a child. You can't imagine how much I regret that decision.'

Elizabeth looked as though she were on the brink of tears; she clearly could imagine how Sonia felt. She reached over and put her hand on Sonia's shoulder, offering some silent comfort.

Several of the women I contacted and interviewed could not attend the reunion because of geographical distance; they now lived in Atlanta, Los Angeles, Chicago or Dallas. Many of them had moved to follow husbands or boyfriends. The special trials of relocation dominated the telephone calls, lunches and dinners I had with my far-flung ex-students.

Paula,* class of '79, is now an editor in the publications department of a museum in Los Angeles. She earns $19,000 a year, which is less than what she earned two years ago when she was the managing editor of a New York journal. She left this job in 1982 to follow her husband (then fiancé) when he joined a private law firm in Los Angeles. When Paula arrived on the West Coast she did not find a job for eight months, and her memories of this period are painful.

'I followed every lead there was in the West Coast publishing industry, but despite the fact that I had skills and experience, all anyone ever asked me was "How is your typing?" It had a bad effect on my self-esteem, and even my relationship with Bob changed as I felt so much less attractive as a person. Some days it took an incredible amount of energy to get dressed and make myself beat on some more doors. Finally I got this job at the museum. It's low-level work – mostly copy-editing – and I do not have nearly as much responsibility as I did in my last job, but I am thankful to be working.' Paula thought for a while and then added, 'You know, I used to be ambitious, but the move and that period of unemployment have really shaken my confidence.

'The thing that really worries me is that there is now this huge economic gap between Bob and myself. In New York he was a law student with much less money to spend than I did. Now he earns four times as much as I do. I can see that over the last two years there have been all kinds of changes in who does what around the house. It used to be that he would do the laundry and shopping while I would cook and clean. Now we have a fairly conventional division of labour since his work takes up more of his time and is more "important" than mine. And we don't even have children! Imagine how skewed things will become once there is a baby. Sometimes I wonder how a liberated seventies woman like myself ever got into such a traditional scene.'

The loss of career opportunities and the loss of earning power were recurring themes in the conversations I had with ex-students who had followed their men to distant cities.

Dana,* class of '78, now lives in Chapel Hill, North Carolina. She moved there in 1981, when her husband accepted a tenured appointment at the University of North Carolina. Dana is a well-qualified woman. She obtained a master's degree from North-western University in 1980 and had just started a job at a prestigious private foundation in Chicago when she and her husband upped sticks and moved to Chapel Hill. As Dana put it, 'There is nothing to do in Chapel Hill except teach, and I can't compete for the regular teaching jobs because I don't have a PhD. The chair of the political science department has promised me that I can teach one course next academic year. But do you know what that means? It means a few weeks of work and about three thousand dollars in pay. To think that I was earning $32,000 a year in Chicago!'

What did I learn from my Barnard reunion?

Most of the facts I uncovered are quite predictable. With the exception of Dana in North Carolina, all the women are either working or doing post-graduate training. This is to be expected given the fact that none has a child and only half of them are married. The average salary for the working women in the group is $28,000, a figure which easily places them within the top 10 per cent of all women workers in America, although it is not very high considering their qualifications and experience.

Most of my other findings are also unsurprising. Remember Kathryn, the law student? Her failure to integrate the two role models in her life is commonplace since most American women her age have inherited from the fifties and the seventies two contradictory models of what women should do. And it is also predictable that most of these women found little support in the women's movement for their family ambitions.

I was even prepared for the degree to which these women were obsessed with the problems of reconciling career and family life (a particularly striking fact since none of them has yet had a child). There is a lot of evidence in this book that supports the perception of these Barnard women that working out how to deal with their double burden might be the central problem of their adult life.

A recent study by the *Wall Street Journal* dramatises the constraints imposed by the double burden and confirms the findings of my small and informal survey.[1] This study took a close look at 722 female executives, each of whom had the title of vice-president or higher, and found:

> As women move into corporate management they're finding it difficult to balance the competing demands of their private and professional lives. Married women, including many who earn more than their husbands, still find themselves doing most of the chores at home. [When there are children] only very few of the husbands – 5 per cent or less – assume chief responsibility for any duty involving children.
>
> Single women worry that they're focusing on their jobs to the exclusion of all outside interests. One way or another, women executives feel that they have made substantial [personal] sacrifices to further their careers.

But perhaps the most significant finding of the *Wall Street Journal* survey was that 52 per cent of these women executives are childless, compared with only 7 per cent of their male contemporaries.[2]

Several recent studies have come up with the same result: half or more of America's high-achieving women today do not find it possible to have children. A 1983 survey by *Fortune* magazine of the women graduates of the Harvard Business School class of 1973 found that 54 per cent had no children.[3] A 1982 report by the *Wall Street Journal* of 300 senior women executives found that 61 per cent of these women were childless.[4] And a 1985 survey of executive women by Basia Hellwig of *Working Women* found that 61 per cent of the women in the sample had no children.[5] In these studies the average age of the women ranges from late thirties on to mid-forties, indicating that most are nearing the end of their childbearing years.

It's a sad commentary on life in the fast track for today's women that so few of them find it possible to have children, or be married for that matter. Many fewer female than male executives are married. In its 1982 study the *Wall Street Journal* found that 48 per cent of the women executives were married, compared with 96 per cent of the men, while in a 1985 *Working Women* study 59 per cent of the women executives were married, compared with 96 per cent of their male colleagues.

Thus many high-achieving women in America do not have children because they are single or because they genuinely cannot work out a way of combining child care with managing the home and high-pressure careers. Only 5 per cent of the husbands surveyed by the *Wall Street Journal* pick up any significant responsibility for their children, and things are just as bad on the housework front. As Philip Blumstein and Pepper Schwartz find in *American Couples*, 'married men's aversion to housework is so intense it can sour their relationship. The more housework they do, for whatever reason, the more they fight about it.'[6] Despite all the talk about men being into parenthood and the home, modern men are failing most tests in these spheres. When a career woman has children, she most surely takes on a double burden.

Many career women end up alone and childless, but it is not because they want it this way. Like Elizabeth and Sonia, they are desperately anxious to find mates and to have children. Some are even prepared to have children on their own. In 1983, thousands of women underwent artificial insemination at private clinics in New York City.[7] In the same year hundreds of single American women adopted children on their own. Most of these women were professionals in their late thirties who had given up on finding Mr Right but could not reconcile themselves to childlessness. Like Elizabeth, they were afraid of the great chasm it would produce in their lives.

In her 1984 book *Sex and Destiny* Germaine Greer accuses modern society of being profoundly hostile to children.[8] She describes motherhood as being 'virtually meaningless in our society'[9] and states categorically that 'there are practically no good reasons left for exercising one's fertility'.[10] She is partially right. In America, at least, work place policy and public policy fail to support women in their struggle to bear and to rear children. It also seems to be true that most men do not give children a very high priority in their lives. But in one respect Greer is way off centre. She accuses individual women of not wanting and of not liking children.[11] She is dead wrong. At the September reunion at my house, if there was one note that rang loudly and clearly through the room, it was that modern women – no matter how ambitious – yearn to have children. They tie themselves into knots, trying to work out how to do this, but despite desperate effort, the odds are that a high proportion of them will fail. Still, it will not be through lack of trying. Modern society in general and America in particular has put all kinds of barriers in the way of these women having children. Laura, the assistant vice-president at Citibank, was well ahead of the game. At the age of twenty-nine she had made significant progress in her career and had a solid marriage, yet as she contemplated having children she was preparing herself for some major sacrifice. Like the women surveyed by the *Wall Street Journal*, the women at my reunion mostly looked forward to a future of compromise.

Despite my knowledge that the experience of these Barnard women was a long way from being exceptional, it did not prevent me from being disappointed in what I found. Perhaps it's because I had shared the youthful aspirations of these women. I had been their confidante when they were eighteen and twenty, when they truly felt the world was at their feet. I remember Laura as a first-year student blithely telling me that of course she would marry a man who would share the housework fifty-fifty, otherwise, how could she realise her ambitions? I remember Elizabeth telling me that she was going to have three children and be a vice-president by the time she was thirty. Somehow I had harboured the thought that at least some of these hardworking, accomplished women would have been able to beat the system. But they were clearly not turning into superwomen, who handle with ease rich, multi-dimensional lives. Instead, these Barnard women were running into all the problems that have dominated my adult life and which permeate the pages of this book.

The mood of anxiety that possesses these young women is impressive. They feel they have so little time to negotiate the central tasks of their lives, and despite their youth, they feel close to failure. Psychologist Willard Gaylin described it very well when he wrote that 'women approaching their mid-thirties feel enormous pressure converging on them from every quarter. They have so much to put together but not much time left to do it, it all must happen now'.[12] They worry about their careers, staying in that fast lane; they worry about their biological clocks, bearing children before infertility problems mount up; and they worry about their mating clocks, for with each passing year the pool of available men shrinks. The truth is that their anxiety is well founded. We have not yet created a context that allows a woman to reasonably expect that she can have both a career and a family.

I am reminded of the writings of Charlotte Perkins Gilman, the nineteenth-century feminist. In 1897 she wrote, 'We have so arranged life that a man may have a house, a family, love, companionship, domesticity and fatherhood, yet remain an active citizen of age and country. We have so arranged life, on the other hand, that a woman must "choose"; she must either live alone, unloved, uncompanied, uncared for, homeless, childless, with her work in the world for sole consolation; or give up world service for the joys of love, motherhood and domestic service.'[13]

Things have not changed very much. A century later women have more choices, but to use Laura's words, they are often 'crummy choices'.

My Barnard reunion serves to underline a major argument of this book: that women need more than equal treatment if they are to find fulfilment in both love and work. They need equal opportunity – in education and in the job market – but they also need a plethora of family support structures that range from job-protected maternity leave to subsidised day care and flexitime. For whether they are in fact mothers or simply have the potential to be mothers, the lives of women are conditioned by and constrained by child-related responsibilities. As the rock star Madonna reminds us in so many of her songs: 'Women aren't like men / They can do things that men can't do.'[14] These differences produce burdens as well as opportunities.

In the 1970s, particularly in America, it was thought that all you had to do was to break down the barriers so that women could fully participate in the mainstream of society. The spirit of the decade was to pretend that there were no differences between men and women. Well, the results are in. More women than ever before are working outside the home, and at least some of them have broken into the previously closed ranks of executives and professionals. But despite all of this 'progressive' change, most women are in worse economic shape than their mothers were. They have lost the protections and guarantees of traditional marriage without improving their earning power in the marketplace.

Author Elizabeth Janeway hit the nail on the head when she told a 1985 gathering of Barnard College alumnae: 'Recently we've been hearing a lot about women "having it all". Myself, I think that is not really an accurate description of female lives today. It seems to me that what we have been up to is – DOING it all.'[15] Doing it all does not turn most women into superheroes; it merely produces strain, stress – and low pay. For swimming in the mainstream and taking your chances doesn't produce equality if you are picking up 75 to 85 per cent of all family responsibilities. Formal equality has to be supplemented by special support systems if women are to become equal participants in the world of work.

The European social feminists got it right when they decided to push not only for equal rights in the sphere of work but also for social benefits to ease the family responsibilities of working women. Both are needed. As Warren Farrell pointed out in *The Liberated Man*, 'Liberation will mean little for men or women if women enter men's world on men's terms.'[16]

The problems of contemporary American women are not the result of some massive or inevitable conflict between work and family life. Rather, they result because the United States does less than any other advanced country to make life easier for working mothers.

*

This is not to argue that supportive social policies would solve the problems of all women. Better benefits and services for working mothers would still not resolve the deeper issue of how anyone – man or woman – with family responsibilities can compete in the most competitive fields, 'where workaholics with virtually no private lives often set the pace'.[17] If you want to be a chief executive you should probably think twice about having children. But this issue should not be confused with the concrete, practical problems most working women face. Most careers are not in the fast lane. Only 7 out of every 100 employed women in America work in the top professions, and even within this small group, most do not need to put in a sixty-hour week in order to fulfil their responsibilities. The great majority of all jobs could be combined quite satisfactorily with child rearing if more supportive policies were adopted in the work place and by governments. If Debbie had access to generous maternity leave, subsidised child care and flexitime, her problems would be greatly eased.

Which brings me back full circle. The impetus to write this book came from my own experience, prompted by the difficulties and frustrations I encountered when attempting to bear two children mid-career. Why should it be so hard? I wondered. Now I know. It shouldn't.

Notes

Preface to the British Edition

1. Alexis de Tocqueville, *Democracy in America* (New York: Vintage Books, 1945), vol. 11, 224.
2. *Wall Street Journal*, 7 September 1983.
3. Ibid.

1. A Personal View

1. Burton L. White, *The First Three Years of Life* (New York: Avon Books, 1975; London: Star Books, 1979), 134.
2. Dr Benjamin Spock, *Baby and Child Care*, 2d ed. (New York: Simon & Schuster, 1967; London: Bodley Head, 1979), 570. This was the edition of Spock I used when Lisa was a baby. A subsequent edition of the book was kinder to working mothers, but even in the later edition Spock still argues that the best caretakers in the first three years of life are the parents. Group care is not considered a good alternative until the child is at least three years old. *See* Dr Benjamin Spock, *Baby and Child Care*, 3d ed. (New York: Pocket Books, 1976).
3. T. Berry Brazelton, *Infants and Mothers: Differences in Development* (New York: Delacorte Press, 1969; London: Hutchinson, 1970), 164.
4. White, op. cit., 148.
5. Ibid., 70.
6. Ibid., 71.
7. Ibid., 73.
8. Rudolph Schaffer, *Mothering* (Cambridge, Mass.: Harvard University Press, 1974), 69.
9. Ibid.
10. *See*, for example, the *Wall Street Journal* report on a survey of 300 senior women executives in the 1,000 largest U.S. industrial companies: '52% of women surveyed are single, compared with only 4% of the men. In addition, 61% of the women are childless, while 97% of the men were parents'; the average age of the women in this survey was forty-six, and most of them were vice-presidents (*Wall Street Journal*, 11 February 1982).
11. Interview, 6 January 1984.
12. At Columbia University the situation in the autumn of 1984 was the following: of the non-tenured faculty, 28.1 per cent were women while only 8.7 per cent of the tenured faculty

were women. (Interview, Caroline Sperberg, Columbia University, 28 September 1984.)

13. At one point in our negotiations the lawyer acting for the Barnard administration suggested that the 1978 Pregnancy Disability Amendment solved the problem since pregnant women were eligible for the same benefits as persons with other physical disabilities. Our committee did not agree. For starters, no one was taking disability for childbirth (the senior faculty and the administration discouraged it). And even if disability was to become a reality, it covered only a few weeks of partially paid leave around childbirth. We felt strongly that we needed to have lighter work loads for the first year of a child's life and the possibility of stopping the tenure clock for this period. Only then would mothers (or parents for that matter) have a reasonable shot at promotion. *See* discussion of the Pregnancy Disability Amendment in Chapter Three.

14. Betty Friedan, *The Feminine Mystique* (New York: Dell, 1963; London: Gollancz, 1971), 237.

15. The classic books on the subject are Fernand Lamaze, *Painless Childbirth* (New York: Pocket Books, 1965; London: Burke, 1958); Frederick Leboyer, *Birth Without Violence* (New York: Alfred A. Knopf; London: Wildwood House, 1975); and Grantly Dick-Read, *Childbirth Without Fear* (New York: Harper, 1953; London: Heinemann, 1954). It is interesting to note that all the founders of this movement were men and therefore couldn't possibly have known whether childbirth hurt or not.

16. Barbara Grizzuti Harrison, 'Men Don't Know Nuthin 'Bout Birthin Babies', *Esquire* (July 1972), 109.

17. Robert A. Bradley, *Husband-coached Childbirth* (New York and London: Harper & Row, 1965), 168.

18. Ibid.

19. Ibid., 18.

20. Ibid., 19.

21. Ibid., 20.

22. Genesis 3:16.

23. Edward Shorter, *A History of Women's Bodies* (New York: Basic Books, 1982; London: Allen Lane, 1983), chap. 5 and 9.

24. Ibid., 59.

25. Franz Boas, *Kwakiutl Ethnography* (Chicago: University of Chicago Press, 1966), 361.

26. Margaret Mead, *Growing Up in New Guinea* (New York: Blue Ribbon Books, 1930; London: Penguin, 1943), 322. In some other primitive societies – e.g. among the Mundagumor – women are abused for becoming pregnant (*see* Margaret Mead, *Sex and Temperament in Three Primitive Societies* [New York: William Morrow, 1935], 189). In others they are forced to practise infanticide (*see* Yolanda Murphy and Robert F. Murphy, *Women of the Forest* [New York: Columbia University Press, 1974], 165–66).

27. Karen Pryor, *Nursing Your Baby* (New York and London: Harper & Row, 1963), 8.

28. Ibid., 9.

29. Ibid., 233–34.

30. Interview with Sheila Kamerman, 27 March 1985.

31. Sheila B. Kamerman, Alfred J. Kahn, and Paul Kingston, *Maternity Policies and Working Women* (New York: Columbia University Press, 1983), 75.

32. It is instructive to note that most women either fail to breast-feed or choose not to breast-feed for any length of time. One survey found that while 51 per cent of infants were breast-fed immediately after birth, numbers dropped dramatically after they were taken home from hospital; at six weeks only 4 per cent of babies were being exclusively breast-fed. (*See* Penelope Leach, *Babyhood*, 22–23.)

33. Interview, 10 November 1983.

34. Marvin S. Eiger and Sally Wendkos Olds, *The Complete Book of Breastfeeding* (New York: Workman Publishing Co., 1972), 174–75.

35. Ibid., 112.

36. *Parenthood in the Balance*: An Assessment of Benefits and Leave around the Time of Childbirth, Equal Opportunities Commission, December 1982.

37. Ibid.

38. 'Report of the Dean of Barnard College', *Columbia University Bulletin of Information*, 33d series, no. 1 (October 1, 1932), 6.

39. Ibid., 7.

40. Ibid.

41. 1982–3 report on more than 2,500 institutes of higher education from the American Association of University Professors, reported in the *New York Times*, 6 February 1984.

42. Interview with Betty Vetter, executive director, Scientific Manpower Commission, Washington, D.C., 8 February 1985.

43. This approximates the gap in salaries in the country at large. In 1983–84 female full professors earned, on average, $33,730 a year while male full professors earned $37,860 a year (*Academe* [July–August 1984], 12).

2. The Economic Fall-out of Divorce

1. In the United States the divorce rate in 1981 was 5.3 divorce decrees granted for every 1,000 persons, while in Sweden the rate was 2.4 per 1,000; in Britain, 3.0; in Canada, 2.6; in France, 1.6; and in Italy, .2. *UN Demographic Yearbook 1981* (New York: UN Department of International and Social Affairs, Statistical Office, 1983), 461–63. *See also* discussion in Robert Chester, *Divorce in Europe* (Leiden: Martinus Nijhoff Social Science Division, 1977), 302–06.

2. *Monthly Labour Review* (December 1983), 18.

3. *New York Times*, 4 October 1984.

4. *Money, Income and Poverty Status of Families and Persons in the US: 1984*, Current Population Reports, Series P–60 (Washington, D.C.: Bureau of the Census, August 1985), 15.

5. Interview, 3 December 1983.

6. In the mid-seventies, as the divorce rate rose steeply, the number of 'displaced homemakers' increased to such an extent that their predicament finally began to penetrate the public consciousness. National magazines ran poignant articles, and several centres to help displaced homemakers appeared around the country. Most of these centres were started and staffed by displaced homemakers themselves. 'Don't agonise, organise' was their motto. They concentrated on career counselling and training, and had considerable success

in preparing women for modest jobs in the labour market. However, the centres were able to reach only a tiny fraction of the women who needed help. In the late seventies the federal government finally stepped in with funding for an umbrella organisation, the Displaced Homemakers Network, which for a short time provided assistance to centres around the country. Unfortunately the network was a casualty of Reagan budget cuts and in 1983 was drastically reduced in its scope. Although there are more displaced homemakers than ever, less is being done for them.

7. Erica Abeel, 'School for Ex-Wives', *New York* (16 October 1978), 97.

8. *What Happens When Homemakers Lose Their Jobs* (Washington, D.C.: Displaced Homemakers Network, Inc., 15 November 1983).

9. Quoted in Lenore J. Weitzman and Ruth B. Dixon, 'The Alimony Myth: Does No Fault Divorce Make a Difference?', *Family Law Quarterly* XIV (Fall 1980), 143.

10. Ibid., 158

11. Ibid., 154–55. The percentage of women awarded monthly payments dropped from 19 to 13 per cent between 1968 and 1972.

12. Ibid., 163.

13. Judge Leander Foley of Milwaukee, quoted in the *Wall Street Journal*, 21 January 1985.

14. Katherine Bouton, 'Women and Divorce,' *New York* (8 October 1984), 36.

15. Ibid., 35.

16. Interview, 10 October 1984.

17. Interview, 25 September 1984.

18. New Jersey Supreme Court Task Force on *Women in the Courts* (June 1984), 80.

19. Ibid., 99.

20. Ibid., 99.

21. Lenore J. Weitzman, 'The Economics of Divorce: Social and Economic Consequences of Property, Alimony and Child Support Awards', *UCLA Law Review* 28 (August 1981), 1254.

22. Weitzman and Dixon, op. cit., 143.

23. Interview, 25 September 1984.

24. Weitzman and Dixon, op. cit., 182.

25. *Globe* (29 May 1984).

26. Interview, 29 November 1983.

27. *Reducing Poverty Among Children* (Washington, D.C.: Congressional Budget Office, May 1985), 6.

28. Joyce Everett, 'Patterns and Implications of Child Support and Enforcement Practices for Children's Well-Being', Wellesley College Center for Research on Women, Working Paper No. 128 (1984), 2.

29. Linda Bird Francke, *Growing Up Divorced* (New York: Linden Press/Simon & Schuster, 1983), 28.

30. Weitzman, op. cit., 1256.

31. Lucy Marsh Yee, 'What Really Happens in Child Support Cases: An Empirical Study of the Establishment and Enforcement of Child Support Orders in the Denver District Court', *Law Journal Denver* 57 (1980), 21–36. The average father for whom data were available paid $136.97 per month for his car and $113.59 per month for his 1.6 children.

32. Information supplied by the Office of Representative Barbara Kennelly (Democrat, Connecticut), 9 March 1985.

33. New Jersey Task Force, op. cit., 100.

34. Between 1978 and 1981 the average child-support payment decreased by 16 per cent in real terms (ibid., 62).

35. The cost of raising a child up to the age of eighteen in 1980 ranged from $71,712 (when family income was less than $10,000) to $159,430 (when family income was in the $20,000 to $40,000 range); these estimates *do not include child care or college education* (New Jersey Task Force, op. cit., 76).

36. Interview, 5 December 1983.

37. Term coined by Marcia Guttentag and Paul F. Secord, *Too Many Women: The Sex Ratio Question* (Beverly Hills, Calif.: Sage Publications, 1983), 18.

38. Noreen Goldman, Charles F. Westoff, and Charles Hammerslough, 'Demography of the Marriage Market in the United States', *Population Index* 50 (Spring 1984), 16.

39. Ibid., 20.

40. Ibid., 16.

41. *American Women: Three Decades of Change* (Washington, D.C.: Bureau of the Census, August 1983), 4–5.

42. Beverly Stephen, 'In Pursuit of Justice for Women in the Courts', *Daily News*, 11 August 1984, 10.

43. Weitzman and Dixon, op. cit., 185.

44. Weitzman, op. cit., 1266.

45. Ibid., 1252.

46. Quoted in Lenore J. Weitzman, *The Marriage Contract* (New York: The Free Press, 1981), 152.

47. Interview with Olga Baudelot, Institut National de Recherche Pédagogique, Paris, 2 February 1985.

48. Interviews with Swedish journalist Karl Ahlenius, 30 May 1984, and West German sociologist Greta Tullmann, 5 June 1984.

49. Frank F. Furstenberg, Jr., and Christine Winquist Nord, 'Parenting Apart: Patterns of Childrearing After Marital Disruption,' *Journal of Marriage and the Family* (November 1985), 874.

50. Study by Dr. E. Mavis Hetherington of the University of Virginia at Charlottesville, reported in the *New York Times*, 13 December 1983.

3. The Wage Gap

1. Roy Rowan, 'How Harvard's Women MBAs Are Managing', *Fortune* (11 July 1983), 64.

2. Jill Bettner and Christine Donahue, 'Now They're Not Laughing', *Forbes* (21 November 1983), 117.

3. *Money, Income and Poverty Status of Families and Persons in the US: 1984*, Current Population Reports, Series P-60 (Washington, D.C.: Bureau of the Census, August 1985), 21.

4. For 1939 figure, *see* Dorothy S. Brody, 'Equal Pay for Women Workers', *Annals of the American Academy of Political and Social Science* 217 (May 1947), 54. For the 1984 figure, *see* Bureau of the Census, op. cit., 17. The wage gap seems to go back a long way. In biblical times, says Leviticus 27:3–4, women of working age were valued at thirty silver shekels, while men were valued at fifty.

5. August 1985 figure released by the Bureau of the Census.

According to Ray Marshall, in the 1981–83 recession the relative position of women improved slightly because of the worsening economic conditions for men, who were heavily concentrated in the declining industrial sector, not because women were improving their absolute positions. (Interview, 3 April 1985.)

6. Bureau of the Census, 1985, op. cit., 17.

7. *Philadelphia Inquirer*, 15 July 1984.

8. *Money and Income of Households and Families in the US* (Washington, D.C.: Bureau of the Census, 1982).

9. Older Women's League, 'Older Women's League Protests Change in Poverty Definition' testimony before the Joint Economic Committee, 6 June 1984, 3.

10. *New York Times*, 22 May 1984.

11. Peter J. Sloane, 'The Trend of Women's Wages Relative to Men's in the Post-war Period in Great Britain', paper presented to the Economic Policy Council's panel 'Parents and Work: Family Policy in Comparative Perspective', Washington, D.C., 12 June 1984, 23–29.

12. Annual earnings of all full-time year-round workers. These figures are comparable to the US figures. See annual report of the Central Bureau of Statistics and various issues of *Allman Manadsstatistik*, Stockholm, Sweden.

13. The Italian, West German, French, and Danish figures refer to manual workers in industry.

Hourly Earnings Differentials in Various Countries of the European Community
Manual Workers in Manufacturing Industry
Female Earnings as a Percentage of Male

	1968	1977	1982
Belgium	67%	70%	72%
Denmark	74%	85%	86% (1981)
France	n.a.	76%	78%
West Germany	69%	72%	73%
Italy	74%	84%	86%
Netherlands	55%	75%	75%
Sweden	78%	87%	90%
Switzerland	64%	68%	n.a.
U.K.	60%	72%	74%

Source: *Eurostat*, 'Hourly Earnings – Hours of Work', various issues (Luxembourg: Statistical Office of the European Community).

Within the EEC there is no systematic collection of nonmanual earnings figures. However, the patchy data that do exist suggest that non-manual earnings follow a similar trend, though at a lower level. For example, in France women in non-manual occupations earned 62 per cent of the male wage in the mid-1970s. In Italy the figure was 68 per cent, and in West Germany it was 65 per cent. *See* United Nations, *The Economic Role of Women in the EEC Region* (New York: 1980).

Australia is another country where the wage gap has narrowed considerably in recent years. Female earnings as a percentage of male earnings rose from 70 per cent in 1968 to 82 per cent in 1977. *See* discussion in the testimony of Robert C. Gregory before the Equal Employment Opportunity Commission Hearings on job segregation and discrimination, 28 and 30 April 1980, 611.

14. In Britain earnings figures are generally presented as average gross hourly earnings. Under this measure working women earned 74 per cent of the male wage in 1982, up from 60 per cent in 1968 (the figures include manual and nonmanual workers and are for both the public and the private sectors). The British data are also available in the form of full-time gross weekly earnings. Under this measure women earned 66 per cent of the male wage in 1982, up from 54 per cent in 1970. The lower figures are due to the fact that weekly earnings take into consideration the effects of overtime and the shorter working weeks typically worked by women workers. These weekly earnings figures can be compared with the US data. *See New Earnings Survey 1970–1982*, part A, tables 10 and 11. *See also* analysis in Sloane, op. cit., 1–43.

15. Smith and Ward, op. cit., 35. Figures are for the birth cohort 1951–54. *See also Employment in Perspective: Working Women*, Report 650 (Washington, D.C.: Bureau of Labor Statistics, 1981); this shows that younger women have a considerable educational advantage over younger men.

16. *Hansard*, vol. 13, 17 November 1981; *UNESCO Statistical Yearbook*, 1982, table 3.10.

17. *The Wage Gap: Myths and Facts* (Washington, D.C.: National Committee on Pay Equity, 1982), 5.

18. Bureau of the Census figures, quoted in the *Wall Street Journal*, 10 November 1983.

19. By Barbara Everitt of the Market Opinion Research Company, Detroit.

20. *Business Week* (1 October 1984), 126.

21. *New York Times*, 16 January 1984. Green's analysis is of all workers who entered the US labour force in 1970 and 1980. He documents the educational gains of women: in 1970, 19 per cent of white women entering the job market had four or more years of college; by 1980 this figure was 27 per cent. For white men the figure stayed constant at 27 per cent.

22. *See* discussion in Barbara R. Bergmann, 'Feminism and Economics', *Academe* (September–October 1983), 22–25. It should be pointed out that much of the disagreement in the economics profession over how to explain the wage gap is over differences in emphasis, not over facts. As Ray Marshall has put it, 'I don't know of a liberal who believes all of the pay gap is due to discrimination or a conservative who believes it is all due to human capital factors. There is a sizeable unexplained residual in most econometric studies.' (Interview, 3 April 1985.)

23. Sloane, op. cit., 27.

24. Bureau of the Census figures, quoted in the *New York Times*, 25 November 1984.

25. The British sources are as follows: Assistant Secretary figures: Civil Service Statistics, 1983. Institute of Bankers figures: Institute of Bankers. Figures on doctors: Health and Personal Social Services Statistics for England.

26. National Committee on Pay Equity, op. cit., 5.

27. 1983 figures from the Bureau of Labor Statistics, quoted in the *New York Times*, 25 November 1984, 32.

28. Preamble from a suit filed against the state of California by the California State Employees Association, quoted in the *New York Times*, 9 December 1984.

29. *See* reports of Washington State case in the *New York Times*, 1 January 1984, and 9 April 1984. It should be pointed out that this decision was overturned by a federal appeals court in September 1985. The case will now go to the Supreme Court.

30. *Washington Post*, 17 November 1984.

31. For a discussion of the conservative viewpoint see Michael Levin, 'Comparable Worth: The Feminist Road to Socialism', *Commentary* (September 1984), 13–19.

32. Interview with Ray Marshall, 3 April 1985.

33. Approximately 15 per cent of the wage gap is due to occupational discrimination. Polachek explains between 12 and 21 per cent of the wage gap using this methodology (*see* Solomon William Polachek, 'Women in the Economy: Perspectives on Gender Inequality', paper presented at the US Commission on Civil Rights Conference on Comparable Worth, 6–7 June 1984). Treiman and Hartmann explain between 11 and 19 per cent of the wage gap this way, and Fuchs explains 6 per cent (*see* Donald J. Treiman and Heidi I. Hartmann, eds., *Women, Work, and Wages: Equal Pay for Jobs of Equal Value* [Washington, D.C.: National Academy Press, 1981], and Victor Fuchs, 'Differentials in Hourly Earnings Between Men and Women', *Monthly Labor Review* 94 [May 1971], 9–15). The explanatory power of this approach depends on how many occupational groups are considered. The larger the number, the higher the proportion of the wage gap explained. However, even with 479 occupations (a degree of disaggregation many economists think is unwarranted) less than half of the wage gap (between 35 and 39 per cent) can be attributed to occupational segregation (*see* discussion in Earl F. Mellor, 'Investigating the Differences in Weekly Earnings of Women and Men', *Monthly Labor Review* [June 1984], 26, 17–19).

34. Interview, 10 October 1984.

35. *See* discussion on Cynthia B. Lloyd and Beth Niemi, *The Economics of Sex Differentials* (New York: Columbia University Press, 1979).

36. Polachek, op. cit., 24.

37. Ibid., 22.

38. Smith and Ward, op. cit., 12. *See also*: Mark B. Stewart and Christine A. Greenhaigh, 'Work History Patterns and the Occupational Attainment of Women', *Economic Journal* (September 1984).

39. Polachek, op. cit., 13–14.

40. Corcoran and Duncan explain 44 per cent of the wage gap by analysing tenure in job, on-the-job training, and number of years of work life at full-time jobs (Mary Corcoran and Greg J. Duncan, 'Work History, Labor Force Attachment and Earnings Differentials Between Races and Sexes', *Journal of Human Resources* [Winter 1979], 3–20). Rytina finds

that work history and labour force attachment account for 25 per cent of the wage difference between the sexes (Nancy F. Rytina, 'Tenure as a Factor in the Male-Female Earnings Gap', *Monthly Labor Review* [April 1982], 32–34).

41. Bureau of the Census data reported in the *New York Times*, 14 April 1984, and 3 August 1984.

42. Interview, 13 April 1985.

43. National Committee on Pay Equity, op. cit., 3.

44. Lester C. Thurow, '62 Cents To The Dollar; The Earnings Gap Doesn't Go Away', *Working Mother*, October 1984, 42.

45. Lester C. Thurow, *The Zero Sum Society* (New York: Basic Books, 1980), 19.

46. Quoted in Barbara A. Brown, Thomas I. Emerson, Gail Falk, and Ann E. Freedman, 'The Equal Rights Amendment: A Constitutional Basis for Equal Rights for Women', *Yale Law Journal* 80, 5 (April 1971), 973.

47. Kathleen Sylvester, 'Women Gaining, Blacks Fall Back', *National Law Review* (21 May 1984), 41, and Kathleen Sylvester, 'Minorities in Firms', *National Law Journal* (21 May 1984), 3.

48. Jill Abramson and Barbara Franklin, 'Are Women Catching Up?', *American Lawyer* (May 1983), 79.

49. Ibid., 84.

50. Much the same pattern is emerging in investment banking. 'It's been a good decade since large numbers of women began emerging from top business schools and embarking in earnest on careers in finance. Yet, with rare exceptions, women have so far failed to achieve that most hallowed of Wall Street goals: being named partner, or in public firms, managing director.' Women now comprise something like a quarter of all professionals in investment banking, but the proportion of female partners and managing directors is a minuscule 1 per cent. Beth McGoldnick and Gregory Miller, 'Wall Street Women: You've Come a Short Way, Baby', *Institutional Investor*, June 1985, 239.

51. Polachek, op. cit., p. 17.

52. Heidi I. Hartmann, 'The Family as the Locus of Gender, Class and Political Struggle', *Signs* (Spring 1981), 366–94. *See* discussion in Dolores Hayden, *Redesigning the American Dream: The Future of Housing, Work and Family Life* (New York: Norton, 1984), 64.

53. Joseph H. Pleck, 'Husband's Paid Work and Family Roles: Current Research Issues', in Helena Z. Lopata and Joseph H. Pleck, eds., *Research in the Interweave of Social Roles*, Vol. 3 (Greenwich, Conn.: JAI Press, 1982), 251–333. *See also* discussion in Joseph H. Pleck, 'Husbands' and Wives' Family Work, Paid Work and Adjustment', Working Paper No. 95 (Wellesley, Mass.: Wellesley College, Center for Research on Women, 1982).

54. Hartmann, op. cit., 380.

55. Hartmann, op. cit., 383.

56. Lopata and Pleck, op. cit., 253.

57. Nora Ephron, *Heartburn* (New York: Pocket Books, 1983; London: Pan Books, 1984), 104.

58. Simone de Beauvoir, *The Second Sex* (New York: Alfred A. Knopf, 1952; London: Cape, 1953), 536.

59. Philip Blumstein and Pepper Schwartz, *American Couples: Money, Work and Sex* (New York: William Morrow, 1983), 53.

60. *See* A. Beller, 'The Impact of Equal Opportunity Policy on Sex Differentials in Earnings and Occupations', *American Economic Review (Proceedings)* (May 1982), 171–75.

61. Sheila B. Kamerman, Alfred J. Kahn, and Paul Kingston, *Maternity Policies and Working Women* (New York: Columbia University Press, 1983), 66. Much of the discussion of maternity leave in America is based on the work of Sheila B. Kamerman.

62. Caroline Little, 'Mother Load or Overload: The Need for a National Maternity Policy', *Journal of International Law and Politics* 17 (1985), 3.

63. Testimony of Dr Lenora Cole Alexander, director of the Women's Bureau, US Department of Labor, before the Joint Economic Committee of the US Congress, 3 April 1984, 9.

64. Naomi Barko, 'Maternity Leave – American Style', *Working Mother* (November 1983), 45–46.

65. Kamerman, Kahn, and Kingston, op. cit., 56.

66. 'When the Mother-to-Be Is an Executive', *Business Week* (11 April 1983), 128.

67. Interview, 10 January 1983.

68. Interview, 18 November 1984.

69. Interview, 1 March 1983.

70. Interview, 6 March 1983.

71. Sheila B. Kamerman and Alfred J. Kahn, 'Company Maternity-leave Policies: The Big Picture', *Working Women* (February 1984), 80. In Europe the minimum paid maternity leave is fourteen weeks, and the most common leave granted is five months. In addition, most European countries provide at least one year of unpaid but job-protected leave, and all European countries have some form of national health insurance to cover the costs of pre-natal and post-natal care. For more details see Sheila Kamerman, *Maternity and Parental Benefits and Leaves* (New York: Columbia University, Center for the Social Sciences, Monograph No 1, 1980).

72. *Equality Between Men and Women in Sweden* (Stockholm: The Swedish Institute, May 1983).

73. 'Parental Leave: A New Proposal for a Directive', *Social Europe* (May 1984) No. 1, Brussels Commission of the European Community, 24.

74. 'Maternity Rights and Benefits: The Current Situation' (London: Equal Opportunities Commission, 1983), 7.

75. Department of Health and Social Security press release (86, 131), 'Government Proposals on Maternity Benefit – Introduction of New Scheme of Statutory Maternity Pay', 18 April 1986.

76. Interview, 20 November 1983.

77. Interview, 30 November 1983.

78. *OECD Employment Outlook* (Paris: OECD Labor Force Statistics, September 1985), 40. The figures are for working women aged 16–64 as a percentage of the working-age female population.

79. Marvin Harris, *America Now: The Anthropology of a Changing Culture* (New York: Simon & Schuster, 1981), 92.

4. Children: The Other Victims

1. The statistics in this paragraph are from the Select Committee on Children, Youth and Families, *US Children and their Families: Current Conditions and Recent Trends* (Washington, D.C.: US Government Printing Office, May 1983), 6; and the National Citizens' Board of Inquiry into Health in America, *Health Care USA* (October 1984), vol. 1, p. 1.

2. Mayor's Task Force on Child Abuse and Neglect, 'Report on the Preliminary Study of Child Fatalities in New York City', November 1983. *See also New York Times*, 23 October 1983.

3. *American Children in Poverty* (Washington, D.C.: Children's Defense Fund, 1984), 14. *See also New York Times*, 2 September 1983.

4. *Money Income and Poverty Status of Persons and Families in the US 1983*, Current Population Reports, Series P-60 (Washington, D.C.: Bureau of the Census, 1984).

5. Quoted in Letty Cottin Pogrebin, *Family Politics: Love and Power on an Intimate Frontier* (New York: McGraw-Hill, 1983), 60.

6. *New York Times*, 2 September 1983.

7. Interview with Michelle Seligson, Center for Research on Women, Wellesley College, 24 July 1985. *See also* 'What Price Day Care?', *Newsweek* (10 September 1984), 14.

8. Interview with Sheila Kamerman, 27 March 1985.

9. Interview, 3 October 1983.

10. Ann C. Crouter, Jay Belsky, and Graham B. Spanier, 'The Family Context of Child Development: Divorce and Maternal Employment', *Annals of Child Development* 1 (1984), 207. See also Select Committee on Children, Youth and Families, op. cit., 14.

11. Barbara Ehrenreich and Karin Stallard, 'The Nouveau Poor', *Ms.* (August 1982), 222.

12. Michael Rutter, 'Protective Factors in Children's Response to Stress and Disadvantage', in *Primary Prevention of Psychopathology*, vol. 3; *Promoting Social Competence and Coping with Children*, eds., M. W. Kent and J. E. Rolf (Hanover, N. H.: University Press of New England, 1978). *See also* E. M. Hetherington, 'Divorce: A Child's Perspective', *American Psychologist* 34 (1979).

13. Interview, 12 February 1984. *See* Linda Bird Francke, *Growing Up Divorced* (New York: Linden Press/Simon & Schuster 1983). This book contains vivid portraits of the children of divorce.

14. Joyce Everett, 'Patterns and Implications of Child Support Practices for Children's Well-being', Wellesley College Center for Research on Women, Working Paper No. 128 (1984), 2.

15. *Money, Income and Poverty Status of Families and Persons in the US: 1984*, Current Population Reports, Series P-60 (Washington, D.C.: Bureau of the Census, 1985).

16. Bishop's Pastoral, 'Catholic Social Teaching and the US Economy,' *Origins* 14 (15 November 1984), 363.

17. Mayor's Task Force, op. cit.

18. Interview, 2 March 1984.

19. *New York Times*, 20 July 1983.

20. *Child Care Arrangements of Working Mothers*, Current Population Reports, Series P-23 (Washington, D.C.: US Bureau of the Census, 1983), 22.

21. *New York Times*, 3 September 1984.

22. *Child Care: The States' Response* (Washington, D.C.: Children's Defense Fund, 1983–84), 1.

23. *New York Times*, 2 September 1984.

24. Myron Magnet, 'What Mass-produced Child Care is Producing', *Fortune* (28 November, 1983), 157–58.

25. Sheila B. Kamerman, *Parenting in an Unresponsive Society: Managing Work and Family* (New York: The Free Press, 1980), 58.

26. Interview, 5 March 1983.

27. Sheila B. Kamerman, 'Child Care Services: A National Picture', *Monthly Labor Review* (December 1983), 36.

28. *See* discussion in Eugenia Kemble, *Starting Off on the Right Foot*, Publication No. 625 (Washington, D.C.: American Federation of Teachers, 1974), 12.

29. Kamerman, 'Child Care Services', loc. cit., 37.

30. *Nation at Risk: The Imperative for Educational Reform* (Washington, D.C.: National Commission for Excellence in Education, April 1983), 32.

31. Interview with Michele Seligson, 24 July 1985. *See also Employers and Child Care: Development of the New Employee Benefit* (Washington, D.C.: Bureau of National Affairs, 1984), 1.

32. Helen Blank, testimony of the Children's Defense Fund Before the Joint Economic Committee Concerning Child Care Problems Faced by Working Mothers and Pregnant Women, 3 April 1984.

33. Lynette and Thomas Long, *The Handbook for Latchkey Children and Their Parents* (New York: Arbor House, 1983), 174.

34. Interview, 2 June 1983.

35. *New York Times*, 8 September 1974.

36. Long, op. cit., 283.

37. Interview, 1 March 1983.

38. *Fact Sheets on Sweden* (Stockholm: The Swedish Institute, October 1982), 86.

39. National Plan of Action for Equality, *Step by Step* (Stockholm: 1979), 76.

40. Ibid., 76–105.

41. Olga Baudelot, 'Child Care in France', paper presented to the Economic Policy Council, 11 December 1984. The cost data are from 1980–81. In this paper Baudelot draws on the research she did for the Kamerman-Kahn study. *See* note 47.

42. Sheila B. Kamerman, 'Child Care and Family Benefits: Policies of Six Industrialised Countries', *Monthly Labor Review*, November 1980, 26.

43. Interview with Fabrizia Mauro, Ferrara, Italy, 10 November 1983.

44. The Case for Workplace Nurseries, press release issued by the Equal Opportunities Commission, 1986.

45. Ibid.

46. Quoted in the *New York Times*, 4 September 1984.

47. Ibid.

48. Interview, 9 November 1983.

49. Nicole Questiaux and Jacques Fournier, 'France', in Sheila B. Kamerman and Alfred J. Kahn, eds., *Child Care, Family Benefits and Working Parents: A Study in Comparative Policy* (New York: Columbia University Press, 1981), 161.

50. *American Children in Poverty*, op. cit., 9.

51. *The Stake of the Public Schools in Early Childhood Education*, Publication No. 626 (Washington, D.C.: American Federation of Teachers, 1974).

52. *See* discussion in Marilyn Rauth, *A Review of the History, Current Conditions and Future Prospects of Child Care Programs in America*, Publication No. 630 (Washington, D.C.: American Federation of Teachers, 1974), 6.

53. Ibid.

54. Ibid.

55. *Wall Street Journal*, 29 November 1984.

56. *Nation at Risk*, op. cit., 5.

57. Ibid., 8.

58. Ruth Leger Sibard, *World Military and Social Expenditures, 1982* (Leesburg, Virginia: World Priorities, 1982), 30–32.

59. John Betjeman, 'Norfolk,' *Collected Poems* (London: John Murray, 1958; Boston: Houghton Mifflin, 1971), 211.

60. E. Nesbit, *The Railway Children* (London: ·Puffin Books, 1960), 9–10.

61. Betty Friedan, *The Second Stage* (New York: Summit Books, 1981), 100.

62. *Business Week*, 28 January 1985.

63. Figures for 1982, GHS.

5. *Image and Reality*

1. *New York Times*, 10 December 1983.

2. R. W. Apple, Jr, 'New Stirrings of Patriotism', *New York Times Magazine*, 11 December 1983.

3. Quoted in Marvin Harris, *America Now: The Anthropology of a Changing Culture* (New York: Simon & Schuster, 1981), 76.

4. Ibid.

5. Eleanor Smeal, *Why and How Women Will Elect the Next President* (New York: Harper & Row, 1984), 26–32. When Eleanor Smeal was re-elected to the presidency of NOW in the summer of 1985, she reaffirmed her prime commitment to the ERA and legalised abortion. *New York Times*, 22 July 1985.

6. Interview, 7 March 1984.

7. *New York Times*, 22 July 1984.

8. Quoted in the *New York Times*, 5 November 1984.

6. *Equal Rights Versus Social Benefits*

1. William H. Chafe, *Women and Equality: Changing Patterns in American Culture* (New York: Oxford University Press, 1977), 24.

2. Quoted in Elisabeth Griffith, *In Her Own Right: The Life of Elizabeth Cady Stanton* (New York and London: Oxford University Press, 1984), 54.

3. Chafe, op. cit., 29.

4. Griffith, op. cit., XV.

5. Phyllis Chesler, *Women and Madness* (Garden City, N.Y.: Doubleday, 1972), 243–44.

6. Colette Dowling, *The Cinderella Complex* (New York: Pocket Books, 1981; London: Michael Joseph, 1982), 8.

7. Ibid., 21.

8. Ibid.

9. Ibid.

10. David Bouchier, *The Feminist Challenge: The Movement for Women's Liberation in Britain and the United States* (London: Macmillan, 1983; New York: Schocken Books, 1984), 45.

11. William L. O'Neill, *The Woman Movement: Feminism in the United States and England* (London: Allen & Unwin, 1969, Chicago: Quadrangle, 1971), 31.

12. H. L. Mencken, *In Defense of Women* (New York: Alfred A. Knopf, 1922), 132.

13. Emily Blair, 'Are Women a Failure in Politics?', *Harper's* (October 1925), 513–22.

14. Gayle Yates, *What Women Want: The Ideas of the Movement* (Cambridge, Mass.: Harvard University Press, 1975), 77.

15. Ibid., 102.

16. Carolyn Teich Adams and Kathryn Teich Winston, *Mothers at Work: Public Policies in the United States, Sweden and China* (New York: Longman, 1980), 132.

17. *New York Times*, 3 November 1975.

18. Anna-Greta Leijon, 'Equality in the Labor Market, in Political and Trade Union Organizations, and in the Home', *Current Sweden* 75 (April 1975), 4.

19. Interview with Birgitta Karlstrom, foreign correspondent for Swedish Broadcasting, 22 February 1983.

20. Adams and Winston, op. cit., 116.

21. It should be pointed out that just after the Civil War an organisation called the American Equal Rights Association (AERA) was formed to push for both black and female suffrage. But the rights of blacks took precedence over the rights of women. In 1868 the Fourteenth Amendment gave black men the vote but excluded black women from citizenship and voting rights. After this date the women's suffrage movement was self-consciously separatist (Griffith, op. cit., 118–25).

22. Adams and Winston, op. cit., 117. *See also Equality in the Labour Market: Programme Adopted by the Labour Market Board* (Stockholm: Avbetsmarknadsstyrelsen, September 1977).

23. Interview, Anna-Greta Leijon, 7 March 1984.

24. *Guardian*, 28 October 1983.

25. Sheila Lewenhak, *Women and Trade Unions: An Outline History of Women in the British Trade Union Movement* (London: Benn; New York: St. Martin's Press, 1977), 60.

26. Norbert C. Soldon, *Women in British Trade Unions 1874–1976* (Dublin: Gill and Macmillan, 1978), 70.

27. Gladys Boone, *The Women's Trade Union Leagues in Great Britain and the USA* (New York: Columbia University Press, 1942), 121.

28. Louise A. Tilly and Joan W. Scott, *Women, Work and Family* (New York: Holt, Rinehart & Winston, 1978), 173.

29. Bouchier, op. cit., 57.

30. Ibid.

31. Ibid., 37.

32. Interview, December 1984.

33. Interview, Ruth Spellman, National Economic Development Council, London, 3 October 1984.

34. *See* discussion in Anna Coote and Beatrix Campbell, *Sweet Freedom: The Struggle for Women's Liberation* (London: Pan Books, 1982), 143–49.

35. *Guardian*, 10 May 1984.

36. Remato Giancola, ed., *Italy: Documents and Notes* (Rome: Presidency of the Council of Ministers, 1975), 401.

37. Daniela Colombo, 'The Italian Feminist Movement', *Women's Studies International Quarterly* 4, 4 (1981), 467.

38. Giancola, op. cit., 421–27.

39. Interview, 17 November 1984.

40. Interview, 1 March 1984.

41. Interview with Fabrizia Mauro, Ferrara, Italy, 10 November 1983.

42. Interview, October 1984.

7. *Women's Liberation and Motherhood*

1. *American Women: Three Decades of Change* (Washington, D.C.: Bureau of the Census, August 1983), 4. In 1950 more than 20 per cent of forty-year-old American women were childless.

2. *See* discussion in Chapter One, especially Note 10.

3. Bureau of the Census, op. cit., 7.

4. Interview, 28 January 1985.

5. Paul Bagne, 'High Tech Breeding', *Mother Jones* (August 1983), 23–27.

6. Interview, Roxanne Felshuch, IDANT Laboratories, 4 January 1985.

7. *Wall Street Journal*, 21 May 1985.

8. Elisabeth Griffith, *In Her Own Right: The Life of Elizabeth Cady Stanton* (New York and London: Oxford University Press, 1984), 184.

9. Shulamith Firestone, *The Dialectic of Sex* (New York: William Morrow, 1970; London: Cape, 1971), 73.

10. Ibid., 202.

11. Griffith, op. cit., 51.

12. Ann Dally, *Inventing Motherhood: The Consequences of an Ideal* (New York: Schocken Books, 1983; London: Hutchinson, 1982), 133.

13. Ibid., 136.

14. Dolores Hayden, *The Grand Domestic Revolution: A History of Feminist Designs for American Homes, Neighborhoods and Cities* (Cambridge, Mass.: MIT Press, 1981), 189.

15. Dally, op. cit., 140–41.

16. Hayden, op. cit., 197–98.

17. Ibid., 281.

18. Ibid., 284.

19. Ibid., 286.

20. Valerie Solanis, 'Excerpts from the SCUM (Society for Cutting Up Men) Manifesto', in Robin Morgan, ed., *Sisterhood is Powerful* (New York: Vintage Books, 1970), 577.

21. 'Redstocking Manifesto', in Morgan, op. cit., 598.

22. Ann Koedt, Ellen Levine and Anita Rapone, eds., *Radical Feminism* (New York: Quadrangle Books, 1973), 219.

23. Quoted in Benjamin R. Barber, 'Beyond the Feminine Mystique', *The New Republic* (11 July 1983), 27.

24. Betty Friedan, *The Second Stage* (New York: Summit Books, 1981; London: Michael Joseph, 1982), 203.

25. Gloria Steinem, *Outrageous Acts and Everyday Rebellions* (New York: Holt, Rinehart & Winston, 1983), 131.

26. Ibid.

27. Betty Friedan, *The Feminine Mystique* (New York: Dell; London: Gollancz, 1963), 52.

28. Juliet Mitchell, *Women's Estate* (New York: Vintage Books; London: Penguin, 1971), 162.

29. Ibid., 156.

30. Firestone, op. cit., 15.

31. Morgan, op. cit., vii–xiii.

32. *See* account in the *New York Times*, 21 November 1977; Barbara Howar, 'Waxy Yellow Build-up at the Houston Women's Conference', *New York* (5 December 1977), 39–42; and 'What Next for US Women', *Time* (5 December 1977), 19–25.

33. National Commission on the Observation of International Women's Year, *Declaration of American Women* (Washington, D.C.: IWY Commission, 1977), 7.

34. Dally, op. cit., 177.

35. Interview, 4 April 1985.

36. Friedan, *The Second Stage*, loc. cit., 103.

37. Dally, op. cit., 174.

38. Ibid., 175. *See also* Suzanne Arms, *Immaculate Deception: A New Look at Women and Childbirth in America* (Boston: Houghton Mifflin, 1975), 25.

39. Interview, 15 February 1984.

40. Federation CECOS, D. Schwartz and M. J. Mayaux, 'Female Fecundity as a Function of Age', *New England Journal of Medicine* (18 February 1982), 404–06. *See also* L. Westrom, 'Incidence, Prevalence and Trends of Acute Pelvic Inflammatory Disease and Its Consequence in Industrial Countries', *Epidemiology*, 138, 7 (December 1980), 880–92; Westrom explains increased infertility by 'the current epidemic of sexually transmitted diseases'.

41. Interview, 6 January 1984.

42. Quoted in Dally, op. cit., 179.

43. Firestone, op. cit., 188–89.

44. Friedan, *The Feminine Mystique*, loc. cit., 290.

8. *The ERA: A Test Case*

1. Elizabeth Pleck, 'Notes on the Defeat of the ERA', Wellesley College Center for Research on Women, Working Paper No. 103, Wellesley, Mass. (1983), 9.

2. Barbara A. Brown, Thomas I. Emerson, Gail Falk and Ann E. Freedman, 'The Equal Rights Amendment: A Constitutional Basis for Equal Rights for Women', *Yale Law Journal* 80, 5 (April 1971), 887.

3. Phyllis Schlafly, *The Power of the Positive Woman* (New York: Jove/HBJ, 1977), 88–9.

4. Carol Felsenthal, *The Sweetheart of the Silent Majority* (New York: Doubleday, 1981), 237.

5. Paul A. Freund, 'The Equal Rights Amendment is Not the Way', *Harvard Civil Rights–Civil Liberties Law Review* 6 (March 1971), 234.

6. Schlafly, op. cit., 92.

7. Felsenthal, op. cit., 243.

8. Bella Abzug, *Gender Gap* (Boston and London: Houghton Mifflin, 1984), 50.

9. Felscnthal, op. cit., 247.

10. Ibid., 251.

11. Ibid., 250.

12. Ibid., 253.

13. Lisa Cronin Wohl, 'Phyllis Schlafly: The Sweetheart of the Silent Majority', *Ms.* (March 1974), 55.

14. Felsenthal, op. cit., 265.

15. Pleck, op. cit., 6. Schlafly spent $100,000 over the same time period, and even when you add in $300,000 in PAC donations by the STOP ERA movement, it is hard to approach the NOW figure. Jane O'Reilly, 'The Big-Time Players Behind the Small-Town Image', *Ms.* (January 1983), p. 59.

16. *Eagle Forum Newsletter*, the STOP ERA official newspaper.

17. Wohl, op. cit., 55.

18. Ibid.

19. Betty Friedan, *The Second Stage* (New York: Summit Books, 1981; London: Michael Joseph, 1982), 100.

20. Felsenthal, op. cit., 289.

21. 'What Next for US Women?', *Time*, 5 December 1977, 22.

22. Felsenthal, op. cit., 290.

23. Ibid., 291.

24. Ibid., 292.

25. Alice Kessler-Harris, *Out to Work: A History of Wage-Earning Women in the United States* (New York: Oxford University Press, 1982), 206.

26. Ibid.

27. Henry R. Seager, 'Plan for Health Insurance Act', *American Labor Legislation Review* 6 (March 1916), 25.

28. Kessler-Harris, op. cit., 207.

29. Kessler-Harris, op. cit., 212.

30. David Bouchier, *The Feminist Challenge: The Movement for Women's Liberation in Britain and the United States* (London: Macmillan, 1983; New York: Schocken Books, 1984), 18–19.

31. Kessler-Harris, op. cit., 286.

32. *New York Times*, 31 December 1983.

9. *Ultradomesticity: The Return to Hearth and Home*

1. Interview, 3 May 1983.

2. Lou Cannon, *Reagan* (New York: Perigee Books, 1982), 31.

3. John Russell Taylor, *Ingrid Bergman* (New York: St. Martin's Press; London: Hamish Hamilton, 1983), 90.

4. Ibid., 84.

5. Ibid.

6. Betty Friedan, *The Feminine Mystique* (New York: Dell; London: Gollancz, 1963), 52.

7. Ibid., 53.

8. Quoted in Carl N. Degler, 'Revolution without Ideology: The Changing Place of Women in America', in Robert Jay Lifton, ed., *The Woman in America* (Boston: Beacon Press, 1967), 193.

9. Fredrika Bremer, *Hertha* (New York: G. P. Putnam, 1856), iv.

10. Lucy Freeman and Herbert S. Strean, *Freud and Women* (New York: Frederick Ungar, 1981), 199.

11. Joanna Stratton, *Pioneer Women: Voices from the Kansas Frontier* (New York: Simon & Schuster, 1981), 57.

12. Degler, op. cit., 193.

13. Stratton, op. cit., 14.

14. Comparative figures obtained from Degler, op. cit., 194.

15. Alice Kessler-Harris, *Out to Work: A History of Wage-earning Women in the United States* (New York: Oxford University Press, 1982), 276–77.

16. Ibid., 276.

17. William H. Chafe, *The American Woman: Her Changing Social, Economic and Political Roles, 1920–1970* (New York: Oxford University Press, 1972), 170.

18. Degler, op. cit., 207.

19. Chafe, op. cit., 217.

20. Degler, op. cit., 202, and Alva Myrdal and Viola Klein, *Woman's Two Roles* (London: Routledge and Kegan Paul Ltd, 1969), 66.

21. John B. Parrish, 'Professional Womanpower as a National Resource', *Quarterly Review of Economics and Business* 1 (February 1961), 58.

22. Myrdal and Klein, op. cit., 12.

23. William Manchester, *The Glory and the Dream: A Narrative History of America, 1932–1972* (Boston: Little, Brown, 1974), 42.

24. Joseph Pleck, *The Myth of Masculinity* (Cambridge, Mass.: MIT Press, 1981), 159.

25. A. G. Mezerik, 'Getting Rid of the Women', *Atlantic Monthly* (June 1945), 80.

26. William E. Leuchtenberg, 'Consumer Culture and the Cold War', in William E. Leuchtenberg, ed., *The Unfinished Century: America Since 1900* (Boston: Little, Brown & Co., 1973), 754.

27. Kessler-Harris, op. cit., 287.

28. Margaret Barnard Pickel, 'How Come No Jobs for Women?', *New York Times Magazine* (27 January 1946), 46.

29. Agnes Meyer, 'Women Aren't Men', *Atlantic Monthly* 186 (August 1950), 33.

30. Quoted in Chafe, op. cit., 207.

31. Nell Giles, 'What About the Women?', *Ladies' Home Journal* LXI (June 1944), 23.

32. Kessler-Harris, op. cit., 287.

33. Mezerik, op. cit., 81.

34. 'The Roots of Home', *Time* (20 June 1960), 15.

35. Betty Friedan, *The Second Stage* (New York: Summit Books, 1981; London: Michael Joseph, 1982), 100.

36. Christopher Finch, *Norman Rockwell's America* (New York: Harry N. Abrams, 1975).

37. *See* discussion in Leuchtenberg, op. cit., 741–57.

38. Gilbert Steiner, *The Children's Cause* (Washington, D.C.: The Brookings Institution, 1976), 115.

39. Chafe, op. cit., 187.

40. Nathan G. Hale, Jr., *Freud and the Americans* (New York: Oxford University Press, 1971), 304.

41. Ferdinand Lundberg and Marynia F. Farnham, *Modern Women: The Lost Sex* (New York: Harper and Brothers, 1947), 235.

42. Ibid., 370.

43. Helene Deutsch, *The Psychology of Woman: A Psychoanalytic Interpretation* (New York: Grune & Stratton, 1944), 290–91.

44. Freeman and Strean, op. cit., 109.

45. Betty Friedan, 'Smith College – Class of 1942, Questionnaires, 1957', Friedan Papers, Schlesinger Library, Harvard University, Microfilm No 78–1.

46. Friedan, *The Feminine Mystique*, loc. cit., 52.

47. Ibid.

48. Mirra Komarovsky, *Woman in the Modern World* (Boston: Little, Brown, 1953), 258.

49. Friedan, *The Feminine Mystique*, loc. cit., 53.

50. Chafe, op. cit., 205.

51. Friedan, *The Feminine Mystique*, loc. cit., 51.

52. Lundberg and Farnham, quoted in Chafe, op. cit., 204.

53. Molly Haskell, *From Reverence to Rape: The Treatment of Women in the Movies* (New York: Holt, Rinehart & Winston, 1974), 141.

54. June Sochen, 'The New Woman and Twenties America: Way Down East', in John E. O'Connor and Martin A. Jackson, eds., *American History/American Film* (New York: Frederick Ungar, 1979), 13.

55. Alain Silver and Elizabeth Ward, eds., *Film Noir – An Encyclopedia Reference to the American Style* (Woodstock, N.Y.: Overlook Press, 1979), 187.

56. Haskell, op. cit., 270.

57. Ibid.

58. Sochen, op. cit., 17.

59. Philip E. Slater, *The Pursuit of Loneliness* (Boston: Beacon Press, 1970; London: Allen Lane, 1971), 62.

60. Kessler-Harris, op. cit., 302.

10. The Rise of a Cult of Motherhood

1. The article referred to appeared in the *New York Times*, 1 February 1984.

2. Play group meeting, 3 February 1984.

3. N. I. Kugelmass, *Wisdom and Children* (New York: John Day, 1965), 292.

4. John B. Watson, *Psychological Care of Infant and Child*, 1928 (New York: Arno Press, 1972), 87.

5. Quoted in Christina Hardyment, *Dream Babies* (New York: Harper & Row; London: Cape, 1983), 9.

6. Philippe Ariès, *Centuries of Childhood* (New York: Knopf; London: Cape, 1962), 38.

7. Quoted in Ann Dally, *Inventing Motherhood* (London: Hutchinson, 1982; New York: Schocken Books, 1983), 28.

8. Winston Churchill, *My Early Life: A Roving Commission* (London: Butterworth; New York: Charles Scribner & Sons, 1930), 4–5.

9. Ronald Steel, *Walter Lippmann and the American Century* (Boston: Little, Brown, 1980), 1–12.

10. Joanna L. Stratton, *Pioneer Women: Voices from the Kansas Frontier* (New York: Simon & Schuster, 1981), 145.

11. Willystine Goodsell, *A History of the Family as a Social and Educational Institution* (New York: Macmillan, 1919), 422.

12. Luther Emmett Holt, M.D., *The Care and Feeding of Children* (New York: D. Appleton and Co., 1900), 92.

13. *See* discussion in Dally, op. cit., 81.

14. Watson, op. cit., 87.

15. Ibid., 82.

16. Ibid., 83.

17. Erich Fromm, *The Sane Society* (New York: Holt, Rinehart & Winston, 1955), 38–9.

18. Philip Slater, *The Pursuit of Loneliness* (Boston: Beacon Press, 1970; London: Allen Lane, 1971), 64.

19. *See* Sigmund Freud, *The Sexual Enlightenment of Children*, 1907 (New York: Collier Books, 1978). Interestingly enough, Freud himself had a nanny for the first three years of his life, and Freud's own children had a nanny and a nurse. *See* Lucy Freeman and Herbert S. Strean, *Freud and Women* (New York: Frederick Ungar, 1981), 48.

20. Interview with Jerome Kagan, 1 April 1985.

21. Jean Piaget and Barbel Inhelder, *The Psychology of the Child* (New York: Basic Books; London: Routledge, 1969), 3. Piaget himself did not think it a good idea to hasten a child's development. In fact, he criticised those who were saying that one should accelerate development.

22. *Wall Street Journal*, 29 August 1984.

23. Interview, 25 September 1983.

24. Burton L. White, *The First Three Years of Life* (New York: Avon Books, 1975; London: Star Books, 1979), 105.

25. Jerome Kagan, *The Nature of the Child* (New York and London: Basic Books, 1984), 108.

26. Dr Benjamin Spock, *Baby and Child Care* (New York: Pocket Books, 1977; London: Bodley Head, 1979), 286.

27. Selma H. Fraiberg, *The Magic Years* (New York and London: Charles Scribner's Sons, 1959), 93.

28. Ibid., 94.

29. Ibid.

30. Nancy Pottisham Weiss, 'Mother, the Invention of Necessity: Dr Benjamin Spock's Baby and Child Care', *American Quarterly* 29 (Winter 1977), 525.

31. Ibid.

32. Ibid.

33. White, op. cit., 100.

34. Ibid.

35. Weiss, op. cit., 526.

36. Spock, op. cit., 358.

37. Spock, op. cit., 2d ed. (1969), 570.

38. Spock, op. cit., 36.

39. T. Berry Brazelton, *Toddlers and Parents* (New York: Delacorte Press, 1974), 122.

40. Selma H. Fraiberg, *Every Child's Birthright: In Defense of Mothering* (New York: Basic Books, 1977).

41. Burton White, 'Should You Stay Home with Your Baby?', *Young Children* (November 1981), 3–5.

42. White, *The First Three Years of Life*, loc. cit., 104.

43. Interview, 1 March 1983.

44. Ruth E. Zambrana, Marsha Hurt, and Rodney L. Hite, 'The Working Mother in Contemporary Perspective: A Review of the Literature', *Pediatrics* 64 (December 1979), 862–70.

45. Penelope Leach, *Babyhood* (London: Penguin; New York. Alfred A. Knopf, 1983), 121–34.

46. Jerome Kagan, Richard B. Kearsley and Philip R. Zelazo, *Infancy: Its Place in Human Development* (Cambridge, Mass.: Harvard University Press, 1978), 260.

47. Claire Etaugh, 'Effects of Non-maternal Care on Children: Research Evidence and Popular Views', *American Psychologist* 35 (April 1980), 312. In another survey Belsky and Steinberg find that middle-class children neither gain nor lose in the long run from day care, while disadvantaged children gain (Gay Belsky and L. D. Steinberg, 'The Effects of Day Care: A Critical Review', *Child Development* 49 [1978], 929–949).

48. Claire Etaugh, 'Effects of Maternal Employment on Children: A Review of Recent Research', *Merrill Palmer Quarterly* 20 (1974), 85.

49. Ibid.

50. Kagan et al., op. cit., 165.

51. Kugelmass, op. cit., 292.

52. *New York Times*, 3 September 1984.

53. *See* 'Population and Employment 1950–76', *Eurostat* (Luxembourg: Statistical Office of the European Community, 1977), 130; and *Statistical Abstract of the U.S., 1980* (Washington, D.C.: Bureau of the Census, 1985).

54. 'Women in the Labor Market', *OECD Observer*, May 1980, 4.

55. Slater, op. cit., 56. Anthony Trollope protested that 'American babies are an unhappy race, they eat and drink as they please, they are never punished, snubbed and kept in the background as children are kept with us.'

56. Quoted in Spock, op. cit., 12. *See also* discussion in David Riesman, *The Lonely Crowd* (New Haven, Conn.: Yale University Press, 1950), 42.

57. Interview, 2 February 1984.

58. Libby Purves, *How Not to be a Perfect Mother* (London: Fontana, 1986).

59. *The Working Mother's Handbook* (London: The Working Mothers' Association, 3rd edn 1985), 39.

60. Olga Baudelot, paper presented to the Economic Policy Council, New York, 11 December 1984.

61. Robert H. Bremner, ed., *Children and Youth in America: A Documentary History*, vol. III, *1933–1973* (Cambridge, Mass.: Harvard University Press, 1974), 704.

62. Spock, op. cit., 13.

63. Bremner, op. cit., 718.

64. Quoted ibid., 718.

65. Quoted ibid., 719.

66. Marian Wright Edelman, 'A Political-Legislative Overview of Federal Child Care Proposals', in Nathan B. Talbot, ed., *Raising Children in Modern America: Problems and Prospective Solutions* (Boston: Little, Brown, 1974), 316.

67. Ibid., 305.

68. Interview, 3 May 1983.

69. Weiss, op. cit., 545.

70. Ibid., 520.

71. Interview, 25 February 1985.

72. Edelman, op. cit., 316.

11. The Unravelling of the Fifties

1. David Bouchier, *The Feminist Challenge: The Movement for Women's Liberation in Britain and the United States* (London: Macmillan, 1983; New York: Schocken Books, 1984), 31.

2. Interview, 12 January 1983.

12. The Male Rebellion

1. J. M. Barrie, *Peter Pan* (New York: Charles Scribner's Sons, 1950), 228.

2. C. Wright Mills, *White Collar* (New York: Oxford University Press, 1953), 282.

3. Arthur Miller, *Death of a Salesman* (New York: Viking Press; London: Cresset, 1949), 22.

4. Herman Wouk, *Marjorie Morningstar* (New York: Doubleday; London: Cape, 1955), 47.

5. Ibid., 48.

6. Warren Farrell, *The Liberated Man* (New York: Random House, 1975), 74.

7. Sloan Wilson, *What Shall We Wear to This Party? The Man in The Gray Flannel Suit Twenty Years Before and After* (New York: Arbor House, 1976), 11.

8. William H. Whyte, Jr., *The Organization Man* (New York: Simon & Schuster, 1956; London: Cape, 1957), 306.

9. Charles A. Reich, *The Greening of America* (New York: Random House, 1970), 163.

10. Ibid., 209.

11. Wilson, op. cit., 183.

12. Bruce Bliven, Jr., 'Life and Love in the Split Level Slums', *Reporter* (7 February 1957); Anthony Winthrop, Jr., 'The Crab Grass Roots of Suburbia', *New Republic* (11 February 1957); 'On the 5:19 to Ulcerville', *Newsweek* (17 August 1959).

13. Quoted in Scott Donaldson, *The Suburban Myth* (New York: Columbia University Press, 1969), 14.

14. Philip Roth, *My Life as a Man* (New York: Holt, Rinehart and Winston; London: Cape, 1974), 169.

15. Ibid.

16. Morris Dickstein, *Gates of Eden: American Culture in the Sixties* (New York: Basic Books, 1977), 63.

17. Richard Yates, *Revolutionary Road* (New York: Dell, 1961; London: Four Square Books, 1964), 12.

18. Ibid., 23.

19. Betty Friedan, *The Feminine Mystique* (New York: Dell; London: Gollancz, 1963), 261.

20. Betty Hannah Hoffman, 'Through All My Housework in an Hour', *Ladies' Home Journal* (October 1960), 184–90. The portrait of Janice Crabtree featured in this issue was meant as a serious treatment of an efficient housewife, but it succeeded in stirring up a great deal of anger around the country. Irate readers wrote to the editor of the magazine complaining about Mrs Crabtree. Housewives felt misrepresented, and men felt taken for a ride.

21. Bob Norman, 'Miss Golddigger of 1953', *Playboy* (December 1953), 12–71. © Playboy.

22. Charles Perry, *The Haight-Ashbury: A History* (New York: Random House/Rolling Stone Press, 1984), 245.

23. Shulamith Firestone, *The Dialectic of Sex* (New York: William Morrow; London: Women's Press, 1980), 30.

24. Quoted in David Bouchier, *The Feminist Challenge: The Movement for Women's Liberation in Britain and the United States* (London: Macmillan, 1983; New York: Schocken Books, 1984), 52.

25. Dickstein, op. cit., 203.

26. Ibid., 207.

27. Marge Piercy, 'The Grand Coolie Damn', in Robin Morgan, ed., *Sisterhood is Powerful* (New York: Vintage Books, 1970), 483.

28. Robin Morgan, 'Goodbye to All That', in *Going Too Far* (New York: Random House, 1977), 122–28.

29. 'Take a Memo, Mr Smith', in Morgan, op. cit., 69.

30. Andrea Dworkin, *Right-wing Women* (New York: Perigee Books; London: Women's Press, 1983), 91.

31. Ibid.

32. Ibid., 94.

33. 'Redstocking Manifesto' in Morgan, op. cit., 598.

34. Herb Goldberg, *The Hazards of Being Male* (New York: Signet Books, 1977), 67.

35. Farrell, op. cit., 151.

36. Quoted in Joseph H. Pleck, *The Myth of Masculinity* (Cambridge, Mass.: MIT Press, 1981), 317.

37. The Playboy Report on American Men, *A Study of the Values, Attitudes and Goals of U.S. Males, 18–49 Years Old* (New York: Louis Harris & Assoc. Inc., 1979), 59.

38. Dan Kiley, *The Peter Pan Syndrome: Men Who Have Never Grown Up* (New York: Dodd, Mead, 1983), xvi.

39. Interview, 9 October 1984.

40. Betty Friedan, *The Feminine Mystique* (New York: Dell; London: Gollancz, 1963), 363.

41. Donald H. Bell, *Being a Man: The Paradox of Masculinity* (Lexington, Mass.: Lewis Publishing, 1982), 97.

42. 'Cat's in the Cradle'. Music and words by Harry Chapin and Sandy Chapin. © 1974 Story Songs Ltd. Courtesy of the Chapin estate.

13. Contemporary Women in America: Two Hostile Camps

1. Marilyn French, *The Women's Room* (New York: Harcourt Brace Jovanovich; London: Deutsch, 1978), 267–68.

2. Grace Baruch, Rosalind Barnett, and Caryl Rivers, *Lifeprints: New Patterns of Love and Work for Today's Women* (New York: McGraw-Hill, 1983), 106.

3. Mirra Komarovsky, *Women in The Modern World* (Boston: Little, Brown, 1953), 108–110.

4. William H. Whyte, Jr., 'The Wives of Management', in Sigmund Noscow and William H. Form, eds., *Man, Work, and Society* (New York: Basic Books, 1962), 548–55.

5. Philip E. Slater, *The Pursuit of Loneliness* (Boston: Beacon Press, 1970; London: Allen Lane, 1971), 74.

6. Sloan Wilson, 'The Woman in the Grey Flannel Suit', *New York Times Magazine* (15 January 1956), 15.

7. Alice Lake, 'The Revolt of the Company Wife', *McCall's* (October 1973), 22.

8. Ibid., 24.

9. Interview with Greta Tullmann, 9 September 1984.

10. Midge Decter, *The New Chastity* (New York: Berkley Medallion Books, 1972), 78.

11. Quoted in Susan Lyndon, 'The Politics of Orgasm', in Robin Morgan, ed., *Sisterhood is Powerful* (New York: Vintage Books, 1970), 222.

12. Ibid., 219.

13. Simone de Beauvoir, *The Second Sex*, 1952 (London: Cape, 1968; New York: Vintage Books, 1974), 438.

14. Betty Friedan, *The Second Stage* (New York: Summit Books, 1981; London: Michael Joseph, 1982), 47.

15. George Gilder, *Sexual Suicide* (New York: Quadrangle Press, 1973), 6.

16. Phyllis Schlafly, *The Power of the Positive Woman* (New York: Jove/HBJ, 1977), 81.

17. Andrea Dworkin, *Right-wing Women* (New York: Perigee Books; London: Women's Press, 1983), 69.

18. Schlafly, op. cit., 16.

19. Marabel Morgan, *The Total Woman* (New York: Pocket Books, 1975), 17.

20. Ibid., 60.

21. Ibid., 112.

22. Ibid., 113.

23. Ibid., 115.

24. Ibid., 116.

25. Ibid., 17.

26. Ruth Carter Stapleton, *The Gift of Inner Healing* (Waco, Texas: Word Books, 1976), 32.

27. Anita Bryant, *Bless This House* (New York: Bantam Books, 1976), 51.

28. Dworkin, op. cit., 72.

29. Nora Ephron, *Heartburn* (New York: Pocket Books, 1983), 104.

30. Beverly Lahaye, *To Manipulate a Housewife*, prepared by Concerned Women for America, San Diego, California, 1983.

31. Ibid., 2.

14. What Can Trade Unions Do for Women?

1. Interview, 26 March 1985.

2. *New York Times*, 8 February 1985.

3. Ibid.

4. British figures: *Employment Gazette* 91, 1 (January 1983), 26. Swedish figures: Gunner Quist, Joan Acker and Val R. Lorwin, 'Sweden', in Alice H. Cook, Val R. Lorwin and Arlene Kaplan Daniels, eds., *Women and Trade Unions in Eleven Industrialized Countries* (Philadelphia: Temple University Press, 1984), 267.

5. Interview, 5 November 1983.

6. Larry T. Adams, 'Changing Employment Patterns of Organised Workers', *Monthly Labor Review* (February 1985), 25.

7. *Pay Equity on Trial* (Washington, D.C.: AFSCME, 1984), 2.

8. Ibid., 2.

9. *Winning the Fight for Pay Equality* (Washington, D.C.: AFSCME, 1984), 11–12.

10. William H. Chafe, *The American Woman: Her Changing Social, Economic and Political Roles 1920–1970* (New York: Oxford University Press, 1972), 77.

11. Cited in Alice Kessler-Harris, *Out to Work: A History of Wage-earning Women in the United States* (New York: Oxford University Press, 1982), 153.

12. Bettina Berch, *The Endless Day* (New York: Harcourt Brace Jovanovich, 1982), 41.

13. Adams, op. cit., 30.

14. Interview, 25 March 1985.

15. Adams, op. cit., 25.

16. Ibid., 26.

17. *New York Times*, 8 February 1985.

18. Ibid.

19. Interview with UAW member at Ford assembly plant, 28 August 1984.

20. Adams, op. cit., 26.

21. Interview, 23 November 1983.

22. Gunner Quist et al, op. cit., 267.

23. Ibid., 264.

24. Ibid., 269. *See also* Annual Report of the Central Bureau of Statistics and various issues of *Allman Manadsstatistik*, Stockholm, Sweden. *See* discussion in Chapter Three.

25. Bianca Beccali, 'Italy', in Cook et al., op. cit., 193.

26. 'Equal Opportunity for Women', *OECD Observer* 97 (March 1979), 9, and *Eurostat*, 'Hourly Earnings – Hours of Work', various issues, Statistical Office of the European Community, Luxembourg. *See* discussion in Chapter Three.

27. Chiara Ingrao, 'Feminism and Trade Unions in Italy', mimeograph, New York, May 1981, 6.

28. Interview, 11 February 1984.

29. *Wall Street Journal*, 28 March 1985.

30. *Employment Gazette* 91, 1 (January 1983), 26.

31. Lindsay Mackie and Polly Patullo, *Women at Work* (London: Tavistock Publications, 1977), 166.

32. Catherine Bodard Silver, 'France: Contrast in Familial and Societal Roles', in Janet Z. Giele and Audrey C. Smock, eds., *Women: Roles and Status in Eight Countries* (New York: John Wiley & Sons, 1977), 276.

33. Ibid., 277.

34. *Social Europe* (Luxembourg: Commission of the European Community, May 1984), 120.

35. Adams, op. cit., 21.

36. Interview, 13 January 1983.

37. CWA staff member (New York) interview, 4 September 1984.

38. Adams, op. cit., 28.

39. *New York Times*, 31 July 1984.

40. *New York Times*, 2 April 1985.

41. Interview, 5 April 1985.

15. *The Establishment Gropes for an Answer*

1. The Economic Policy Council (EPC) of the United Nations Association of the USA was founded in 1976. Its mission is to sponsor a systematic and constructive involvement in international economic problems by the American private sector. The EPC is committed to representing the views of both management and labour. Its membership comprises eminent individuals from the corporate, labour and academic communities. The EPC is co-chaired by Robert O. Anderson, chairman of the Atlantic Richfield Company, and Douglas A. Fraser, president emeritus, United Auto Workers. Its steering committee consists of: Charles Barber (former chairman, Asarco, Inc.); Henry Kaufman (executive director, Salomon Brothers, Inc.); Ray Marshall (Bernard Rapoport Professor of Economics and Public Affairs, University of Texas at Austin); Jack Sheinkman (secretary-treasurer, Amalgamated Clothing and Textile Workers Union, AFL-CIO); Thomas A. Vanderslice (president and CEO, Apollo Computer Inc.); and Lyn R. Williams (president, United Steelworkers of America). The EPC has approximately 100 members.

EPC members are brought together in study panels to analyse important international economic issues. Every year the EPC branches out into two or three panels, each of which addresses a specific problem area. The EPC both identifies critical policy questions and makes recommendations, which are then published and presented to officials within the executive and legislative branches of the United States government.

The EPC maintains a close working relationship with the executive branch and with leaders in Congress. Council members have regularly presented panel recommendations at hearings in the House of Representatives and in the Senate; cabinet-level officials attend the annual plenary sessions of the EPC to engage in an informal exchange of views; and several study panels have met with and advised presidential task forces.

2. Statements of Albert Shanker, president, American Federation of Teachers, AFL-CIO, before the Senate Subcommittee on Children and Youth, 5 June 1975, 11.

297

16. Epilogue: Voices from the Post-Feminist Generation

1. *Wall Street Journal*, 30 October 1984.

2. Ibid.

3. *Fortune* (11 July 1983), 58. In 1983 60 per cent of these women were married and 46 per cent had children. The average age of the women in this sample was thirty-seven.

4. *Wall Street Journal*, 11 February 1982. The average age of the women in this survey was forty-six, and most were vice-presidents.

5. Basia Hellwig, 'The Breakthrough Generation: 73 Women Ready to Run Corporate America', *Working Women* (April 1985), 98–146. *See also* Mary Anne Devanna, 'Male/Female Careers: MBAs a Decade into Their Careers', Center for Research into Career Development, Columbia University School of Business Administration, 1983. Devanna sampled several hundred MBAs who received their degrees from Columbia University in the period 1969–72: '72% of men in the sample were married as opposed to 58% of women ... Less than 10% of the married men have no children, 22% of the married women are childless', 108. To round out one's picture of top women in America today, a study in the late 1970s of women scientists showed that 50 per cent were unmarried, compared with 10 per cent of their male counterparts; among married women scientists 33 to 50 per cent were childless, again compared to 10 per cent of the married men. According to this study, 'women more than men must compromise their family lives for the sake of career'. *See* Ruth E. Zambrana, Marsha Hurst and Rodney L. Hite, 'The Working Mother in Contemporary Perspective: A Review of the Literature', *Pediatrics* 64 (December 1979).

6. Philip Blumstein and Pepper Schwartz, *American Couples* (New York: William Morrow, 1983), 146.

7. Interview, Roxanne Felschuch, IDANT Laboratories, 4 January 1985.

8. Germaine Greer, *Sex and Destiny: The Politics of Human Fertility* (New York: Harper & Row; London: Secker & Warburg, 1984), 2.

9. Ibid., 29.

10. Ibid., 458.

11. Ibid. 2.

12. Quoted in Erica Abeel, 'Dark Secrets', *Esquire*, June 1984, 262.

13. Quoted in Dolores Hayden, *The Grand Domestic Revolution* (Cambridge, Mass.: MIT Press, 1981), 197–98.

14. *Time*, 27 May 1985, 81.

15. *Barnard Alumnae* (Summer 1985), 9.

16. Warren Farrell, *The Liberated Man* (New York: Random House, 1975), 26.

17. Ann Critenden, 'We "Liberated" Mothers Aren't', *Washington Post*, 5 February 1985.

Index

abortion, 87, 102, 105, 106, 111, 113–14, 124, 125, 126, 138, 139, 192, 217, 218, 220, 261, 263
Abramson, Jill, 52, 53
Abzug, Bella, 135
Accords Matignon, France, 240
Addams, Jane, 93
adoption, 115–16, 131, 229, 266
Aetna Life and Casualty Company, maternity policy, 58
AFDC (Aid for Families with Dependent Children), 66
AFL (American Federation of Labor), 230, 231
AFL-CIO, 228
alimony, 28, 29–33, 34, 38, 137, 195, 208, 209, 225; and equitable distribution laws, 30–32, 33, 136
Amalgamated Clothing and Textile Workers Union, 242
American Association of Labor Legislation, 140
American Civil Liberties Union, 102
American Economic Association, 133
American Equal Rights Association, 284n
American Federation of State, County and Municipal Employees, 229, 242
American Federation of Teachers, 76
amniocentesis, 6
Anderson, Mary, 141, 142
Anderson, Robert O., 297n
ante-natal clinics, 140
Anthony, Susan B., 86, 93–4, 117–18
Anti-Discrimination Act (1977), Italy, 45

anti-slavery movement, 92–3
Apple, R. W., 85
Ariès, Philippe, 168
Arnbom, Susan, 61, 77
artificial insemination (A.I.), 116–17, 266
Atlanta, canvassing for ERA in, 133–4
Australia, wage gap in, 277n

baby boom, US post-war, 147, 153, 181
baby clinics, 106
baby-sitters/child minders, 3, 4, 49, 59, 66, 69, 71, 72, 74, 77, 79, 110, 232, 233, 234, 238
Bailey, Liz, 79
Ball, Lucille, 187
Bane, Dr Mary Jo, 220
Barnard College, 2, 4, 6, 10, 20, 155, 254; maternity policy, 11–12, 22, 120–21; reunion of ex-students (1984), 254–68; 'The Scholar and the Feminist' conference, 11, 261; tenure system, 6, 11, 20; Women's Center, 11–12, 261
'Barrett, Nancy' (pseudonym), 191–5, 205, 216
Barrie, J. M., *Peter Pan*, 199
Barroso, Rose, divorce case of, 34–5
battered wives' shelters, 107
Baudelot, Olga, 248–9
beats and beatniks, 204
Beauvoir, Simone de, 56; *The Second Sex*, 216
Bell, Donald, *Being a Man*, 209
Bergman, Ingrid, 148–9, 150
Berkeley, Dr Alan, 8, 128
Betjeman, John, 81

Index

Garland, Lillian, 89–90

Gaulle, Pres. Charles de, 249

Gaylin, Willard, 267

Gaynor, Abby, divorce case of, 36–7

gay rights, 217, 218

genital mutilation in Third World, 124

GI Bill (Serviceman's Readjustment Act: 1944), 156–7, 162

Gildersleeve, Dean Virginia, 22

Gilman, Charlotte Perkins, 118–19, 267

Ginsberg, Allen, 204

Ginsberg, Eli, 50

Goldberg, Herb, *The Hazards of Being Male*, 207

Goldwater, Barry, 131

Gompers, Samuel, 230

'Gorden, Lisa' (pseudonym), 231–3, 241

Graham, Katharine, 244

Great Depression (1930s), 154, 201

Green, Bob, 219

Green, Gordon, 44

Greer, Germaine: *The Female Eunuch*, 121; *Sex and Destiny*, 266

Gudger, Lamar, 135

guest worker schemes, 236

Guggenheimer, Elinor, xv

Haight-Ashbury psychedelic community, 191, 192, 204, 205

Haltes-garderies, French, 78

Harris, Marvin, 63

Hartmann, Heidi, 54

Harvard Business School, 41, 265

Harvard Law School, 52, 53, 134

Harvard Preschool Project, 179

Haskell, Molly, 161

Hayden, Senator Carl, 132

Hellwig, Basia, 265

Helms, Senator Jesse, 249

Hepburn, Katharine, 148, 161

Highway Act (1944), 156, 157, 162

Hirsch, Katrina de, 80

Hitschmann, Edward, 158

Hoffman, Dustin, 209

Hoffman, Nicholas von, 139

Hofstadter, Richard, 154

Holdern, Cathy, 237–8, 240–41

Holmes, Dorris, 138

Holt, Luther Emmett, 169, 170, 171, 177; *The*

Care and Feeding of Children, 169–70

home ownership, 120

homosexuality, 137, 138–9, 172, 202, 219

Hoover, President Herbert, 120

housewives, American: disillusionment of, 212–15, 216; and relocation, 214–15; support roles of, 214; traditional women, 217–21; ultradomesticity in 1950s, 147, 152–63, 166, 212; *see also* motherhood, cult of

housewives co-operatives, 118

housework, 54–5, 213–14, 266, 267; wages for, 112, 118

Hull fishermen's wives' movement, 108

Hunt, Jane Master, 117

hygiene, 169, 170, 171

I Love Lucy (TV series), 162, 186

Ilchman, Alice, 244, 247, 248

illegitimate birth, 148, 149

Independent Union of Flight Attendants, 226–7, 243

Industrial Workers of the World (IWW), 230

Infant Care (pamphlet), 177–8

infant mortality, 16, 127, 167–8, 171

infertility, 8, 23, 128, 255

inflation, 63, 147

International Ladies Garment Workers Union (ILGWU), 141

International Women's Year conference, Houston (1977), 124–5, 138–9

investment banking, women in, 279n

Italian Women's Centre (CIF), 110

Italy, women in, xiv, 150; child rearing, 182–3; divorce, 27, 111; education, 44, 76; *femminista* movement, 111–12; Family Charter, 110, 111, 237; maternity policies, 22, 61, 63, 78, 79, 90, 111, 112, 140, 237; protective legislation for working women, 140; trades unions, 110, 236–7, 240, 241; wage gap, 43, 233, 277n; women's movement, 110–12; working mothers, 22

IUDs, 128

Jagger, Mick, 206

Janeway, Elizabeth, 268

job evaluation, 46, 229

job-sharing, 232, 250